D1479079

THE RISE AND FALL OF A PALESTINIAN DYNASTY

ILAN PAPPE

# The Rise and Fall of a Palestinian Dynasty

## The Husaynis 1700–1948

UNIVERSITY OF CALIFORNIA PRESS

*Berkeley Los Angeles*

University of California Press, one of the most distinguished university presses
in the United States, enriches lives around the world by advancing scholarship in
the humanities, social sciences, and natural sciences. Its activities are supported by
the UC Press Foundation and by philanthropic contributions from individuals
and institutions. For more information, visit www.ucpress.edu.

University of California Press
Berkeley and Los Angeles, California
Copyright © Ilan Pappe 2010
Translation copyright © Yael Lotan 2010

ISBN: 978-0-520-26839-5 (cloth : alk. paper)
Library of Congress Control Number: 2010925507

First published in Hebrew as *Azulat Haaretz: HaHusaynim Biographia Politit*
by the Bialik Institute, Jerusalem, in 2002

Published in 2010 in the United Kingdom by
Saqi Books, London
www.saqibooks.com

Manufactured in the United States of America

19 18 17 16 15 14 13 12 11 10
10 9 8 7 6 5 4 3 2 1

This book is printed on Cascades Enviro 100, a 100% post consumer waste,
recycled, de-inked fiber. FSC recycled certified and processed chlorine free.
It is acid free, Ecologo certified, and manufactured by BioGas energy

# Contents

# Foreword

This book is a political biography of the Husaynis, the leading clan in Palestine for many years. The family appears here as an informal political organization whose activities have dominated Palestine's political history for almost 250 years.

Although historians have followed the trajectories of such elites quite successfully in the past, they have never focused on one particular family.[1] Historians' central interest has shifted over time from families as political elites to families as identifiably crucial social units. Historicizing a family is a fairly new scholarly approach, although one quite familiar in fictional works from both the Arab world (such as those of Naguib Mahfouz) and in Europe (such as those of Thomas Mann). In this respect, the scholarly venture is orientated toward the non-elite – part of an attempt to write 'a history from below'.[2] This biography of the Husaynis is inspired by, but does not reflect, the new scholarly focus on the Middle Eastern family and its place in the local society.

Since this book focuses on elite history, it therefore does not examine the family's internal dynamics, structure, rivalries and other features that characterize social research on the family in Middle Eastern history. These are all worthy subjects that will surely be explored by others in the future. The purpose here, however, is to analyze this Palestinian family, the Husaynis, as the most significant informal political association prior to the appearance of national movements and political parties – a political organization whose narrative is representative of Palestine and the Palestinians over a period of two and a half centuries.

The family became an affiliation, and its name allowed individuals to wield influence and establish leading positions in their local and later national society. All the positions that could affect society in Jerusalem and eventually in Palestine as a whole could only be obtained through the family's power base. As such, its members are considered here according to their political weight inside and outside the family. The central figures of this narrative are those individuals who held official and unofficial positions as the heads of the family. Only a few Husaynis who were less politically significant are mentioned (for instance, poets, writers and successful businessmen). This leaves, of course, much research to be done in order to achieve a more focused view on the social history of the family.

A political biography of a large family offers a historical perspective with many advantages for writing a fresh historiography of Palestine. It enables historians to detect patterns of continuity over fault lines that, in hegemonic narratives of Palestine, seem decisively to divide the country's history into modern and pre-modern periods or Zionist and pre-Zionist histories. The family's political history is one way, by no means the only one, of telling the story of the continued human and cultural presence in the land of Palestine. By focusing on the Husaynis throughout their transformation from a provincial Ottoman elite into the leadership of a national movement, this biography is, I hope, a constructive way to demonstrate how Palestinian society existed and developed before the Zionist settlement or the British occupation began.

Which brings me to the second principal motivation for writing this book. I wanted to tell the story of Palestine through the history of its leading family as a way to correct the common so-called truisms and to challenge some of the conventional mythology about its past. There is no need to elaborate here on why Palestine's past is relevant to the contemporary Middle East and beyond, but it is still necessary to gain a better understanding of this history.

By studying the Husaynis, one recognizes that Palestine was never an empty territory waiting for a landless people to inhabit it. Palestinian and other historiographies already show that this land had long had a society and an economy. This book hopes to complement such historiographies by humanizing a landscape described by travelers such as Mark Twain as arid and uninhabited. The Husaynis' continuous presence at the top of a complex social structure in Jerusalem throughout Ottoman rule (1517–1917) attests to the falsity of the common view of Palestine on the eve of Zionist settlement (1882).

A third reason for choosing the Husaynis as the focus of this narrative was their leading role in the Palestinian national movement from its inception around 1908 until the end of the British Mandate in 1948. By looking at the family, I hoped to gain much greater insight into the Palestinian struggle after the country was colonized by the Zionist movement and occupied by the British Empire. The family's dominant political role in Mandatory Palestine forms a link in a continuum stretching back to the early Ottoman years. From the Husaynis' perspective, one can better comprehend how the Palestinian political elite regarded the British presence and the Zionist movement: this point of view highlights the Palestinian predicament and failure, and consequently the tragic catastrophe of the 1948 Nakbah.

Finally, this book is specifically geared towards a 'Western' readership. It was originally written in Hebrew in an attempt to challenge hegemonic Israeli–Jewish perceptions of the country's history. In contemporary Israel, pre-1882 Palestine is still commonly viewed as having been an uninhabited land that was developed only when Zionism, and with it Western modernity, reached its shores. Moreover, Palestinian political life after 1918 has been portrayed in both scholarly and popular literature as that of primitive tribesman, fanatic Muslims and hateful *sheikhs*. The text in Hebrew attempted to humanize, not idealize, the Husaynis, both because of their paramount position and because they are relatively well-known (due to the accusation that al-Hajj Amin was allied with the Nazis in the Second World War, and more recently because of the politics of Faysal al-Husayni).

In the West, and particularly in the US, similar views reign, and thus similar attempts are required to redress a biased and hostile image of Palestine and the Palestinians. This seemed to me an especially urgent task after 11 September 2001 and the second *Intifada*.

Hopefully, other more scholarly benefits will emerge from this work as well. One such byproduct, but by no means its principal objective, is that it is among the few histories of Arab Jerusalem that cover both the Ottoman period and the mandatory era. There are focused monographs on Ottoman Jerusalem and a very few others on post-1918 Jerusalem, but there are hardly any continuous urban histories of the city.[3]

*Ilan Pappe, London, 2009*

# Introduction

## The Narrative

This book is a narrative, the story of a family. In general it is purposely light on analysis. It moves along slowly in the hope of allowing the reader a closer look at the life of the Husaynis. It is also a descriptive narration. It leaves the reader to draw the more obvious conclusions about the patterns of continuity in the history of Palestine.

I chose a descriptive rather than an analytical approach because I wished to zoom in on the dramatic events that shaped the lives of people in Palestine and to try to reconstruct how these events were experienced by individuals with names, distinct locations and discernable emotions. From Napoleon's invasion to the Tanzimat, the British occupation and Zionist colonization, events are examined through the eyes of the family and not just from an 'objective' historical perspective. This means that some events that look important to us in retrospect were not important in the eyes of the family, and some we disregard today were life and death issues then. (A locust invasion could have been seen at the time as more disastrous than French occupation.) For this reason the book goes into minor details while the dramatic, well-known historical events are sometimes left in the background.

The wish to tell a narrative transcends the choice of a family as a subject. There is a desire to plot a tale that is loyal to the facts but that has its own rhythm, flavor and color. Hence, I allow myself, not too often I hope, to speculate – using common sense – about people's feelings, emotions and considerations. I feel this is part of the humanization of history.

But this subject does also deserve an analytical context. So I would like briefly to introduce the proposed analytical context for this narrative, some historical background information that will benefit the reader's understanding of the narrative and the sources I have relied on in constructing this story.

## *The Analytical Context*

Apart from being a political biography, this book is also very much an urban history – both Ottoman and mandatory. Although the book does not pretend to rise to the level of micro urban social histories such as André Raymond's on Cairo, Kenneth Cuno's on Mansura, Abraham Marcus's on Aleppo, James Reilly's on Hama, Leila Fawas's on Beirut, Michael Reimer's on Alexandria or Dina Khoury's on Mosul, amongst many others,it has something in common with these works.[1] They helped us to challenge the notion of Ottoman decline that allegedly began in the sixteenth century and continued with the economic stagnation of the eighteenth century before the advent of the Napoleonic expedition to Egypt in 1798. The narrative of this book hopefully challenges the notion of 'decline' in that period by showing how Arab-Ottoman elites maintained their position through a complex web of relationships with the center of the empire as well as with European powers and their representatives. This is a reality that cannot easily be reduced to the notion of 'decline'.

## *Notables and Their Political Role in History*

The Husaynis were part of the urban elite in the Arab world. This elite dates back to the pre-Ottoman period and was present when the Ottomans conquered the Arab world in the early sixteenth century. Nor were these local elites replaced by the Ottomans' 'open occupation'.[2] But with time, when the new rulers of the Arab world realized the benefits of taxation and direct power, they installed a more complex administration, many significant members of which were brought from the center of the empire. The Ottomanization of the provinces in the Arab world included, among other things, the reshaping of the local urban elite. But even within this restructuring, the families, which Gibb and Bowen and later Albert Hourani called the 'notables', continued to play a crucial role.[3] These notables, to which the Husaynis belonged, were an informal elite consisting of the richest, the most influential and most prestigious families of merchants, *ulama* and civilian and military officers. This was not a well-defined class, and 'notables' are not a sociological concept but rather a political one. The term denotes those who play a role in the political system and suggest how this role is implemented.

In the early eighteenth century, the system stabilized and the local elite were included within the imperial matrix of control and sovereignty. As Ehud Toldano remarks, this was not systematic planning on the part of Istanbul but rather a piecemeal, *ad hoc* policy responding to events on the ground. An elite position in the empire required a high office, which enabled the holder to acquire wealth (although wealthy people did not necessarily win high positions).[4]

Ira Lapidus taught us that the core of this elite was the pool of Islamic scholars, the *ulama*. They appeared in nineteenth-century Syria as notables who descended from prominent eighteenth-century families who supplied the officials for the religious posts of *mufti*, *khatib* (preacher) and Syndic of the Descendants of the Prophet. They also managed the *awqaf* and had strong support from merchants, artisans, Janissaries, and the town quarters.[5] The Husaynis belonged to the Syndic of the Descendants of the Prophet – the Ashraf families. This was the family's main source of power, and through it its members held hereditary offices throughout the Ottoman period.

## The 'Politics of Notables'

A more focused look at how the notables remained in a high position for so long can be obtained with the help of a concept developed by Albert Hourani for describing and analyzing their political career: the 'politics of notables'.[6] In many ways these 'politics' are the key for understanding the urban politics of the Ottoman provinces (at least in the Muslim provinces). The 'politics' were a mode of behavior, a 'practice', a Weberian concept put forward by Hourani to explain their prolonged political survival. The wider context of this kind of urban history is European patrician history. It is tempting indeed to use the term 'patrician' for these people, but it is safer to employ the term 'notables' as it is probably the closest to the term *'a'ayan'* used at the time. There are other possible terms from the period as well as new ones, but for the purposes of this book I am content to use 'notables'.

This practice is in essence the 'politics of dependence and coalitions', practiced by people in the city and the area around it with their notables and through them with their ruler. Such a mode of behavior can work when there are 'great' families or 'grandee' families – more akin in the greatness accorded to them to the medieval families of Italy than to that enjoyed in medieval France and Britain, as Hourani remarks.[7]

The notables enjoyed considerable independence in running the affairs of the cities in the Arab Ottoman world. These families won this relative autonomy because they had access to the rulers of the empire – in the case of Jerusalem, to regional capitals such as Damascus, Acre and Beirut as well to Istanbul and Cairo. This enabled the notables to represent their society before the powers that be. Their prestige in the eyes of the empire stemmed from their standing within their own society.

Other factors also affected the relative independence and authority of the urban notable families. The Husaynis' ability to compose effective coalitions with forces within and without the city is a major feature of this political biography. The key word is 'coalition', and it was such a powerful asset that it served the Husaynis as well in the eighteenth century as it did in the twentieth.

As Hourani sensed even before going into a particular case study, the need to form coalitions increased the tendency 'towards the formation of two or more coalitions'.[8] These formations are traced in this book and are indeed a vital factor in the political history of Palestine in the period under review. In this context, Hourani makes additional remarks that are relevant to the history of the Husaynis: the coalitions were challenged because they were not institutionalized and were fragile because they demanded an almost impossible balancing act between the families' interests and the policies of the rulers. But it is exactly this balancing act that explains why the Husaynis were leaders of such coalitions for so long: they had the support of the other families in Jerusalem and access to the rulers.

The formation of coalitions was part of the habitual circumspection built into the 'politics of notables'. These coalitions were not part of a fixed institution; they were far more fluid formations. Occasionally, one party left the coalition for another, disappointing an ally and aligning with a former foe. These shifts also occurred because of the 'divide and rule' policies of the central government. Therefore the notables' 'modes of action must in normal circumstances be cautious and even ambiguous', as illustrated by how the Husaynis led revolutions against rulers or shunned others or left them behind when convenient.

As it had been a century before, at the beginning of the nineteenth century 'the politics of notables' was very much a politics of *ulama*. Hourani remarks that their scholarly background placed the *ulama* notables closer to the ruler than to society.[9] But this changed with the secularization of the notables at the beginning of the twentieth century. The notables of religion became the notables of nationalism.

Within society the notables were at the top of the hierarchy, and in the empire they were a substratum below the officials governing the provinces from the capital of the main province or, later on, directly from Istanbul. Among the notables, *primus inter pares* seemed to be the rule of the game

– one family would hold this advantageous position. The position of seniority was the *naqib al-ashraf*, which until the 1860s was one of the most coveted in Jerusalem next to that of the *mufti*, the most senior religious position to which a notable could aspire. An appointment as *naqib al-ashraf* carried with it certain duties as an arbitrator, as a representative of certain *awqaf* and as an objective witness in matters involving local elite groups.

The titles and functions of notable families were inherited from father to son, making the Husaynis a kind of hereditary aristocracy. This aristocratic status was won with religious respectability and a prestigious lineage. Fur-· thermore, families such as the Husaynis augmented their power by establishing alliances with the military chieftains (*aghawat*) whose power was based on clientele and the control of suburban quarters and the grain trade that passed through them.

### The Economic and Financial Basis

But prestige, alliances and connections were not enough to sustain the clan as a political force; they also needed financial resources. Most of these resources came with the appointments rather than ensuring them. The tax-farming system in the Ottoman Empire was such that it enabled the notables both to be enriched by and to accumulate political power. In a way, it was an alternative to the European banking system. As Sevket Pamuk explains:

> While loans to kings, princes and governments were part of the regular business of European banking houses in the late medieval and early modern periods, in the Islamic world advances of cash to the rulers and the public treasury were handled differently. They took the form of tax-farming arrangements in which individuals possessing liquid capital assets advanced cash to the government in return for the right to farm the taxes of a given region or fiscal unit for a fixed period.[10]

At first this right was given for a year to three years, but during financial crises the tendency was to grant it for longer periods. The Ottoman Empire relied on tax-farming for urban taxes in particular, and hence the importance of notables who could serve as tax collectors. A different system was at work in the rural areas until the sixteenth century, but it was replaced by tax-farming thereafter, the concessions for which were auctioned in Istanbul.

Another source of income, and probably the most profitable one, was the ability of the notables to benefit from supervising, and later on breaking up, religious endowments – the *awqaf* (plural of *waqf*).

Before the emergence of municipal services, the authorities attended to the essential needs of the urban population through the *waqf,* the source for funding the restoration and maintenance of religious buildings and centers, educational systems and social services. Moreover, the *waqf* financed the expansion of infrastructure, the construction of bridges and the introduction of more systematic water supplies to the cities. The *waqf* was not invented by the Ottomans but was used more extensively by them as the best means of catering to the urban society's concerns and requirements.[11]

Usually, Ottoman officials such as local governors founded the *awqaf* and appointed notables to look after them (as *mutawallis* and *nazirs*). At the beginning of the nineteenth century, the Husaynis established three *awqaf* of their own, while others of the family were appointed as *mutawallis* and *nazirs,* which meant the family as a whole became the beneficiary of the *waqf.*[12] Gabriel Baer, who investigated the period from 1790 to 1801, discovered that the Husaynis had a larger share than any other group in founding new *awqaf* and in being appointed *mutawallis* (one third of the former and half of the latter).[13]

*Awqaf* that were endowed by the state for public services included profitable assets such as *muzara'* fields (lands cultivated on a permanent basis), the total cultivated lands of several villages, factories, workshops, etc. Out of the profits salaries were paid. Sons of the notable families in Jerusalem were already receiving generous allowances from the profits of the *awqaf* in the early nineteenth century. Among them were the Husaynis, who were given the title *wujah-i-murtazaqa* (those who benefit most in several lists of *awqaf*). But they were not the only ones; they had to compete with many other families. There were about 1,000 to 1,500 notables in Jerusalem at the end of the eighteenth century, and they were about 20 percent of the overall population of several thousand. (Figures are not easily attainable for that period, and there is no room here to enter the debate about them.) Their high proportion within the overall Muslim community explains why they were so numerous among those enjoying the profits of the *awqaf.*[14]

At the end of the eighteenth century, the Ottoman central government found they could use the *awqaf* to reward families who cooperated with them.[15] Supervision at the beginning of the nineteenth century was lax, and therefore families could expand their financial benefits from the endowments, which in principle were meant to serve the public. One imperial decree, a *firman* from 17 April 1797, decries the excessive number of beneficiaries drawing on these sources without the sultan's permission, which led to growing debts that disabled the proper functioning of the endowed institutions.[16]

Inclusion on such a list required authorization from either the governors of the province or the city – or those who represented them: the supreme *qadi* (Islamic judge) in the region, the *qadi* of Jerusalem or his deputy. This explains the networking a notable family needed to do to sustain its economic prosperity. In the eighteenth century, an innovation was introduced: the beneficiary documents could be passed to the next of kin, a fact that expanded the lists and overburdened the debts of the *awqaf*. The notables themselves approached the governor from time to time and asked him to limit the lists so as to ensure smoother operations in the field of charity and aid to the poor.[17] Of course, they made this request without giving up their own privileged positions.

In 1777, after a period of political upheaval, the central government transferred the right to grant beneficiary status exclusively to the Ottoman officials dealing with the finances of the empire. The ministry was ordered to consider further documents only on a purely economic basis. There was worse to come. The move annulled past documents, which generated a strong protest and a demand to return the old system. The outcry worked, and the old system was reinstated.[18]

The *waqf* became a particularly profitable asset in the beginning of the nineteenth century when it was broken up. Gaining control of public *waqf* domains and making them a family's own private property was legal. Some cases were sanctioned by the local *qadi* and the properties registered in the *sijjilat* as privately owned land. Alongside the Khalidis, Nammaris, Nusaybas and al-Dajanis, the Husaynis were the most important family to amass wealth in such a way. These families held high posts in the *waqf* administration and in the Shari'a judicial system and other Islamic institutions, so they exploited their economic power. But there were those who truly meant to help develop an endowment, and thus they re-endowed their investments.

This redistribution was executed in more than one way. The most common was followed by the deterioration of the asset so that it could be dismembered in a long-term, or perpetual, lease. This was a down payment of a lump sum by the tenant to cover the debt owed by the *waqf*, or from expenses on repairs and restoration in the form of long-term (90-year) leases at a very low rent. Transactions of this and similar kinds enriched the Husaynis considerably in the early nineteenth century.[19]

Assets that were not leased or dismembered still benefited the Husaynis. Being a *mutawalli* of other people's endowments promised the family a large share in those assets, as well as a prestigious position in society.[20] Again, research shows that for the first part of the nineteenth century, the Husaynis had a proportionately larger share in transactions involving endowments.

Apart from the *waqf*, the urban notables of Palestine also relied on the rural economy to thrive. In the nineteenth century, Palestine was a largely rural country, and revenues were directly connected to agriculture. Through the process of centralization that characterized the Tanzimat period, power shifted from rural lords to urban notables such as the Husaynis. Before the Tanzimat, the lords of the Palestinian hills owned a large share of the rural hinterland and received a considerable share of the land taxes and custom posts. These assets were now transferred to the urban elite.[21]

But generally speaking, in the eighteenth and nineteenth centuries, Jerusalem was not very important to the Palestinian economy either as a trading center or in its commercial activity. It was less its connection to the land and much more its holiness that provided income for many in the city, as did the frequent pilgrimages.[22]

Matters changed somewhat with the promulgation of the Land Law of 1858, which transformed the basis for landownership in the empire. The law required the registration and categorization of land for the sake of greater taxation. The Husaynis acquired land in many areas and became one of the leading landowning families. (However, since it took time for the Land Law to be applied in Jerusalem, the initiatives of the family occurred later on.)[23]

The sources of power varied with time. Once they held power, they found ways of maintaining it. By the time the Husaynis were both a religious and landowning elite, their fortified position in society was reflected in the educational orientation they chose for their children, who during the nineteenth century were sent to Ottoman professional schools to compete for places in Ottoman governmental service.

But while the nineteenth century brought with it new sources of power, it also set in motion processes that limited the notables' influence in society. During their rule (1831–40), the Egyptians tried to overcome local independence, establish a centralized government and promote economic development. The Egyptian rulers tried to disarm the local population and introduced conscription, forced labor and new head taxes, as well as economic monopolies. The position of the notables was challenged again by the Ottoman programs of centralization, the Tanzimat.

When the Ottomans returned to Syria in 1840, they introduced some reforms that weakened the family Husayni to fulfill the reformers' wish to centralize power, eliminate intermediary notables and mobilize mass support for the state. The family was also negatively affected by central authorities' drive to secularize the judicial system and to introduce formal equality between Muslims and non-Muslims. However, they benefited from the local and municipal councils that were created to counterbalance local governors – councils within which they enjoyed important fiscal and administrative powers.[24]

With the advent of the age of nationalism, social standing no longer ensured the maintenance of financial and economic gains. Family wealth was now also part of the nation.

## *The Politics of Nationalism*

This book tries to avoid the conventional school of thought that views nationalism as merely a product of modernization with a clear date and location of origin. Lebanon is typically singled out as the cradle of Arab nationalism, which is seen as an influential concept early on that then moved from Beirut to Jerusalem via Damascus.[25]

This is, of course, only one possible way of looking at it. Relying on more updated theoretical analysis of the phenomenon that has inspired a few intriguing volumes on Arab nationalism, this book treats the emergence of a nationalist point of view as a much more enigmatic subject. It examines nationalism before it became such a powerful feature dominating life in Palestine and Israel in the second half of the twentieth century – a period that is beyond the historical scope of this work.

The theoretical literature views nationalism in various contradictory ways: as an ideology, a product of the imagination, a cultural product or an act of social engineering. But there is a common thread running through recent critiques of nationalism. National identity, whether imagined, engineered or manipulated, is shown to be a recent human invention born of the integration of conflicting ethnic or cultural identities or the disintegration of such identities. This is the process described here.

Nationalism appears in this book as a modern invention that provides a new axis of social and political inclusion and exclusion that is neither organic nor natural. An artificial identification emerged, as in the case of the last years of Turkish rule, amongst those who belonged to the nation and more importantly amongst those who were excluded from it.

Late in the life of the Husaynis as notables of nationalism, Zionism came along and started a process that caused the Palestinians to construct an 'other' to their newly born national identity, an 'other' that became crucial to the formation of their national self. Hence, as is shown in the book, a Zionist threat was necessary to clarifying the uniqueness of the Palestinian national experience within the overall Arab one. But Zionism was not necessary for the emergence of such nationalism.

This book illustrates how national identity demands the subordination of other identities – communal, religious, ethnic, etc. This subjugation defines the parameters of 'otherness' and the degree to which it is constituted as a source of menace to the prevalent or hegemonic identity. The Husaynis followed through to the end of this process and in so doing delayed this subjugation – a disaster in the face of Zionism but a potential blessing for those who wished Palestine to continue benefiting from the more cosmo-political and pluralist air of the previous Ottoman era.

## Sources

Since the Husayni family was an integral part of local government, its political history can be traced with the help of the *sijjilat*, the records of the Shari'a court in Jerusalem. This is a useful source for many who research Jerusalem's history in the nineteenth century. The *sijjil* in Jerusalem is still kept in the storeroom of the Shari'a court, and it covers the period from 936 to 1948. Like many other scholars much more experienced in using this type of source, I was fortunate to be able to see them with the help of the loyal staff of the Haram al-Sharif.

Reports by European diplomats and travelers were another important source. Albert Hourani believed the diplomats to be more reliable than the travelers.[26] But in the context of our subject, some travelers' reports seemed to be more trustworthy than the diplomats' summaries, such as the ones sent by the British consul in Jerusalem, James Finn, in the mid-nineteenth century. These sources served me well into the mandatory period and provided depth that drier sources lacked.

Palestinian biographical and autobiographical works complemented the very thorough archival material found in both the Public Record Office and the Central Zionist Archives. Together these sources helped me to reconstruct the mandatory period. I also relied on the the valuable and amazingly vivid memories of Amina al-Husayni and other family members who recall this period.

The Arab Studies Society, which was headed by Faysal al-Husayni for many years, hosts a small family archive. I was fortunate enough to be helped by Faysal al-Husayni and Dr Budeiri, the chief librarian, with the materials present there (mainly secondary sources that relate to the family, as well as some letters and documents).

I also used quite a few sources in Hebrew – mainly secondary historiographical works that are unavailable in English. This may seem strange since this work seeks to challenge the scholarly and popular narrative common to most Israeli historiographies. The reason I used these sources is that industrious Israeli scholars have mined, and continue to mine, this relevant archival material in a systematic and admirable way – though their conclusions and interpretations follow the Zionist metanarrative very closely. Hence, while there are many references in this work to the empirical data they gathered, the plot woven here seriously challenges many of their conclusions and ideological assumptions.

# Prologue

In the middle of the night between 28 and 29 October 1705, Muhammad ibn-Mustafa al-Husayni al-Wafa'i, *naqib al-ashraf* of Jerusalem, fled the holy city. (The *naqib* was the head of the families who claimed descent from the Prophet Muhammad in the city of Jerusalem, and his position was one of the highest to which a local could aspire in the Ottoman Empire.) The *naqib* and a group of his followers opened the Nablus Gate in the wall of the Old City and fled under cover of darkness to the Mount of Olives. Halfway up the hillside they met other rebels who had come out of the city by way of the Mughrabi Gate. By daybreak, the rumor had spread throughout the city: the great uprising against the representatives of Ottoman rule had been crushed.

Though the revolt did not break out openly until May 1703, worrying information had been reaching the court of Sultan Mustafa II since early 1702. Ever since a new ruler was appointed the previous year, Jerusalem had been in turmoil – not only the city but also the nearby districts of Gaza and Nablus. The new governor was sent to collect taxes more efficiently.[1] The Porte hoped that this would serve as an example to others, showing that the empire was still the mighty force that made Europe tremble – despite its unprecedented losses to Europe at the end of the seventeenth century – and was respected by its multitudinous subjects.

The new ruler brought with him extra troops to help him enforce the new collection. Any attempt to avoid paying taxes was dealt with by the governor's troops at once. The troops, however, were not content to collect the due tax, and so they also periodically robbed the citizens. Any failure to pay the demanded tax was punished with a severe fine, and the general burden of taxation increased. The combination of taxation and looting was enough to drive the inhabitants to the verge of an uprising.

In May 1703, the burden of taxation and the savagery of the governor's emissaries the year before had provoked general resistance, which intensified with the imminent arrival of the tax gatherers in the spring. Led by two young and inexperienced notables, a revolt broke out that was unique in the history of the district of Jerusalem in that it allied peasants and Bedouins with dignitaries and notables. The revolt went on for two and a half years (1703–5), centered around the mosque of al-Aqsa and the citadel. The governor's limited troops were unable to subdue the determined rebels, and the *naqib* became the city's *de facto* ruler.[2]

Inside the beleaguered citadel, the *qadi* of Jerusalem breathed a sigh of relief once the revolt had ended. One of the worst years of his life had drawn to a close – or so he hoped. He had come to the city from Istanbul towards the end of the previous year, on a mission that had filled him with anxiety before he even sailed into the Port of Jaffa. He had been appointed to represent the sultan's law and order in a city dominated by the *naqib* and his cohorts, who were rebelling against Ottoman rule. The *naqib* received him courteously, but in effect confined him to the citadel, along with other government officials. Now at last the *qadi* might be able to administer the holy city in accordance with the Shari'a, and perhaps win the sultan's approval, as well as a more exalted post closer to his home in Istanbul.

As soon as he heard that the *naqib* had fled, the *qadi* ordered the drawbridge linking the citadel with the city wall to be lowered. The bridge had been raised from the start of the revolt, for fear of attack by the populace. Now the *qadi* crossed the moat with ostentatious ceremony, on his way to the fortress commander. On his left and right, evidence of Istanbul's claim to sovereignty over Jerusalem was displayed in the form of engraved plaques noting the contributions made by the sultans through the ages to the city's fortification. The most prominent plaque, the one over the fortress gate commemorating the building of the fortress by Sultan Suleiman I in 1531, was a reminder that the *qadi* represented the power that had ruled Jerusalem for more than a century and a half. The *qadi* hastened to consult the fortress commander about whom they would recommend to Istanbul to be the new *naqib* of Jerusalem. Walking confidently down the path from the city wall to the tower, he no doubt recollected the stirring events of the *naqib*'s revolt.

The *qadi* went to the Dome of the Rock, where he was met by the commander and the notables of the city. Before the meeting started, the *qadi* had the uncomfortable thought that most of his predecessors had been killed by rebels. And no wonder – the *qadi* was always the most tangible symbol of the sultan's rule, for better or worse. Those *qadis* who survived were forced to obey the will of the mob rather than God's holy law. He was determined to recommend to the authorities in Istanbul that the next *naqib* be someone loyal to the sultan's representatives, and certainly someone who had his personal approval.

Many of the city's notables had already turned against the rebellious *naqib* a year earlier, when they heard that the sultan was sending a large army to suppress the revolt. The *naqib* did not hesitate to confront this loyalist camp and fought a bloody battle against it in the city in 1704. The climax of the confrontation, involving many combatants, took place in the Bab al-Huta quarter, in the northern end of the Old City. By the time it was over, corpses littered the narrow, crowded alleys of the quarter that was named after the Sinners' Gate, through which prayerful penitents entered. After this civil war many abandoned the *naqib*'s camp and joined the beleaguered faction in the citadel, who were waiting for the sultan's army. The rebellious *naqib* chose to flee the city before the arrival of the imperial army.

A representative of that army, which was still a few days' journey from the city, took part in the meeting. He brought the *qadi* greetings from the commander of the dispatched force and congratulated him on his resolute stand in the besieged citadel. Then the *qadi* reported that he was about to recommend that Istanbul appoint Muhib al-Din Effendi, of the Ghudayya clan (later to be known as the Husayni family), as the next *naqib*. He explained that, unlike the *naqib* who had fled, Muhib al-Din had been loyal to the government from the start of the uprising. In actual fact, Muhib al-Din had at first contemplated joining the rebels, but at this time he could certainly be counted among the loyalists, rather than the opponents of the sultan's rule.

In the days that followed, the notables gave much thought to the reversals among the ruling officials. Now they were free to indulge in the pleasures of the *hammamat* (the baths), which they had been deprived of for some time. Most of them favored the Hammam al-Sultan, on the corner of al-Wadi (Valley) Street, which is also one of the first Stations of the Cross. There, amid the scent of rose water and the aroma of coffee wafting from the loaded trays of sweetmeats, they discussed the vicissitudes of their times, continuing their talk long into the night in the city's cafes. The poets sang the praises of the new *naqib* and speculated about the future in between puffs of their *nargilehs*. These were the customary ways of the notables of Jerusalem, which Muslim travelers described as a lively city, quite unlike the picture that would be drawn by many Christian travelers, among them Gustave Flaubert and Mark Twain, who advanced the myth of the empty land and the desolate city.[3]

This was the city in which the Ghudayyas, the family of the fortunate Muhib al-Din, had resided for four centuries. The high points of life in Jerusalem, for them as for other notable families, were the *mawlid* – the religious festivals – weddings and births, and the occasional appearance of famous Muslim travelers, who were admired for their great learning in religion and the sciences as much as for their literary style. At their house – which at least one manuscript describes as a 'palace', so impressed was the visitor – the Ghudayyas entertained some of the great men of their era.[4]

But nothing was as momentous as the day of Muhib al-Din's appointment, which in all likelihood was marked by a great feast. If so, it must have been attended by all the notables, who doubtless discussed the division of the spoils. The Ottoman authorities had expropriated the estate of the fugitive *naqib* and were about to distribute it to the loyal notables. The lion's share was sure to be given to the two branches of the Ghudayya clan – the family of the new *naqib* and that of his cousin Abdullah, who had for years held the post of *sheikh al-haram* (*sheikh* of the Jerusalem holy sanctuary). Abdullah was greatly admired in the city for his work and his great learning in theology and *i'lm al-fiqh*, the Islamic religious precepts. But though his father had been *naqib al-ashraf,* he himself did not win the post and had to be content with being *sheikh al-haram.*[5]

We focus on Abdullah al-Ghudayya because his son Abd al-Latif is the central figure of the present story, a story that begins in 1703 and ends in our time and one that may indeed continue so long as the family is represented in the political life of Jerusalem and of the surrounding country, Palestine.

As far as we know, Abd al-Latif's youth was uneventful, and he makes a rare appearance in the writing of a Sufi traveler, Mustafa Ibn Kamil al-Bakhri, who visited the city quite often.[6] On his visits, al-Bakhri stayed near the mosque of al-Aqsa, where he settled for long spells after his second visit to the city in 1710. It seems that Abd al-Latif and al-Bakhri first met in 1724 at one of the city gates where al-Bakhri, about to enter, was reading the Fatiha before passing through, as was customary in those days. Having read the opening verses of the Qur'an, he changed his rich traveling apparel for the simple garments of purity, expressive of the visitor's reverence for the city's sanctity.

The *naqib* was welcomed by the Ghudayyas and by *sheikh al-haram* Abdullah and his son Abd al-Latif. After praying together and exchanging lengthy blessings, the august company walked through the city, composing a *qasida* (a poem in the classical style) at every noted site:

In the name of God, if you meet us, we
shall tell you it is the day of Jerusalem.
Together let us go to this city and visit it.
The Good will be with us forever.[7]

Each time al-Bakhri returned to Jerusalem he brought books from his library in Damascus, thereby enriching the lives of his companions in Jerusalem. His visits also had a certain missionary quality. Al-Bakhri was a member of the mystic Sufi Kheloti order, which he would eventually head. But it seems that his hosts were more impressed by the order's ostentatious self-mortification and accompanying ceremonies than by its theological message of approaching God via Muslim mysticism.[8] Members of the family were entranced by the spectacular exercises and the dancing in a circle that culminated in intense excitement. Al-Bakhri never arrived on his own: as a man of high position, he was always surrounded by an entourage, and his frequent visits demonstrated the great importance of Jerusalem in the Muslim world of the early eighteenth century.

Hosts and guest alike passed the time discussing the mysteries, showing off their abilities as religious mystics. Al-Bakhri was deeply influenced by one of the great medieval Sufi philosophers, Ibn al-Arabi. Al-Arabi had written about the creation of the world and of understanding it, and consequently al-Bakhri wrote a good deal about such subjects. It is possible that not only members of the religious elite took part in such gatherings but also others such as the *sheikh al-tujjar*, the leader of the city's merchants.[9] During his visit, al-Bakhri gave the customary guest lecture; he liked to quote from 'The Praises of Jerusalem' – the literature lauding the city, which had grown following the Crusades. He also visited the graves of holy men, among them that of Nabi Musa (the Prophet Moses) near Jericho, where he spent the week of festivities in the prophet's honor.

The Ghudayyas took to al-Bakhri. He was invited to be the guest of honor at the dinner celebrating *Mawlid al-Nabi* (the Prophet's birth), and they offered him a chair in the courtyard of al-Aqsa mosque, where most of the guests reclined on cushions on the ground. The public dinner was a widely attended occasion in which all walks of life took part: the rich and the poor, the learned and the ignorant. In a travelogue he wrote after an earlier visit in 1690, al-Bakhri expressed his wonder at seeing that among the throng 'there were also veiled women in the corner of the mosque, and with them young and small girls'. The *muezzins* trilled the verses. Servants of the *haram* circulated through the multitude, offering sweets and fragrant pastries and finger bowls of rose water for the guests to rinse their sticky hands in, and at last the crowd dispersed, well-fed and contented.[10]

The years that followed al-Bakhri's visit were disappointing for the Ghudayyas. During the 1730s, the key posts in the city were given to other families. The Alami clan, for example, won a number of lucrative positions at the expense of the Ghudayyas, causing the rivalry between the two clans to continue for some time. Like the Ghudayyas, the Alamis had made good use of the *naqib*'s revolt in the early years of the century, and persuasion combined with money won them the position of *mufti*, which the Ghudayyas had coveted.

The *mufti* was a state official who wrote opinions (*fatwas*) on legal subjects for judges and common believers. Some of his opinions became binding precedents. He also belonged to an Ottoman hierarchy that was supervised by the *mufti* of Istanbul, who had the power to appoint and dismiss local *muftis* around the empire.

But this was a temporary decline – Abd al-Latif's family would later recover the *mufti*'s post, and the three most important positions held by local personages under Ottoman rule would be theirs: *naqib al-ashraf, mufti* and *sheikh al-haram*. No wonder they became the most important family in Jerusalem and perhaps in all of Palestine.

For a short while it looked as if all this glory would fall to the Alamis. In January 1733, when Muhib al-Din of the Ghudayyas died and his son Amin was appointed in his place as *naqib al-ashraf* of Jerusalem, the Alamis moved into action. Amin was a pleasant man, but even his family recognized that he did not have the necessary qualities to serve as *naqib*. As soon as it became known that he had failed to settle a feud between two city families, the Alamis began to agitate for the post. They bribed the Grand Vizier and the governor of Damascus, and with their support obtained it.

It took Abd al-Latif twelve years of continuous effort to wrest the prestigious position from his rivals. Bribery, intrigue and considerable personal charisma restored the Ghudayyas to the apex of the local hierarchy. Having won this position, Abd al-Latif launched a successful dynasty that would drop the name 'Ghudayya' and adopt that of the fugitive *naqib* – 'al-Husayni'. This dynasty would lead Palestinian society for the next two and a half centuries, up to the present day.

Appropriating the name and lineage of another clan requires great ingenuity and the ability to exploit uncertain political circumstances. It is unclear exactly when this happened, but thanks to Adel Mana'a we do have the genealogy that was used to create the family's new identity. It is hard to determine whether it was a deliberate takeover of another family's lineage, as one would be inclined to imagine, or an error due to the families having an ancestor with the same name back in the seventeenth century. The rebellious *naqib al-ashraf* was the head of the Wafa'i Husaynis, and he had a great-grandfather by the name of Abd al-Kader ibn al-Karim al-Din. The Ghudayyas also had a great-grandfather by that name.

The Ghudayyas' lineage was fairly lackluster compared to that of the Wafa'i Husayni. The latter family arrived in Jerusalem in the early fourteenth century, with a family tree stretching back to the Prophet Muhammad – to be precise, to Hussein, the son of Ali, husband of the Prophet's daughter Fatima. A direct line of succession leads from Hussein to one Muhammad Badr al-Din, who made his way in the fourteenth century from the Arabian Peninsula to Jerusalem and built a house in Wadi al-Nusur on the city's outskirts.

The Wafa'i Husaynis appear in records from the sixteenth century onwards, and they are certainly not the forefathers of today's Husaynis but rather their adoptive ancestors. Another theory ascribes to them a different, anonymous ancestry. There evidently was a hiatus in the grand 'family history' that was doubtless quoted and repeated whenever the family's fortunes either faltered or rose to new heights.[11] The adoption of the new family name was followed by closer ties with Jerusalem families of more esteemed lineage. Daughters were married to the sons of the al-Khalidi and Jarallah families, considered to be the noblest in the city. In this way the family kept its position in the front rank of the city's notables, even if it did not always retain all three leading posts in Jerusalem.

It appears that the name change had already taken place by the 1770s, when Abd al-Latif was in his forties. Documents show that by that time he was already a respected figure – *rais al-Quds ayn aayanuha* (the leader of Jerusalem and its notables), as he was dubbed by contemporary historian al-Muradi. Abd al-Latif was famous for his generosity and modesty. And though al-Muradi lavished such praise on almost every notable, in this case he offered various testimonies to back it up. Abd al-Latif served his guests with his own hands, reported the amazed al-Muradi, 'and always smiled at his children and preferred the poor over the rich'. He was renowned beyond the confines of the city as one who provided food for pilgrims and indigent visitors. The poets of the time, al-Muradi goes on to say, sang his praises in their poems.[12]

We have a slightly different version of the story about the name. Butrus Abu-Manneh proposes opening the narrative not with the Ghudayya clan but with Abd al-Latif's father, the scion of an important family whose name is unknown, because prior to the eighteenth century, Abu-Manneh claims, people did not use surnames.[13]

Members of the family, however, have asked that we begin their history with the Prophet Muhammad, since the link between the Husaynis and the Prophet's family was the basis for their claim to a senior position in Palestine – and who is to say that this claim is or is not valid? Max Weber argues that the identity of a given organization is the sum of its subjective and objective definitions. During most of the period covered in this account, the local population accepted the Husaynis' claim to notability, and this acceptance was used to advance its status. Towards the end of the period, however, the situation changed – by the late Ottoman era, and *a fortiori* in our time, a family's lineage is of secondary importance.

We cannot tell if the Ghudayyas' claim of having descended from the Wafa'i family, whose positions they inherited, was a deliberate act. Be that as it may, it was a very proud claim. The Wafa'is owned, among other properties, the *zawiyya* that bore their name: *al zawiyya al-wafa'iyya*. This was a room, usually in the corner of a mosque, for the accommodation of the dervishes, who with their unkempt beards and worn sandals slept on straw mats and subsisted on charity. The Wafa'i *zawiyya* was exceptionally highly regarded, because it was also known as '*dar al-Mua'wiyya*', after the *khalif al-Mua'wiyya*, who had stayed there with his daughter Fatima. A stone memorial engraved with her name still stands there. It was in this *zawiyya* that the Wafa'i Sufi order came into being.[14]

In the latter half of the eighteenth century, the various accounts converge into one that describes the rise of the Husaynis in parallel with the decreasing power of the Ottoman center. This enabled the family not only to win the most important posts in the city but also to wield influence in the religious and secular centers of power. The post of the *naqib* was theirs for a while, and the function itself grew in importance in the latter half of the eighteenth century; it was equal and in certain cases, as we shall see in our narrative, even greater than that of Istanbul's official representatives. By that time, the Husaynis were unquestionably one of the leading notable families together with the al-Khalidis, the Jarallahs, the al-Jama'is and others. But the post of the *naqib* was not assured, and the Husaynis would lose it from time to time. Nevertheless, in any history of Jerusalem from the eighteenth century onward, they figure more centrally than any other family or clan.[15]

# Maps

## CHAPTER I

# The Making of a Family

## From al-Ghudayya to al-Husayni

On the first day of the year 1765, Mehmet Aga, the chief eunuch in the harem of the sultan, was awakened by a strong but pleasant odor. It was the scent of soap, familiar to him ever since that 'Arab Abd al-Latif' (Abd al-Latif II) was appointed *naqib al-ashraf* in Jerusalem. The latter had a small soap manufactory in Jerusalem, and many in the palace had become partial to its soaps and vials of rose water. The chief eunuch was especially fond of soaking in a rose water bath, but his supply had recently run out. Now he got out of bed as briskly as his great bulk allowed and prepared to meet Abd al-Latif's emissaries. He gave his sleeping servant, a young black eunuch recently arrived from Egypt, a little kick to wake him and sent him to the major–domo to help him sort out the presents intended for the various dignitaries who were regular recipients of Abd al-Latif's largesse.[1]

The majordomo found the delegation from Jerusalem standing beside the guardhouse that had sprung up near the eunuchs' quarters and watching open-mouthed as builders and masons completed the conversion of the harem from a traditional Ottoman structure into a baroque-rococo one.[2]

Abd al-Latif's son Abdullah was the delegation's leader. After the usual greetings, he addressed the chief eunuch as follows: 'We urge our glorious son, Mehmet Aga, to do his utmost to distribute these gifts in accordance with our wishes, and may Allah prolong his days. To our benefactor, *sheikh al-islam*, a chest of soap, a jar of rose water and six head-coverings ...'[3]

The list went on: former chief *qadis*, past and present *naqibs al-ashraf* of Istanbul, all received one or two fragrant chests and soft linen caps with the dignitaries' names embroidered on them by daughters of the family. As on previous occasions, Mehmet was asked to obtain receipts showing that the gifts had reached their destinations. The list was usually made up of eighteen of the imperial capital's dignitaries. Two chests were always assigned to the *sheikh al-islam* (who appointed local notables to the highest religious posts) to make sure he remembered Abd al-Latif's four sons and would obtain plum positions for them in the city's religious hierarchy.

Abdullah spent several days in the bustling capital and called on Zayn al-Abidin, Istanbul's *naqib al-ashraf*, an exalted official empowered to appoint and discharge any *naqib al-ashraf* in the provincial capitals throughout the empire. Zayn al-Abidin assured Abdullah that the *niqaba* – the post of *naqib al-ashraf* of Jerusalem – would remain in the family, or, more precisely, remain his.[4] The authorities also confirmed Abdullah in his post as supervisor of the sanctuary of Nabi Musa.

This time the mission was driven by some urgency: the governor of Damascus harassed the family by threatening to pass the *niqaba* to the Alami family. As noted before, ever since the appointment of Muhib al-Din al-Ghudayya to the post of *mufti*, the Alamis had coveted the post and had actually filled it for a while.

## Abd al-Latif, Founder of the New Family

But all that was in the past, and in 1765 Abdullah was thinking about the future. Would he be able to repeat his father's achievements?, he wondered.

Zayn al-Abidin clearly remembered Abdullah's father. *Al-Qudsi* – 'the Jerusalemite' – was the nickname of the notable who sent him chests of fragrant soaps, sweet rose water and exquisite caps almost every year. The first such delivery arrived in 1740, accompanied by a letter begging for the post of *naqib* to be restored to the Ghudayyas. The letter vilified not only the Alamis but also their allies the Jarallahs, likewise one of the grandest families in the city. With amazing boldness, Abd al-Latif asked not only to have the post of *naqib* restored to him but also his father's old post of *sheikh al-haram*, guardian of the city's holy shrines. The letter was kept for several years in the Istanbul *naqib*'s office, until one day the loyalty of the Ghudayyas during the 1703 uprising was brought to mind and the decision was made to accede to Abd al-Latif's request. Perhaps the sweet scents of the soaps and rose water helped.[5]

The letter of appointment arrived in the beginning of February 1745, and Abdullah could still quote it verbatim: 'We hereby command that you be appointed *naqib al-ashraf* of the holy places in Jerusalem, Nablus, Gaza, Ramallah and Jenin. You are to treat respectfully all persons of high lineage. You are to preserve their legal rights ...' and so on and so forth. It was signed: 'In all humility, the Honorable Ottoman *naqib al-ashraf*, Sayyid Zayn al-Abidin.'[6]

Once he held these two posts, Abd al-Latif's sphere of influence stretched beyond Jerusalem. More importantly, the Alamis could not compete with his status and power. Khalil al-Muradi, the *mufti* of Damascus, who knew him personally, would write that Abd al-Latif controlled every aspect of life in Jerusalem, so powerful and dominant had he become.[7] But it was not blind fortune that preserved Abd al-Latif's exalted position – it was his tireless efforts to maintain good relations with the governor of Damascus and the authorities in Istanbul that ensured his standing and influence. He followed closely everything that took place at the sultan's court, and every possible opponent of the sultan or the *vizier* received gifts from Abd al-Latif.

But times were changing. Abdullah complained to the high official in Istanbul that the source of the trouble lay in Damascus. In 1760 the sultan had appointed a new governor of Damascus, Othman Pasha, a harsh, tyrannical man who had been sent to the region in order to suppress the revolt of Dahir al-Umar, dubbed the 'King of Galilee' by the Franciscans in the country. Al-Umar was in fact much more attuned to the people and less ambitious as a king, but he did become a thorn in the empire's side. This young Palestinian *sheikh* had sprung up and grown strong in the town of Saffuriya, and with his personal charm and well-placed bribes he persuaded the Ottoman authorities to make him governor of Galilee as well as its imperial tax collector. In 1735 he expanded his rule to Nazareth, Marj ibn Amr (the Jezreel Valley) and Nablus.[8]

When al-Umar expanded his sphere of influence, he threatened the valuable *Hajj* routes, which provided substantial revenues from levies on transit and encampment on the pilgrimage route to Mecca. (They also conferred honor and prestige on the person who protected the journey of the believers on their way to perform one of the five basic commandments of Islam.) Yet despite his grave infringement of Istanbul's power, no one could defeat this man. In 1750 he expanded his rule to include Haifa and Tantura. His success encouraged other local potentates to encroach on Ottoman control of the Syrian districts. But it should be understood that what appeared to be the crumbling of imperial control was in reality a struggle for the representation of the empire and the collection of its taxes rather than attempts to displace it as the sovereign power. When a local potentate sought a larger share of the tax revenue, he was not actually challenging the empire. Istanbul's decen-tralized, delegated power made such moves possible; only when the empire began to weaken would the rules of the game change, and then the central power would try to deter dominant figures in the provinces from embarking on independent courses.

Decades before, al-Umar had created enough uncertainty to allow relief from tax collection and other forms of annoying governing policies directed from Damascus. This was now over, and with the help of the new governor Damascus restored its position as the center of regional author-ity. At the time of Abdullah's visit, the new governor in Damascus began to show satisfactory results in the attempt to contain Dahir al-Umar. He succeeded in strengthening Jerusalem's attachment to Damascus, and hence to the empire.

But Abdullah complained in Istanbul that the new governor was more concerned with increasing his own wealth at the expense of the local notables than in suppressing the rebellious al-Umar. What Abdullah did not tell his host was that some months before going to Istanbul, he himself had sent emissaries to al-Umar in Acre, proposing cooperation against the tyrannical governor. However, the governor did hear about it, and forbade Abdullah's father to leave his house – a punishment that was still in force for some time after Abdullah entered the imperial capital. So tyrannical did Damascus's rule seem to Abdullah that he would have preferred to let his beloved city fall into Dahir al-Umar's hands. Economic considerations combined with political ones prompted the family to support the Galilean ruler. Abdullah feared that more money would be taken by the governor in Damascus than by al-Umar. Moreover, the family's fortunes were in decline due to the 1760 earthquake that shook Jerusalem and, although causing little loss of life, destroyed many of the family's properties.[9]

Zayn al-Abidin reassured the young man, saying that his father's connec-tions in the capital would secure the family's predominance in Jerusalem, even if they were at odds with Damascus. The Istanbul *naqib*, like other high imperial officials, habitually made such promises, not only to the Ghudayyas but to their rivals. The old imperial method of divide and rule enabled the central government to maintain control over its outlying provinces. Still, the family's great wealth and generous gifts served to secure an advantage over its rivals. This was a ruthless competition for limited resources and properties capable of sustaining only a handful of aristocratic families in Jerusalem.

The power of these families derived from the income they received for managing the sanctuaries and for the religious services they provided to the populace, and they strove to pass these posts and their properties on to their heirs. Abd al-Latif succeeded in conferring a prime position on his offspring, and his son had to work to keep it. The fate of the family hung in the balance. Since the Ghudayyas' income came indirectly from the sultan himself, their lavish gifts were a kind of *quid pro quo*. Since the reign of Suleiman the Magnificent, the sultans had invested greatly in the holy places in Jerusalem, a good deal of their investment being in the form of rewards to the people who looked after the shrines, such as the *sheikh al-haram*, the *mufti* and others. So far as we know, the Ghudayyas had no sources of income outside the city walls. Still, the management of holy places and clerical posts was sufficient to make them wealthy by both contemporary and modern standards.

Muslim notables such as the Ghudayyas also accrued economic power from the debts owed to them by the Jewish and Christian communities. All members of the family lent money, and the debts increased from one generation to the next, enriching the family's capital. Abd al-Latif himself passed on this kind of financial asset – not unlike modern bonds or shares – to his son Hassan and his daughter Budriya. The creditors were also the benefactors and patrons of the non-Muslim communities in the city. For example, the creditors of the Jews had the right to veto the community's chosen leaders.

But there was no satisfying the governor of Damascus: the accrue-ment of debts meant that the Ghudayyas were richer than before, and the governor thus expected them to pay more taxes. Despite Zayn al-Abidin's assurances, Abdullah returned to Jerusalem with a heavy heart and a pre-monition that his family could expect a difficult time. His worries were confirmed as soon as he returned. Before he had rested from the journey, his family informed him that the situation had worsened. The governor of Damascus had openly allied himself with the rival families to depose Abd al-Latif from his post.

The campaign against Abd al-Latif had begun before Abdullah's journey to Istanbul. It was led by the Dajani family, who headed the Shafi'i school in the city. (Each of the four canonical Islamic schools of law had its own judiciary.) The rumor that was spread in the city would not seem defamatory to us today, but at the time it could seriously damage Abd al-Latif's standing. It began with an undeniable act that was typical of the man. Not far from his house lived the Jewish rabbi Aharon, who used to beat his son Hayim mercilessly. Abd al-Latif could not bear to see this and demanded that the rabbi stop the beatings, and indeed they stopped. The grateful lad must have decided that only Islam could save him from his abusive father, and asked to be converted. But Abd al-Latif refused to convert him. It was here that the slander began. Some claimed that Abd al-Latif was not interested in protecting the boy but was motivated by greed, and that he had been paid handsomely by the leaders of the Jewish community. Abd al-Latif had no choice but to petition the court, which decided that he was 'a religious man and a true believer' and that the slander was groundless.[10]

But the campaign went on, and it was only thanks to the *mufti* of Damascus, Khalil al-Muradi, Abd al-Latif's devoted old friend, that the rival families were unable to carry out their scheme. The family enterprises were now being run by Abdullah, since his father was still confined to his house for the crime of corresponding with the Galilean rebel Dahir al-Umar. In effect, Abdullah had become the city's *naqib al-ashraf*. Counseled by his friends in Damascus and Istanbul, he hoped to be successful in the post, which he had wanted but had not expected to take on so soon.[11]

In fact, Dahir al-Umar unwittingly saved the family from the hostile governor of Damascus. In September 1771, he routed the governor's army in the Huleh Valley. To replace the defeated governor, Istanbul appointed Muhammad al-Azm, a scion of the chief notable family in Damascus, with whom the Ghudayyas had cordial relations. Al-Azm was no more successful than his predecessor in the fight against Dahir al-Umar, who continued to expand his kingdom. In 1773 al-Umar seized the entire area west of the Jordan (from the Litani River in the north to Bir Saba in the south); only Jerusalem and its environs remained under effective Ottoman rule.

Fortunately for Jerusalem, al-Umar had no interest in the city, but he did take a brief interest in the Ghudayyas. He believed that their status as a leading family – possibly already known as the Husaynis – could be useful to him in the regional power play. He therefore sent the heads of the family a letter asking them to mediate between him and Damascus.[12] The family only rarely supported rebels against Ottoman rule; mostly they remained loyal to the central government, and they did so in this case too. In any event, Dahir al-Umar's rise did not force them to become involved in regional political machinations, and since their local rivals showed no interest in the matter, they felt no need to deal with such a mighty force as Dahir al-Umar.

In November 1773, a new local figure successfully challenged both al-Umar and Istanbul. This was Ahmad al-Jazzar, or 'Cezzar Ahmet' as he was known in Turkish. (Since he knew no Arabic, it would be appropriate to call him by his Turkish name, but we will use his more common Arabic name.)

Al-Jazzar would become a major figure in the region. He quickly rose from being a mercenary soldier to the position of provincial governor, betraying others who helped him along the way, such as Dahir al-Umar. During his ascent to power he visited Jerusalem, but we have no evidence of any contact with the Ghudayyas.

Dahir al-Umar and al-Jazzar were part of a general challenge from within to the empire's authority in the Middle East. In the 1770s Istanbul was hard-pressed by its prolonged, bloody war with expansionist Russia, and this encouraged potentates in the provinces to try to unseat their Ottoman overlords. In Palestine, this new reality was manifested in a constant struggle for the land amongst Egyptian rulers, who gradually seceded from the empire, and ambitious governors in Damascus, Saida and Beirut.

Al-Jazzar added a new regional center, the city of Acre, which was responsible for most of Syria's southern regions. After consolidating his role, al-Jazzar, in the service of the empire, succeeded in containing the Egyptian drive into Palestine.

During those years of regional strife, Jerusalem was not sought after by any of the warring parties. Nevertheless, its inhabitants were prey to more zealous tax collection every time one of the rivals gained the upper hand. However, because of all the confusion and ambiguity, this meant escaping the need to pay customary annual taxes. The city was also immune to the destruction wreaked by invading armies on towns in the adjoining districts of Jaffa, Gaza and Ramla. This urban space was quite often a battlefield for the belligerents.

These troubled times were relatively short and came to an end in the mid-1770s. During those years of unrest, the Husaynis, like other urban notables, were more concerned with financial matters than local politics. They were affected by the Ottoman monetary reform declared in the late seventeenth century, but only many years later. Until 1690 most of the Ottoman economy had been based on foreign rather than local currency, which limited the government's ability to control its economy in the capitalist era, and the frequent wars in the late seventeenth century had further depleted the treasury. They decided to base the economy on a new imperial currency, the *akce*, a silver coin later replaced by the *piastre*. People began to buy the new currency from the government, paying in old specie, but the government preferred jewelry, diamonds and the like. The notables were ordered to hand over silver objects, as the metal was needed to mint the new imperial coins. The inhabitants of all the cities were obliged to pay for the Ottoman currency with gems and gold.[13]

The regional and local agitation subsided once Istanbul ended its long, bloody war with Russia with a peace treaty in 1774. With the capital at peace, it was possible to concentrate on pacifying the provinces. Al-Jazzar's position was solidified alongside a loyal governor in Damascus.

In that year of relative calm, Abd al-Latif's health began to decline. Perhaps he was worn out by the struggle against the governor of Damascus in addition to the rivalry with the other great families. But his failing health had to be kept secret. While Abdullah conducted most of his father's business, by all appearances Abd al-Latif was still the city's *naqib al-ashraf.*

He finally died in 1775, aged eighty-one (though some sources say he was ninety years old). The funeral was low-key. His body was placed in a casket and followed by the family and close friends. Dervishes and sheikhs bearing palm fronds murmured prayers, and everyone called out repeatedly: 'There is no God but Allah!' The casket was taken to the Haram al-Sharif, where it was placed on a stone plinth for people to walk past it before it was taken to the cemetery facing the Mount of Olives.[14]

While walking down to the cemetery, Abd al-Latif's four sons discussed the future and shared out their father's posts without dispute. Two of them will appear later in our narrative as they were the ones who were given a role in public life: Abdullah and Hassan. The other two were not given any posts or particular honors (their part of the family played no role in the public life of Jerusalem or Palestine but instead followed private careers in business or the sciences). Abdullah inherited the *niqaba,* which would remain in the family for a long time. In 1776 he was also appointed Sheikh al-Haram, a position that had always been in the family (that is, in the 'appropriated' Wafa'i family). However, Hassan had to wait five years for his post, and only in 1780, at the age of thirty-eight, was he appointed *mufti* of Jerusalem. Now the family had almost complete control of Jerusalem's religious and social systems.

Before the eighteenth century came to an end, the family would once again have to defend its prominence in the city. It was thanks to Hassan and his brothers that the family made it through this challenge.

### Hassan al-Husayni: The Making of a Family Narrative

Towards the end of the eighteenth century, Hassan al-Husayni finished writing *The Biographies of the Jerusalemite Families in the 12th Hijra Century,* the histories of forty-three Jerusalem notables of his time. He had labored for over a year on this composition about 'the Jerusalemites', including his own family. A few years later, the *mufti* of Damascus, Khalil al-Muradi, wrote a directory of the notables in his district, modeling it on that of Hassan. A hundred and fifty years later the two books would end up at the British Museum Library and enable modern historians to trace the history of the Arab-Ottoman elite of the Greater Syria area.[15]

With these two books the family's takeover of the al-Husayni al-Wafa'i lineage became a fait accompli, and its members could proudly hang a drawing of their family tree in the entrance halls of their homes, as was customary among notable families in Palestine.[16] But Hassan did more than that. He studied a variety of other subjects. The post of *mufti* required considerable learning – his rulings allowed him to interpret and expound on Islamic law (the Shari'a). His interpretations were rulings (*fatwa*) sent to those who asked questions about Islam, and they relied on precedents or Muslim religious texts or occasionally on the *mufti*'s own inclinations. Hassan's familiarity with the intricacies of Muslim religious rules was famous throughout the region, and many students from al-Azhar University visited him and consulted his library. Hassan owed his great learning to his father, who had not only hired local religious scholars for his studious son but had also sent him, at the tender age of thirteen, to study with the leading al-Azhar scholars of his time. He spent 1755 and 1756 in Egypt and was so impressed by one of his tutors that before returning to his country he composed a short poem in his praise. His education at home and abroad introduced him not only to Islamic learning but also to Ottoman culture. In time, Hassan would write his memoirs and name all his teachers and mentors.[17]

During the 1770s and 1780s Hassan was able to devote himself to religious scholarship because his brother Abdullah was still managing the affairs of the family. Abdullah's successful trip to Istanbul had ensured good relations with the sultan's court in the Ottoman capital. Nevertheless, it would have been impossible to sustain the family's political standing without recourse to Hassan's religious status. Whenever it seemed that the rulers of Damascus, the al-Azm family, were plotting against the Husaynis, it fell to Hassan to tackle the problem. And indeed he not only managed to sort out difficulties with Damascus but also established such good relations with the al-Azms that he became an informal adviser to the Syrian governor.

The most notable political event in the lives of Hassan and Abdullah was the failed attempt, in about 1790, by other notable families to dispossess them of their official posts. It was only a matter of time before such an attempt would be made. Throughout the eighteenth century no single family held such a position in the city. It was no secret that this was due to alliances with Damascus and Istanbul. To maintain their position it was necessary to win the trust of the local *qadi*, then the approval of the governor of Damascus and finally that of Istanbul's *naqib al-ashraf.* The latter would not confirm an appointment without a magnificent gift, and the list of people expecting largesse kept growing longer. It reached a point where the family had to employ a regular agent in Istanbul to deliver boxes of soaps and vials of perfume to any person with potential influence on the family's position. Needless to say, the rival families envied the Husaynis' wealth, because it was impossible to satisfy the greed of all the senior functionaries in the Ottoman capital without considerable means. The Husaynis' ability to obtain the post of *naqib* was especially impressive because, although it passed from father to son and was in theory an appointment for life, it had to be confirmed annually. It especially rankled that the appointment was supposedly approved by all the notables of Jerusalem, whether they agreed or not. They would all be summoned to the courtyard of the Hanbaliya mosque in the city to hear the town crier announce the appointment of a Husayni to the post.

So strong had the family become that inevitably some of the other notables resented it. The most hostile was the al-Khalidi family (with a reputed and well-established lineage that could be traced back to the Prophet Muhammad and a high position in the city and beyond) when it was headed by Sheikh Musa al-Khalidi. Musa was not only a greatly respected *alim* (religious scholar) with good connections in Damascus and Istanbul; he had climbed higher than any Jerusalemite in the Ottoman hierarchy and become a chief *qadi* of Anatolia, second only to the Sheikh al-Islam, the empire's Grand Mufti. Musa al-Khalidi was well positioned to harm the Husaynis now and then, and to close ranks with the other families.

The year 1790 was an especially tense one in the city. The list of recipients of gifts in Istanbul had grown inordinately long and included persons who were potentially, though not actually, powerful. At first the Khalidis succeeded in removing the Husaynis from their three important posts. Their main allies were the Alamis and al-Jama'is. They got a member of the Alami family appointed as *naqib al-ashraf* in place of Abdullah, and brought about the dismissal of Hassan from the post of *mufti* and of one of his brothers from the post of *sheikh al-haram.* The Alami notable Muhib al-Din was a suitable candidate for the post of *naqib*, which both his father and grandfather had filled. As for Hassan's replacement there was some poetic justice in it, since the latter had been the most serious candidate for the post of *mufti* when Hassan was appointed to it in 1780.[18] Hassan had observed in his book about

Jerusalem's notables that this man was among the best qualified for the highest posts in the city. Then Hassan himself became *mufti*, and nine years elapsed before he was displaced by his rival.

However, like the displacement of his brothers, this setback did not last long. Hassan remained in Jerusalem while his brothers lived in exile in Homs. But for two individuals so entrenched in regional politics, exile was a high road to their return to Jerusalem. To create the impression that they were in the authorities' good books, the two spread rumors that they had the support of the governor of Damascus before they actually had it. Once they actually obtained it, their way home was open.[19]

We lack sufficient information to reconstruct the exact circumstances in which the Husaynis recovered their dominant positions in Jerusalem in 1796. Presumably lavish gifts and good contacts helped restore the family to its former status. That year most of the notables went to the *qadi* and the city's governor to declare their support for Hassan. As soon as Hassan was appointed, they all – even his opponents – came to congratulate him, since he was now in a position to harm them and, even more important, to protect them from the whims of the governor and the *qadi*.

The *qadi* sometimes ignored the custom of allowing the members of a notable family to be judged solely by their peers. Only a strong *naqib* could prevent such an indignity. In its turn, the government demanded that Hassan put a stop to some of the notables' habit of wearing the white tarbush with the green stripe, which was officially the prerogative of Istanbul-appointed judges. This habit was widespread in other provinces too, and it infuriated the Ottoman administration. In past centuries this prestigious tarbush had been worn by all notables, thus giving rise to the misunderstanding. This stylish vogue was viewed as deliberate defiance of the imperial power, and the *naqib* was expected to maintain the delicate balance between local pride and the honor of the central authority.

Abdullah died in July 1797, and his son inherited the *niqaba*. But the new appointee died after a few months, and the post passed to his brother , who also died soon after assuming the *niqaba*.[20] And so once again Hassan stood in the mosque of al-Aqsa to hear the *qadi* declare before the multitude: 'We have accepted the recommendation of the notables of Jerusalem, who have chosen you, Hassan ibn Abd al-Latif, to be *naqib*, like your father and grandfather before you. Knowing of your good qualities and abilities, we appoint you accordingly.'[21]

The series of misfortunes that had led up to the rise of Hassan doubtless aroused suspicions that he had had something to do with it, but no one dared to express them in public and they were probably groundless. When Umar, the son of one of the boys who died in 1797, reached the proper age, Hassan passed the post of the *naqib* to him. Theirs was a complex relationship: Umar was not only Hassan's nephew, he was also his grandson, being the son of Hassan's daughter who had married his nephew. Such matches were customary in those days, and no one discredited their motives. Certainly the clan as a whole had no doubts about the revered *sheikh*.

The reversals in the family's status reflected upheavals in the empire, and times of uncertainty and transition prompted people to change the ground rules. The stable, continuous regime in Istanbul ended, and a period of instability ensued. A new century began in which the Middle East would change almost beyond recognition, plunged into a maelstrom of wars and revolutions that continue to the present day. The drama was so high that one would have expected it to drastically alter the life of the Jerusalemites in general, and the Husyanis in particular. But continuity rather than transformation seemed to be the rule in those anxious times.

The high drama in the empire began in 1789 with the accession of Sultan Selim III, who ruled until 1807. He dared to challenge some of the more conservative power bases of the empire – the military and religious institutions – and thus destabilized the center. As always in such critical situations, the small players on the regional stage had to exercise the utmost caution and exert the greatest effort. Both camps in Istanbul demanded that these regional players commit to a side.

Which brings us back to Hassan sitting in his library, reconstructing the genealogies of Jerusalem's notables. While the enterprise satisfied his intellectual curiosity, it was also driven by the exigencies of the rivalry in Jerusalem. Responding to Istanbul's demand for loyalty, the family now asked to be paid in advance for its support. Hassan wrote to the *naqib al-ashraf* in Istanbul, asking that the sultan approve all of the family's posts, so as to consolidate its religious and social standing. Hassan sought to persuade the great *naqib* that the Husaynis' lineage was not inferior to that of the Khalidis. The latter's name, as has been noted, was engraved in the collective consciousness as pure and proven. Hassan's highly regarded books, and later al-Muradi's prosography, had completed the usurpation of the lineage of the al-Husayni al-Wafa'i. The sultan's renewed recognition was thus needed not only for reappointment but also as a final unqualified recognition of the new family name. 'After almost a hundred years in which the family has filled such important posts,' Hassan wrote in his letter to the *naqib al-ashraf* of Istanbul (which was accompanied by an especially generous gift), 'it deserves to be known by the name that attests to its noble lineage.'[22]

But the Ottoman power was not satisfied with the generous gift – it wanted political results. The family had helped to put down a tax revolt in 1789 in the villages of Banu Hassan (the area around modern-day Beit Safafa, in the south of the city). Damascus tended to regard the family as responsible not only for Jerusalem and its environs but also for Gaza, Nablus, Ramla and Jenin. In 1796, when one young Husayni after another was appointed to the post of *naqib*, those towns and cities were mentioned explicitly in their letters of investiture. During the time of Umar, Lydda and Jaffa were also included in the family's sphere of influence.[23] These places were always named in the family's investitures, though its position in them was not invariably strong. But as the eighteenth century drew to a close, the family was seen as an important factor in these urban centers, and its prestige grew beyond the leadership of the Jerusalemite nobility to encompass a broader field. This would be one of several reasons for the family's future position at the head of the Palestinian national movement.[24]

During this period, marriage with another family was also used to strengthen the Husaynis' position. In the summer of 1792, Abdullah's eldest daughter married the heir of the head of the al-Jama'i family. The match sealed the alliance between the two families, though only two years earlier the al-Jama'is had taken part in the coalition that had driven the Husaynis from their dominant posts. But the women of the family were more than diplomatic assets in consolidating its position. As we shall see, the Husaynis helped to advance a progressive Muslim attitude regarding the position of women. Hassan was the first to do so: one of his decisions stated that whoever failed to bequeath to his daughters their proper portion in the inheritance, or who robbed them of their dowry, could not be considered a Muslim. This statement appears as part of his wider criticism of the condition of Islam in the villages surrounding Jerusalem.[25]

This is not to suggest that Sheikh Hassan was a feminist ahead of his time: he, too, thought the birth of sons a blessing and the birth of daughters, if not a curse, certainly a disappointment. His first wife bore only daughters, and it was thought that the *sheikh* would have to sustain his family's position by marrying them off well. But he followed the custom in such cases and married a young woman who bore him his first sons. By the time he died, he had grandchildren by his daughters, and one of them, Umar al-Husayni, was appointed guardian of his half-siblings who were still minors – eight boys and three girls.

The position of women had some weighty economic aspects. From the time he reached adulthood, Hassan had to appear before the Shari'a court in connection with the estate of his mother, and his sister. Their estates included the debts owed his family by the Jewish and Christian communities in Jerusalem – among them the Ashkenazi and Sephardi Jewish communities, as well as the Armenians. Appearing as the creditor on behalf of his family was not, incidentally, an indication of hostility towards these communities. Indeed, his very first decision as *mufti*, in a dispute between the Muslim inhabitants of the village of Silwan and the Jews of Jerusalem, came down in favor of the latter. The Jews of Jerusalem traditionally bought stone for their tombstones from Silwan, where it was quarried on land belonging to the village's religious authority. The complaint was that the sale had been carried out without a permit from the guardian of the religious lands, but Hassan ruled that the vendors – namely, the villagers – had been at fault, and not the Jewish purchasers. This was the first of many decisions that revealed the complexity of Hassan's worldview, including the issue of Muslim-Jewish relations.[26]

The high drama continued with Napoleon Bonaparte's invasion of Egypt in 1798 and his journey into Palestine and Syria a year later. This, too, was a climactic event that did not affect the lives of the Husaynis, unless one considers the invasion as the onset of modern times in the Middle East and the starting point of its Westernization (a somewhat anachronistic concept with students of the Middle East, who prefer a more synthetic picture of internal and external dynamics to explain transformations in the area over the last 200 years). Certainly, the next century saw the economic and political integration of Palestine into the European scene and exposed the family to the impact of foreign interests and agendas. How the family responded to these new developments is not easy to assess. The evidence from the past is open information: we know what difficulties they faced but less, if anything at all, about how they responded.

What mattered in the early years of the nineteenth century was that Jerusalem's fate depended greatly on the policies of al-Jazzar, with whom the family maintained good relations. Even while French soldiers were marching on the Palestine coast, the Husaynis corresponded with Acre on trivial and routine issues that reflected Hassan's agenda. During these dramatic days, Hassan wrote a letter beseeching Ahmad al-Jazzar to ease the burden on the *jaballiya*, the mountain people, poor peasants from the mountains of Hebron, Jerusalem and Nablus who worked as servants of the Haram. The letter sang their praises. We cannot say whether this was typical of the family's attitude towards the unfortunates in the city and the surrounding country or the expression of a social conscience, but we do know that such tendencies would not always persist in later generations.[27]

The notables of Jerusalem as a whole were loyal to al-Jazzar. When the Ottoman government attempted to limit his rule but allowed the governor of Gaza more authority in Jerusalem (translating mainly to the power of collecting taxes), they encountered a rebellious opposition of notables led by the Husaynis. In 1801, the notables caused the representative of the pro-Ottoman Gazan governor to flee and seek refuge in King David's tomb on Mount Zion. Faced with such determined resistance, the Gazan governor, Abu Maraq, gave in, perhaps also because he was interested in Umar's sister. The family had never objected to politically advantageous matches, but we have no way of knowing how Zaynab, the young woman in question, felt about it.[28]

As in the 1770s, it was the coastal towns that took the brunt of the high ambitions of local and foreign invaders. When Bonaparte occupied Gaza for a short while, French soldiers rampaged through the city and many of the inhabitants met a horrible death. Twenty years after Egyptian invaders had committed dreadful slaughter, the French troops showed that they were just as capable of cruelty and indifference to human life.

The greatest difficulty during this period for the Husaynis was the presence in Jerusalem of a member of the original clan al-Husayni al-Wafa'i, known as al-Maqdasi. Though that family's standing had declined since the *naqib*'s revolt of 1705, Hassan and most of Jerusalem's notables felt a great regard for and attachment to this remarkable man. After the *naqib*'s revolt, his family settled in Gaza, and some of them went on to Egypt. Al-Maqdasi became one of the most outstanding scholars of al-Azhar and from time to time would visit Jerusalem, where he became Hassan's teacher. Moreover, his family was connected by marriage to the Ghudayyas.

In 1798, al-Maqdasi led the popular revolt against Napoleon in Cairo. After the French troops had searched for him in vain for three days, he fled to Jerusalem. There he immediately took a wife, because he had left his family behind in Egypt and would return only after Napoleon had been driven out. In the meantime, it was feared that his presence in Jerusalem would attract the French. This fear grew when al-Maqdasi made it plain that he did not intend to remain anonymous. He was too active a man to sit still. He served as *imam* at Friday worship, gave lessons on the Qur'an and received from the local *qadi* the guardianship of some important properties of the religious authority. He spent three years in Jerusalem, during which time he helped Hassan but was also a dangerous lure to the French forces.[29]

Once again, as during the time of Dahir al-Umar, the city's marginality saved it and its inhabitants from the heat of battle. Strategic considerations prompted the foreign invader to proceed elsewhere into the last stage of his failed journey of conquest.

As Karl Marx noted, a political vacuum never lasts. Indeed, no sooner had the French withdrawn than Abu Maraq of Gaza and al-Jazzar of Acre began to fight for control of Palestine. The Sublime Porte preferred Abu Maraq and handed over Jerusalem to him (together with most of al-Jazzar's previous possessions as well as Egypt). The notables and the Husaynis leading them wished the city to belong once more to Acre's sphere of influence. And no wonder: unlike Abu Maraq, the Grand Vizier's protégé, al-Jazzar had never taxed them oppressively or sought to limit their power. Not wishing to enter into conflict with the powers that be, however, the notables wrote to Istanbul praising the Acre magnate and maligning the Gazan. This was a bold move, considering that Abu Maraq governed Jerusalem. Yet their position mattered, since the governor's appointment came into force only after the notables had been informed of it. Abu Maraq was not of their class but a man of the people. During the struggle against Napoleon, he had not even approached the notables but had appealed directly to the villagers, some of whom responded to his call to mount a *jihad* against the invader. His demand that the notables raise a certain number of troops for the war also alienated them.[30]

The ignominy continued when the heads of the families and the notables were forced to hand over to the wife of the governor's chief aide all the weapons that they had received from al-Jazzar or obtained as spoils. This humiliating scene took place in the *qadi*'s presence and greatly intensified the resentment against Abu Maraq. Here, too, he showed his sympathy for the lower classes. He also used his power over Egypt and the districts of Palestine to strengthen trade relations between them. While harassing Jerusalem's notables, he wrote to the city's merchants: 'The evil days are over, to be followed by days of blessing and joy.' The merchants were regarded as a lower class in Arab-Ottoman society, and most of them were non-Muslim.[31]

But Abu Maraq's standing also rose and fell. In 1802, despite the Grand Vizier's solid support, he was eventually defeated by al-Jazzar. He lost his position in Egypt to local forces and his other regions in a field battle with al-Jazzar, who simply ignored the Grand Mufti's and Grand Vizier's support for his foe. The alliance with the governor of Damascus gave al-Jazzar sufficient military strength to force Istanbul to give in to him, and so Jerusalem fell once again under Acre's rule.

But only for two years. For in 1804 al-Jazzar died, and the city's status changed again. Officially it was once more subordinated to Damascus, which received a new governor but which in reality continued to be ruled from Acre. For a brief while, the Jerusalemites even felt nostalgic for Abu Maraq, since al-Jazzar's heir, Suleiman, immediately raised taxes. The inhabitants rebelled and – this should sound familiar by now – imprisoned the ruler's representatives in the city fortress. In response, Suleiman dispatched the commander of his army, who sent for the ringleaders, some fifty men, on the pretext of negotiations and, having caught them, had their heads cut off in public. Suleiman was content to receive the heads, and the city became quiet. Thus neither Suleiman nor Abu Maraq looked like an attractive proposition.[32]

But Abu Maraq's shadow still hung over the city, or rather over its notables, for whom he had no use. He was highly regarded in Istanbul, where it was hoped he could help create a buffer between the empire and the Wahabiyya – a Salafi movement on the Arabian Peninsula that challenged the sultans' right to rule over the Muslim world. The notables of Jerusalem, fearful that 'the commoner' planned to humiliate them again, began to agitate intensively in Istanbul for their city to be ruled directly either by Acre or Damascus.

Strangely, there is no record of the Husaynis playing a significant part in the 1804 struggle between Acre and Gaza for control over Jerusalem. The family seemed anxious not to attract attention, so as to cope with whatever developments took place in the country and their city.

The *qadi*'s deputy, a Khalidi, wrote personally on behalf of the city's notables to the governor of Jerusalem, appointed in al-Jazzar's days and thus loyal to Acre, to ask him to remain in his post: 'For fear of disorder in the collection and administration of taxes, and concerned about the need to protect the poor and weak and the general populace, the revered *ulama* and the notables of the city beg you to remain in your former post.'[33] This intervention by the local notables was exceptional, but in the course of the nineteenth century it would become more frequent, and the Husaynis would also gradually take part in such interventions.

Only Hassan al-Husayni, by virtue of his high position, was partly involved. Fearful that Abu Maraq would penalize the city for its support for al-Jazzar, he appealed to the governor of Damascus, who was staying in Jenin during the annual tax collection. The governor hastened to reassure Hassan: 'We are aware of your concern about the forthcoming visit of our brother, Muhammad Pasha Abu Maraq, but he will only be passing through your district. We wish to make it clear that Jerusalem is still under our [Damascus's] rule, and we have no intention of letting Abu Maraq rule over the city.'[34] To further reassure the families, in 1805 the governor came to the city and publicly noted that that he was forgoing that year's *Hajj* in order to visit al-Aqsa mosque. But this governor's support proved useless: while he was visiting Jerusalem he was deposed by Istanbul.

But Abu Maraq, too, soon vanished from the scene – Suleiman had him killed in 1807. The imperial *firman* sent by the sultan to the notables of Jerusalem must have reassured Hassan that the bad times were over. Even if he did not agree with Suleiman that the assassination of Abu Maraq was 'part of the *jihad* for Allah,'[35] he must have felt greatly relieved.

In 1806, as part of the struggle in Istanbul between the religious establishment and the reforming Sultan Selim III, religious leaders such as the Grand Mufti of Istanbul began dismissing *muftis* throughout the empire whom they suspected of sympathizing with Selim III. Hassan was such a person. In winter 1806 came the order the Husaynis had dreaded since the unrest had begun in Istanbul. Hassan's nephew Tahir, the current *naqib*, was also deposed. Fortunately for the family, the crisis lasted only a year, thanks to the help of Yusuf Kanj Pasha, the governor of Damascus at the time and an old family friend. Kanj was popularly known as 'the Kurd' (whether or not he himself was a Kurd, certainly his guard were Kurds).[36] In the family's collective memory, he occupies a very favorable place. He was indeed a real friend of the family, an ally who helped them to pass in relative calm the twilight zone between the rule of Acre and the old-new rule of Damascus.[37]

Kanj persuaded the Grand Mufti that the Husaynis were perfectly devout Muslims who would never have supported the former sultan if they had realized that he proposed to violate the sanctity of their religion and tradition. There was some truth to this argument, because the family's loyalty to Selim III stemmed not so much from enthusiasm for his innovations or for the ideas of the French Revolution as from traditional loyalty to the head of the Muslim world.[38]

The year 1808 was the last of Hassan al-Husayni's life, and it was as tumultuous as all the rest. The summer had been unusually hot, and in September the Church of the Holy Sepulchre went up in flames – one more chapter in the endless feuds among the rival Christian denominations in Jerusalem. This time the struggle for control over the church reached new heights. The blaze broke out in the middle of a thronged service. The place was more crowded than usual, and an Armenian pilgrim set the place on fire – whether by accident or by design is not known. The unusual crowding was due to that year's great increase in the number of pilgrims, who almost outnumbered the locals.[39]

The blaze revealed the strength of the Husaynis' position. Hassan was the *mufti*, and Umar had just been appointed as *naqib al-ashraf*, replacing his grandfather. They were asked to spend the night in tents in the churchyard in order to prevent looting. They responded willingly and showed that their mere presence in the place ensured obedience to the Prophet's commandment to respect the Christian 'People of the Book'. They also benefited from the reconstruction of the church, which began immediately and as always in those days entailed bribery to everyone authorized to approve the reconstruction of Christian houses of worship – namely, representatives of the Ottoman government and the Husaynis.

The era of Hassan ended. His fascinating personality is crucial to an understanding of how and why the Husaynis came to be the leading family in Palestine throughout the nineteenth century and the first half of the twentieth century. Almost every contemporary testimony about prominent persons in the region, including Egypt, mentions Hassan as an important religious scholar and a charismatic figure who maintained exceptional contacts with the intellectual elites of Syria and Egypt. It was he who succeeded in keeping the three most important posts in his family and who created a solid structure that would crumble only in 1948, when all of Arab Palestine fell.

The three religious posts remained in the family after his death. His nephew Tahir, inherited the post of *mufti* of Jerusalem, while Hassan's other position as *sheikh al-haram* was passed to the grandson of his other brother Abdullah, Umar, who had already been appointed *naqib al-ashraf* during Hassan's lifetime (in 1800). As before, the three most important positions in the city were held by two members of the Husayni family.

While the post of *mufti* was higher in the Ottoman hierarchy than the other position and would make its holder the more powerful member of the family, most people regarded the *naqib al-ashraf* as the head of the family. It is hard to know in the case of Tahir and Umar who was the informal head. As it happened, Tahir's great learning made him the dominant figure. The records of the Shari'a court in Jerusalem note: 'We have elected Tahir because of his great learning and wisdom, and his outstanding service of the *ifta*' – meaning that he had made brilliant decisions on problems of religious practice and

questions posed by the faithful.[40] Even in Hassan's lifetime, and doubtless
under his influence, Tahir spent several years at Cairo's al-Azhar University,
where he acquired his vast knowledge. He was often seen sitting in a corner
of the Dome of the Rock – the corner facing the Mount of Olives was his
favorite – teaching students the Qur'an and its interpretations.[41] Umar, by
contrast, was the worldlier of the two and took little interest in spiritual
matters. As leaders, they formed an unusual team.

Umar acted as guardian of his grandfather Hassan's young children – that
is, Umar's uncles and aunts, who were also his second cousins. As a result,
Hassan's own offspring had no share in the public honors. But Umar kept
his promise to his grandfather and made sure that the 'Hassans' among the
Husaynis would return to the center of the public stage no less than the
descendants of Abdullah.

By now the family was clearly made up of two branches – the 'Tahiri'
one, which would retain the *mufti*'s post down to al-Hajj Amin al-Husayni,
and the 'Umari' one, which would inherit the *niqaba* until the position lost
its meaning with the end of Ottoman rule. The two branches were independent families who maintained their unity by marriage, inheritance and
solidarity. Whenever the *naqib* and the *mufti* cooperated *vis-à-vis* the central
and regional government, and later foreign invaders from Europe – which
occurred quite frequently – they formed a single entity.

CHAPTER 2

# In the Shadow of Acre and Cairo

## The Third Generation

In 1813 Umar al-Husayni's daughter married Musa Tuqan, the governor of Nablus and scion of one of its leading families, and Musa Bey's daughter married Umar's son Abd al-Salam II. The weddings were held together in Jerusalem. That evening (Muslim weddings were usually held in the evening) the two young couples walked under an immense canopy carried by house servants in a procession that marched towards the Haram al-Sharif. It was illuminated by blazing tar-dipped torches, also borne by servants, and followed by a drummer thumping a great tin drum, giving the beat to a deafening band of pipers. The Husaynis and Tuqans walked serenely behind the musicians, accompanied by many notables and other friends.

A double wedding was a great joy, especially when it consolidated the family's standing. Circumstances in the new century required the Husaynis to expand the family's power base, and once again the daughters were mobilized for the purpose. Musa Bey was not the most important member in the Tuqan family, but he was very close with his brother Khalil, the head of the family, and was on excellent terms with the regional ruler, the governor of Damascus. The family had friendly relations with the former ruler, but had so far failed to establish their position with his successor. Now, thanks to the newly forged link with the Tuqans, Tahir al-Husayni retained his post of *mufti* of Jerusalem, and the new governor sent a heartwarming letter congratulating him on his reappointment: 'We shall not allow any harm to come to the Husaynis under our rule, and we wish them all the prosperity and success due to their status.'

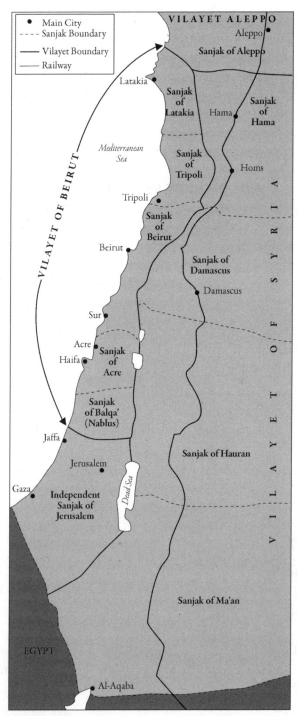

Legend:
- • Main City
- ---- Sanjak Boundary
- —— Vilayet Boundary
- — Railway

VILAYET ALEPPO

Aleppo

Sanjak of Aleppo

Latakia

Sanjak of Latakia

Hama

Sanjak of Hama

Mediterranean Sea

Sanjak of Tripoli

Homs

Tripoli

Sanjak of Beirut

Beirut

Sanjak of Damascus

Damascus

VILAYET OF BEIRUT

Sur

Acre

Haifa

Sanjak of Acre

Sanjak of Balqa' (Nablus)

Jaffa

Jerusalem

Sanjak of Hauran

Gaza

Independent Sanjak of Jerusalem

Dead Sea

VILAYET OF SYRIA

Sanjak of Ma'an

EGYPT

Al-Aqaba

*Adminstrative boundaries under the Ottomans*

But that year the Husaynis also received a reminder that a family's power was liable to fluctuate. A Jerusalem family by the name of Abu al-Suʿud had become very prominent, and in 1813 the sultan invited its head to his court – an honor never bestowed on a Husayni. The following week the sultan himself called on Abu al-Suʿud in Jerusalem, with regard for his great age (he died later that year) and as a gesture of respect.[1]

Such reminders prompted the Husayni family to strengthen their connections in the imperial capital and their position in the region. The ties with the Tuqans helped them to cope with the upheavals on the regional stage after al-Jazzar finally died at a ripe old age (frustrating both his supporters' hopes and his enemies' wishes).

As noted in the previous chapter, Jerusalem was formally restored to the rule of Damascus, but in practice the governors of Acre acted as proxies. Thus the network of contacts needed to maintain the family's position in Jerusalem had to include not only the rulers in Damascus but also the potentates of Acre and al-Jazzar's heir, Suleiman Paşha, with whom the Tuqans had useful contacts. But such a dual rule fueled the ambitions of the regional opposition. Jaffa potentate Muhammad Aga Abu Nabut rose up against Suleiman, helped by the unchallenged strongman of the Jerusalem mountain region, Sheikh Uthman Abu Ghosh. The cause of the insurrection was the usual one in the region: they sought economic power based on tax gathering. Their immediate aim was to restrict the range of Acre's power, and since Abdullah was weakest in Jerusalem, this became their first target. Once again, the Husaynis of both houses had to take a stand.[2]

So long as there was no hint of defiance against the rule of Istanbul, the Husaynis tended to stay out of these often bloody local politics. But now the Abu Ghosh family's involvement made neutrality impossible. Its position in the village of Einab – where it had settled upon its arrival from Kurdistan hundreds of years before – preceded the Husaynis' and intimidated them. The younger Husaynis admired the Abu Ghosh men as models of bravery in the face of regional and even imperial power. The older Husaynis saw them as a liability, as the Abu Ghoshes were rather unpopular in the ruling circles.

The year 1813 was especially pleasant, and not only on account of the double wedding. Naquib Umar al-Husayni renovated a covered area in the Old City and built shops and a soap factory there. This enterprise would be the sound basis of the Umari branch of the family's wealth for years to come. Breaking with a tradition of conservative business dealings, the family also expanded its interests beyond the city and invested in Jaffa and its environs.[3]

The family's economic prosperity enabled it to devote time and thought to the restoration of the Muslim holy places in Jerusalem. In 1816 the governor of Acre, Suleiman Pasha, ordered the restoration of the al-Aqsa mosque. He dispatched a special messenger to Umar, who showed the visitor the ruinous and dilapidated condition of the shrine. They were accompanied by Ahmad Arif Hikmet, a minor Ottoman official who served as *qadi* in Jerusalem and was a close friend of the Husaynis on account of his claim that he was also a descendant of the Prophet. Hikmet was Tahir's age, and the two young men became bosom friends. This connection would be very important in the middle of the century, when Hikmet was appointed the Grand Mufti of the empire. He would be the person who assured the family's continued predominance in Jerusalem through one of the worst times in its history, perhaps the very worst until the catastrophe of 1948.

Following this visit, Sultan Mahmud II issued a decree demanding that the governor of Acre expand the restoration works in the mosque. In keeping with the custom, the inhabitants had to pay for their ruler's generosity. Tahir and Umar were among the first appointed to collect taxes, and later they imported builders and engineers. Bashir II, the ruler of Lebanon, was also roped in, and he and the governor of Beirut held a special tax–collection tour in their territories for the project. Ships laden with cedars of Lebanon were sent to the Port of Jaffa, where Abu Nabut took part in the enterprise. When the restoration was complete, details of the contributions of the sultan and Suleiman Pasha were engraved on a wall of the mosque. The Dome of the Rock was restored at the same time, and there, too, the name of Suleiman was engraved. But Tahir and Umar did not restrict their building activities to religious institutions. As early as 1810 they began to construct and maintain various public buildings. That year Umar received a substantial donation from the governor of Damascus with which he constructed a water conduit leading from the Pools of Solomon into the city.[4]

Times were good for the Husaynis. Umar's house, adjoining the wall of the Haram, attracted important visitors, just as Abd al-Latif's house had done a hundred years earlier. Sheikh Hassan al-Attar, who would later become the *sheikh al-azhar*, came calling, and he noted the warm cultural atmosphere at the Husaynis'. Like many visitors before and after him, he accompanied them at the head of the procession when they led celebrants to the tomb of the Prophet Moses in Jericho.

It was also during this time that the first European visited the Husaynis: Scottish physician Richard Richardson repaid Umar's hospitality by curing him of an eye infection that had troubled him for years.[5] Richardson was also the first European to be admitted to the Haram al-Sharif more or less formally – that is, with the permission of the Sheikh al-Haram, who happened to be Umar al-Husayni. Wearing a black turban lent him by Umar, the Scot sneaked into the Haram in the dead of night. Later he complained that he had been unable to appreciate the beauty of the place in the dark, and Umar relented and smuggled his guest into the place in broad daylight in 1818. But Richardson did not keep the secret, and Umar came to regret the gesture, because then more Europeans asked to be allowed in. His consent suggests either that he was aware of the changing circumstances or that he did not consider the matter vitally important. Be that as it may, historians of the Middle East would later discover how flexible Islam was in Ottoman times, unlike some of its more rigid radical forms that sprang up in the latter half of the twentieth century.

It was not so easy for Mrs Belzoni when she wished to visit the Haram. Her husband, Giovanni Belzoni, was a prominent explorer of Egyptian antiquities, but his English wife was not content to follow his expeditions to the Pharaonic past and wished instead to observe the contemporary Middle East. In her memoirs she recounts proudly that by emulating Richardson's bold act she proved that she was not afraid to risk death. Ottoman law permitted the execution of any Jew or Christian who presumed to enter the Haram, though in practice the penalty was much less severe. Mrs Belzoni befriended a group of Christian builders and craftsmen whom the governor had brought in to restore the Haram shrines, and persuaded them to allow her to join them as though she were the wife of one of their team. But they dithered, and by the time they agreed the work had been finished. Then she tried to bribe Umar al-Husayni to let her go in, but he was under no obligation to her as he had been to Richardson, and he threw her out of his house. In the end, she put on traditional local dress and went in on her own. Richardson and Mrs Belzoni blazed a trail that would be followed by many, and their incursions into the sacred enclosure marked the decline in the status of the Husaynis and the disappearance of the world they had known for 400 years.[6] Later Sarah Berkeley Johnson, the daughter of an American missionary, would imitate Mrs Belzoni. Dressed as a local Muslim woman, she entered not only the Haram but also the Tomb of David, which was also sacrosanct.

Easy times came to an end under the son of Suleiman, al-Jazzar's grandson, known as Abdullah Pasha (in power from 1818 to 1831). The rulers of Acre were determined to dominate all the potentates of southern Syria, obliging the Husaynis to act very circumspectly. Taking advantage of Istanbul's inability to cope with each successive crisis in its far-flung empire, Abdullah Pasha proceeded to change the divisions in the region. Before long he reduced Damascus to his rule and transferred the governance of Jerusalem to his own districts of Acre and Sidon. Now Jerusalem's notables were squeezed by both Damascus and Acre. The main pressure was financial, as both capitals periodically raised the taxes they demanded from their subjects, and every *dura* (the annual tax collection) was likely to stimulate a revolt somewhere. The Husayni family apparently helped these insurrections only when its own interests were affected.

While the Husaynis' relations with Suleiman caused them to become involved in regional politics, they were also drawn willy-nilly into the greater political sphere – namely, the conflict with the Janissaries, the elite Ottoman military corps that had outgrown its usefulness and was threatened with being disbanded by the reformists. When Sultan Mahmud II proposed creating a new army, the Janissaries all over the empire went on the offensive. In 1819 it was Jerusalem's turn.

The Janissaries succeeded in provoking a crisis between the government and society. The pretext was their demand to stop the restoration of the Church of the Holy Sepulchre, which had burned down in 1808.[7] Some of the townspeople fell for their incitement, since any excuse would do to resist higher taxation, and together with some outsiders they converged on the governor's office in the city's fortress. They demanded that he appoint Janissaries as exclusive guards around the fortress, since only they could be trusted to protect the honor of Islam against the Christian encroachment represented by the restoration work at the church. If their demand was not met, they threatened, they would kill everyone inside the fortress. When the governor hesitated, the rebels closed the gates of the city and overran the fortress. If nowadays the seizure of a broadcasting station or presidential palace symbolizes an assault on or overturning of the ruling power, in those days in Jerusalem or other provincial capitals seizure of the fortress meant a putsch. On their way the rebels demolished the restorations at the church and killed some of the monks. Then they elected one of their own, an unknown individual of no special rank, as governor of Jerusalem.

The Husaynis reacted very cautiously, as they had done during the revolt of Abu Nabut. The uprising was aimed at a friend of the family, the governor of Damascus, Yusuf Kanj, whom they did not wish to alienate. Moreover, they wanted the work at the church to continue, since they received a constant stream of gifts and grants that would cease with the suspension of the restoration. Why, then, did they hesitate to oppose the revolt? Presumably because they were being made to pay a special and onerous tax to fund the new imperial army.

Since 1813 the Husaynis, whose exalted status had generally kept them exempt from taxation, had paid a special impost of a considerable sum to the new army fund. Mahmud II was casting around for every possible source of income, up to and including the notables of Jerusalem. It seemed to be a question of simple arithmetic – the tax burden was likely always to be greater than the donations of the Christians, but the family appreciated the stability of the new government after a long period of upheavals and thus avoided clashing with it.[8]

The sultan's response to the uprising was predictably harsh. On the initiative of the governor of Damascus and with the support of the governor of Acre, a regional commander, Abu Zari'a al-Maghrabi, was dispatched to put it down. He stormed the fortress in the middle of the night and slaughtered the rebels. It was said that the governor of Jerusalem accompanied him and with his own hands strangled to death twenty-eight of the rebels. The following day the ringleaders were decapitated and the rest strangled, and their bodies were lined up outside the Bab al-Khalil (Jaffa Gate).

Amid this violent political turmoil the notables of Jerusalem were at a loss about whom to support – Abdullah, the governor of Acre, or the governors of Damascus, who were closer to Sultan Mahmud II. Some opponents of the Husaynis spread a rumor – probably not unfounded – that Umar al-Husayni was inclined to support Abdullah. Early in 1820 this led to an open accusation, as a result of which Umar was briefly exiled, but his status remained unaffected.[9]

For Jerusalem this was a small sample of the political drama unfolding at the heart of the empire. In the early decades of the nineteenth century, life in the holy city was periodically jarred by the concussion of political explosions in the centers of Ottoman or European power. The local manifestations of these detonations were sometimes quite strange, but the family's standing meant that it was more readily embroiled than other Jerusalemites. Such was the case with the chain of events associated with the Greek revolution.

The Greeks were the first to assert their national identity in rebelling against Ottoman power, which had ruled over their lands for nearly 400 years. The revolution broke out in March 1821, and when the news reached Jerusalem, every actor on the local stage used it to promote interests that had nothing whatsoever to do with the uprising.

Every Christian in Jerusalem who felt solidarity with the Greeks and failed to disguise his joy was viewed by the authorities as an active supporter of the rebels. The principal adversary of the Greek Orthodox subjects was the governor of Damascus, Darwish Pasha, whose representative in Jerusalem called on the townspeople to take up arms against the Greek threat. The tension grew with the arrival of a company of soldiers dispatched by Darwish to occupy the fortress 'in preparation'. The Christian inhabitants were ordered to surrender their weapons, to wear black and to drag heavy guns from place to place for no apparent reason. Their humiliation was aggravated by looting and attacks against the Greek Patriarchate. A rumor spread that the townspeople had been commanded to kill every Christian who was caught bearing a weapon.[10]

The governor of Jerusalem might have massacred all the Greek Orthodox inhabitants if the Muslim notables had not intervened. They published a statement condemning the action and reassuring the Christians. The statement quoted the Qur'an on the legal status of *ahl al-kitab* (the Christian 'People of the Book') in the Muslim nation. The governor of Damascus also recovered his wits and intervened to stop the harassment. The government's attitude towards the Roman Catholics was quite different: because of its links with France, it permitted the Catholics to restore and reconstruct the Church of the Holy Sepulchre, and they were exempt from wearing the *qawqa* (the distinctive turban imposed upon the rest of the Christians and the Jews).[11]

At the time, the events of 1819–21 did not seem extraordinary. Then rebellion came to Palestine, and since the land had been quiet for a century this was decidedly unusual. Moreover, these rebellions covered almost all of Palestine and included all the social groups living on the land, which was also unusual. The first occurred in 1824, and the second a decade later in 1834. Some historians consider these the awakening of a Palestinian national, or proto-national, identity (we shall have more to say about this later). In the present context, these political tremors had a greater impact on the life of the Husayni family than those that shook the center of the empire, such as the Greek revolution and the other national uprisings that followed it.

We have chosen to denote the 1824 uprising as the first Palestinian revolt rather than the better-known peasant uprising of 1834, which has lately been described in a book of history as 'the first Palestinian revolt'.[12] The events of 1824 are usually described as a *fitnah* (sedition). It all began in 1823, when Abdullah, the governor of Acre, sent a representative to Jerusalem to demand, in addition to the usual taxes collected by Damascus, a substantial chunk of the family's property. This was a time of decision for the family. Tahir took the lead in formulating the family's response. Ever the scholar, Tahir was thoroughly familiar with the city's history and had also learned from his forefathers to pay close attention to proceedings in Istanbul. This combination of historical and political knowledge gave him his answer. Faced with the new threat, he thought of repeating past victories. He recalled the events with which this account opens – the revolt of the *naqib al-ashraf* al-Husayni al-Wafaʾi that began in 1703. In the long run it had failed, but at its climax it had spilled out of the city walls to the surrounding villages. Tahir realized that the revolt had failed because it had challenged the sultan. The current situation was different: Tahir was rebelling against someone who was himself a rebel against the empire, and Tahir could expect the empire to support him. He decided to mount the rebellion with the help of the local peasants, brave and stubborn men oppressively taxed by the governor of Acre. This was a wise decision, and the Husaynis weathered yet another crisis.

During those same years even more meaningful developments took place. We know this only in hindsight; Tahir could not have realized it at the time. Foreign visitors who arrived during the days of the revolt would alter the country's character beyond recognition.[13] Protestant missionaries, both British and American, came to spread Christianity among the Arabs and to convert the Jews. Two American missionaries were especially active. They concentrated their activity around the Church of the Holy Sepulchre and tried not only to Christianize Muslims and Jews but also to attract lapsed Protestants and win over Greek Orthodox and Armenian Christians. This was an unprecedented presence in Jerusalem that would have far-reaching effects on the evolution of national awareness and on political developments in Jerusalem.[14] Christian messianism would lay the groundwork for the rise of the new Jewish messianism, namely, Zionism. But this, too, is obvious only in hindsight, and the Husaynis had no inkling of it.

The full extent of the missionary activity in the city was not generally known, or else tensions between Muslims and Christians would have grown worse. The Greek revolution, as we have seen, contributed directly to the restless atmosphere, and constant rumors made it harder to maintain the delicate status quo. The city governor, Suleiman Pasha, was unable to calm things down, and while the uprising of 1824 was quite unrelated to events in Greece, all these developments created unease and uncertainty and a feeling that there was no firm hand on the government helm.

The personal biography of this Suleiman is not documented, but it was evidently well-known in the city. He was rumored to be a Jewish convert and was suspected of sympathizing with the Christians in Jerusalem during the conflict between the Greeks and the Ottomans. Indeed, his very presence in the city exacerbated the tendency to rise up against the government. His common epithet was 'the nineteenth century's Pontius Pilate'. In addition to these rumors, there were also reports that a European navy had reached the coast of Palestine, bringing an advance force for the conquest of Jerusalem. Whenever this story came up, the Christian inhabitants of Jerusalem were confined to their churches.[15]

The Husaynis were still occupied with the struggle to survive the greed of local rulers in Acre and Damascus. In 1824 this pressure doubled: Damascus demanded its pound of flesh from Jerusalem, which was officially under its rule, and Acre did not let up either. The family's friend in Damascus was replaced by a new governor, Mustafa, nicknamed 'the Criminal' because of his penchant for imposing unprecedented taxes. The Husaynis, along with the rest of the notables, felt that if they gave in to all these demands they would soon be left penniless. In the spring of 1824 things went too far, and a full-blown revolt broke out.

Mustafa 'the Criminal' arrived in April for the annual tax collection and camped outside the Jaffa Gate. The mood in the city was already very grim, but the visit might have passed without overt trouble if the governor had not been seized with a fit of 'Jerusalem madness' and launched a wild assault on the city and its inhabitants, the likes of which had not been seen since 1700. This time the governor of Damascus went too far, stayed longer than was customary and behaved in an unheard-of manner. He had the leaders of the Christians, Jews and Muslims brought to his camp and held them ransom until their communities paid the amounts he demanded.

Early on 5 April the governor's troops came to the gate of the Husaynis' residence, and before the family could gather its wits, Umar al-Husayni was seized and taken to the governor's camp. There he found Abd al-Rahman, the brother of Mustafa Abu Ghosh, who had also been taken hostage in order to force the Abu Ghosh family to share with the government the income from the impost paid to them by Christian pilgrims on the road between Jaffa and Jerusalem. As representatives of the Jews, 'the Criminal' seized Rabbi Mendel and his son, both French nationals hitherto protected by the special agreements signed by the government with the European powers (the Capitulations of the Ottoman Empire). Evidently the Damascus governor meant to demolish personally the special status granted to Christians and Jews of European nationality. The last hostage taken was the abbot of the Greek Orthodox monastery of Mar Elias.

To demonstrate his determination to humiliate these men until their communities paid the vast sums he had demanded, Mustafa submitted the Greek abbot to torture. The monk was dragged to a pole stuck in the ground, and his legs were thrust through a ring attached to it that was tightened until he bled. Then the pole was pulled out of the ground and hung on two hooks in front of the governor's tent, so that the abbot's head rested on the ground. Next, ten soldiers began to flog his feet. The soldiers were replaced again and again. Umar counted four shifts and trembled. He feared that Mustafa would dare to flog the *naqib al-ashraf* of Jerusalem, as the governor was clearly out of his mind and there was no telling how far he would go. The abbot remained lying on the ground with his head uncovered was given nothing but water for three days. The other hostages were confined to the governor's camp pending payment by their communities.

On the third day, the governor tied a rope around the abbot's neck and threatened to hang him if he did not confess that the treasures of the inhabitants of Bethlehem were hidden under his monastery. Now the reason for these mad proceedings became clear to Umar: many of Bethlehem's inhabitants had fled to the mountains just before the tax collection. The governor threatened to wipe the monastery from the face of the earth. While the abbot was being tortured, the governor's soldiers invaded Jerusalem, broke into houses, beat up the residents and arrested some of them for tax evasion. They made no distinction between Muslims, Christians and Jews. Tahir al-Husayni and the other notables found a way to halt the devastation, if only temporarily: they pawned the valuables of the Orthodox Church in Jerusalem to an English Jew for 50,000 *piastres* as a down payment on the debt to the Pasha.[16]

But still it was not enough. The learned governor had discovered that in the distant past it had been customary to present the governor with robes and shawls made of camel hair, and he demanded the same. He finally left on 15 April, but not without a parting blow – he took Umar al-Husayni and Abd al-Rahman Abu Ghosh with him. 'You will be my guests in Damascus until this unruly city does its duty,' he explained.[17] Curiously, he let the Christians and Jews go. Abu Ghosh's furious family seized some sixty Christian pilgrims and held them hostage. Umar was fortunate: the governor changed his mind at the last moment, deciding to wait in Nablus until the Husayni and Abu Ghosh families paid the ransom, penalty, tax – whatever payment that all Jerusalemites, regardless of religion or class, were obliged to remit.

But here he went too far. In July the people of Abu Ghosh rebelled, and they were soon joined by the Christians of Bethlehem. Together the peasants and townspeople succeeded in driving the military out of Jerusalem. The governor's troops fled to Nablus and remained there with him for twenty days. The unfortunate inhabitants of Nablus were forced to pay double to make up for his loss of Jerusalem's taxes.[18]

But the rebels did not have only the governor in mind – they were determined to oust the Albanian troops stationed in the city. That day Tahir al-Husayni sent a youngster to the fortress, which was occupied by 450 men of the Albanian guard known as the Arnauts. The lad had memorized his speech to the commander of the Arnauts, which said that the inhabitants of Bethlehem had declared war on the city's southern villages and, 'If you please, Your Honor, send a large force out there to prevent bloodshed.'[19]

The commander agreed and at once set out with most of his troops on the main road to Nablus, leaving only a small number of officers and men at the fortress. As they drove out, Tahir summoned a large crowd to al-Aqsa mosque and roused them to march on the fortress. The fortress immediately surrendered to the throng, and one of the Albanians was forced to load and fire the cannon to warn the population that something was afoot. The commander, who had not yet gotten very far, heard the explosion and understood that he had been tricked. Apparently deciding that prudence was the better part of valor, he proceeded to Damascus to await the return of Governor Mustafa.

Tahir summoned the families of the notables and the heads of the Christian communities to his *naqib*'s office and informed them that the tax demands on the city had been lifted. The meeting was attended by the leaders of the *masheikh*, the strongmen of the mountains and outlying country, the sons of the Abu Ghosh, Qassem, Jarar and the Nablus Tuqan families, who reported that they had proclaimed 'independent republics'. For a brief while Jerusalem, too, became an independent entity, as it had been in 1704. This time the rebels even had a flag, which they flew from the top of the fortress. It is not known who decided to spare the lives of the commander of the fortress and the governor. The latter would later be captured by the rebels when he tried to attack the city after his exile in Nablus.

Jerusalem was now administered by two men: the commander of the local force, who had joined the rebellion (as the Janissaries had done), and a local resident. The leading notables, including the Husaynis, supported the rebellion but for obvious reasons avoided leading it openly. This brief regime was one of the strangest the city had ever known. On the one hand, 'non-resident Arabs' were executed, while on the other hand, the cancellation of the special taxes imposed on the Christians apparently brought the Christians and Muslims closer together. Thus not only peasants and *effendis* but also Christians and Muslims had a share in this historical moment.

The cooperation between these communities was all the more extraordinary in 1824, in view of the titanic conflict that had broken out between them in Greece. Palestinian historians would later point to this cooperation as proof that this was the moment when the Palestinian national movement began and that it therefore preceded the advent of Zionism. More recently, a historian wrote that the leaders of the revolt in Jerusalem behaved like the rulers of the *sanjaq* (an administrative division of the Ottoman Empire). Like all new rulers, they were generous to their protégés and exempted the villages in the vicinity of Jerusalem from paying taxes that year. Yet everyone knew that the imperial government would not tolerate these developments, and less than a month later, in August, the troops of the governor of Damascus appeared on the Mount of Olives and began to bombard the city.

When the Greek revolution ended with the establishment of an independent Greece, Sultan Mahmud II turned to the rebellious Jerusalemites. The first national uprising against Ottoman rule would serve as a model for several other nations, first in the Balkans and later in the Middle East. But now the sultan ordered Abdullah Pasha to crush the Jerusalem rebellion. Abdullah sent a representative to warn the rebels, but they were euphoric and vowed to remain in power.

When Rabbi Yehoseph Schwartz came to Jerusalem nine years later, he heard horror stories about the thick smoke and the fires that had been started by the exploding shells. 'Nevertheless,' he wrote in his journal, 'the Lord in his mercy protected the city and the shells did not harm anyone.' The Jews of Jerusalem would not forget the day when the Husaynis capitulated – it was on the last day of the festival of *Sukkot* (Feast of Tabernacles) that the guns fell silent and Jerusalem could rest.[20]

The siege had lasted five months, and only the shelling of the city from the summit of the Mount of Olives drove Tahir to negotiate with Abdullah. An agreement was reached at length, which, if not improving the plight of the surrounding peasantry, at least lifted the threat that had hung over the Husaynis. Umar went back to his house, and life seemed to return to normal, though Abdullah's shadow would hang over the family until the Egyptian occupation of the country in 1831. Abdullah had been reined in thanks to the family's good connections in the Ottoman capital; the reformist Sultan Mahmud II had not forgotten the family's support for his predecessor and patron, Selim III.

Once the rebellion was over, life went on smoothly enough, despite being disrupted now and then by the whims of the governor of Acre. In the late 1820s, he issued several edicts forbidding people to enter or leave the city without his express permission. Modern life unfolding in Jerusalem brought injustices as well as marvels. The Turks, British, Jordanians and Zionists all followed Abdullah of Acre in periodically restricting the movements of the inhabitants on some pretext. But this practice was suspended in 1831 when Ibrahim Pasha invaded Syria. It was one of those military events that alter the political reality at a stroke and in the long run induce profound changes in society and its way of life.

Once again a man from the Balkans overturned the Ottoman order. The Albanian Muhammad Ali, an Ottoman army officer who had fought brilliantly against Napoleon, employed one of the most sophisticated, elaborate campaigns of intrigue in modern history to achieve the governorship of Egypt. Before long, he expanded his realm, first in the service of the empire and then in defiance of it. His first goals were Sudan and the Arabian Peninsula, and when the sultan summoned him to help put down the Greek revolt, Muhammad Ali demanded the Syrian provinces in payment. But the Egyptian Pasha was unable to fulfill his side of the bargain. Aided by France and philhellenic Britain, the Greek David defeated the imperial Goliath, trouncing the Ottoman-Egyptian allies. The sultan, therefore, felt free to break his promise to the Egyptian Pasha, but this was not, from the imperial viewpoint, a good moment to turn down an ally. The sultan had just resolved to create a new army and physically annihilate the commanders of the Janissaries, who had prevented him from turning the empire into a modern, European-like state. Without the old army and not yet in possession of a new one, the empire presented an irresistible temptation.

When Muhammad Ali persisted in demanding compensation for his efforts against the Greeks, the sultan ordered the governor of Syria to launch a preemptive strike against Egypt. But his letter was intercepted by Muhammad Ali, and it strengthened his resolve to move north. His pretext for the action was feeble enough: 5,000 Egyptian peasants had deserted his army for Syria during the Greek war, and the Syrian governor was refusing to extradite them. Still, a pretext was essential in those chivalrous times. Moreover, the Pasha claimed that the governor of Acre owed him a large sum of money from the Greek war and therefore his campaign was a punitive one against a defaulting debtor. Encouraged by the French king Charles X and his foreign minister Chateaubriand, Muhammad Ali began to prepare his campaign to the Levant, possibly even to Istanbul, and in 1831 tens of thousands of soldiers crossed the northern Sinai Peninsula under the command of his nephew Ibrahim Pasha, whom he treated like a son.[21]

Ibrahim reached Jerusalem that year. The Husaynis had heard from their relatives the Tuqans that someone was already preparing for the political reversal – the Abd al-Hadi family, or rather its head, Hussein Abd al-Hadi, who offered concrete help to the invader. This would turn out to be a fateful error on the part of the Abd al-Hadis, because once Ottoman rule was reimposed they would lose status. Thus Hussein felt so attracted to Ibrahim's family that he conducted a love affair with the latter's sister, who would eventually poison her Nablusi lover.

The Husaynis, however, not only avoided such colorful and dangerous liaisons, they were also extremely cautious politically. When Ibrahim Pasha besieged Acre and, like Napoleon before him, was unable to storm it, he asked the notables of Jerusalem to support him. But Umar and Tahir persuaded their fellow notables to send a courteous refusal and declare sympathetic neutrality.

When the Egyptian Pasha defeated Acre and came to Jerusalem, Umar and Tahir were among the first to greet him. But the Egyptian, presumably remembering Umar's wavering, treated him with hostility. It was a traumatic encounter. The heir of the famous Pasha addressed the notables with meticulous care, spelling out their titles and past deeds, all in accordance with protocol. Then he declared that times had changed – henceforth the notables and *qadis* would not rule supreme, and the administration of the district would be entrusted to an advisory council that would include Christians and Jews. And this was not all. The Christians and Jews would henceforth be allowed, for the first time since the Arab conquest, to ride horses in the city, to wear Muslim garments and to repair and restore their houses of worship. When he went on to say that the testimony of foreigners would also be admissible in court, Umar, who occasionally served as *qadi*, could not believe his ears. Shortly after this meeting town criers circulated through the streets of Jerusalem proclaiming: 'We hereby abolish the special penalties and taxes imposed upon the churches in Jerusalem, and the tax imposed upon Christian pilgrims, and undertake to protect the lives and honor of the Christians.'[22]

Historians are divided about Ibrahim's motives. Some attribute to him a modern egalitarian outlook, while others argue that the abolition of special taxes was part of his agreement with France, or at any rate a conciliatory gesture to induce France to support him and his adopted father against the other European nations, which were less than happy about Muhammad Ali's conquests.

To add insult to injury, Ibrahim obliged Tahir, in his role as *mufti* of Jerusalem, to accompany him on a visit to the Church of the Holy Sepulchre.[23] Hitherto it was the Christian notables who called on the Muslim clergy to pay their respects on Muslim festivals, reflecting the hierarchy and balance of power in the Muslim empire. Ibrahim expressed his admiration for the beautiful church and was fascinated by the eternal flame that burned inside. There, in Tahir's presence, he announced that Christian pilgrims would no longer pay a special impost. This, like his decision to abolish the *jizya* (the special poll tax paid by Christians and Jews), was a severe blow to the Husaynis since this tax paid Umar's salary as keeper of the holy shrines. Worse was to come. The Egyptian rulers were intensely suspicious of anyone who was close to the sultan's court, and the elaborate edifice of connections to Topkapi Palace was a liability under their rule.

Now the Khalidis and their associates were the favorites, while the Husaynis were regarded as enemies. The Egyptians made a point to promote those notable families whose star had waned under the Ottomans and to sideline those who had been predominant. Thus in Nablus the family of Abd al-Hadi became powerful at the expense of the Tuqans, who were allied with the Husaynis.

The worst year for the Husaynis was 1833. The ambitious Ibrahim, wishing to outdo Sultan Mahmud II in Istanbul and Muhammad Ali in Egypt, sought to turn Syria into a showcase modern Middle Eastern state. Safe roads, advanced agriculture and commerce, industrialization and a secularized judiciary – Ibrahim's advisers regarded these as the principal features of such a new political entity. And it all cost a great deal of money. The wealthy Husaynis were among the first to be hit by the Egyptian ruler's methods of financing.

Six different taxes were imposed on the population. Jerusalem was also required to provide cannon fodder for Ibrahim's army – one fifth of all adolescent boys were conscripted (a total of several hundred in the city, and several thousand from all of Jerusalem's districts). The conscription did not proceed very well: the peasants fled in all directions, and the Egyptian army soon suffered a serious shortage of manpower.[24] But the main purpose of the operation was to seize all the weapons in the possession of the dignitaries, which symbolized their standing *vis-à-vis* the government and society. The largest arsenal in the area of Jerusalem belonged to the Abu Ghosh family, the Husaynis' allies. But the Abu Ghosh family were not the only ones who called on the Husaynis to help them resist the weapons roundup – the Tuqans, who were their allies and relatives by marriage, had a substantial quantity of arms that the Egyptians had their eyes on.[25]

If asked to pinpoint which was the most resistance-provoking aspect of the situation, we would probably concur with the historian Arif al-Arif that it was the financial blow to the notables, including the Husaynis. Not only were they compelled to pay taxes, they were denied the right to collect them. The Egyptian ruler's abolition of imposts on the roads to Jerusalem also caused a major reduction in the income of their collectors.

By the end of the year, Tahir and Umar had formulated the family's position. Up until then, they had tended to support the Egyptian's rule, however harsh. In 1832 they had actually endorsed a manifesto drawn up by the *sheikhs* of al-Azhar against the sultan and in favor of Ibrahim. Tahir had gone even further. Escaping the heat of Palestine in the summer of 1832, he stayed as a guest of Ibrahim Pasha in the encampment of Bashir II, governor of Mount Lebanon. There he quoted to the two potentates, who shared power over the areas stretching between the Taurus Mountains and the Sinai Peninsula, the well-known *hadith* (Prophetic tradition), 'May God curse the weak sultan' – namely, Mahmud II.[26] This act, and the signatures on the manifesto, would not help the Husaynis when confronted by Muhammad Ali a few years later, nor would the sultan forget it after he regained Syria.

In any event, in 1833 the heads of the family were ready to rebel. The revolt broke out the following year. But although Umar and Tahir were regarded as its leaders, they did not initiate it. Perhaps they helped to set off the rebellion known as 'the second peasants' revolt' by encouraging the surrounding rural population and the populace of Jerusalem to close ranks against the foreign invader. The burden of taxation enraged the peasants, as did the compulsory military service imposed on them by the Egyptians. Moreover, the efficient new rulers made it difficult to evade either tax payment or military service. And on top of it all, the improved situation of the Christian community exacerbated the Muslims' feelings of grievance and helped bring the rebellion against the Egyptian ruler to the boil.[27]

The success of the insurrection depended on the cooperation of the village *sheikhs*, especially those who dominated the northern areas of the Jerusalem *sanjaq*. Each of these *sheikhs* could rally hundreds of peasants armed with muskets or cold steel.[28] When the Husaynis joined the revolt, they were able to call on those groups that had demonstrated their loyalty to them during the previous revolt of 1824, and these in turn helped to rally everyone who had ever served the Husaynis. Impelled by loyalty to the Ottoman government and by the injury to their status, many other notables supported the revolt.

But the initiative for the revolt against the Egyptian occupation of the Syrian districts lay elsewhere. Ostensibly the time was ripe for it in 1833, since in May of that year Ibrahim was 300 km from Istanbul, beside the city of Konya. However, though Ibrahim was far away, Muhammad Ali was present in person. With his army not far from Damascus, he demanded and obtained control over Syria's districts, and now he came to inspect the booty. He arrived in Jerusalem on Easter Sunday, when there were more pilgrims (20,000) than residents in the city. Accompanied by a caravan with banners, he alighted at Nabi Daud. His first order was to open another gate in the city wall, one that had been filled with earth since the days of Umar ibn al-Khattab (586–90).[29] It was difficult to revolt while the ruler was making such symbolic gestures. A vast throng filled the streets, and an eyewitness reported that some 500 persons were crushed to death during the official reception.[30] Needless to say, the reception did nothing to improve the situation, and insurrection remained the only solution.

If anyone still doubted it, a new Egyptian decree in early 1834 impinged directly on the grandees. Ibrahim announced his intention of conscripting the sons of notables. The Husaynis, and others like them, had to send their sons to the mountains. All at once, *fellahin* and aristocratic sprigs hid together in the caves and *wadis* in terror of the brutal Egyptian recruiting officers.[31]

It seems easy in retrospect to analyze the causes of a revolt, as we have done here by summarizing the general consensus among historians some 100 years after the outbreak. But in fact we cannot be sure that we truly understand the course of events more than a century and a half ago. Undoubtedly, the Egyptian army was perceived as alien and hated as such, and the forced conscription of young men and the confiscation of personal weapons may have been sufficient to cause people of all classes and communities – rural and urban, Christian and Muslim, peasants and notables – to rise up, risking their lives, their families and their properties. Some historians, however, have been so impressed by the dangers faced by the rebels and the breadth of their coalition that they describe the revolt as the uprising of a national movement – that is to say, of a population motivated by a spirit of solidarity and patriotism rather than the particular interests of its members. In 1993 sociologists Kimmerling and Migdal described it as the first Palestinian national revolt (as the Druze Lebanese historian Sulayman Abu Izz al-Din defined it back in 1929). Indeed, in the territory that would later be called political Palestine, the resistance against Egyptian rule was unprecedented in scope and intensity. The whole country backed Jerusalem. Though no one proposed an independent nation state and clearly the intention was to restore Ottoman rule, it may be possible to regard the events as the first signs of a national consciousness.[32]

It is hard to determine exactly where the revolt erupted, but we know that Jerusalem did not immediately join the other Syrian cities. It seems that it all began with an order from Egypt that may not have been to Ibrahim's taste. Muhammad Ali ordered him to implement the tax policy and disarm the population throughout Syria. The first clash was with Bedouin tribes near the Jordan River who had never paid taxes to the Ottoman government. Later, in the spring of 1834, these were joined by aggrieved peasants, first in Transjordan and then in the village of Sa'ir near Hebron, and soon after by the peasantry of the hills of Nablus. It was only a question of time before the notables would decide to confront those who had turned them from creditors into debtors. The first of these were the Tuqans and al-Jarars in Nablus, followed by the Abu Ghoshes, owners of the village of Einab whose chief source of income had been the impost on pilgrims en route to Jerusalem, now taken over by the Egyptians.

At this time Ibrahim was staying in his hilltop residence at Zawiyya al-Ibrahimiyya on Mount Zion, his favorite abode in Jerusalem because of his fear of the epidemics that periodically raged in the crowded alleys below. In April, before departing for his usual residence in Jaffa, he made an effort to defuse the imminent outbreak of revolt by inviting the ringleaders to discuss a compromise on the issue of arms. He proposed that only every other man surrender his weapons. It seems that only one family in the district accepted the deal – not surprisingly, this was the Abd al-Hadi family, which would continue to support Ibrahim throughout the revolt and would be rewarded with the governorship of Nablus until the end of the Egyptian occupation.[33]

The other families rejected the compromise and waited until the end of the month, when Ibrahim would return to Jaffa, where he usually spent the month of May. Qasim al-Ahmad, a Hebron grandee, came to Jerusalem at the head of a large contingent that has been variously described as between 5,000 and 20,000 strong. Together with the men of Abu Ghosh they formed a human barrier on the Jerusalem–Jaffa road to prevent Ibrahim from coming back. When al-Ahmad's messenger called on Tahir al-Husayni, the *mufti* willingly gave his blessing to the revolt and even recruited other notables in the district of Jerusalem. Even Jaber Abu Ghosh, the governor of Jerusalem – the *mutasalem* – joined the insurrection. On 28 April 1834, the revolt erupted in Jerusalem, Nablus, Hebron, Galilee and even Transjordan.[34]

On 8 May the villagers began marching to the city, and the following day some 10,000 more armed men arrived from Nablus and Hebron. They all camped outside the city gates, and the following morning an impressive sight met the eyes of the Jerusalemites: all around the city's southern and eastern walls were hundreds of peasants armed with pitchforks and clubs. That evening the rebels penetrated the city by the biblical ruse of slipping in through a disused water channel, and before long they seized control of the whole city except the fortress. They set up their headquarters in the Saraya

Building, the seat of the Egyptian governor on the Via Dolorosa. They also besieged the fortress, which was occupied by an Egyptian force between 600 and 1,000 strong. As in 1703, the fortress held out, and the rebels could not declare a complete victory, though the rest of the city was in their hands.

On 10 May the besieged soldiers demonstrated their own ingenuity. Using a brilliant guerrilla tactic, they seized some of the city's dignitaries and imprisoned them in the fortress. Then the pendulum swung again, and for the second time the men of Nablus came to the aid of the Jerusalemites. They not only freed the imprisoned men but also captured the fortress with all the soldiers in it. Unlike the rebels in earlier uprisings, they hardly touched the captured soldiers, perhaps because they knew that reversals were not impossible and they did not wish to arouse Ibrahim's vengeance. Instead they let off steam by sweeping through the city, breaking into some Jewish and Christian houses and looting them (though by and large they did not discriminate between Muslims and non-Muslims) and robbing shops and market stalls and peaceful citizens.

It was a heady victory, but not without underlying anxieties. The leaders knew that in the long run a peasant army could not stand up to Muhammad Ali's formidable forces. It is possible that such doubts also began to trouble Umar and Tahir al-Husayni. Umar was worried about the unstable personality of the Hebronite Qasim al-Ahmad, one of the leaders of the revolt. This Qasim had become a close friend of the frivolous Ibrahim Abu Ghosh, whose father Uthman was imprisoned in Acre. These, Umar felt, were neither easy nor trustworthy allies.[35]

Without stirring from Jaffa, Ibrahim asked Muhammad Ali to send him reinforcements of 9,000 troops. The reinforcements arrived only at the end of June and consisted of 15,000 men. (These figures, or their close approximations, are significant, especially for historical comparisons. For example, in 1948 some 100,000 Jewish troops fought against a similar force from the Arab countries.) The rebels clearly had no intention of surrendering, and Ibrahim grew impatient and decided to assault the rebellious city before his father's troops arrived.[36]

The Abu Ghosh clan had been waiting for precisely this move. Though Ibrahim was able to get across the Qastel Hill on his way to Jerusalem, he arrived there in a poor state, worn out by the harassments of the Abu Ghosh. In Jerusalem his camp was besieged by the enthusiastic popular army, and some report that he considered surrendering. In desperation he appealed to the Abd al-Hadi family, who were indebted to him for giving them the governorship of Nablus in place of their old rivals, the Tuqans. The head of the family, Hussein

Abd al-Hadi, distributed gifts and promises among the Nablusi rebels, with the result that a gap appeared in the besieging ring, enabling Ibrahim to slip out. His famous army having been beaten twice since the outbreak of the revolt, Ibrahim decided to turn his attention to the village of Einab, the seat of the Abu Ghosh family. After a battle that lasted a day and a night, the villagers surrendered to Ibrahim's 6,000 men.[37]

After his triumph over the villagers, Ibrahim proceeded to Jerusalem and defeated the city he had abandoned in April. He approached from the north, having beaten the men of Nablus, who then joined his forces in droves. But the Hebronite Qasim al-Ahmad did not yield, and though he retreated from the city, he remained determined to free Hebron, Nablus and Jerusalem from the Egyptian occupation.[38] When Ibrahim concluded early in June that he had brought rebellious Jerusalem to its knees, he returned to the coast to prepare for the greater confrontation with the Ottoman sultan. But like a bushfire that flares up again after it appears to be extinguished, the flames of rebellion began to flicker once more around the walls of Jerusalem.

At the end of June, Jerusalem was once again up in arms against the Egyptians, thanks to the urging of Qasim al-Ahmad and Ibrahim Abu Ghosh. Then something strange happened. Whereas in May Tahir and Umar al-Husayni had hesitated to continue the insurrection, this time, against all odds, they joined the men they had previously mistrusted. Perhaps the earlier successes distorted their thinking or, however unusual for them, they underestimated the Egyptian ruler's dogged determination.

Muhammad Ali had no intention of giving up Jerusalem. On the contrary, despite the city's marginal strategic value, he meant to devote an unusually large military force to the purpose. The European powers were beginning to assume that Jerusalem was no longer in Egypt's possession because of its belated response to the revolt, and Muhammad Ali was determined to show the Europeans that the Christian holy places were ruled by Egypt and not the Ottoman Empire.[39]

Just when the Husaynis had made up their minds to risk supporting the hopeless revolt, Muhammad Ali landed in Jaffa from Egypt with 15,000 men.[40] The experienced Egyptian started his campaign by contacting the rebels and proposing a compromise on the questions of weapons and conscription. He promised Ibrahim Abu Ghosh that he would release his father from prison in return for the Abu Ghosh family's support. Remarkably, Qasim al-Ahmad stood his ground. On the very day when the naval guns of Jaffa announced the arrival of Muhammad Ali, the rebels stormed Ibrahim's palatial residence on Mount Zion and looted it.

Muhammad Ali put great pressure on Tahir and Umar al-Husayni to withhold their support for the rebellion, and invited them to negotiate with him in Jaffa. After a sleepless night of consultation, the two men set out, accompanied by representatives of other leading families. Had they been more familiar with Egyptian history, they would have known that the last conciliatory meeting proposed by the imperious Pasha had ended with his opponents having their throats cut. In 1811 he had invited to his fortress some 300 Mamluk princes, members of the Turco-Egyptian aristocracy with whom he had shared the government of Egypt since 1805. He gave them dinner, after which they were all put to the sword.

One cool morning a caravan of donkeys, camels and mules waited outside the Husayni residence near the Haram. Members of the family said good-bye to Umar and Tahir, expecting to see them back home soon. After riding hard for a day and a half, the men arrived in Jaffa to be met by the corpulent, white-bearded Pasha. Reclining on cushions, one leg folded under him and his hand resting on a long, curved scimitar, he paid little heed to the Jerusalemites' explanations, and a few moments later they were arrested and dispatched to Egypt in the belly of an Egyptian ship.

Fortunately for them, they were not confined in the *qala'as*'s prison in the Salah al-Din fortress that dominates Cairo, from which few ever came out alive, but rather they were exiled and kept under heavy guard. Tahir's close friendships with the scholars of al-Azhar and Umar's reputation as a gener-ous host to many Egyptian visitors to Jerusalem, to whom he had shown its mosques and saints' tombs, stood them in good stead.[41] Two years later, the Pasha suddenly freed them and sent them to Jerusalem. Perhaps he hoped they would be grateful and support him in the event of another insurrection, or maybe he was concerned about Tahir's popularity, in view of the many peti-tions sent by Jerusalem residents begging him to restore Tahir to his former post. Another less likely possibility is that the Egyptian Pasha was moved by a letter written by seventeen women in the *mufti*'s harem in April 1835 saying that since their master's exile they had no one to provide for them.[42]

Qasim al-Ahmad was captured a few days after the Husaynis, and his fate remains unknown. Having reconquered Jerusalem, Ibrahim punished the city by sealing up the Mughrabi Gate (also known as the Dung Gate), near the quarter inhabited by a North African community that had supported the revolt. (It would be reopened in 1841, after the Egyptians had been driven out.) This was not merely a symbolic gesture. It was the nearest gate to the spring of Silwan, and sealing it made it harder for the townspeople to fetch water. Also, a large jail was built near the fortress – Jerusalem's famous Kishleh

– and anyone who dared to resist the ruler was thrown into one of its tiny cells. The Ottomans, when they returned, and later the British, Jordanians and Israelis, all kept up this institution and its practices.

In the latter days of Egyptian rule, the Husaynis made their peace with Ibrahim and even agreed to help administer the city on his behalf. The rulers were willing to forgive Tahir, due to the high regard in which he was held by the scholars at al-Azhar in Cairo, but Umar was not so fortunate. The Husaynis had to agree to let Umar's son, Muhammad Ali (whose name no doubt appealed to the Pasha), fill his father's post as *naqib al-ashraf* of Jerusalem. He retained the position after Umar returned from exile in 1836. But the Egyptian authorities, who wished to be reconciled with the family, did not cancel any of Umar's honorary titles or the stipends that went with his former position. Thus the Husaynis grew still stronger despite the unfortunate gamble they had taken in the final stages of the revolt. Their reconciliation came just in time, because by then the standing of the Khalidis had surpassed theirs, and good relations with the powers that be were, as always, translated into important posts and rich emoluments.

Muhammad Ali al-Husayni played an active part in the creation of the first representative and constitutional body in the district of Jerusalem – namely, the *Majlis al-Shura* (the general council of Jerusalem). It was set up as an advisory council to the Egyptian ruler and represented the leading groups in local society. The council was headed by Mahmud Abu al-Saud; Muhammad Ali al-Husayni was a member by virtue of his position as *naqib al-ashraf*, and from the beginning so was Tahir al-Husayni as the *mufti*.

Curiously, Tahir al-Husayni, whose political instincts were generally acute, failed to discern the approaching end of Egyptian rule in Palestine and chose to steer close to the Pasha. This was not a minor matter in those days, least of all for a *sheikh* who had been out of favor and even exiled for his part in the revolt. In recognition of his belated loyalty to the regime, Tahir received the title *nazir al-diwan* (chairman of the city council). In this way the Husaynis were associated with the cancellation of the special taxes imposed on the Christians and Jews, though apparently they were able to restrict the scope of the reforms.[43] Led by Tahir, the city council forbade the Jews to engage in agriculture, buy grazing land or deal in soap (which the Husaynis manufactured); Jews retained their right to engage in commerce. In Egypt, Muhammad Ali Pasha ratified the resolution: 'We shall not allow the Jews to purchase land in Jerusalem and its environs, as this would constitute a legal precedent.'[44] Nor did the *majlis* accede to the Jews' request to be allowed to pray aloud; they stated that the old arrangements on this matter remained in force. Likewise, the question of the status of the Western ('Wailing') Wall – which would be a major bone of contention between future Husayni generations and the Zionist movement – came up in the last days of Muhammad Ali's rule in Jerusalem. The Jewish community hoped to gain from the Pasha's lenience towards non-Muslim minorities and asked permission to build a structure near the Wall and to pray aloud. But the *majlis* decreed that since the Wall adjoined the Haram al-Sharif the Jews could have no legal right to it or to the road leading to it, which passed through the Mughrabi quarter.

In its final stages Egyptian rule created some new facts that displeased the Husayni family. For example, Muhammad Ali permitted the foreign consuls in Jerusalem to build business premises, though in response to the protest of the Husaynis on behalf of the populace, he did not allow the American consul to fly his country's flag. Pieces of colored cloth were important symbols of presence and dominance long before the country was caught up in the heady mood of nationalism.[45] The Pasha also permitted foreign merchants to trade in the city and canceled the tax that had been paid by the guardians of the churches since the time of Saladin, as well as the tithe paid by the *fellahin*.

Ibrahim also left his imprint on the city's architecture and introduced some technological innovations. Historians theorizing about the rise of nationalism argue that such innovations induce a new attitude to the environment, which in turn enhances the development of a national identity.[46] Among the new structures were a windmill and the first flour mill of its type, both built in 1831.

In 1839 Muhammad Ali was driven out of Syria and the familiar Ottoman rule returned. These changes of government frayed the people's nerves. Muhammad Ali left Jericho first, and rumors spread in Jerusalem that he had destroyed it. People feared that he would do the same to their city. Tahir and Umar called for the city gates to be closed, and recommended that the people hide their money in the cemeteries and shut themselves up inside their shops. The Ottoman forces, backed by the navies of the European powers, had already landed in Jaffa, but by the time they reached Jerusalem Muhammad Ali had already left. Later it transpired that he had not harmed Jericho.[47]

The old rulers returned to Palestine bursting with a new resolve: the empire was to be turned into a modern state capable of standing up to Europe, which was eager to grab any part of it that seemed attainable. At the same time, Istanbul was anxious to nip in the bud the ambitions of the various communities that drew inspiration from the Greek revolution of 1821 and from Muhammad Ali's relative success.

The Ottomans also had to contend with a European 'fifth column' – namely, the European consulates that Ibrahim had permitted to be established in the imperial provinces, many of which were set up in Jerusalem. These consulates changed the city: European buildings housing foreign families that, as the foreign powers consolidated their presence in the city, gradually became regular ports of call for all the socialites in town. Towards the end of the nineteenth century, the Husaynis would be among the regular guests of these foreign representatives.

This was the dawn of the Tanzimat – the reforms loathed by the Husaynis. The winds of change tended to weaken the power of the local notables, to grant positions of power to those who were willing to relearn the rules of Ottoman administration and to replace lineage with a diploma from one of the new schools of administration that had opened in Istanbul. The Khalidis were quick to take up this proposition, but the Husaynis lagged behind. It would be some years before the family regained its prominence in the city and its environs.

Success in the local political arena was of prime importance. Before the reforms, Jerusalem had been a small Ottoman district between Gaza and Nablus administered from Damascus. At the end of the period it would be an autonomous district that encompassed a large part of Palestine. It would become a strong economic and political entity led by a substantial city, not a small town as it had been when Muhammad Ali retreated from it. Before the reforms, the city's population had been about 12,000; twenty years later it had grown to 20,000.[48] The district, which before the reforms had been mainly rural and dominated by mountain potentates like Mustafa Abu Ghosh, became more urban in character, and the Husaynis were at its social and political center.

CHAPTER 3

# Struggling with Reform, 1840–76

## *Redefining Jerusalem and Palestine*

The return of Ottoman rule to Jerusalem in the winter of 1840 was a noisy affair. The old-new rulers immediately began to reconstruct the city and to reinforce its walls for fear of the rural *sheikhs* whose power had noticeably increased under the Egyptians. The walls surrounding the city were made higher, and it looked as if the division between the townspeople and the surrounding villages would continue unchanged. Hoping to assuage the angry authorities, the Jerusalem notables joined a petition sent by the notables of Syria to the young sultan, Abdul Macid (Majjid) II, describing the wrongs suffered under Muhammad Ali's rule and begging to be taken back into the imperial fold.

They were indeed looking at a new order once the power of the empire was reasserted. New, smaller districts were decreed, and a government representative was stationed in every administrative unit down to the village. Jerusalem, which had been sidelined for years, was made the capital of the southern sub-region of the *vilayet* of Sidon. Not only was Jerusalem detached from Damascus, the districts of Gaza, Jaffa and Nablus were placed under it (in 1858 Nablus would become a separate district). The *sanjaq* of Jerusalem, defined by the reformers as a sub-region of a *vilayet*, spread from the Marj ibn Amar (Jezreel Valley) in the north to Rafah in the south (a large portion of what is Palestine and Israel today). The Ottoman rulers hoped to end the situation in which large tracts of southern Syria were not subordinated to the empire, and wished to weaken Damascus's influence on the Mediterranean coast. Trade with Europe became one of Istanbul's prime objectives, and

78

under the new order all the port cities began to enjoy a prominence they had not experienced since the Roman Empire.

Even though Jaffa and Gaza were on the coast, Jerusalem was more important, possibly because it was the most populous of the three – with some 20,000 inhabitants (about half of them non-Muslim) at the start of the reform period and 68,000 at its end.[1] Moreover, Jaffa and Gaza were more vulnerable, as history had shown. Above all, Jerusalem's primacy was reinforced by the high regard in which it was held by the European nations, whose consuls in the holy city would become a major factor in local politics. The European interest in Jerusalem forced the sultan to show his commitment, as the head of the Muslim nation, to the third holiest city in Islam.[2]

But the governor of Damascus was still a post to reckon with, and during the Tanzimat period his influence was still felt in Palestine as well in Jerusalem.[3] It was only in 1872, when the administrative map was yet again redrawn, that Damascus's role weakened considerably. In that year, Jerusalem became a separate district of equal standing to Damascus, and it incorporated the districts of Nablus and Acre. The British consul in Jerusalem reported to his government: 'Palestine has become a separate district' – it was called the District of Holy Jerusalem. A new governor, Mustafa Surayya Pasha, arrived to rule over it, but he was soon cut down to size.

'Holy Jerusalem' became an ordinary district, no different from the district of Mount Lebanon. It was shorn of Nablus and Acre but retained Gaza, Hebron and Jaffa. Nonetheless, Jerusalem had a higher status than these sub-provinces as it reported directly to Istanbul. This state of affairs persisted right up to the First World War – the northern part of Palestine, the districts of Nablus and Acre, were ruled from Beirut, and the southern part from Jerusalem (in this period, Vilayet Sidon was renamed Vilayet Beirut).[4]

## Early Bids for Nationalism

Western historians ascribe this important Ottoman reorganization in 1872 to the growing influence of Western powers that wanted to raise the status of the holy city. But Palestinian and Turkish historians argue that the reformulation was an internal Ottoman initiative and only partly shaped by European pressure. Behind this debate lies a more substantive one about timing, or more precisely about the exact date of the birth of Palestinian nationalism. A clear definition of geopolitical units in a proto-nationalist era is quite often mentioned as a precursor of modern nationalism; hence the importance attributed to this particular act by the Ottoman government in 1872.[5]

Indeed, though updated scholarship on the birth of a modern nation requires other ingredients to detect a clear emergence, this particular criterion – a well-defined space – is crucial. During the same period, another ingredient was thrown into the national pot: a transformation in the conceptual perceptions of space and time amongst the local elites. Simultaneous with the local elite constructing, devising or inventing (depending on the scholar's point of view) the idea of nationhood, the society as a whole developed a new perception of the space in which it lived. This was a perception triggered by administrative changes such as the one that occurred in 1872 – the creation of a new district, regardless of whose initiative it was – as well as by economic, social and cultural processes.

The economy of the new district became linked to that of Europe, leading to an influx of Europeans – merchants, speculators, medical men, tourists, missionaries and Zionists. The Western powers followed, greatly enlarging their influence in the region, affecting the local society and its culture.

As the geopolitical entity they were living in increased in size, it was given clearer definitions by Ottoman reformers, visitors, geographers and various interested Europeans. This is how 'Palestine' was defined for the first time in a British travelers' guide from the late reign of Muhammad Ali:

> Palestine is the name by which the 'moderns' designate that part of the Ottoman Empire in Asia that lies between latitudes 31 and 34, extending from the River Jordan in the east to the Mediterranean in the west.[6]

Here, as Benedict Anderson puts it, was a fusion of discrete processes that gave rise to a new conception, a new vision, of the region inhabited by people who had formerly been the subjects of a small district in the *vilayet* of Damascus. At some indefinable stage – this being a collective process that affected individuals at different times – the *shamis* (the inhabitants of the Syrian districts) living in the newly created district began to think of themselves as Palestinians.[7] At some point in time, the Husaynis too changed their self-reference in a similar way.

### A Temporary Decline, 1840–56

The Ottomans assigned the notable families to an important position in the management of the renewed government by inviting them to take part in the council of the *sanjaq*, called *Majlis al-Idara* in Arabic or *Mecelis-i-idari* in Turkish, as well as the council of the city. The Husaynis aspired to add the city council to the other three major centers of power they controlled – the *niqaba*, the *ifta* and the position of Sheikh al-Haram – but did not always succeed. The struggle to win the new post was still carried out by the old rules and tactics. And while the new council had a democratic element that the city's government had previously lacked, it nevertheless granted primacy to the notables. The new situation actually suited the Husaynis' slow adjustment to the dramatic changes wrought by the Tanzimat.

Only the *mufti* and the *naqib al-ashraf* did not have to be elected to their posts, as they were appointed on the basis of social standing; all the other positions required a run for office. Thus Tahir al-Husayni and Muhammad Ali al-Husayni retained considerable power so long as they filled their posts. Tahir headed the council in the final year of Egyptian rule, but apparently not for long; having started with a flourish, he soon declined. Muhammad Ali al-Husayni's position was also precarious. At first he lost the post of *naqib*, which was given to the al-Alamis. But before long he regained the position and managed to keep it until shortly before his death in 1869.[8]

The temporary decline in the family's standing lasted from 1840 to 1856. Rival families such as the Khalidis and the Alamis benefited from this and for a while took over some of the Husaynis' positions.[9] Losing a position such as the *naqib* or *mufti* quite often resulted in short-term, forced or voluntary exiles in Damascus or Istanbul.

Tahir al-Husayni effectively used his forced stay in the capital to retain the good connections that would return his family to power despite the relative decline in the period mentioned.[10] The most precious position lost to the Alamis in 1856 was that of the *mufti*, but it was returned as a result of Tahir's efforts and remained in the hands of the Husaynis until 1948.

## Economic Compensations

The temporary waning of the Husayni family's political standing did not affect its economic welfare. On the contrary, it seemed to provide an impetus for growing richer. Generous governmental compensations for positions lost during Egyptian rule and the expansion of the family's profitable soap factory and flour mill provided the necessary security.[11] Though properties were usually confiscated when their owner was deported, Umar was actually paid compensation, thanks to his excellent contacts in Damascus and Istanbul. He was therefore able to leave a rich estate that would consolidate the prosperity of the Umari branch of the family. Even in his old age, he engaged in commercial transactions that extended beyond the city or even the district and enlarged the family fortune.[12]

The Tahiri branch of the family did not do badly either, and Muhammad Ali al-Husayni – who had at one time been both *naqib* and *mufti* – showed business acumen. He was also exiled at the time of the rift with the Alamis. After his return from exile, he took advantage of his position and began to develop the religious properties his family managed. On certain properties near the village of Sarafend, he built a new village named Fuja. This investment would pay off in later years and benefit his descendants.[13]

Once all the deportees returned home – except Tahir, who remained in Istanbul to the end of his life – the family could regroup and prepare for future challenges. They faced the hostility of various governors, representatives of the Ottoman reforms, who believed that it was their duty to reduce the power of notable families and did all they could to stir up enmities among them. The family dealt with this policy with a dual tactic. On the one hand, they created new matrimonial ties – most importantly with the Darwish family, which held several important positions in the city – thus neutralizing some of the rivalries. And on the other hand, they used past alliances to overcome the power of opposing clans (primarily the Alamis and the Khalidis). In fact, the Husaynis were becoming so powerful that marrying into them became a goal for former rivals such as the Alamis and the Nashashibis.[14]

### The End of Countryside Rule and its Effect on the Husaynis

Rural chieftains were the main victims of the new centralization and taxation policies in the age of reform. In the greater Jerusalem area, the decline in the fortunes of such families between 1840 and the mid-1870s benefited the urban elite of Jerusalem as a whole and the Husaynis, as its leading family, in particular.[15]

These policies in greater Jerusalem were challenged by the Abu Ghosh family, and for a while the protests turned into a series of insurrections beyond Jerusalem and throughout the countryside. However, this time the Abu Ghoshes could not rely on the urban families, and the Ottomans succeeded in enlisting other strongmen in the mountains who had been antagonized by the Abu Ghosh family in the past over issues of taxation and territory. It would not be an exaggeration to claim that urban families such as the Husaynis helped implement the centralized Ottoman policy and benefited from it.[16]

The younger generation of Husaynis was initially enthused by the rebellious mood. And thus we find Muhammad Ali al-Husayni joining the Abu Ghosh insurrection in the 1840s.[17] He was arrested and exiled for this role, but when released in 1847 he was reinstated as *naqib al-ashraf*. This was due not to any change of policy in Istanbul but to the family's friendship with the Grand Mufti in Istanbul from 1846 to 1854, Arif Hikmet, who time and again came to the Husaynis' aid. After this incident, the family kept out of the conflict and did not support the Abu Ghoshes, while sensibly refraining from voicing loyalty either to their enemies or to the government.[18]

## Back in Power

At the start of the sixth decade of the century, the Husaynis could congratulate themselves on having survived the severe tests of the previous decade. They retained the post of *naqib*, though that of *mufti* was less secure. Until 1856 the latter was periodically filled by Muhammad Fadhl Jarallah instead of Mustafa al-Husayni. But after Jarallah's death that year, the government stopped playing divide-and-rule, at least with regard to the post of *mufti* of Jerusalem. Yet government policy did not cause the change so much as marriage connections with the Jarallah family that ensured it would no longer compete for the post of *mufti*. That is, until 1949, when King Abdullah of Jordan appointed a Jarallah to the post in place of al-Hajj Amin al-Husayni.[19] Mustafa remained in the post with the approval of the Jarallahs until 1893, the year of his death.

Two decades after the return of Ottoman rule, the Husaynis were once again at the political and social hub of Jerusalem. This was not blind fortune's doing – the family's skillful use of such traditional means as prudent matrimonial and other social ties, as well as more modern ones like economic power, restored their preeminence. Even before the passing of Tahir and Umar, both of whom died at a ripe old age in the 1850s, the family was guided by the younger men: Muhammad Ali, who would be either *naqib al-ashraf* or a serious contender for the post throughout most of the time of reform, and Mustafa, who was *mufti* for much of that period or likewise a strong candidate for the post. Umar and Tahir remained official heads of the family but had not been involved in the cardinal decisions taken during the very difficult times.

Once they felt secure in their relations with the governor and the other notables, and even in the face of the authorities' centralizing drive, the heads of the Husayni clan turned their attention to the increasingly problematic presence of foreign consuls in Jerusalem. This was particularly true of their relationship with the British consuls, with whom the Husaynis were in constant, bitter conflict.

The first British consul, William Tanner Young, arrived in Jerusalem in 1838 and perceived the city notables to be a group hostile to his country's interests and to himself personally. It seems he failed to understand their world and mindset. While they certainly resented the consuls' intervention in city affairs, they were not a dynamic or a conspiratorial group and rarely tackled diplomats head-on. Only when the latter went so far as to intervene in judicial matters or the status of the notables did disagreements rise to the surface.

After some time, the notables realized that every such incident ended with the consuls' position becoming stronger. Within a decade of coming to Jerusalem in the late 1830s, they had grown into a force to contend with.

More than any of them, British consul James Finn personified the disturbing effect of the European presence. Stationed in Jerusalem between 1845 and 1863, he has been lauded by Israeli historians for helping Jews to settle in their 'ancestral land', and his memoirs have been translated into Hebrew. He is not the only historical figure who appears in one nation's pantheon and in the rogues' gallery of another. Finn detested Islam as a whole and the notables of Jerusalem in particular. He never learned to speak Arabic and communicated via an interpreter, which did nothing to smooth relations.

He was especially hostile to the Husaynis, whose main seat of influence, the Haram al-Sharif, he dubbed 'a site of special fanaticism'.[20] Probably his worst offense in the eyes of the family was his repeated attempts to smuggle foreigners into the Haram. The place had been out of bounds for non-Muslims for more than five centuries, and those who tried to get in were stopped by the Sudanese guards who were the principal defenders of the shrines.[21] Finn tried for some time to change this custom, at first without success. But slowly the prohibition began to weaken, and Sheikh al-Haram Mustafa al-Husayni was unable to prevent it.

In general, it seemed to the Husaynis that Finn was working more eagerly than any other European to establish a permanent Western presence in Jerusalem, mainly through the purchase of lands and real estate for missionary and, later, commercial groups.[22]

## The Crimean War and its Impact

Although a minor incident in Jerusalem served as a pretext for the Crimean War, which embroiled many of Europe's powers, the conflict did not have an immediate impact on Jerusalem or its people's lives. Politically, the crisis exposed the weakness of the central government – since the war was fought in the capital's vicinity. The temporary vacuum was not filled by one particular group but rather increased tensions between the foreign consuls and the notables over issues of honor and control.

As far as the Husaynis were concerned, the years of the war were the last phase of the serious inter-clan feuds that had threatened their grip on the powerful positions in the city. The next fifty-two years – 1856 to 1908 – would favor the family as a social and political force in the Ottoman world.

The signing of the Treaty of Paris, which ended the war in March 1856, had important implications for the political life of Jerusalem. Britain and France used their wartime assistance to the Ottoman Empire to obtain further privileges for its Christian subjects and greatly strengthened the position of their consuls.

The consuls were influential in other ways as well. They gave the city a more cosmopolitan look, but the process entailed various humiliations of the local inhabitants. For example, Ottoman soldiers and guards had to stand in the presence of a consul's son, a gesture of respect that had never been accorded even to the notables.[23] Eventually the Husaynis were able to cope with this challenge too.

The family's ability to contend with the power of the consuls after the Crimean War was due to their greatly increased wealth as well as their political standing. One of their financial resources was the money paid by the various Christian denominations fighting amongst themselves for possession and management of their sacred sites. Their political rise was due to frequent changes of governors in Jerusalem, much as it had been in Damascus. As each new man came in, he had to quickly establish a *modus vivendi* with the notables, whose power and self-esteem grew accordingly. Their principal field of operations was the city council, whose composition had hardly changed since the days of Egyptian rule, and this continuity gave it added power.

## Adding a New Power Base: The Municipality

Considering their situation in the late nineteenth century, it may be said that the Husaynis did better in the new world of the twentieth. In the short term, their main rivals, the Khalidis, adapted more successfully to the new realities, benefited from their support for the existing regime and their connections among the new forces in Istanbul and won a dominant, if short-lived, position in the new power base created by the reformists – namely, the municipal council. When the term of the first mayor of Jerusalem, Abd al-Rahman al-Dajani, ended, it seemed only natural that the government would offer the post to Yusuf Daya', a bright young Khalidi who was only twenty-five. His friendship with the Ottoman foreign minister also helped consolidate the Khalidis' standing in Jerusalem. (This same Yusuf would later overcome the Husaynis in the contest for another powerful post devised by the reformists, that of district representative in the parliament launched in 1876.)

In 1863 the opening of the first municipality building – a fine edifice, and only the second municipality in the empire after Istanbul – gratified all the other notables as much as it did the Khalidis, and it seems they all took part in the ceremony. The event also marked the start of a new sartorial fashion among the elite: many of them appeared wearing the tarbush ('headgear' in Persian), a hat that had been introduced in Jerusalem in 1861 after it made its first appearance in Istanbul and Cairo.[24]

Before long the Husaynis realized that if they wished to maintain their position in the city, they had to have some control over the municipality.[25] Yet only in the sixth round, during the 1880s, did they put up a candidate of their own. Since it was a secular post, they chose someone from the Umari branch, the family's social side. Umar Fahmi, the son of Muhammad Ali, was elected as the sixth mayor of Jerusalem, and thereafter the post often remained in Husayni hands. Yet the Umari branch did not retain the post for long, and Umar Fahmi's successor was Salim, the son of Abd al-Salam. In fact, since the two main branches had formed more matrimonial bonds between them, Salim Hussein – known as *al-Shaqir* ('The Benefactor') – belonged to more than one branch of the family. His own son and successor, Hussein Salim, was a scion of the family as a whole, though after him the post of mayor passed to the religious Tahiri branch of the family, which also held the post of *mufti*. Centralizing reforms caused the two Husayni posts of *naqib al-ashraf* and *sheikh al-haram* to lose their elevated status (in Palestine at any rate and certainly in Jerusalem), and these were held by the Umari branch (Bashir, the son of Umar Fahmi, would be *sheikh al-haram*). In contrast, the Tahiri branch filled two powerful positions – the old one of *mufti* and the new mayoralty.

Future historians, many of them Israelis and some – for example, Elie Kedourie – unsympathetic to the Palestinian nation, would argue that al-Hajj Amin al-Husayni became a powerful figure in Palestine by deceiving the new rulers, particularly the British. This ignores the tremendous power of the Husayni branch to which al-Hajj Amin belonged. The British rulers did not ignore this but took it into account. At any event, in the final stages of Ottoman rule there were other senior posts to be had in the local officialdom.

It seems that the administrative pie was fairly evenly divided between the branches of the family.

In the period under discussion, only the municipality was added to the array of coveted local posts. Though in future the mayoralty would become a significant institution, it was less influential during the 1860s, if only because its budget was too meager for it to carry much weight. Nevertheless, after the promulgation of the *vilayet* law in 1864, the municipality became more important, and it became even more so in 1872 when Jerusalem became a district in its own right.

The situation changed in 1875 when the prerogatives of the municipality were enlarged to include exclusive control over the city's budget and development. Two years later it changed still further when the new institution became more powerful following the promulgation of the law of municipalities. From that point on, the mayoralty was usually in the hands of Husaynis.[26]

In the late 1870s the Husaynis and other families, notably the Khalidis, waged an unprecedented, intense contest for the post of mayor. The mayor was chosen first by the city council, which consisted not only of notables but also of the leaders of non-Muslim communities and representatives of the poorer classes. Then the chosen candidate had to win the support of all the townspeople who were Ottoman citizens. This contest took place during the reign of Sultan Abdul Hamid II (1876–1909), who favored the Husaynis more than had his predecessor, Abdul Aziz II. Perhaps it was thanks to this imperial favor that the family took over the institution and retained it.

## Growing Affluence and its Price

For the Husaynis, the 1870s were also a time when property and commerce became very significant factors. Until the previous decade, they had still been very cautious about economic expansion and, as we have seen, about the reforms, which – at least until 1875 – tended to favor Jerusalem's Christian and Jewish merchants. The conservatism of the Muslim elite constrained their development, but once they shed their traditional stance the notables also began to reap the financial benefits of the increasing integration of the local and European economies. Following the deaths of Muhammad Ali and Mustafa in 1869, a younger and bolder generation of Husaynis came to the fore, and in 1870 they began to look beyond the city walls.

Rabah al-Husayni, the son of Muhammad Ali and grandson of Umar al-Husayni, was more interested in the accumulation of wealth than in local politics. He was a scion of the Umari branch of the family, whose decline in public affairs may have spurred its members to succeed materially. At first Rabah did quite well. His great wealth gave him political influence, and it was only natural that he was appointed *naqib al-ashraf* like his father and grandfather before him. Like his kinsmen Salim, Shukri and Ismail, who had headed the family in the reign of Abdul Hamid II, he discovered that continued social prominence and the guardianship of Muslim sacred properties could be profitable. Personal wealth became another weapon in the arena of the local economy, which was increasingly linked to that of the world at large.

The chief losers in this struggle were the Palestinian farming community – that is, most of the population – which was obliged to turn from cultivation for personal consumption to cash crops. The Christian and Jewish merchants, and later the great Muslim families who also mediated between the cultivators and the outside world, could withstand the sweeping process by acting as middlemen in the export of raw materials (chiefly from neighboring countries) or by importing manufactured goods. Towards the end of the century they also took up speculating and dealing in real estate, including properties of the Muslim religious council.

Rabah al-Husayni enlarged the family holdings in the neighboring villages and bought lands in the villages of Ayn Sinniya and Ajul. He was also the first to display the family's wealth and to change its residential habits. During the 1860s, young members of the family who returned to the city late often found themselves threatened by wild animals and bandits. (Since the time of Governor Surraya [c. 1700] the city gates were closed every evening at nightfall.) Rabah came up with the idea of moving the family's residences adjacent to the religious properties they managed – mostly beside the Haram – outside the walled city. Perhaps the move was also prompted by the desire to live among orchards and groves, rather than in the increasingly crowded walled city, whose population doubled in the closing decades of the nineteenth century.[27] In 1870 Rabah built himself a palatial home near the mosque at Sheikh Jarrah, making him the first Husayni to live outside the city.

These buildings outside the walls of Jerusalem, to which new Jewish neighborhoods would later be added, were changing the character of the city. During the reign of Abdul Aziz (1861–76), there was a dramatic surge in construction, including the Russians' extensive purchase of lands both inside and outside the city. The process entailed the westward extension of water pipes and roads as well as gardens. The Austrians contributed by paving the road to Jaffa, improving the link between Jerusalem and the rest of the country. The first carriages appeared in Jerusalem in 1860 and gradually replaced the traditional covered litters.[28]

Rabah lived in his new house with his four wives. Since none of them bore him a son, the *niqaba* passed to the Tahiri branch of the family, that of the *muftis*. It did not pass directly: first Rabah's brother Abd al-Latif won the post, but since there was an open contest for it, the government (or perhaps the family itself) preferred Hassan's grandson Ahmad Rasim al-Husayni to be the *naqib*. Thus at the end of the century the Umari branch of the family lost another power base (having already lost the mayoralty to the stronger Tahiri branch). In reality, by this time the post of *naqib* no longer carried any political weight and was chiefly a vestige of the old nobility. Rabah lost not only the nostalgic title but also his entire fortune in a miscalculated land transaction, in which he sold his palatial home and its surrounding land to an American family who would later establish the American Colony on the site.[29]

Two of Rabah's kinsmen did much better and made the most of the new opportunities created during the Tanzimat. One was Umar Fahmi al-Husayni, whose fortunes recovered extremely well after the incident that had led to his exile in Rhodes late in the reign of Abdul Aziz. As Umar Fahmi's name indicates, he was a scion of the Umari branch of the family, which had lost much of its political power. His own financial acumen was as poor as that of his kinsman Rabah, but his family's decline drove Umar Fahmi, like many of his younger relatives, to opt for an administrative and parliamentary career. The imperial constitutional reform did not separate these powers, and it was possible to combine them. Umar Fahmi was one of the first to study at the new Ottoman schools of administration, where he was a brilliant student. In 1872, his first appointment was as chief of the land registry in Jerusalem, where he received a handsome *baksheesh* for every registered land transaction – which frequently led to rows with the Europeans. But Umar Fahmi soon rose higher, and under Abdul al-Hamid II (1876–1909), the last effective sultan, he became a member of the Ottoman Parliament and Mayor of Jerusalem.[30]

The other Husayni who made the most of the new system was Musa, the son of Tahir and younger brother of Mufti Mustafa al-Husayni. Strictly speaking, Musa belonged to the Tahiri branch, that of the *muftis*, but in reality he figured in on a different track entirely – that of individual members of the family who broke out of the old confining framework and followed their own path. In Chapter One, we saw how in the middle of the eighteenth century the first Mustafa, the son of Abd al-Latif, had no share in the family fortunes but chose to follow a purely religious career. Musa al-Husayni was cast in the same mold. But where Mustafa had devoted himself to religion, Musa chose commerce and construction. Starting from the solid economic foundation left to his branch of the family by Tahir al-Husayni, Musa became one of the most important businessmen in the district of Jerusalem. He was elected head of the local chamber of commerce, and this led to a senior position on the district council. Though he did not seek a political career, his material success obliged him to accede to the request of the governor of Jerusalem, Kamal Pasha, to serve as the city's mayor in 1874.[31] During the 1880s Musa al-Husayni also sat as chief magistrate of the secular court that dealt with criminal cases.

Another of their contemporaries was Tahir II, the son of Mustafa – to be distinguished from his grandfather Tahir – who succeeded Mustafa II as *mufti* of Jerusalem. Born during the Tanzimat in 1842 when his grandfather was in exile in Istanbul and his young father assumed the post of *mufti*, Tahir II is remembered as the father of al-Hajj Amin al-Husayni but deserves to be known in his own right. He was only twenty-three when he became *mufti* himself (his son Amin would repeat this achievement by becoming *mufti* at the age of twenty-five). Tahir II remained in the post for forty years – an astonishing feat in itself – and would leave his imprint on the religious atmosphere in the city, which had recently become, as it had been during the Crusades, a lodestone for the three monotheistic religions and the five European powers.

The history of the Husaynis during the Tanzimat may be divided into ebb tide and flood tide. During the first part, which ended in 1856, the Husaynis had difficulty adapting to the changes imposed by the reforms of the sultan and his ministers that some other families managed to cope with. In fact, the Husaynis missed a historical opportunity when the balance of power in the district of Jerusalem shifted in favor of the urban notables at the expense of the mountain potentates. At high tide, a new generation adjusted fairly easily to the new Ottoman state and, by combining the economic fortune created by their predecessors with the new education, was able to restore the family's power.

Though the Tanzimat created additional power bases, the family was able to seize control of most of them. Other families underwent a similar process – for example, the Nashashibis, whose relationship with the Husaynis in the twentieth century has been likened to that of the Montagues and Capulets. But none of the other notables achieved such status and prestige, largely because the family had built a power base unequalled in the city or district, thanks to the cousins Umar and Tahir I.

At their high tide after the Crimean War, the Husaynis began to fit into the new Ottoman administration. However, this did not put an end to the politics of notables, as Albert Hourani called them. The modern Ottoman state recognized the genuine social power of the local notables, who continued to command all the religious posts (except that of the *qadi*, which was reserved for men from Istanbul). The sultans valued their connection with holy cities such as Jerusalem and ensured that the guardians of the sacred sites retained their status.[32]

For a moment in the late 1860s, it looked as if the Ottoman policy was becoming so Westernized that the mediating function of these families would come to an end. Motivated by the need for greater efficiency following the military defeats, or by economic difficulties, and certainly by European influence, a group of more radical reformers sought to launch new reforms that would tighten the link between the government and its subjects. These were democratically orientated groups of intellectuals hoping to advance reform beyond the limits imposed by the high bureaucrats running the show. This was not what the Husaynis were looking for, and they were quite happy when a more cautious reformer, Sultan Abdul Hamid II, came to the throne.

The historian Beshara Doumani has noted that the situation in Palestine was not merely a reflection of the reformist laws. Every reformist law, when promulgated, set off negotiations regarding the new relationship between the government and the districts and brought about the creation of a new reality. This made it possible to adapt and survive in a changing world.

During the reign of Abdul Hamid II, the Husayni family assured its survival by sending its sons to take up administrative posts in the empire. To achieve this, they took advantage of Jerusalem's private Christian educational system. This was entirely a missionary system that the family had previously resisted as a crude Christian infiltration of the holy city. One important institution was the Zion School for Boys, established in 1853 on Mount Zion by the Anglican bishop Samuel Gobat, who had come to Jerusalem in the 1840s to provide free education to indigent students. Eventually many of the Husayni men were educated by him.

As in the past, survival still depended on good contacts in Istanbul, but it was a very different capital from the one that the family patriarch, Abd al-Latif II, had known. It was divided between the Westernizing reformists and the 'reactionary' guardians of tradition. It was not enough to be on friendly terms with someone in a senior position – political acumen and a sound understanding of the relative strength of the warring factions was also essential. In this setting the Husaynis, unlike many of the Arab elites in the empire, were not passive pawns in the hands of the chess players in the capital but rather active elements in shaping the process of the reforms.

## CHAPTER 4

# The Death of the Old World

## Towards the End of the Ottoman Era in Palestine

During the 1870s the pace of change increased dramatically. In the early years of the decade the Ottoman reforms reached their peak. Divinely inspired Shari'a law was converted into a modern codex, the *Majala*, while the 'Young Turks' – that dynamic group of Ottoman statesmen who sought to turn the empire into a modern state with a constitutional monarch – drafted a constitution and proposed the creation of a Western-style parliament.

The Young Turks supported Abd al-Hamid II, the younger brother of Sultan Abd al-Aziz II, and when the latter died as a result of falling from his bed, they were widely suspected of having conspired to bring this about. Abd al-Aziz had been a very large man, and it was not surprising that his bed collapsed under him; though by the same token his bulk should have protected him from a fatal injury. Be that as it may, in 1876 the throne was inherited by Abd al-Hamid II – destined to be the last real sultan of the great house of Uthman.

It soon became obvious that he was not a trustworthy ally of the constitutional reformists. Though he permitted the first parliamentary elections in the history of the empire, he soon suspended both the parliament and its constitution. Presumably he felt that the time had not yet come for the sultan to share power with others or to be accountable to a sovereign people instead of to God – a shocking reversal for one who has ruled by divine will. But, as Benedict Anderson notes, even autocratic rulers like Abd al-Hamid II could not ignore the age of nationality in which they found themselves, or turn the clock back. Indeed, the one Western cultural product that the sultan warmly embraced was nationalism – an Ottoman variety thereof. Applying his supreme religious status to the national feelings animating many of his diverse subjects, he offered pan-Islamism to the Muslims, while to the non-Muslims he offered that invention of the Young Turks: 'Ottoman patriotism'. It would soon become clear that neither tactic worked during the volatile turn of the century.[1]

The Husaynis who occupied various positions in the Jerusalem city council were among the first to hear about the reversal in Istanbul. Initially they did not appreciate its full significance, but later it would become obvious that this historical development enabled the family to consolidate its position and complete its recovery, which had begun after the Crimean War.

The family needed time to adjust to the Ottoman constitutional system, as illustrated by its failure to obtain the post of representative of the Jerusalem district in the new parliament. Eventually they would obtain this important new post too, but in 1876 Umar Fahmi lost the contest to Yusuf Daya' al-Khalidi, who had also won the mayoralty. The district governor placated Umar Fahmi by appointing him briefly as mayor and then as governor of the district of Gaza. Unfortunately he died suddenly, and according to the historian Adel Manna, the demise of this gifted man was a grievous loss to the family and the whole of Jerusalem.[2]

The contest for parliamentary representation took place while the Husaynis were adapting to the profound changes that had taken place on the local political scene and in its social makeup. In the months following the accession of the new sultan, the entire family, as a political entity, was occupied with a renewed struggle against the foreign consuls. The principal arena of this conflict was the city council.

### *The 1870s – The Municipality and Salim al-Husayni*

From 1870 on, the European consuls increasingly intervened in the work of the city council, in which they represented almost all the non-Muslim inhabitants of Jerusalem. Utilizing to the utmost the changed legal status of non-Ottoman residents in the empire, they pressured the municipality to adopt resolutions that improved the situation of the Christians and Jews in Jerusalem, especially those who had obtained European nationality and protection.

The council met twice in 1876 and dealt primarily with the demands of the consuls to improve the conditions of the Christian pilgrims in the city. The number of pilgrims kept growing, especially when Jerusalem was connected by newly laid roads to Jaffa in 1867 and to Nablus in 1870. Under pressure from the consuls, a new gate was opened in the city wall on the northwest side to enable the pilgrims to enter directly into the Christian Quarter. Thus in the Hamidi period – the reign of Abd al-Hamid II – Jerusalem was newly connected to much of the country, and Europeans and Ottomans helped to turn it into a geopolitical center whose influence spread far beyond the administrative boundaries of the Jerusalem *sanjaq.*

The consuls did not always attend the council's sessions. When an issue important to them was on the agenda, they would wait outside the conference room and their interpreters, who were inside, would keep them informed about the proceedings. There was only one small room for guests at the municipality, used not only by the consuls but by anyone who was concerned with the council's agenda. When the room became overcrowded, the connecting door to the council chamber sometimes burst open and the visitors pushed their way in, even causing the meeting to be suspended. The consuls regarded themselves as allies of the district governor, who was present at the council sessions, and together they opposed the notables on issues concerning their governments' positions or their own personal status in the city.

In the first years of the new reign, the Husaynis developed a fairly intricate set of relationships. Their relations with the British consulate improved greatly, especially after Finn's departure. His successor, Moore, became a friend of the family, and perhaps the seeds of the future alliance between the Husaynis and the British government, which lasted till the late 1920s, were sown at that time. Towards the end of Abd al-Hamid's reign, the family relied on Moore in the face of the hostility of the Ottoman governor, Rauf Pasha.[3]

During the first decade of the new reign, the European impact on the city was so profound that the family had no choice but to cooperate to some extent and certainly to avoid the confrontations that had marked Finn's tenure. The consuls became much more powerful thanks to their construction projects on the lands they had acquired in the 1850s. New buildings kept cropping up, demonstrating that the political balance of power in Jerusalem had changed beyond recognition. As well as new monasteries, there were new hostelries, such as the New Grand Hotel and Joachim Fast's hotel, which appears in almost every contemporary photograph. These hotels accommodated the consuls' foreign guests, who were given Ottoman citizenship for the duration of their stay.

One contemporary described the Husaynis as better adjusted to the new reality than were the Khalidis. Yitzhak Rokah, who had business dealings with the Husaynis, noted that they 'strive to respond gracefully to learning various languages', and that unlike the Khalidis, they 'have grown accustomed to learning, and appreciate that there is a world outside the boundaries of Islam'. It was this pragmatism, said Rokah, that enabled the Husaynis to rise at the expense of the Khalidis. But Rokah was aware that it was not only ideological pragmatism that enhanced the Husaynis' position. Their connection with the Hamidi monarchy was unmatched by any other Jerusalem family due to the marriage of Musa al-Husayni's daughter to the Grand Vizier in Istanbul. The historian A. Droyanov also quotes a letter written by a Jew from Jaffa referring to Musa al-Husayni as the Grand Vizier's father-in-law. Such a connection, if true, undoubtedly strengthened the Husaynis early in the reign of Abd al-Hamid II.[4]

The members of the family who served on the city council appreciated the importance of taking the consuls' views into account. They also considered what might be called public opinion, which reflected the general attitude towards the consuls and could sometimes be used against them. At that time the Husaynis learned to use the Nabi Musa festivities as a way of demonstrating to the consuls their own and the public's protests. The German journalist Klaus Volken, who witnessed the celebrations in the late 1870s, reported to his paper that some 10,000 had taken part in the Nabi Musa procession.[5] He noted that the heads of the Husayni family used the occasion to express for the first time their objections to the excessive intervention of European consuls in Palestine, particularly in Jerusalem, but that even without their public declarations, the great throng that took part in the festivities protested against the consuls' meddling in matters large and small. The sight of the processions and groups of European pilgrims – chiefly from Russia, France and Austria – that filled the city streets during the Nabi Musa celebration made it a natural occasion for expressing displeasure. The new governor of the city, who came into office in 1876 and remained until 1888, tried to prevent the holiday from turning into a political occasion but only succeeded in averting violent clashes. Year after year, until the end of Ottoman rule, while a semblance of order was maintained, the event retained and even intensified its political character. And from the eighteenth century on, the Husayni family was at its center.[6]

Public opinion affected more than the issue of consuls; demands from below were beginning to have an impact on municipal issues as well. For example, in 1875 the municipality responded to the clamor of the residents in the Bab al-Huta neighborhood and opened the Flowers Gate, which had been bricked up for many years.[7] The combined effect of the consuls' demands and pressure from the local populace altered the sense of responsibility – or rather the scope of responsibility – of the Husaynis who engaged in politics. In the past, obeying the traditional concept of charity and welfare, they responded to the personal petitions and group demands of those who depended on their material or political benevolence, whereas now their official functions obliged them to accept responsibility for the entire community. They continued to exact payment for their generosity and responses, and only rarely did they initiate action to benefit this or that group or the community as a whole. But in the 1880s, they began to act on behalf of groups that were not their particular clients. Starting with the mayoralty of Salim al-Husayni, the family tackled issues that concerned the city's general population. Voluntarily or not, some members of the family began to regard it as a 'national' responsibility (the word is in quotation marks because only in the twentieth century would it become a true national responsibility). Indeed, it seems that the Husaynis fulfilled this 'national' role very well before the formal birth of the national movement – that is, before World War I. They did less well in the role after the war than they had done before it, thus calling into question the notion of progress over time.

The history of the family in the first decade of the Hamidi reign is the history of the municipality of Jerusalem, and in particular that of its mayor Salim. He was the grandson of Abd al-Salam and Musa Tuqan's daughter, and the brother of Mufti Mustafa. His father, Hussein, was a prosperous merchant whose wealth enabled Salim to build up his political power. Salim was very much the head of the Tahiri branch of the family, though strictly speaking he descended from both branches, which may account for his special strength. He was more powerful than his nephew Tahir II, who had been *mufti* since 1865. Salim was regarded by the people of Jerusalem as the head of the citizenry – a novel title to replace the obsolete one of *naqib al-ashraf*. One of his sons was governor of the district of Jaffa, while the governor of the district of Jerusalem was a close friend of his immediate family.[8] These two power bases, that of mayor and *mufti*, both held by the Tahiri branch, would be consolidated by the 'politics of notables'. During the British Mandate, Mufti al-Hajj Amin al-Husayni was always at odds with Mayor Musa Kazim. When they cooperated they achieved advances for their families and their people, and when they fought – as they did much of the time – they sowed dissension and reaped failures.

We have noted that the Tahiri branch of the family acquired great power while the Umari branch lost a great deal, especially when the post of *naqib* also passed to the Tahiri branch. At the end of the century, the post of *naqib* passed from Rabah to his brother Abd al-Latif al-Husayni, a man of many facets, remembered by Jerusalemites as the man who paved the road from the Jaffa Gate around the city wall to the Mount of Olives. Paved in honor of the German Kaiser Wilhelm II, who came into power in 1898, the new road extended to Augusta Victoria, a huge edifice named after the Kaiser's wife.[9] Abd al-Latif was a member of the district's administrative council, hence his considerable influence over the management and development of the city. But he was the last Umari to hold the post of *Naqib* – the city council transferred it to the Tahiri branch, namely, to Ahmad Rasim, the son of Said, the grandson of Hassan and the father of Said II (about whom we will learn much more below). At the turn of the century the post was still in the hands of Ahmad Rasim, who kept it until his death, when it passed to his son, Said II. However, as we have seen, the post had already lost much of its significance in the reign of Abd al-Hamid II, and the secular revolution of the Young Turks in 1908 rendered it quite meaningless.

The Umaris did not vanish entirely from the political landscape, but they did grow weaker and apparently poorer. They recovered thanks to a move that had proved useful in the past. This time it was Umar Fahmi's daughter Aisha – fittingly named after a woman famous in Muslim tradition for her financial shrewdness and political audacity – who saved the Umari branch. Her marriage to al-Hajj Amin al-Husayni reunited the two branches of the family. Such matches had not been customary in previous generations, when they were usually made within the branch. Modern Husayni women say that the family had previously preferred to form matrimonial alliances with other clans rather than marry between the branches. Aisha inherited a substantial estate from her father, which would be very useful to al-Hajj Amin. As previously noted, Umar Fahmi himself (in those days known as 'Little Umar', to distinguish him from his namesake in the time of the Egyptian Muhammad Ali) had married a daughter of Musa Tuqan. (A sister of hers had married Abd al-Salam, the son of the first Umar, whose wedding was described at the opening of Chapter Three.) The matrimonial ties with the Tuqans linked the elite of Nablus with that of Jerusalem, enhancing the alliance between these two important cities and forming an urban connection that would become a stronghold of Palestinian nationality.

Though fifty years separated the weddings of grandfather and grandson, the ceremonies were the same. Marriages were agreed upon in advance and took place when the bride reached puberty.[10] The mother of the groom would come to the girl's house accompanied by her relatives, but only if the girl accepted the groom did the men begin to negotiate. (The role of the women was not as passive as often depicted.) In the evening, the male contingent would arrive and ask the girl's father for his approval, after which the betrothal could proceed. In the following days the families negotiated the written contract, the bride price and so on. The wedding preparations consumed two hectic months. After the betrothal, the bride and then the groom took a traditional bath of purification, followed by the henna party, and only then came the wedding night. The evening began at the *hammam*, followed by an elaborate dressing ceremony, and concluded with the groom walking to the bride's house. A month or two after the wedding, the bride's father would hold a feast, but the guest list was made up by the groom's family. In years to come, the women of the family would describe tensions that arose between the branches of the family because certain individuals of this or that branch were not invited to the post-wedding party.[11] These events, like the new family homes built outside the city walls, were the highlights of the lives of those members of the family who did not take part in the high politics associated with the Husaynis' aristocratic status.

However, Salim al-Husayni needed no matrimonial ties to preserve his standing, either in the family or in the city. His physical appearance in a photograph from the period gives no indication of his forceful personality. A short man, unusually dark-complexioned, he wears a grizzled beard and looks older than he actually was when the picture was taken. His reputation stemmed mainly from his being a *qadi asha'ir* – one who adjudicated Bedouin tribal conflicts – but he was above all the family's foremost entrepreneur, a talent he had inherited from his father, Hussein. Thanks to his abilities, the family could sail through the upheavals in the Jerusalem *sanjaq* as the local economy became linked to the rest of the world. The whole city benefited from his expertise: it was he who developed the concept of municipal services, and with the government's help, he built a hospital in the Sheikh Badr neighborhood (the building still stands in the Mahaneh Yehudah market), paved roads, sank wells and laid sewage pipes. He even tried, unsuccessfully, to solve the problem of the water supply to the poor, but this would only be achieved under British rule.[12]

For eighteen years, between 1879 and 1897, Salim was on-and-off mayor of Jerusalem, and he is still credited with many improvements. It was his initiative to plant trees along Jaffa Road, install the first streetlights and employ the first garbage collectors. This last service was not strictly enforced.[13] The numerous draft animals in the city made street cleaning difficult – even the square in front of the municipality, where the animals were habitually tethered, was full of dung. The British mandatory government could take credit for carrying out some of the cleaning operations and relieving the city of the excessive livestock and dung. Already in 1894 the British representatives complained that the new railway from Jaffa was causing the city to become overcrowded, and deliveries of goods were a problem. In response, Salim ordered barriers to be placed at the entrance of many streets, preventing camels and horseback riders from entering. Though photographs from 1900 show that there were still quite a few animals, during Salim's mayoralty serious efforts were made to improve the cleanliness and sanitation in Jerusalem, and to cleanse its choked drainage channels.[14] As well as caring for the city during the Hamidi period, the Husaynis also built themselves a family neighborhood.

It was during this reign that they began to feel the economic transformation that was affecting the entire Near East. For example, the aforementioned Musa al-Husayni, brother of Mufti Mustafa, personally benefited from the railway project since he was responsible for the supply of timber for the rail sleepers. The project brought him fame and one of the highest imperial decorations, which he was invited to Istanbul to receive ceremoniously. He died before the project was complete and left his sons – the fairly well-known Ismail and Shukri and the less-known Arif – great wealth and a priceless network of contacts in the Istanbul administration.[15] At the start of the twentieth century, Arif would gain some renown by being appointed chief treasurer of the Ottoman Ministry of Education in Istanbul, a senior post that he filled successfully.

Profits from the guardianship of Muslim holy properties, notably the sale of their agricultural lands, enabled the Husaynis to bequeath a handsome estate to the next generation. It is worth noting that this was an extensive range of religious properties, many of them of all-Islamic importance. Even after selling some of these, the family still owned considerable real estate in and around Jerusalem, and like others of their class they were buying property in the lowlands. Musa, Ismail and Rabah al-Husayni all owned lands in what is today called the inner plain. Many villagers registered their lands in the Husaynis' names, or the names of other notables, because they could not afford the cost of registration and ownership. The first to do so were the villagers of Bait Nequba. In the 1870s, as a temporary measure, they registered village plots in the name of Ismail al-Husayni, who paid the land taxes. But they discovered that the temporariness was questionable, and the dispute between the villagers and Ismail over those lands continued throughout the Ottoman period and was not resolved even during the British Mandate.[16] Proprietors of medium-sized lands preferred to deposit their properties in the *waqf*, which also yielded the Husaynis a handsome income.

## The 1880s – Settling Outside the City Walls

The first to realize these profits was Rabah al-Husayni. In 1870 he broke out of the city confines and built himself a house near the mosque of Sheikh Jarrah. In its time, Rabah's palace had a novel style – spacious halls and rooms embellished with marble arches and carved wooden doors, built around a hexagonal patio full of climbing plants, variegated shrubs and fruit trees surrounding a hexagonal stone cistern. It was roofed with lightweight ter-racotta pipes to insulate it from extreme temperatures and faced with nari stone. The architect must have been partial to the six-sided form, which also dominates the main hall with its magnificent chandelier. A two-storey house with a basement, it covered two acres including the garden, and each of Rabah's four wives had a separate wing. The first floor was the grandest, containing Rabah's apartment and those of his wives, but it was the reception room, with the coffered wooden ceiling topped by a brightly painted dome, that most impressed visitors.[17]

The family remained here until the house was closed down at the end of the twentieth century by the Israelis. However, the palace still stands: it is now the American Colony Hotel. It was a striking architectural gem, especially in those days, when the surrounding area was still largely unbuilt. But even today, amid the dense Israeli construction sites all around the city, it remains unusually attractive – as visitors to the hotel can testify.

In 1882 Mayor Salim joined Rabah and built a house next door. There, on the slope leading to the village of Sheikh Jarrah, the Husaynis began to establish a stronghold, a springboard for family members who wished to play major roles in the new world created by the Ottoman reformists, the European powers and the national movements of Jews and Palestinians. By 1894 the family already had six houses outside the walls, and in the early twentieth century it would be known as the Husayni neighborhood.

Salim's house was also a grand structure for its time. Two-storied like Rabah's house, it was more traditional. (Today it is the House of the Arab Child, an orphanage supervised by the family.) They had chosen the site well: the steep hillside near the mosque of Sheikh Jarrah faced Mount Scopus and overlooked a landscape of vineyards, strips of cultivated land, olive groves and fruit orchards and the road leading to Abu Tur. A handsome central edifice predated the arrival of the Husaynis, including Qasr al-Mufti and a few other palaces known as *qusur*. These were buildings originally designated for religious purposes, and some of them dated back to the time of Salah al-Din al-Ayubi (known in English as 'Saladin'). Sheikh Jarrah and Abu Tur had sprung up around these structures, which had served Saladin's warriors.[18] Some of this land fell within the Husaynis' religious properties and was used to build summer houses. Although a common practice, this was disapproved of by the public, who had a saying: 'He who builds his house on the *waqf* risks having his roof fall down on the heads of his family.'

Completed in 1711, Qasr al-Mufti was originally the residence of Sheikh Muhammad al-Khalili (the Shafi'i *mufti* of Jerusalem in the early eighteenth century). Built north of the city wall, it may be seen today in the courtyard of the Rockefeller Museum. In the 1860s, it was used by the Husaynis as a summer house. There the family, accompanied by their servants, would enjoy the fresh air and open spaces through much of the summer, until the end of the British Mandate.

Today it is called the Mufti's Palace, and the surrounding gardens the Mufti's Vineyard. Tahir II made it into a permanent residence in 1864 and lived there until the 1890s, when he moved into a new house nearby. His new home was a grand two-storey villa built of Jerusalem stone, which like Salim's and Rabah's villas had its own water supply and a fountain in the central courtyard. Tahir's house was one of Jerusalem's cultural centers: poets came to read their poems and talk about literature, and debates were held about politics, both local and imperial. Here Tahir's son, the future al-Hajj Amin al-Husayni, would grow up. In 1966 the house became the Arab Academics' Club, and it currently serves as a club and meeting place for Palestinian academics in Jerusalem.[19]

Muslims began to build permanent structures outside the walls after the Christians and the Jews. They had always had temporary buildings outside, but permanent structures required large amounts of ready cash, which they did not have. In the 1870s, wealthy Muslims began to construct permanent dwellings in various places outside the city walls. The Husaynis' neighborhood prompted other wealthy Muslims to follow in their footsteps. By 1918 there were thirty buildings, including the homes of other prominent families like the Nuseibahs, al-Afifis and others. Eventually the Nashashibi and Jarallah houses would outnumber those of the pioneering Husaynis – another indication of the family's decline. The houses were usually preplanned by European architects, and all of them were built of stone and designed to allow for an independent water supply. Few of them exhibited classical Muslim architectural features, except for Ismail's house – the future Orient House – which included the classical Muslim perforated screen, the *qamriya* (though this is more orientalist than oriental). The furniture was heavy and European, notably in Rabah's house, which would become the property of the

American Colony (first leased, then purchased). The furniture in the reception rooms and bedrooms in Ismail's house was also of the heavy European kind, reflecting the vogue for conspicuous wealth and the process sweeping over the entire empire.

In Istanbul, too, the sultans moved from the Topkapi Palace, their residence until the reign of Abd al-Aziz II, into the rococo Dolmabahce Palace, built by that sultan in 1867.[20] The penchant for ostentation did not affect the notables' apparel; until the end of the Hamidi period, they continued to wear modest long robes with fine white linen cloth, called *yans*, wrapped around the tarbush. A period photograph shows many of the public figures of the day standing before the Khalidiyya library in Jerusalem, all dressed in this traditional style.

The villas in the Husayni neighborhood were not the family's only real estate. Between the start of the twentieth century and the outbreak of the First World War, Imam Yunes al-Husayni, a son of Musa and brother of Ismail – who was, as noted, the guardian of the Nabi Musa religious properties – built a number of houses on Salah al-Din Street, increasing the family's wealth. The Alamis settled at the eastern end of the street while the Husaynis occupied the western end.[21]

By the end of the war, a new neighborhood known as al-Sahra had sprung up there at the intersection of Salah al-Din and Ihwan al-Safa Streets, where the family constructed some more houses. By 1918 this neighborhood consisted of about fifty houses.

The buildings outside the city walls demonstrated the family's high status. Only some 200 families lived in these new neighborhoods, and they formed the nucleus of the class from which the municipal council was chosen. They enjoyed the best higher education and were the first to benefit from Western training and the Ottoman reformist institutions. Thus they continued to dominate the traditional education system in Jerusalem. Their training made them highly useful to the Hamidi government, and indeed in the 1890s members of the family filled various posts, not only in Jerusalem but all over the empire. Ahmad Rasim was educated in the traditional manner, proceeding from the religious primary school to the Islamic college, where he studied Muslim religious law, but his son Said received a Western education at the Jewish school, Alliance Israelite. Yet it should be noted that the traditional education received by Ahmad Rasim was not the same as that which his father, Said I, had received, much less his grandfather, Hassan al-Husayni. Perhaps that was why he did not join the *ulama*, despite his profound religious learning, but went into business and even became the head of the city's chamber of commerce.[22] Thus both the traditional and the Western kinds of schooling helped pupils to advance in the changing world of the Ottoman Empire, as shown by the career of two other Husaynis – Ismail and Shukri.

## Serving the Empire: Between East and West

By the 1890s it was clear to see that the reign of Abd al-Hamid II, for all its rigidity, pan-Islamic pretensions and whims, suited the Husaynis immeasurably better than the reformists, who viewed the notables as inveterate obstacles to progress and change.

The family was again at the peak of its power. Salim was mayor of Jerusalem, Mustafa and after him Tahir II were *muftis*, Rabah was the *naqib* and Musa was the head of the chamber of commerce – each a major power base in that decade. Their position was even stronger than it had been in Hassan's lifetime. This was confirmed by the Egyptian visitor Abd al-Jawad al-Qayati, who stayed in the tent of Mufti Mustafa al-Husayni during the Nabi Musa celebrations in the early 1890s.[23] This was a great honor, sought by many who clustered around the tent in the unusually wet spring. The road to Jericho was unpaved since it was used only for the celebrations, and mud, fierce winds and pouring rain caused great hardship. The single building at the holy site offered no shelter to the thousands of celebrants, and the small tents they erected were either swept away by rushing water or blown away by the wind. Some of the participants did not return to Jerusalem, and though for a while it was feared they had been swept away by the flash flood, they were eventually found safe and sound. But no one gave up, reports the Egyptian visitor. They all obeyed Mustafa's directions and trusted his judgment. The admiration for the *mufti*'s persuasive powers in the face of natural hardships was undoubtedly helped by his generous hospitality to the many guests from Arab countries, but it also reflected his reputation in the Muslim community in Jerusalem, which enhanced the family's power.

The family were powerful not because they were 'reactionary' but because they were flexible. Moreover, the ruler they supported, Abd al-Hamid II, was not a thoroughgoing reactionary. He continued to construct the modern state with new power bases like the municipalities and the new Ottoman administration. He also continued the construction of a diverse educational system, which gave the Husaynis the means to make the most of their excellent relations with the Hamidi regime.

Especially in the provinces, the Ottoman educational system offered a variety of tracks, both traditional and modern, to individuals who wished to make their way in the Ottoman world. However, in the Hamidi period education was not the decisive factor that made a man a 'traditionalist' or a 'modern', and the empire provided a choice of religious or administrative trajectories without a formal educational career. In 1869 the government passed a law of compulsory primary education in the empire, to be implemented by local boards of education. However, there was no stringent enforcement, and the vague supervision made it possible to negotiate a compromise between local reality and the provisions of the law. In the Jerusalem *sanjaq* there were 234 primary schools, the traditional *kuttabs* where boys were taught the Qur'an, the Sunna, arithmetic, Arabic and Turkish. Before their migration to the Husayniyya, the boys of the family attended the *kuttab* adjacent to the Haram al-Sharif, and later various schools near the Lions' Gate.[24] From the *kuttab* it was possible to proceed to one of the new secondary schools, such as the one that opened in 1891. Only in 1906 did a reformist secondary school open, the Rashidiyya (probably named after Ahmad Rashid, the governor of Jerusalem), which was modeled on the French *lycée*. Every sub-district had two such schools, one for boys and one for girls, in which they learned Ottoman Turkish, Arabic and French.[25]

The Husayni sons were among the first to attend European schools, notably the nearby school of the American Colony, run by the Spafford family. The Americans had arrived shortly before the start of the Hamidi reign, after an odyssey that began with the Great Chicago Fire in 1871. Horatio Spafford, a successful attorney and church leader, and his Norwegian-born wife devoted themselves to helping the survivors and reconstructing the devastated city. After three years of exhausting toil, they set out on a pleasure trip to Europe, but the ship on which they sailed sank on 21 November 1874, and the only survivors were the Spaffords' daughter Anna and her husband. Seven years later, moved by these tragedies and their deep religious faith, Anna, her husband and their daughters went to the Holy Land, along with sixteen likeminded friends, including three children. That was the start of the American Colony, and then the hand of fate – whether Muslim or Christian – intervened. Rabah al-Husayni went bankrupt and sold them his beautiful residence.

The range of possibilities open to the Husaynis may be illustrated by the lives of Musa's two sons, Ismail and Shukri, who were educated differently yet followed similar careers. This is another individual example that confounds the widespread theories of Westernization – for example, that of the important scholar John Szyliowicz – which assume that a Western education assured one a great career in the Ottoman Empire. In fact, the Husaynis repeatedly fail to bear out the theories of scholars of the period who maintained that a Western education led to secularism and nationalism. Ismail received a Western, possibly American, education, whereas Shukri received a traditional one. Yet Ismail was very conservative and avoided nationalism, while Shukri was in the vanguard that sought to secularize his society.

Nor does another theory propounded by the scholar of Arab nationalism George Antonius fit the case. According to Antonius, American education in the Middle East catalyzed the rise of nationalist thinking among the local elite. Therefore Ismail, who had come into contact with American missionaries, should have been infected with nationalism, but he was not, while Shukri promptly picked it up. It is true that at the age of sixteen he, too, was exposed to a little French education, so perhaps the West did have some influence on him.

Shukri's brilliant administrative career began in 1881, when he was eighteen, with his appointment to the district of Jerusalem's Board of Education. A young product of a traditional religious education, Shukri was devoted to the practice of *zakkat*, the Muslim duty of charity. In 1885 he launched a charitable organization called the Association of Muslim Welfare Society (Maqasid). In it he combined a traditional institution with a Western concept of social welfare, a fact that illustrates how nuanced the individual personality is compared with the sharp distinctions proposed by the many theories about transitions in human society in the modern age.

In 1885 Shukri's religious devotion earned him an invitation to Istanbul. At this time Sultan Abd al-Hamid II began to backtrack and to maintain that pan-Islamism would save the empire from total collapse. Shukri was given a senior post in the Ottoman treasury, that of chief paymaster of the Ministry of Education in the capital, one of the most important economic posts in the Hamidi bureaucracy. Money, and the people in charge of it, turned the creaking wheels of the empire, and Shukri was able to help his family out of trouble when necessary. He also served as its bridge to the rich and diverse Arab cultural world of the late nineteenth century. He became acquainted with many of the contemporary figures of Arab literature and philosophy. This, no less than his position in the administration, stood the family in good stead in 1908, when secular forces came to power in the Ottoman Empire.

As already noted, Ismail received a more Western education. In addition, he had the eldest son's advantage of inheriting the family lands in the villages around Jerusalem. Due to his connection with the *fellahin*, his first appointment was as a tax collector. This was followed by a career in the Ottoman administration. The highest post he held was that of chief of education in Idna, then part of Jerusalem. During the Hamidi reign, he was the most influential person on the Board of Education assigned to implement reforms in the district of Jerusalem.

Though he was a scion of the Tahiri branch, during the Hamidi period Ismail was regarded as the head of the two Husayni branches. However, by this time the family had already lost its clear hierarchical structure. What makes Ismail the central figure of this chapter is not only his status as head of the family but his interesting relations with the sultan and the Europeans and with the newcomers on the scene, the Jewish settlers. He was the last major figure to be untouched by nationalism, and he judged townspeople and visitors not according to their religious or national affiliation but according to familial or possibly class interests.

Ismail liked to relax on the flat roof of Rabah's house when it was still his cousin's, and even after it had been leased and then sold to the Americans. It had a broad view of the lovely surrounding landscape and a small *bayt sayfi* (summerhouse), in which it was possible to rest and enjoy the fresh air. Beginning in the 1880s, the young people of the American Colony would come up to Rabah's roof every day, from spring to fall, to take part in a summer feast.[26]

It was on that same roof, at the end of March 1897, that Ismail made a major contribution to Palestinian society. He had just been appointed head of the Ottoman Department of Public Instruction. On this occasion he did not pass the time aimlessly with members of the household and other colonists but spoke privately with Anna Spafford's young daughter, Bertha. He talked to her about the education of girls in Jerusalem and said he was looking for a teacher from the American Colony to supervise the only Muslim girls' school in the city. It is doubtful he was aware of the precedent he was setting by asking a Christian to supervise the education of Muslims. He lived in a world that the Turkish sociologist and scholar Sherif Mardin described as bureaucratic Islam – that is, Islam in the service of Ottoman bureaucracy rather than bureaucracy in the service of Islam. In that doomed world, religious ideology was not a prescription for life, it was an abstract discussion and only inspired action when it was politically or socially expedient in advancing someone's personal interests.[27] Ismail, with his Western education, Ottoman training and brilliant administrative career, did not need that ideology when interpreting the reality around him. When he needed to choose suitable individuals in the cause of education, he picked them on the basis of their qualifications and his connections with them or their families. Bertha Spafford was a natural choice – Ismail had been her father's pupil and had known her since she was a child.

As Bertha herself recalled, Ismail cared greatly about the education of girls (as had Hassan in the previous century). He had been impressed by the extensive education Bertha had received from her father, and now he asked her to give him her answer the following day, her eighteenth birthday. When Ismail came to call, he heard that although Bertha wanted the post, her mother adamantly refused. 'You're too young and have no experience,' she said. But the other candidate, a Miss Brooks, who had been headmistress of a Christian girls' school in the city, was too old to take on the post by herself. In the end Bertha's mother gave in to Ismail's urging and allowed her daughter to be Miss Brooks's senior assistant. The following day Ismail took both Miss Brooks and Bertha to see the school, which stood in its own grounds bordering the Dome of the Rock. According to tradition, it had been built by Saladin and had served as a *madrassah* (Muslim school). Its renovation took some time, but finally the first female pupils arrived. Six years later, Bertha Spafford became sole headmistress, and after she married Frederick Vester in 1903, the two ran the school together.[28]

The Spaffords and Ismail shared another interest, that of archaeology. When Ismail became head of the Board of Education, he began to collect ancient artifacts found by foreign archaeologists. He picked six finds and arranged them in a handsome permanent display at the Sultaniyya school opposite Herod's Gate. This was the first Palestinian museum, which Ismail hoped would encourage the study of the history of Palestine from the Canaanite period to his days.

Ismail and his young nephew Said (son of Ahmad Rasim and great-grandson of Hassan) were the first Husaynis to lead their society not only into the traditional religious track but also into the tracks of the Ottoman reformist world and Western education. Said did so as a twenty-year-old school teacher, ostensibly teaching only the art of writing but in fact teaching much more. He was his uncle Ismail's right hand and principal aide. By 1901 Ismail's department included Said and Said's brother Husam al-Din, who served as deputies, as well as fourteen other officials.[29] Thus, the educational department became another power base in the growing empire of the Husayni family. And it was mainly due to Ismail that this influence has grown so greatly.

It should be noted, however, that visitors from the region, mainly Egyptians and Istanbulis, were divided on Ismail's achievements. Some seemed unimpressed by the standard of education compared with that in their own countries, but it is difficult to determine the relative quality of education in the various cities at that time. Georgi Zaydan, who visited Palestine, wrote that education 'in the principal city Jerusalem' was even poorer than in other districts, especially in the government schools. Having visited the constitutional secondary school of Khalil al-Sakakini and the Rawdat al-Ma'arif ('Educational Garden') run by Muhammad Salah al-Husayni, he concluded that their standard was equivalent to that of primary schools in Egypt. Muhammad Salah was a wealthy man who owned most of the houses near the Herodes Gate, and devoted some of his capital to the schools. Zaydan noted that the schools run by foreigners were of better quality – for example, the Schneller orphanage school, established in 1860, and Zion, the school of the Anglican bishop Gobat. Yusuf al-Hakim of the Syrian national movement thought so too. Though he was impressed by the number of schools in Jerusalem, he described only the foreign ones as 'first-rate'.[30] On the other hand, Muhammad al-Shanti, the Palestinian editor of the Egyptian paper *Al-Aqdam*, visited the 'Educational Garden' in 1914 and was favorably impressed.[31] But he was moved by the school's commitment to the Palestinian national struggle against the Zionists and did not comment on its educational standard.

Ismail's historical standing as an educator is therefore controversial. Nor is his public and social work clear-cut. Each of the individuals and groups that had dealings with him remembers him in a different way – always as an important figure though not always as a positive one. In the tragic history of the village of Qolonia (present-day Mevasseret Zion), some of whose lands were sold to the Zionist settlement Motza at the turn of the century and most of whose inhabitants became refugees in 1948, Ismail's behavior in early 1871 was probably not the worst chapter. But his conduct tells us much about the social outlook of the Palestinian aristocracy, or rather the limitations of that outlook. While the early Zionists began to show an interest in the village lands, so did Ismail al-Husayni. Some of the best land was owned by one Khalil Salim, and despite the heavy taxes, he did not want to sell it to Ismail's agent. Thus Ismail reported to the authorities that Salim was a deserter from the Ottoman army who had joined the forces of the Egyptian rebel Muhammad Ali. Salim fled to the mountains, and his family could not resist the Ottoman soldiers who arrived at Ismail's behest and forced them to sell the land to him. Needless to say, the price he paid was barely a fifth of its value.[32]

Be that as it may, by the turn of the century Ismail had become the most important figure in Jerusalem. His standing and that of his entire family were demonstrated when Kaiser Wilhelm II came to Jerusalem in 1898. The kaiser's reception, conducted by Ismail, was of great importance to Sultan Abd al-Hamid II, whose relations with Britain and France had deteriorated as these powers displayed their territorial appetite in the guise of support for the liberation of nations under Ottoman rule. It began with the British conquest of Cyprus in 1876, continued with the British occupation of Egypt – one of the empire's most important regions, which had been practically independent since 1805 but nominally, and crucially, an Ottoman territory – and culminated in France's firm grip on North Africa. Wilhelm II also dreamed of an empire to call his own, but he did not expect to obtain it at the expense of the Ottomans. The conservative and impulsive kaiser was willing to confront the hegemony of Britain on the high seas and French hegemony on land. After establishing a cordial relationship with Russian Tsar Nikolai II, he set out to consolidate his alliance with the Ottoman Empire. He sent the sultan military experts to help build up a strong army that would resist the constant nibbling at his provinces, dispatched engineers to expand the Ottoman railway system and placed at the sultan's disposal capitalists to help him save the empire from the financial bankruptcy it had undergone in 1875.

On his journey through the sultan's empire, the kaiser treated his visit to Jerusalem as a demonstration of their alliance. Moreover, his visit to the holy city symbolized his struggle against the secularization of Europe and his support for the conservative values of Christianity. He hoped that this support would halt the disintegration of the conservative empires, including his own.

Ibrahim al-Aswad, who accompanied the royal procession, described the event.[33] The cannons roared in honor of the Christian visitor, he reports, as was common with visits of such august people. The Husaynis and several other Jerusalem notables waited at the Jaffa Gate. Al-Aswad had never seen the city so bedecked with flowers or so full of armed guards. The royal couple's carriage drove through the city and passed between the former Joachim Fast Hotel near the gate – just outside the city wall on the corner of the Jaffa and Mamilla Roads – and the New Grand Hotel, a handsome three-storey building inside the wall above a fine colonnade of shops owned by the Greek monastery. (Fast's hotel had become the seat of the municipality in 1896.)

As it approached the gate, the kaiser's carriage passed under two decorative arches displaying his imperial standard beside the Ottoman crescent. At the gate he was greeted by Mayor Yasin Khalidi, who made a speech in his honor. The kaiser repaid him with a half-hour speech at the Church of St Savior, opening with the words, 'I have not come with political intentions. This is a purely religious visit.'

The following day the notables, including the Husaynis, gathered for yet another ceremony, this time on Mount Zion, where the sultan's representatives gave the kaiser the title to a half-acre plot.[34] Starting in the afternoon and ending in the brilliant sunset, the ceremony began with a solemn procession led by Tawfiq Bey, the sultan's ambassador to Berlin, and concluded with a pompous handing over of the title deed from the original owner, Said al-Daudi, to the kaiser in the presence of the city governor. The kaiser then laid the cornerstone of the prospective church, the Dormizion, which would be built in 1910 to rise above the city as a symbol of the new era. The municipality also gave the royal visitor a collection of drawings of the views along the road from Jaffa to Jerusalem, bound in mother-of-pearl, and a gilded Qur'an, presented to him by Ismail al-Husayni. The kaiser also visited the Dome of the Rock.

The entire city had brightened its face to welcome the sole remaining European ally of Sultan Abd al-Hamid II. The city council tore down a section of the wall between Jaffa Gate and the Citadel and filled in the moat so that the kaiser could enter the city on horseback. But it also took other measures to improve the life of the inhabitants: increasing the number of streetlights, renovating the cotton market and, most important, enlarging the water supply by extending pipes into the city from the Pools of Solomon and the nearby spring, so that water again flowed into the cistern beside the Mahkameh near the Chain Gate at the entrance to the Haram al-Sharif. The water supply to adjacent houses was also improved. But, as said above, only after the British took over the city did the population as a whole begin to enjoy a decent supply of water.[35]

Having been completed the previous year (1897), the house of Ismail al-Husayni was a focal point during the kaiser's visit. Smaller than Rabah's house – Ismail was not as wealthy as he – it stood on an acre and a quarter of land, the garden planted less with fruit trees than with young olives. Ismail's son Ibrahim supervised the construction. This fine house would become a hotel, which opened in 1914 under the name Orient House. Like the American Colony, it too would lose some of its architectural beauty amid the dense modern construction around it, but it is still possible, looking at the graceful colonnade leading to the entrance, to imagine Kaiser Wilhelm II and Ismail al-Husayni walking up the staircase to the entrance hall. Many eyewitnesses described the occasion as a splendid reception in which all the city's notables and Ottoman officials took part.[36]

A newly built house was a cause for celebration – one of the three major events in the life of a family, after marriage and the birth of sons. A series of ceremonies marked the occasion, and the presence of such an august visitor made for even greater solemnity. Had the occasion not been marred by a horrible tragedy, it would have been remembered by the family as one of its finest days.

Some weeks before the kaiser's visit, the Ottoman Department of Education ordered the Muslim school for girls in Jerusalem to prepare a gift for Queen Augusta Victoria. The gifts chosen were a diamond brooch and a box of sweets. The headmistress, Bertha Spafford Vester, had to choose a pupil to present the gift. With many parents fearing the evil eye, she turned to her friend Ismail, who agreed to let his eight-year-old daughter, Ruwaida, do the honor. The night before the presentation, the little girl, greatly excited, tried on the fine white muslin dress that had been made for the occasion. She was wearing it as she followed the servant who went up to the roof to light the candle lamps, as was done in the other five houses outside the walls at nightfall. A spark from the servant's lamp fell on her dress, which immediately went up in flames.[37]

To round off the picture of the Husayni family's adaptation to the changing Ottoman world, we need to look at the career of a third family member – after Shukri and Ismail – who served in the empire's bureaucracy. Musa Kazim al-Husayni, a scion of the Tahiri branch, would be the first mayor of Jerusalem after the British conquest of Palestine. He will figure largely later in this book when the British Mandate is discussed. His path resembled that of his kinsman Shukri. Like him, Musa Kazim attended a religious primary school in Jerusalem, where he had been born in 1853. At an early age he was admitted to the *maktab malkiya* (state school) in Istanbul, the school of administration that trained men for service as provincial governors and officials. Upon graduation, Musa Kazim was third amongst all students from the Arab world – an impressive achievement that gave him an auspicious start. He was put in charge of the local Department of Health and was later appointed *qaymaqam* (governor) of Jaffa – all before he was thirty. Between 1892 and the outbreak of World War I, he served as governor in a number of places, including Safed, Akkar (Lebanon), Irbid (Transjordan), Asir and Najd (Arabia), Thalis (Anatolia), and the Hauran (Syria). The height of his career was the governorship of the al-Muntafaq region in Iraq.

Musa Kazim was one of the first of the urban notables to become integrated into the Ottoman administration, right up to its highest echelons. The historian Yehoshua Porath has noted that the government's decision to send him to such remote regions showed his high standing: it was precisely in those remote places that the sultan needed men he could count on.[38] If Shukri reached the highest rank at the heart of the Ottoman Empire, Musa Kazim achieved the highest posts in the provincial administration. These two men would advance the family and enable it to cross the Rubicon of the First World War. The historian Philip Mattar noted that during the reign of Abd al-Hamid II the notables chose to follow bureaucratic careers and became an 'aristocracy of service'.[39] Like many of the Husaynis, Musa Kazim not only enhanced the family's standing but also added to its wealth – for example, in 1872 he acquired at an auction 1,000 acres of fertile land, including two thirds of the land of Jericho in the Jordan Valley.[40]

It was not only through the careers of these three central figures that the family expanded its influence. Another member who contributed was Abd al-Salam II (1850–1915). He was the son of Umar Fahmi, who had been governor of Gaza, while Abd al-Salam III was governor of Jaffa. This is not the place to expatiate on his life, except to note that he was also known as a poet and left a respected volume of poetry about Jerusalem.[41]

This Umari sub-branch illustrates the Husaynis' spread throughout Palestine – Gaza, Jerusalem and Jaffa – and the wide range of their influence in the administration and in cultural life.

## Facing Old and New Challenges

The declining status of the *qadi*, in Jerusalem as in other cities, revealed the power acquired by the family due to its integration into the Ottoman administration. Again, the *qadi* was the only outside appointee other than the governor. The *muftis* and *naqibs* – most of whom during the Hamidi reign were members of the Husayni clan – now began to move into areas that had previously been the *qadi*'s purview. The latter's position was already weakened, as the Tanzimat had created a secular judiciary that functioned alongside the religious one.[42] This reversal in the relations of *qadi* and *mufti* concluded in 1913, when Ottoman law decreed that 'The head of the local hierarchy is the *mufti*.'[43] During that period, as previously noted, the post of *sheikh al-haram* also reverted to the Husaynis: Bashir, the son of Abd al-Salam and grandson of Umar Fahmi – that is, a scion of the Umari branch – was appointed to the post. But it had lost its significance, and possessing it did not help the weakened branch of the family.

The historian Yusuf al-Dabagh comments that the family's dominance of the city's life was fairly limited. He describes the period as 'democratic': the aristocratic families did not really control the life of the city but were concerned with particular aspects that affected the townspeople as a whole. The Ottoman government, however, seemed to regard it as considerable dominance.

The increasing power of the Husaynis aroused the resentment of the Ottoman governor of Jerusalem, especially Rauf Pasha, the last governor during the reign of Abd al-Hamid II. Over the last two years of the sultan's reign (1907–9), Rauf Pasha repeatedly complained that the Husaynis were inciting the populace against the sultan. Fortunately, he said, the sultan had a servant who was the right man in the right place, who was able to overcome them 'for the good of the people'. He told the central government that he had succeeded in controlling the 'parasites' – namely, the Husaynis, Khalidis and Nashashibis.[44]

The family's growing power also reawakened the tension in its relations with the foreign consuls, who had become much stronger since the kaiser's visit. As the British consul John Dixon reported, this was due to Jerusalem's growing importance in the eyes of the world, and as a result the Western consuls became an even more dominant element in the city than they had been in Finn's time. In the past fifteen years the city's population had doubled, as had its area, and since the opening of the railway link with Jaffa, commerce had also doubled.[45] As the consul walked around the market, he rejoiced to see the finest British goods on display and to hear English spoken everywhere, both by the many missionaries living in the city and the numerous tourists who frequented it. 'Hundreds of British tourists come here twice a year, spring and autumn,' he wrote. He also complained about his numerous duties and his low salary. Most of the European consuls had been promoted to consuls-general, but not Dixon – not because Britain was less interested in Jerusalem than the other powers but because of bureaucratic parsimony.[46]

During the final years of Abd al-Hamid's reign, which ended in 1909, the European influence was so dominant that the sub-district of Nazareth was detached from the district of Acre and attached to the Jerusalem *sanjaq*, thus putting all the Christian holy places under one umbrella and 'facilitating the services to the pilgrims'. But near the end of his reign, the sultan restored Nazareth to the district of Acre.[47]

The process of economic and technological transformation driven by the foreign presence in the city accelerated in the early twentieth century. European influence was visible everywhere, and the increasing trade with Europe affected the patterns of life in towns and villages throughout Palestine. The new destination of the external trade and its growth in the three districts that would later form the British Mandate of Palestine – Jerusalem, Nablus and Acre (the last two being part of the Vilayet of Beirut, with its capital in Sidon) – would promote a certain economic unity among them. These districts did not need to use the Port of Beirut, and their external commerce could operate from within their territory. Foreign trade meant an increase of cash crops, with cultivators turning into hired laborers and agriculture being modernized. In the city, the effects could be seen in the growing number of foreign banks, in the postal services and in insurance companies.[48]

Though the Husaynis became wealthier in the early twentieth century, they were not affected by the capitalist trend and did not join the world of finance. The capitalization of Jerusalem's economy sustained three principal groups – Jerusalemites of Greek and Italian origin who operated energetically and accumulated fresh capital, a small number of Jewish settlers who arrived at the beginning of the century and the German Templers.[49]

But if the rules of the capital market did not directly affect the Husaynis, other European imports did reshape their world. For example, the installation of a clock tower over the Jaffa Gate, one of the many towers built in honor of the sultan throughout the empire, revolutionized the perception of time and space among the people in Jerusalem and elsewhere in Palestine. According to the intriguing analysis of Benedict Anderson, a scholar of nationality, the clock caused people to relate differently to the reality around them and gave rise to a new political-cultural relationship that eventually became known as nationality. Until the end of the First World War, younger people in Jerusalem set their daily timetable by the clock tower, while the older people continued to live by a dual timetable – a Western one when required to fix a precise time, and the traditional one determined by prayers and meal times.

The more traditional scholars of Arab nationalism agree that the encounter with Europe catalyzed the formation of national identity. It was a complex encounter that included several economic aspects and the advent of new technology which enabled speedy physical access to information and new places and made it possible for people to compare cultural worlds in terms of values. For the Palestinians in general, and the Husaynis in particular, this phenomenon was personified by a new kind of Jew, the Zionist.

The Zionists saw themselves as a national movement that acted as a colonialist project, and they therefore claimed ownership over Palestine and attempted to occupy it by force. This new actor on the ground obliged the Palestinians to think in a totally different way about their own survival and existence. But it was too early to realize this. At this stage, what Zionism did seem to trigger on the Palestinians' side was an impulse to sharpen their local national identity – and here the Husaynis had a major role to play.

## First Encounters with Zionism

Individual Husaynis encountered Zionism in various circumstances and reacted in a variety of ways. It is hard to know to what extent the association of the family with the pre-Zionist Jewish elite in Jerusalem affected its attitude towards Zionism when it appeared. Apparently it had little or no effect, just as there was little or no connection between the world of the old Jewish community in Palestine and the new world that the Zionist immigrants were trying to create.

The first Husayni to confront the new phenomenon was Mufti Tahir II, who found himself at the forefront of the struggle against Zionism in its earliest manifestations. Like other Muslim clerics in the empire, he viewed the Zionist movement as part of the concerted Western effort to undermine Ottoman rule in the shrinking empire. Already in 1882, these clerics prevailed on Sultan Abd al-Hamid II to pass a law banning Jewish immigration. From the day the law was passed – even before he became *mufti* in 1883 – and for the rest of his life, Tahir cooperated with the Ottoman religious establishment and, working like a one-man research institute, studied Zionism's nature, meaning and aims. It was at his initiative that the authorities in Istanbul decided in 1889 to limit Jewish immigration and permit foreign Jews to spend no more than three months in Palestine, and then for religious purposes only.

Tahir was thus in the vanguard of the anti-immigration front. The issue of land was more problematic, at least in the first decade of the Zionist presence. It is doubtful he succeeded in persuading his kinsmen of the importance of this issue, especially as he himself sold some land – though not a great deal – in the vicinity of Jerusalem to Zionist groups.

On the other hand Salim, who said nothing about immigration, took his time when asked to sell land or to approve land transactions in the city council, which he headed. In 1890 the council first discussed the possibility of Jewish immigrants settling in the city and the desire of some of them to purchase plots of land. As usual, the council's summer session dealt with the population figures, and it discovered that a full third of the registered inhabitants were Jews – a marked increase over the number reported in previous sessions.[50] The city began to take on a Jewish character, at least according to the Ottoman records of the time. During the Hamidi reign, Jews who owned properties and houses paid taxes, and so every annual report revealed the demographic change in the city. Salim was convinced that this was not accidental and that it might indicate a plot to take over the city. Together with the Jerusalem notables, he organized a petition to the authorities to forbid the purchase of land by Jews and to the sultan to issue a *firman* to that effect.[51] A year later the sultan did issue such an order, but pressure from the British government made it ineffectual.

But while Salim believed that such action was necessary, he did not apparently see Zionist immigration as something new. He had become accustomed to the growing foreign presence in the city since the Crimean War and tended to view it as a general European scheme to take control of the city, a drive that had begun with the first consuls. His was not, therefore, a specifically anti-Jewish attitude. The family as a whole and Salim in particular had good relations with the Jewish community, notably in the economic sector. Before becoming mayor, Salim had had commercial and real-estate dealings with some Jerusalem Jews and business associations with several, primarily the Rokah family. In the 1870s he and Yitzhak Rokah were partners in a hotel in Bab al-Wad. Rokah had leased it in 1877 with Salim's help (that is, the lease was registered in Salim's name) and managed it, and the profits were divided between them. These profits derived from the taxes levied on travelers from Jaffa to Jerusalem and were endorsed on the tax receipts. This partnership persisted until the opening of the Jaffa–Jerusalem railway.[52] (The hotel, by the way, is still there along Route 1 connecting Tel Aviv and Jerusalem, just as you begin the ascent to the city.)

When Salim became mayor of Jerusalem amid an influx of Jews into the municipality, this did not damage these relations but in fact improved them, if only because the Jewish vote was needed. In the municipal elections of 1892, for example, 700 of the enfranchised Muslims cast their votes, as well as 300 Christians and 200 Jews, who among them elected ten representatives to the city council.[53] Salim's first mayoralty had been by appointment, but in 1892 the post was obtained by election, and he needed the Jewish votes. (Both systems were used irregularly until the end of the century.) Then, as now, votes were won by responding to the demands of the various communities. One of the main demands of the Jewish community was the enlargement of the space in front of the Western Wall. The Husayni family were guardians of important religious properties whose sale or lease could have eased the crowding at the Wall. In 1887 Mustafa al-Husayni agreed to sell to Nissim Bakhar and Edmond de Rothschild part of the Abu Maidian religious property. Named after a Maghrebi saint, this property was under the Husaynis' guardianship and included the Western Wall area. But the deal fell through for unknown reasons.[54]

The Husaynis were able to respond favorably to the less far-reaching demands of the Jewish community and thus obtain their votes for the mayoralty. For example, Salim acceded to the request of three Jewish notables to pave the Western Wall square so that some sewage work being carried out nearby would not sully the Jewish holy site.[55] In fact, this was the last time that the Jewish presence at the Wall was treated as a communal-religious, rather than national, issue. In 1897, when the Baron de Rothschild wished to buy the Western Wall square from the Muslim religious authority and the mayor almost agreed, both branches of the family became alarmed, especially the *sheikh al-haram*, Bashir al-Husayni, the son of Abd al-Salam II, who managed to block the sale. The Husaynis' ability to do so was due to the fact that the purchase of lands required the approval of the city council as well as the governor.[56]

It would seem that Salim did not distinguish between the influx of Jews and the growing foreign influence in Jerusalem. He regarded Jewish immigration as another aspect of the same problem. The British consul John Dixon reassured him. He had seen the correspondence between Beirut and Istanbul, which stated that very few Jews were arriving in Beirut and Haifa. Still, he admitted that it was extremely easy for a Jew to enter Palestine: 'Five pounds are enough to ensure admission to a Jew of any nationality whatsoever' (most were Austrian, Russian and American nationals). The influence of those countries' local consuls meant that the authorities could not bar the entry of many of the Jews. Nevertheless, from time to time the Ottomans managed to put obstacles in their path, as when the 1880 decree forbidding Jewish visitors to stay longer than three months became law in 1901. After a while, Jews who were British nationals could evade the law because their passports did not indicate their Jewish origin. In this way, the British emancipatory spirit assisted the movement that fought against Jewish assimilation in Europe.

An individual's reaction to Zionism often depended on his official position. The mayor was ambivalent; the men of commerce and finance, far from opposing it, made business deals with the newcomers, while the Tahiri branch linked Jewish immigration to the European challenge to the city's Muslim sanctity. Indeed, it was the British consul James Finn, not a popular figure in the Husaynis' historical memory, who connected the arrival of the Jews with the restoration of Crusader glory. It is no wonder, then, that Mufti Tahir II led the opposition to this immigration, with a special emphasis on the sale of land, not only within the family but among the Jerusalem notables as a whole. He knew that possession of land indicated a prolonged stay and a claim of ownership, whereas immigration without settlement was transient pilgrimage. There is no point in searching for a non-national motive for this opposition to the permanent settlement of foreigners in your country. While it is true that it arises – as the scholar of nationality Anthony Smith has shown – from the desire to preserve the purity of the tribe, or the religious or geographic community, it is equally true that it is especially forceful when it bears a national character, as Smith's colleague Benedict Anderson argues.[57]

Tahir al-Husayni II was the first national *mufti* to react to Jewish immigration. At the time, there were half a million inhabitants in the territory that would later be demarcated as the British Mandate for Palestine – 80 percent Muslim and only 5 percent Jews – yet Tahir saw every additional Jew as a threat to the holy city. He was especially incensed that the foreign consuls were unreservedly helping Jewish immigrants to buy land by enabling them to do so as European nationals unconstrained by the laws of the Ottoman Empire. Thus the Zionist presence began to establish itself in Palestine despite the Ottoman government's hostility.

In 1897 the government responded to Tahir's urging and appointed a committee to examine the question of land purchases. This was the year that the First Zionist Congress was held in Basel, Switzerland. The committee recommended that strict limitations be imposed on Jewish land acquisition, and the government adopted the recommendation.

But while Tahir was fighting to stop the process, Rabah was selling land to the highest bidder. In 1891, for example, he sold the lands of the village of Qaluniya, lying between Abu Ghosh and Jerusalem, to the founders of the Motza settlement, led by Yehoshua Yellin. We have seen how Ismail al-Husayni had abused one of the villagers, and it seems that the relations between the villagers and the Husayni family had not improved since. Not only did Rabah sell the land, he helped the Jewish buyers evade the Ottoman law under which the tract in question, categorized as uncultivated, had reverted to state property after three years and was barred from sale. Rabah purchased the land from the village headman and promptly sold it to the Jews. Twenty years earlier Yehoshua Yellin had been one of the Jewish bidders who had competed with Musa al-Husayni for some land in the valley of Jericho, but the government had stopped the Jews from buying it.

It is difficult to determine to what extent members of the family grasped the future potential of Jewish immigration. No doubt they read the newspapers of the time and took in the insights they offered (namely that we cannot analyse how it was received only how it was produced). In 1897 the local press in Jerusalem and Gaza mentioned the opening of the Zionist Congress.[58] It published a letter from Frankfurt reporting that a movement of Jews wishing to return to Palestine had been founded six months previously. The movement, which the letter said was viewed favorably by the United States, Britain and Germany, was called Zionism. It went on to say that, if given permission by the Ottoman Empire, the Zionists proposed to establish in Palestine *masakin* (housing) for Jews who were being persecuted in Russia, Bulgaria and Romania. They promised to develop the agriculture and industry in Palestine, reduce the number of poor people in Europe and promote trade between Europe and the Orient. A correspondent of the newspaper *Al-Muqtataf al-Mufida* reported that the British press was sympathetic to the idea, and stated that there was no reason for the Ottoman Empire to reject such support from Europe or for Europe to object to a reduction of its poor population. The Europeans believed that the Jews, being utterly loyal to the West, would spread its culture and expand its trade and industry.

This extended report came in response to frequent questions from readers in the Arab press about the significance of Jewish immigration. An editorial noted that the Jews who had arrived so far had not fulfilled the above promises. While they had indeed developed trade and industry, they had failed badly in agriculture – and no wonder, since they were not farming people. But the principal failure was that the Jewish capitalists were doing nothing to help. 'We local people', the editorial concluded, 'must hope that the situation of the Jews in Europe will improve.'[59]

The Egyptian newspaper *Al-Manar* was the most emphatic, calling on the local population to resist the vicious European decision to export the weakest of its peoples to Palestine. The indigenous people should rise up and fight for *watan* and *umma* (which some translate as 'homeland' and 'nation', while others argue that those concepts were far from clear at a time when the Ottoman and Classical Arabic discourse was turning into a national one). The newspaper urged its readers not to ignore the problem, but it also showed understanding for the plight of the Jews. It explained that the Jews had competed with the Europeans, which was why they were subjected to persecution. The Jews, it stated, were like the Japanese – 'Orientals who successfully competed with Europe' – whereas the Muslims were failing to do so, a theme that the Egyptian press had harped on repeatedly since the end of the previous century.[60]

But unlike Salim and Tahir II, the grandest member of the Husayni clan, Ismail Bey, did not understand what the fuss was all about. While some of his kinsmen were issuing public calls against the sale of land to Jews, in 1906 he himself sold an estate, a steam-driven mill and an olive press in the village Ayn Siniya, on the Jerusalem–Nablus road, to the family of Jacob Chertok, a member of the early Zionist Bilu group and the father of Israel's future prime minister Moshe Sharett. As noted above, Ismail had inherited his father's extensive properties, including the Ayn Siniya land and more.[61]

To begin with, Ismail's brother Shukri regarded the Zionist issue as a purely economic one and offered the Zionists land near Petah Tikvah and Hulda. Representatives of the Jewish Agency used to visit him at his office in Istanbul, where he was a high official in the Ottoman Department of Education. He spent most of his life in the imperial capital and was a tower of strength for the family during the dramatic transition from Ottoman rule to the centrist national government of the Young Turks.[62] He was there when Theodore Herzl, the founder of political Zionism, came to see the sultan, and heard that Herzl proposed buying Palestine for billions, though Abd al-Hamid II refused. To Shukri this was merely an amusing anecdote, but the future *mufti* al-Hajj Amin al-Husayni would speak of this episode – which occurred a year after he was born – as the most decisive event for him and his family, with the exception of the Balfour Declaration.[63]

The family could not tell whether Herzl was a serious person or a mountebank, since in those days there was no shortage of charlatans who presented themselves as deliverers of Judaism and Christianity. The so-called Prince Emmanuel, for example, was an eccentric Jew who asked the Husaynis to help him set up an Anglo-Zionist college. Before receiving an answer he proclaimed that he had founded the first Zionist college in Jerusalem, then vanished as suddenly and mysteriously as he had appeared.[64]

Said al-Husayni's attitude towards Zionism was unusual. His father, Ahmad Rasim, had sent him to study for some time at the Jewish school, the Alliance Israélite, where he learned Hebrew. This did not induce him to support the notion of the Jews' return to their ancient homeland, but it seems to have prevented him from adopting an unequivocal anti-Zionist stance. Said had several Jewish friends from his school days, and perhaps these personal relationships gave rise to mixed feelings. His knowledge of Hebrew provided him with an unusual career as the local censor of the Hebrew press in Jerusalem, which entailed daily reading of the Hebrew newspapers that had appeared in the city since the middle of the century. Eventually his familiarity with the language and political trends led him to adopt an anti-Zionist, though not anti-Jewish, position.

His field of endeavor combined with his being a Husayni shaped Said's attitude towards Zionism. In 1891, when he ran for the post of representative of Jerusalem in the Ottoman Parliament, he made public statements warning against continued Zionist immigration. It was not an easy position for him to take, since at the time his son Ibrahim Said was employed by ICA (the Jewish Colonization Association), the body created by Baron Edmond de Rothschild to supervise his investment and develop the economy and settlements of the Zionist enterprise in Palestine. When Ibrahim Said resigned from the company, it became easier for his father to come out publicly against Zionism. That year Said and Salim al-Husayni, together with some other Jerusalem notables, sent the sultan a telegram to that effect. It seems that Said's eventual decision to oppose Zionism was taken in 1905, when he organized a conference against Jewish immigration and land purchases by the Zionist movement. The following year he said in an interview with *Al-Aqdam* that he and Salim had been rallying other Arab members of parliament to urge the sultan to take stronger action against Zionism in Palestine.[65]

It was also in 1905 that the first hostile incident took place between a member of the Husayni family and a Zionist representative. Salim was visiting his nephew Abd al-Salam II, who was a government official in Jaffa, when David Lewontin, the manager of the local branch of Anglo-Palestine Bank, publicly insulted him. Abd al-Salam fired off an angry letter to the president of the bank in London, and the family noted another proof of the arrogance of Zionism and the dangers it represented.[66] Yet a very different interaction took place the same year when Musa Kazim, then the *qaymaqam* of Jaffa, sent armed guards to protect the new Jewish neighborhood of Neveh Zedek, which adjoined Jaffa on the north and which had been founded by Eliezer Rokah at the beginning of the century. Rokah and Musa Kazim had been friends since childhood, and thanks to Musa Kazim the new neighborhood, which had been plagued by highway robbers, could now feel secure.[67] The Husaynis had always been on excellent terms with the Rokah family, and the gesture was personal, not political (though in those days the difference between the two was not yet sharply defined).

Curiously, a much lesser-known member of the family, Sheikh Yusuf al-Husayni, was the family authority on Judaism. But he was interested in the Jewish religion and tradition, not in Zionism, so his insight did little to heighten the family's political awareness. He was especially interested in the connection between Judaism and Islam, and in conversations with Jewish religious scholars he tried to convince them that the story of Abraham and Ishmael contained coded predictions of the future appearance of the Prophet Muhammad.[68] But even this open-minded view of the two religions could not avert the forthcoming struggle for the country.

## The Fall of Abd al-Hamid II

Before the family could quite grasp the significance of the Jewish longing for Jerusalem and Eretz Israel that would become a vast colonialist project of dispossession, their world was badly shaken when Abd al-Hamid II lost his place in Istanbul and in history.

Though in terms of Western historiography Ismail al-Husayni was the most progressive (given his treatment of his daughters and his Western education), he regarded the sultan's fall as an unmitigated disaster for the family. Throughout the Hamidi reign, Ismail had given his unqualified support to Ottoman rule, and of all of his family he was the most loyal to the ruler. Ismail had been largely responsible for supervising and controlling the 'new' invention that most worried Abd al-Hamid II, namely, the printing press. The sultan recognized the power of the printed word and of the press to incite and spread unrest. Just as the clock is seen as one of the signs of the age in which the concept of a national community was born, theoreticians of nationalism consider mass printing to have been another technological and material innovation that contributed to the concept's development.

Abd al-Hamid II correctly identified the problem, but his response to it was a failure. He tried to promote pan-Islamic and Ottoman nationalism in the face of the national movements that were cropping up everywhere, and failed. Now he had to contend with the internal national revolution that had begun to take shape when he ascended the throne – that of the Young Turks.

Four medical students who met in Istanbul in 1889 started a process that would change the face of the entire Ottoman Empire. They formed an association they named 'the Young Turks', whose avowed goal was to topple the tyranny of Abd al-Hamid II and replace it with a free, progressive, national Turkish regime. A mixture of romantic nationalism, admiration for the strong modern state and vestiges of liberalism made up their creed, but above all they worshipped 'progress' – technological progress based on reason and science to overcome all obstacles, primarily tradition and religion. No more slow, partial and vague reforms – instead, a single revolution with miraculous solutions for all the ills of society. The first attempt to bring it off in 1897 had failed miserably and was followed by the sultan's repressive measures.

In Jerusalem these measures had taken the form of a relentless resistance to the new printing presses. This was where Ismail had a major role to play. As supervisor of the printing industry, he was in effect the long arm of tyranny's drive to restrict the freedom of expression. He was the first to fight the Arab printing press in Jerusalem, though in times to come it would serve the family during the transition to the national stage. The first Arab press in the city was established in 1906 by George Habib Hananya, who had to prove the machines were not designed to make bombs before he could get a license.[69]

Ismail was party to the moves against the press, particularly the Egyptian newspapers distributed in the districts of Beirut, Nablus and Jerusalem spreading sharp criticism of the government. Near the end of Abd al-Hamid's rule, the order was given to seize all the copies of *Al-Manar* in those districts. This was the journal of Sheikh Rashid Rida, one of the leading Islamic philosophers and activists who would later inspire a future generation of Muslim Brothers and likeminded political organizations. *Al-Manar*'s first issue had accused the Ottomans of not doing enough to raise the level of education and culture in the Arab countries, so the second issue was confiscated. Naturally, the accusation was leveled at Ismail himself, who was responsible for the education system in Jerusalem. The paper also blamed the government for allowing an influx of foreigners into the region and called for a holy war against them and the expulsion of their collaborators. Above all, Sheikh Rashid Rida's newspaper called for reforms based on a stricter reliance on Islamic sources. Ismail was not sufficiently religious or nationalistic for this publication, in sharp contrast with the future image of al-Hajj Amin al-Husayni.[70]

Yet Ismail was not exceptional amongst the local notables, many of whom were faithful to the sultan. The Gaza Husaynis, however, who were apparently linked to the Wafa'i and therefore to the Jerusalem family, displayed a very different attitude to Abd al-Hamid that nearly led to their destruction. In February 1898 the Gazan *mufti*, the head of the family there, his brother and his son were arrested and exiled to Anatolia. They had been about to accept Egypt's rule in El Arish, thus allying themselves with one of the sultan's chief enemies. The opposite was true of Ismail – his standing was badly damaged by the sultan's fall, though he remained a prominent figure and was regarded as the head of the Jerusalemite family. But it would be Said and Shukri, his more dynamic cousins, who would skillfully steer the family through the dramatic upheavals of the first decade of the twentieth century.

## The End of the Hamidi Era

The last family occasion to take place under Ottoman rule – which had lasted more than 350 years – was the coming-of-age celebration of Muhammad Amin, the son of Mufti Tahir II and his second wife, Zaynab. Held on a roof in the heart of the Haram al-Sharif reached by a spiral staircase, it was attended by a large crowd of women and children. The important guests reclined on bolsters on a dais made up of large cushions, while the poorer ones sat on bare wooden benches. The wife of the deputy governor of Jerusalem, a pious, bulky lady, was the guest of honor. Her English companion, the wife of the painter Stanley Inchbold, provided future historians with a detailed description of the event, though unfortunately she was more interested in clothes than in the traditional ceremony. Her painstaking description of the guest of honor's dress, for example – an embroidered gown with gold trimming on the sleeves, a green cummerbund, a small diamond tiara – might have been referring to a fashion-plate from Vienna or Paris rather than Jerusalem. There were about 100 women on the roof, some of them in Western clothes but most in traditional robes. There were Sudanese servants, Bedouin children and country girls in headdresses hung with silver coins – the fashion of the mountain villages since the beginning of the reign. Mrs Inchbold assumed that the women who sat on upright chairs had received a European education, while those who lolled casually on cushions had not been exposed to Western influence. Women and girls came to peer at the Englishwoman and from time to time leaned over the openings in the parapet to see what was going on below. The deputy governor's wife translated their questions: 'Are you comfortable? Is there anything you want?' – 'I'm perfectly comfortable,' the grateful visitor replied. Servants kept bringing her jugs of water for refreshment. Then a group of girls appeared to entertain the guests – Jewish girls from Beirut, the hostess explained, who danced to the sound of a flute played by a girl in a long silk robe. The performance included love songs and delightful dances. Now and then the birthday boy appeared among the guests. He was small and delicate-looking, but vividly colorful with his red hair and blue eyes. The party went on until well past midnight, but the painter's wife did not feel up to it. She was about to depart on a long journey through the Syrian lands (*Under the Syrian Sun*, as her husband's travel book was called) in the summer of 1905.[71]

The Hamidi era ended with the death of Tahir II in 1908. The funeral was an exhausting affair, since in burying the *mufti* the family took great pains with the ceremonies.[72] He had hesitated until his last days to decide which of his sons should inherit his position as *mufti*. As well as five daughters, he had three sons – one, Kamil, by his first wife, Mahbuba, and two, Fakhri and Amin, by his beloved second wife, Zaynab. He used to take the three potential successors to the Haram al-Sharif to learn the requirements of the *mufti* of Jerusalem as well as their duties as members of the Ashraf family.[73]

The quiet Zaynab took pains with Amin's religious tuition at their house in the Husayniyya, the home of the Tahiri branch, and he also received a broader education than his two brothers. First he attended the traditional primary school, where he was taught history and religion in the spirit of Islam. Then he attended the French missionary École des Frères, where he learned French, his favorite language, which he also studied with a private tutor, a Miss Hassasin.[74] In the 1890s he was in Istanbul for his higher studies. A small, slender young man, his tendency to mumble and lisp made communication with him difficult, but his physical appearance remained strikingly colorful. In the early twentieth century he was a pupil of Sheikh al-Rida (who at the time taught at the University of al-Azhar), thereby completing the family's connection with the great institution that had begun 200 years before. But when Tahir II died, Amin was only thirteen and could not inherit his father's position. Fakhri was also too young, so the eldest, Kamil, was automatically chosen. The Tahiri branch was somewhat uneasy about this, as Kamil had a pallid personality and lacked connections with the city notables – a worry that would prove to be well-founded. Palestinian historiography paints him in a bad light, chiefly because he did little to fight against Zionism.

Along with Amin's coming-of-age party, Tahir's funeral and Kamil's installation as *mufti*, the end of the Hamidi period was marked for the young Husayni men (excluding Amin, who muttered religious texts on his way home from school) by the advent of a new sport – football. Most of Musa Kazim's sons excelled at football at their school, St George's, known as the Mutran. It had been founded in 1898 by the Anglican Bishop of Jerusalem, George Francis Blyth, and Musa Kazim's sons were among its first pupils.[75] The school was a splendid edifice in the eastern city, near a fine Anglican cathedral. The school's name was not unfamiliar to the Husaynis, as the eponymous patron saint of England had been born in Lydda. The church was ornamented with colorful stained-glass windows, which the boys enjoyed looking at. They depicted the life of another native of the country born in nearby Ayn Karim: John the Baptist. And everywhere was the image of St George in a feathered helmet, striking down the dragon at his horse's feet. Though the dragon supposedly symbolized the enemies of Christianity, to the boys it was merely a story about a hero and a monster.

Six of the Husayni boys attended this school, and each of them would reach the top of Mandatory Palestine's social and political hierarchy. The eldest and most prominent was Jamal, the son of Musa Kazim al-Husayni's sister and Musa Saleh al-Husayni. Jamal was the first boy to come to school dressed in Western clothes – a dark corduroy suit with a collarless shirt –

catching the attention of teachers and students. The historian Izzat Tanus was also a pupil there at the time, hence our information.

The school had only about 100 students, and was very popular with all of them: in addition to offering football, it was the first school in Palestine that did not use the cane. Four of Bishop Blyth's daughters taught there under the direction of the sports-loving Reynolds, who made sure that no other school could match St George's. Proper football had begun to be played in the British Isles in 1888 and reached St George's in only a few years. In the summer, other colonial sports were introduced, such as cricket, basketball and hockey. Every month there was a sports day, which drew parents and other interested parties, and before the First World War there was a football match every Saturday afternoon. The schools league was launched in 1906 with a match between the St George's team and that of the Protestant school. Some of the players still wore tarbushes, which hampered them as they rushed around the pitch at Bab al-Sahra. Tawfiq, the son of Musa Salih, was one of the best players.

Tawfiq also took part in school theatricals. A pleasant, smiling young man, he played the Prince of Morocco in the school production of *The Merchant of Venice*. On a small stage flanked by green doors and windows with their shutters flung open, Tawfiq seemed to personify the cultural riches of the twilight of the Ottoman age, an age in which East and West were blending into a distinctive culture. It was still the culture of the elite and would have needed many years to flourish and spread through the rest of society, but the process was instead thwarted by the searing force of the political and national struggle that overwhelmed Jerusalem and the rest of Palestine in the twentieth century.[76]

This then was the world of the Husaynis during the Hamidi period, a world in which the official language was Turkish but the language of literature and the one in which the people of the Jerusalem district interpreted reality was Arabic. He who commanded the Turkish language dominated family affairs, but he who thought in 'Palestinian' would become the leader of the family in the new century. No wonder, then, that it was said of them that they were 'first and foremost to all that is sacred in Palestine, and all the people of the place admire and bless it with awe and exaltation.'[77]

CHAPTER 5

# Facing the Young Turks
## The Family as Bureaucratic Aristocracy

While young Tawfiq al-Husayni was playing the Prince of Morocco on the stage of St George's, the clouds were gathering overhead for Sultan Abdul Hamid II, heralding a storm that would sweep away four centuries of Ottoman rule over the Arab Middle East. Although the clearest signs of the imminent revolution appeared in Jerusalem in 1906, it is doubtful if any of the city's notables discerned them. The Young Turks had failed in their first attempt to topple the government in 1897, and they understood that they needed to broaden their revolutionary base before rising openly as a political and military force. They did so on a large scale between 1902 and 1906. The movement infiltrated the standing army, especially the officer corps of the Fifth Army who were stationed in Damascus, Jerusalem and Jaffa. In Damascus a young officer by name of Mustafa Kemal, later known as Ataturk, organized the Homeland and Freedom Association – the first military group and the springboard of the 1908 revolution.[1] At the same time officers of the Third Army began to organize in Salonika. These military rebels were assisted by anti-Hamidi elements all over the empire, notably the Armenians (whom fate would in a few years turn into the slaughtered victims of their erstwhile allies).

Why the revolution erupted in 1908 nobody knows. What is clear is that there was a wide enough coalition of unsatisfied sectors that had been bruised by the sultan and that suddenly came together as a critical mass. Be that as it may, the Husaynis were no more prepared for the explosion than the sultan himself was.[2]

On 25 July 1908, both the regular army and the civilian masses rose up in various ways against Abdul Hamid II. It took another eight months before the revolution would finally succeed, due to a counterrevolutionary attempt to restore the sultanate. Historian Bernard Lewis put it thus: 'The long night of Hamidi tyranny was over, the dawn of liberty had arrived.'[3] Revised historiography today totally disagrees with this depiction. Nor does Lewis's comment seem to reflect the way the Husaynis and their peers felt. The Hamidi era was never regarded as especially tyrannical by the urban Arab elite as a whole, and in fact only during the final years of Ottoman rule, towards the onset of the First World War, was Ottoman rule regarded as particularly oppressive – personified by the policies of Jamal Pasha, the military governor of Syria on the eve of the war.

In short order, the Husaynis joined others in developing new hopes for the opportunities created by the change of guard, and this may explain the widely reported spontaneous expression of joy all around Jerusalem when the news of the sultan's fall arrived in the city.[4] There were mass demonstrations in the city streets and squares, described by people who worked in the post office – for example, Izzat Darwazza. There was dancing in the squares, and exuberant cries filled the street when the local poets recited their songs of praise for the new government on every corner.[5] Salim al-Husayni managed the official celebrations in the city in honor of the revolution. He called the city notables and the officials to the square in front of the municipality and made a short speech in support of the revolution, while behind him hung a massive framed emblem of the Movement for Unity and Progress, as the revolutionaries called themselves.[6]

Members of the family who did not attend the rally read about the events in the newspapers, which overflowed with ecstatic articles written by novelists and poets giving lyric voice to the popular hope kindled by the revolution. The leisurely reading of newspapers had become a common custom in the houses of the Jerusalem notables, chiefly the journals published in Egypt and Beirut but also Arabic-language publications from the United States. Unfortunately, they all had limitations: the Beirut papers did not know what was happening in Istanbul, and those published in the capital seemed unaware of the outside world.[7]

But this was not a time for celebrations, as difficult decisions awaited the family. The political situation was highly volatile and caused a sharp argument among the Husaynis. Shukri – brother of the head of the family, Ismail, who had attained a very high position at the center of power – led many of his relatives towards unreserved support for the revolution as the sublime expression of a new and better age to come. He did not confine himself to the family. On 5 August 1908 he reported to his brother that he had rallied the senior Arab officials in the Ottoman administration to support the revolutionaries. Together they formed an 'Arab-Ottoman' association that was to cooperate with the Young Turks in the Arab provinces.

But while Shukri was confident that he knew whom to support, there was great unease in the house of Ismail, whose loyalty to the Hamidi regime was well-known. Indeed, there was some concern for his personal safety, as rumors began to arrive from Istanbul that the new government was about to launch an offensive against individuals known to have served as Abdul Hamid's agents and spies. Representatives of the new regime claimed that many of the notables of Palestine had served the *Khafiya*, the sultan's secret police. However, the suspicion fell on the Nablus families, not those of Jerusalem.[8] It is unlikely that Ismail cared much for the new rulers, but evidently he avoided a confrontation with them. The only time he openly challenged them was in 1913, when he led a group of Jerusalem notables to urge the new government in Istanbul not to neglect the religious properties in Jerusalem and to 'restore them to their original condition in accordance with the terms in which they had been run' – meaning for the use of the public in Jerusalem.[9] As always, Ismail was concerned about the schools, which were deteriorating, and hoped that at least some of the religious properties would be restored and made fit for students.

Shukri was unconcerned. He led the creation of the Arab-Ottoman Fraternal Association, whose platform was simple and succinct: it called for the preservation of the Ottoman constitution, adherence to Ottoman unity, the improvement of the economic and political situation in the Arab regions as well as the other nations of the empire, and the expansion of education in Arabic.[10]

Arab and Palestinian historians have pointed out that the association was but one of a number of groupings that heralded the rise of Arab nationalism in the region. However, it should be noted that it strove to fit into the new order, not withdraw into a separate Palestinian or even Arab entity. Only in hindsight does it appear as a formative chapter in the rise of Palestinian nationalism. Typically, nationalism appropriates any useful historical event that precedes it, whether related to it or not. But the association was only one of many precursors that heralded the emergence of a pan-Arabist national imagination and identification, and later a more focused Palestinian nationalism. Other precursors were the secret societies that promoted the teaching of Arabic and the study of Arabic history and culture. These included some Palestinians and the Salafiyya movement in Egypt, which associated Islamic reform with liberation from British occupation. Foreign and particularly Zionist intrusion accelerated the creation of the Palestinian national identity.

The association became a branch of the Unity and Progress Party, and on the orders of Istanbul changed its name to the Arab-Ottoman Brotherhood Party. Shukri had wished to call it simply 'the Arab Association', and it has been suggested that he added the adjective 'Ottoman' to placate the Young Turk triumvirate (Cemal, Enver and Talat) that had seized power from the sultan. Others maintain that Shukri and his companions were genuinely enthusiastic about the ideas of the Turkish revolution and decided to change the name themselves. All in all, it seemed less crucial to Shukri than national historians later claimed.

Having formed the association, Shukri began to recruit young members from among the enthusiastic Arab students in the capital who created branches throughout the Arab regions of the empire. These students would be the first to rebel against the Young Turks few years later when they were called upon to become Turks themselves. That was the point when the Turkish association became a national Arab one. But this happened around 1913, and the rapid succession of events that turned Palestine into a battlefield in the First World War prevent historians from making a clear judgment on the overall relationship between the Young Turks and the Arab urban elite, including the Husaynis.

The beginnings of that relationship, however, were quite promising. Shukri al-Husayni created the Jerusalem branch, and in August 1908 a meeting was held to decide the family's policy. Ismail willingly took part but asked to bring in two of his influential friends – the family's Christian friend Khalil al-Sakakini and Ghalib al-Khalidi.[11] Al-Khalidi was one of the most prominent Jerusalem notables, a judge of the district court and a member of the Board of Education chaired by Ismail. So high was his standing that the meeting was held at his residence, out of respect and also perhaps because it was he who had informed the people of Jerusalem about the revolution. Governor Ekrem had been so fearful that for two days he suppressed the news about the revolt that had taken place in July. Finally Ghalib al-Khalidi hired a town crier to go around the city and proclaim the news.[12]

After Ghalib was appointed in the 1890s to the Board of Education, relations between the two families had markedly improved. The former rivals resolved to bury the hatchet and turn over a new page. In fact the Arab-Ottoman Brotherhood was very much a bi-clan project. It would be a springboard for a coalition during the mandatory period that the urban elite would try to use to move forward quickly and forge a clear national identity in the face of Zionist aspirations and British occupation. But in the beginning of the twentieth century and later, both families were unable to expand the base, not only into other social classes but even amongst the other families of the urban elite. Even before the national era, in the new regime imposed by the Young Turks, the particular position of the Husaynis as 'first among equals' became more precarious, and their lineage and religious standing proved to be insufficient resources for maintaining what would be become national leadership.

There was a moment in the winter of 1908 when it looked as if Shukri would lead the family to cooperation and success in the new world created by the Young Turks. He urged the family to continue to participate in the parliamentary life of the new regime. About a month after the publication of the new constitution, Istanbul issued directives about the parliamentary elections. There was to be a representative from every district with 50,000 inhabitants – thus two representatives from Jerusalem and one each from Nablus and Jaffa. Every male over twenty-five could vote, provided he had no criminal record; the voters would choose 'electors' who would chose the parliamentary representative. Ruhi al-Khalidi and Said al-Husayni were elected and thereby cemented their new political partnership even further.[13]

In November 1908, at Shukri's initiative, the city of Jerusalem held a formal reception for Said al-Husayni and Ruhi al-Khalidi upon their return from Istanbul.[14] Muslim youths filled the market alleys, flourishing toy swords and firing invisible rifles. On this occasion they were joined by the Christians and Sephardic Jews, and together they went to the railway station. After a five-hour journey from Jaffa, the train arrived at the usual time in the afternoon, by which point the station was packed with people. When Shukri and his friend Khalil al-Sakakini arrived, the poets and speechmakers began to declaim the praises of the returnees. Then the company proceeded to the Arab-Ottoman Brotherhood club for a lavish dinner.

Alhough Shukri would be remembered in Arab historiography as one of the trailblazers of Arab nationalism, in the winter of 1908 he was very far from it. Like many of the Jerusalem notables, he was concerned about the predicament of the empire. His chief public activity in the following months was organizing the townspeople in the futile struggle to stop the shrinking of the Ottoman Empire. People in his social circle were furious about Austria's annexation of Bosnia and Herzegovina shortly after the publication of the constitution and called on the people of Jerusalem to protest against this unilateral Austrian move. At Shukri's urging, many people wrote angry letters to the Austrian consul and boycotted Austrian-made tarbushes. But such symbolic gestures could not stop the historical process – the empire went on losing territories and prestige. The forces of the Greek general Venizelos conquered Crete, and the new Ottoman activists were further frustrated when Montenegro declared its independence from the empire. In the literary clubs an anti-Austrian poem by the Lebanese poet Shibli al-Mallat was recited along with another poet's anti-Greek poem and one by Khalil Mutran mourning the loss of Montenegro.[15]

This period lasted until 1913. The first years of the Young Turks were a continued effort to centralize the empire, which was welcomed by the old guard of the Husaynis. The younger family members were more supportive of those who called for a more decentralized empire.

On the eve of the First World War, there were the first signs of change: a more nationalist policy was adopted by Istanbul and was intensified during the war. In this new atmosphere it was more difficult to form an Arab-Ottoman Brotherhood. On 23 August 1909 the government passed a law banning political organizations based on ethnic or national groupings, or bearing their names, but this was not directed toward the kind of cultural revival that took place in localities such as Jerusalem. But in 1913 it was. And as a result it was more difficult to advocate an Ottoman-Arab identity. Faced with this sharply reduced choice, it is no wonder that educated persons throughout the Arab world chose Arabism, as Turkishness had nothing to do with their past, their heritage or their hopes for the future. New conditions drove them to form secret societies, and it was in these that the idea of Arab nationalism was nurtured.

## Tender Shoots of Nationalism

Individually and as a family, the Husaynis were faced with the same choice, and the outcome was a clear generational division. Shukri al-Husayni represented the older generation, while his son Jamil represented the younger. Unlike most of his friends in the Arab-Ottoman Association who were dismayed by the Young Turks' demand to diminish the vestiges of Arabism in local politics, Shukri remained firm in his decision not to break away from Istanbul and Turkey.[16] He was pleased to have the support of his brother Arif (Shukri, Arif and Ismail were, as noted, the sons of Musa al-Husayni), who during his stay in Istanbul had associated with the Unity and Progress Party.[17]

Unlike the associations in Damascus, Mecca and Medina, the association supported by the middle generation of the Jerusalem notables was cultural rather than political. Its aim was not to sever the connection with the empire but to preserve the Arab character of their city and country within the Ottoman world. In the eyes of the notables, the danger to that world did not come from Istanbul, it came directly from the growing European and Zionist presence in Palestine. If the empire could help resist these intrusions, so much the better.

For the younger members of the family such as Jamil, the Young Turks' reservations about the idea of Arab national identity was sufficient reason to organize as a national group on behalf of all the Arab regions that might be interested. Perhaps impelled by a son's natural reaction to his father, Jamil was, like other young men in his family, very much a product of Istanbul. While a student in the capital in 1909, he had met an Arab intellectual who, in response to the Ottoman policy, formed a secret organization called Al-Fata ('The Arab Youth'). The front for this organization was a literary club in Istanbul in which Arab literature was discussed – a permissible activity. In reality it was a hothouse for extensive political activity. Jamil joined the secret group as soon as the club opened, and was one of its first members.[18] This was one of the first groups to call for the separation of the Arab regions from the world of the Unity and Progress Party and to fight against the Turkification of the new regime. The Young Turks' secret police never detected the true nature of this club or its many branches that sprang up in the Arab world. The dual structure – a literary façade concealing underground activity – also characterized the branch that Jamil al-Husayni set up in Jerusalem.

Jamil's cousin Mustafa II represented the Tahiri branch of the family in the national movement. Mustafa had attended a secondary school in Istanbul, and in September 1912 he was one of the founding members of the Green Flag Association, an organization of Arab secondary school students in Istanbul. Mustafa was even more dynamic than his Umari cousin, and his group published two papers that discussed Arab nationalism: *Lisan al-Arab* (The Language of the Arabs) and *Al-Muntada al-Adabi* (The Cultural Club).

While the younger Husaynis were engaged in developing a pan-Arab identity, others in Palestine, notably the Greek Orthodox, were beginning to consider a more specific national identity in the country. The first indication appeared in the newspaper *Al-Karmil* in 1913, in editor Najib Nassar's response to a Beirut article attacking the Jerusalem notables. The Beirut paper *Al-Mufid* had accused them of failing to contribute their share to the promotion of the Ottoman reforms. Najib Nassar responded with an article entitled 'The Arab-Palestinian League', in which he distinguished between the interests of the people of Beirut and those of the people of Palestine. 'What have we, the Arabs of Palestine, to do with the Beirutis? Our economic and social situation does not resemble theirs. We are in a bad predicament.' He also charged the notables of Jerusalem with political apathy, but called upon them to create a 'Palestinian league', which would channel all the efforts of the notables for the Palestinian people and not serve the Ottoman government. They should establish 'a league to defend the Palestinian homeland', he wrote, 'not only from the Young Turks, but also from Zionism.'[19] In this way he linked support for the Young Turks with support for Zionism. Young members of the family adopted some of the ideas of the Greek Orthodox writers, but until about 1920 most of them persisted in their efforts to create a pan-Arab – or at any rate pan-Syrian – state and did not call for the creation of an independent Palestine.

Not every notable or every senior person in the family felt called upon to adopt a position. Indeed, there were always some in the family who preferred to wait. Musa Kazim of the Umari branch sat on the fence, with notables like Ismail, Shukri and the mayor on one side and the restless young people, including his own offspring, on the other. Until the outbreak of the war, Musa Kazim tended to agree with Shukri and Ismail that nothing had happened to warrant risky new positions. Such a posture was not necessarily conservative: support for the Young Turks often implied support for their modernization. That is why he supported his sister (who married Muhammad Salih) when she sent her son Jamal to the American University in Beirut. This Jamal would later fill the highest position in Palestinian politics under the British Mandate, that of chairman of the Arab Higher Committee.

For most of the Husaynis, especially the Tahiri branch (though not for historians of the period), 1910 marked an important turning point. That year Salim's son, Hussein al-Husayni, succeeded his father as mayor of Jerusalem. It was not an easy win – he received the votes of 648 out of the 1,200 electors.[20] Nevertheless, it proved that the family was as powerful as ever, especially its Tahiri branch. Hussein's triumph also demonstrated that the family was coping well with the dramatic changes in Istanbul.

Hussein's attitude towards the Istanbul government is not easily assessed. In the early days of the revolution, he supported the cautious attitude of the head of the family, Ismail. Once established in the mayoralty, he became an implacable enemy of the new regime – according to the reports of the British consul in Jerusalem, at any rate. In 1912 he organized a petition signed by sixty of the district notables and telegraphed it to the British consulate, calling on the British government to intervene, if necessary by force, against Turkish nationalism and its manifestations in the district of Jerusalem.

Hussein was the moving spirit at all the gatherings that considered various scenarios of a British invasion of Palestine that would put an end to the new face of the Ottoman Empire and lead to the creation of a new state in the Arab provinces.[21]

Shortly before the outbreak of the war, Hussein al-Husayni ran again for the mayoralty, this time making skillful use of the local press to broadcast his sense of responsibility for the public. He was one of the leading reformers of the family. The newspaper *Al-Quds* published the praises of Hussein Hashim Effendi al-Husayni (his full title), who walked about the city streets and markets and concerned himself with public sanitation, much like a modern-day mayor with public relations in mind. According to that report, he personally supervised the mending of potholes in the roads and the quality of the water supply.[22]

The post of mayor was periodically filled by Hussein's brother Abd al-Salih and his relative Said. The latter – mentioned earlier in connection with his parliamentary career – was the better known of the two and served as mayor of Jerusalem between 1902 and 1906, when he was in his mid-twenties. (The term 'notables' should not be interpreted as meaning 'elders'.) Said was the most dynamic of the Husaynis in pioneering activities for Arab nationalism. After Shukri's decline, it was Said's work in the parliament along with the mayoralty that also made him the most political of the Husaynis.

During the summer holidays, the students Jamil and Mustafa III (a scion of the Tahiri branch) returned home and met at Said's house, where they found warm support for their views. A man of the in-between generation, Said encouraged their new national outlook. 'We Arabs are more than half the population of the empire, so Arabic should be the language of common usage and schooling,' he maintained. Together they read the speeches of Talat Pasha, one of the leaders of the Young Turks, as reported in *Al-Aqdam*, in which he rejected the idea of Arab nationalism.[23]

Said supported the idea of Arab nationalism as enthusiastically as the younger men. He too joined the secret organization Al-Fata, which became the vanguard of the national movement. This group gradually attracted educated Muslims and Christians who wanted to break with the Ottoman Empire. Said was introduced to it by the Syrian friends of the Husaynis, the younger members of the famous al-Azm family. Another member was Ali al-Nashashibi, who apparently joined most of the associations, public or secret, that cropped up between 1908 and 1914.[24]

Shukri al-Husayni was horrified by this mutinous movement and tried to persuade Said to support the attempts in Egypt to create a comprehensive pan-Arab national movement that would campaign for decentralization – that is, the preservation of the loose framework of the empire combined with cultural and administrative autonomy in the Arab regions. Although Shukri supported the Turks, in 1912 he approved of the Egyptian group that called itself the Decentralization Party, which he felt was anti-British rather than committed to pan-Arab independence from Turkey. Shukri's chief concern was to support any entity that resisted Western penetration into the Arab Middle East. He had read about the Egyptian group in the papers that reached Jerusalem or heard about it from young al-Hajj Amin, who was studying at al-Azhar with Sheikh Rashid Rida, who was also involved with the Decentralization Party.[25]

Most of Shukri's contemporaries in the family did not share his hostility to Europe and all it stood for, and they were especially reluctant to adopt a strong anti-British stance. For example, like many of his companions in Al-Fata, Said was sympathetic to the British, whom he regarded as potential allies. He was an Anglophile who spoke excellent English – and no wonder, as he had spent much of his adult life among the residents of the American Colony.

Having noted the various routes by which members of the Husayni family reached the idea of nationalism – whether in reaction to Istanbul's forcible Turkification or inspired by the ideas of certain Greek Orthodox individuals or *sheikhs* like Rashid Rida – we should mention George Antonius's argument that American missionaries had contributed much to the national thinking of Arab notables in Syria, Lebanon and Palestine. It stands to reason that all the Husaynis who had come in contact with the people of the American Colony had been exposed to the enticing vision of the American dream of liberty and progress and been inspired by it. Nevertheless, though the group of young men who would form the backbone of the Syrian and Lebanese national movement did learn much from the American missionaries, the most important teachers in the formative years of the Husaynis, who would lead the Palestinian national movement, were local men.

These future leaders had their world shaped at an early age by the teachers of the *kuttab*, the Qur'anic school. The school of Sheikh Lulu stood at Bab al-Amud (the Nablus Gate), and the first lesson was devoted to the history of the gate. The children heard that in ancient times a column had stood in front of the gate that served as the epicenter from which distances to other parts of the world were measured, proving the universal centrality of Jerusalem. Some were taught by Sheikh Rihan, whose school was also nearby. But the best-loved teacher was Hassan Nur al-Din. He was seventy years old and had never raised his voice or hand to his pupils, but rather led them gently through their childhood via the sacred texts.[26]

From the infant school the children passed to secular schools. There local Christian teachers – rather than American missionaries – 'nationalized' their outlook. Three of these teachers stood out: Khalil al-Sakakini, Zurayk Nakhla and Khalil Baydas, who influenced a whole generation of young Muslim and Christian Palestinians. With his thick beard and great nose and severe gaze, Zurayk Bey had a striking appearance. He was a Lebanese who had come to Jerusalem in 1889 at the request of Anglican missionaries to manage their store of religious books. In 1892 he became headmaster of the Gobat boys' primary school on Mount Zion, which later became the English College and which most of the Husaynis growing up during the Hamidi period attended.

One can still visit the school today. If you ignore a no entry sign on your right when you ascend towards the Jaffa Gate in the Old City of Jerusalem and follow the forbidden turn alongside the old Ottoman wall through the Citadel, on the mountain's slope looking west lies the old Gobat School. Today it is an American college, and amongst the beautiful buildings left behind by the Anglicans, modern-day Americans have planted posters supporting the Greater Israel idea and a Zionist Jerusalem, which would not have shamed the most ultra-right Zionist settler movement in Israel.

As mentioned, Samuel Gobat was an Anglican bishop who built a boys' school there in the mid-nineteenth century. The Gobat School became the main preparatory school for the Palestinian elite. Gobat came to Palestine, as Americans still do today, because he believed that the return of the Jews would precipitate the Second Coming of the Messiah and the unfolding apocalypse of the 'end times'. Unlike his successors, however, Gobat fell in love with the local population and helped tie them into the global educational system. In a way, he forsook his missionary task for the sake of granting them a more universal education. His efforts helped the embryonic Palestinian national movement to emerge.

When Zurayk was headmaster and the Husaynis were studying there, the language of tuition at the school was Arabic, which prepared the students for higher studies. They also studied arithmetic, algebra, geometry and biology. Zurayk taught Arabic but did not confine himself to grammar and syntax. He told his students about the great Arab heritage, and together they read passages selected from the glorious periods of Arab history. This charismatic man so appealed to them that they were drawn to listen to him even when he was among adults. *Al-mu'alim* (the teacher) he was called by all and sundry, including graybeards, because of his renown as a scholar. He used to invite some of his students to his house, where they would sit and listen to the gatherings of Jerusalem notables, including Mayor Hussein al-Husayni. In times to come, Zurayk Nakhla would be regarded as one of the pioneers of the revived modern Arabic.

The Husayni family had close relations with the teacher Khalil al-Sakakini, who had been Zurayk's student at the Anglican Mission in Jerusalem.[27] Always meticulous in his dress, a man of noble qualities and courteous manner, he was widely learned and would be the subject of future writings. He had studied in Britain and the United States in his youth, and his command of the English language was impressive. He returned to Palestine directly after the Young Turks' new constitution was published in 1908, and began to work as a journalist and teacher. That year he opened a private school in Jerusalem, the Ottoman Constitutional School, where he sought to inculcate Arabic language and culture but with reverence for the new constitutional empire that reformers in Istanbul wished to build. He combined his particularist activity on behalf of his Greek Orthodox community with work for the emergent national movement. One of his favorite students was Raja'i al-Husayni, the son of Said, who used to come to his house during the summer holidays for private tuition in Arabic language and literature. Like others of his generation of Husaynis, Raja'i studied with all three teachers mentioned.[28]

Khalil Baydas was born in Nazareth, where he attended the Greek Orthodox school. A charismatic teacher, he told his pupils that he had been a very mischievous boy and was subjected to severe physical punishment. His father died when he was five, and he was brought up by his grandmother after his mother remarried. In 1886 the Russians opened a school in Nazareth and invited Khalil to teach in it. Six years later, he was appointed supervisor of the Orthodox schools in Palestine and Syria. He spent two years in Homs and various places in Lebanon, and in 1908 he arrived in Haifa. The new Ottoman constitution prompted him to launch a scientific-literary magazine called *Al-Nafais* (Pearls), a fairly professional publication that came to be widely distributed through the Arabic-speaking world. When a council was created that year to manage the affairs of the Orthodox communities in Palestine and Jordan, his magazine's popularity led to Khalil being chosen as the representative of northern Palestine. Consequently, he resigned his position as headmaster in Haifa and moved to Jerusalem. Khalil would later become known for publishing the best of Russian literature – chiefly Tolstoy – in Arabic.[29]

These teachers promoted a more secular worldview among the mayoral sub-branch within the Tahiri Husaynis – a branch based on the post of *mufti*, but which had an important presence among the Husayni mayors of Jerusalem. Both Nakhla and Sakakini respected and liked Mayor Hussein al-Husayni, whose sons they taught,[30] and the three men would sit together in the afternoons in Anaste's café. The Greek's café and theater were well-known Jerusalem institutions located on the upper floor of a building just outside the city wall near the Jaffa Gate. It was there, beside the *mangal* (the urn on which coffee was kept heated and the coal for the *nargileh* was prepared), that the three discussed an idea that would effect a profound change in the political life of Palestinian society: the creation of a Muslim-Christian association.[31]

The Christian teachers felt that the Tahiri branch of the family, notably its secular members, differed from the other Muslim families and would resist the attempt of the religious leaders (including some members of the Umari branch) to create a local Arab national association dominated by Islamic scholars. Such a move would have led to further divisions between Muslims and Christians. But the idea of Christian-Muslim unity would fully take shape only after British forces clearly defined the boundaries of the country called Palestine and His Majesty's Government gave the Jews a right to the land. That was when the Muslim-Christian Association (MCA) became the foundation of Palestinian nationalism in Mandatory Palestine.

## Confronting Zionism

The 'nationalization' of the Husaynis cannot be understood without putting Zionism in the picture. While contending with the impact of the Young Turks, many of the Husaynis wondered about the significance of the ongoing Zionist-Jewish immigration. Their interest in this new phenomenon suggests that the heads of the family had come to realize that their social position obliged them to look beyond their narrow family interests. Or, to put it more bluntly, the family now had political ambitions on a scale unimaginable during early Ottoman times. We have seen that their attitudes towards Zionism at its inception varied from individual to individual, depending on their respective positions. That of the *mufti* was naturally the most hostile. It should be emphasized, however, that once they understood that Zionism was a real political movement with a large following and one that was rapidly acquiring land, properties and positions, the differences in their attitudes towards it disappeared. They all saw it as an imperialist-colonialist movement whose one purpose was to rob the Palestinians of their country. The history of the Palestinian national movement is full of vain efforts to put an end to Zionism and occasional attempts to blunt its impact by negotiation. But no one, not even the movement's founders, imagined how Zionism would develop or what its true nature would be.

The Palestinians' failure to understand Zionism's dangerous potential was due in part to their tendency to regard it as a component of a familiar phenomenon, that of the European powers' efforts to colonize Palestine. And no wonder – the Zionists, like the Europeans before them, advanced economic projects and settled in well-defined colonies (at this stage the movement closely resembled that of the German Templars). It is only in hindsight that we perceive that it was a different phenomenon: another national group in the process of formation through the colonization of Palestine, and with the aid of European colonialism; a settler project that focused as years went by on the dispossession of the indigenous population and the takeover of the land, or at least most of it. This colonialist nationalism had sprung from nothing – at least so far as the Palestinians were concerned – and concentrated all its efforts and hopes in survival. To begin with, its avowed aim was to save as many Jews as possible by gathering them in Palestine, and when this failed, the Zionists devoted their efforts to strengthening and expanding the small Jewish community that had already taken hold in Palestine. The most moderate Zionist conception of the Palestinian reality was that the Arab inhabitants could, in the words of the rabbi of Memel, leader of religious Zionism in Germany, 'move a little'. If they did not, 'we'll hit them on the head and make them move'. The Palestinians would have to decide how to respond to the blow.[32]

During the Hamidi period it was not easy to distinguish between Zionist fantasies and reality, but in the time of the Young Turks the appearance of seven Zionist colonies provoked real agitation. The newspapers voiced it. First came the press from Egypt and Beirut, which was read by some of the notables and whose contents presumably spread by word of mouth in the cafés, office courts and the like. Later, reports appeared in the newspaper *Filastin*, founded in Jaffa in 1909 by the Greek Orthodox Isa al-Isa, and in its competitor, Najib Nassar's *Al-Karmil*, also under Greek Orthodox ownership. Thanks to all of these, people who had never met a Zionist heard about the movement. The distribution of these newspapers was quite small, but they reached those who saw themselves as the leaders of the Jerusalem *sanjaq*, or of the two southern districts of the *vilayet* of Beirut (i.e. Nablus and Acre) – that is to say, the territory that would later be defined, to some extent because of Zionism, as Palestine.

A serious discussion about Zionism took place in the winter of 1910 at Ismail's house. As previously noted, this was a significant year because of the elections for the mayoralty. The winter of 1910 resembled that of 1855, when the Husaynis first encountered the famous Jewish philanthropist Moses Montefiore. This time they were confronted with a different kind of Jewish presence. Once again snow fell and piled up in mounds, and there was nothing to do but sit at home and discuss current events. At this time, *Al-Karmil* was publishing portions of Theodore Herzl's book *The Jewish State* as well as some of the resolutions adopted by the Zionist Congress in Basel. Being a parliamentary representative, Said was the most vocal against Zionism. Hussein, the mayor, was the most diffident – possibly because he owed his election to the Jewish vote, since the Association of Ottoman Jews, headed by Dr Levy of the board of IPAC in Jerusalem, had campaigned for him.[33] But Hussein's position was apparently more principled than pragmatic, as became evident some years later when he defended his opinion that Zionism did not represent any danger. He wrote in the Egyptian newspaper *Al-Aqdam*:

> I see no danger in the Zionist movement, because it is not a political but a settlement movement, and I am certain that no sensible Zionist would even conceive of the idea of creating a Jewish government in Palestine, as people claim. The Zionists have come to this country to live in it. They are educated and cultured people. They have no grandiose ambitions, and they are united among themselves. It is neither just nor humane for us to hate and resent this nation.

Events during the British Mandate would hardly reinforce this view in the minds of the Husaynis or of the Palestinians in general. And Hussein did show some caution:

> Nevertheless, we must keep our eye on them. If we go on as we do and they go on as they do, all our landed property will pass to them. Our *fellah* is poor and helpless, and a poor man may sell his property to save his life.

Time would show that the *fellah* resisted Zionism fairly stolidly, whereas the landowners, including some of the Husaynis, could not resist the financial inducement. Hussein called for a law that would limit the sale of land to the Zionists.[34]

As noted before, the attitude towards the Zionist settlers was part of the overall confrontation with the Europeans. They appeared as a force during the time of the Young Turks, while Jerusalem was swamped with Christian pilgrims, as though it were altogether a Christian city. It especially lost its multi-faith character during the Christian holidays, above all during the Easter season.[35] Both sides of the Via Dolorosa and nearby alleys were packed with hundreds of people watching the procession. Pilgrims filled the balconies, windowsills and roofs, and wooden boxes, each holding some twenty people, dangled seven to ten meters above the crowd, adding to the overcrowding. The procession was like a human snake five or six kilometers long.

No wonder the Zionists and Europeans appeared to be conspiring. That year the Nabi Musa procession threatened to erupt into violence. It began on 10 April 1910, and before the celebrants returned from Jericho a scandal rocked the Muslim community in Jerusalem. The immediate cause was the activities of a British archaeological expedition that was digging under the Temple Mount. Under the agreement made with the *sheikh al-haram*, the expedition's workmen did their digging in the small hours of the night, when the outer gates were kept locked for four or five hours. They had been working for the past month when a rumor suddenly spread that they were searching for King Solomon's sword and gold and that the excavation had been approved by the government. The rumor reached the Nabi Musa procession, led by Mufti Kamil al-Husayni, who made a fiery speech – though this was unusual for him, oration was an art his father had excelled in and a talent that his brother al-Hajj Amin would emulate. Kamil accused the governor of Jerusalem of taking part in an anti-Muslim conspiracy with the British infidels to turn the Haram into an archaeological site. The festive mood was shattered, the celebrants turned back and the procession was transformed into a mass protest. Kamil and his family received a lesson in popular resistance. Under their pressure the district governor, the district commander and the *sheikh al-haram* demanded a commission of inquiry. Their demand was met, and calm returned to the city after the protest of Mayor Hussein al-Husayni was formally noted.[36]

The debate about Zionism continued in 1911, when the power of the Jews in the districts of Palestine and Damascus was increasingly discussed in print. The notables were uncertain about their number – it appears that at the outbreak of World War I there were in Palestine some 85,000 Jews, including the old community and Zionist immigrants. The Husaynis relied on the data obtained by the parliamentary representative from Damascus, the editor of the daily *Al-Qabas*, Shukri al-Asali, who tabled a question about the precise number of Jews in the *sanjaq*. Getting the answer did not take long – 100,000.[37]

One of the rumors that spread in Jerusalem and that was quoted in the papers referred to the influence of the new Jews in the Young Turks' power centers. The rumor originated among Arab students in Istanbul who heard that there were some Jews in the new Ottoman army's high command who wielded great influence over policies. The Husayni family had at least two sons studying in the capital – the Umari Jamil and the Tahiri Mustafa III, who together with others organized the Arab students against Jewish immigration and land purchases.[38] But most of the family read about the rumors in the Egyptian newspaper *Al-Ahram*. Under the heading 'Zionists in the Ottoman Parliament', the paper discussed the influence of Jewish members of parliament on the government's Palestine policies. Worst of all, the paper said, was Sheikh al-Islam Jawdat Pasha, a Jewish convert believed to be pro-Zionist, who was meeting European bankers and, like Herzl, offering Jewish money for support for the Zionist enterprise. The paper also expressed the suspicion that Talat Pasha, the minister of the interior, was likewise pro-Zionist. It stated that the minister had admitted in parliament that he had met with Jewish bankers from France, Austria and Germany, though he insisted these had nothing to do with Zionism.

As we have seen, the revolution of the Young Turks restored the constitution and recalled the Ottoman parliament, which functioned between 1908 and 1912. During the parliamentary sessions the representatives from the district of Jerusalem, Said al-Husayni and Ruhi al-Khalidi, were often interviewed in Ottoman and Egyptian newspapers (such as *Al-Aqdam*), where they expressed adamant opposition to the continuing Zionist immigration. In reality, Said had not yet formed a rigid attitude towards Zionism. It would be fair to say that as time went by he became more opposed to the Zionist project, especially in his public appearances. On the eve of the elections to the new parliament in 1913, the representatives from Jerusalem again voiced this position (this time Ghalib al-Khalidi replaced Ruhi).

On 16 May, Said al-Husayni raised the question of Palestine for the first time in the newly elected Ottoman parliament, arguing that 'the Jews were proposing to create a state in the region that would include Palestine, Syria and Iraq'. Following the debate, Minister of the Interior Khalil Bey stated that the empire was opposed to Zionism. But Said could not ignore the general indifference to the issue among the other Ottoman representatives.[39] Before the elections to the Ottoman parliament in April 1914, Said again spoke up against Zionism in the Palestinian and Egyptian press. He told the editor of *Al-Aqdam* about his anger at the Ottoman Empire's passivity in the face of the Zionist menace: 'The government should wake up and face what it is happening,' he said. The main danger lay in the Zionist acquisition of the lands of the *fellahin*. Like Mayor Hussein, Said, too, feared the *fellah*'s weakness, though it was the *effendiya*, including the Husayni family, that sold lands to the Zionists.

After his interviews appeared in the Egyptian newspaper, Said discovered that they had been reprinted in the Hebrew newspaper *Ha-Herut* in March 1914. He was in the habit of reading every issue of this paper, and now he made a point of telling some of his former Jewish classmates that the peremptory tone was designed to placate public opinion, or at any rate the electors whose votes he would need to get elected to parliament.[40]

But Said al-Husayni's unease was not only about public opinion. His knowledge of Hebrew and his close friendships with his Jewish friends from schooldays, some of whom were Zionists, made for some tension between his personal feelings and his principles. It was also due to the difficulty of appraising the Zionist phenomenon. Until the end of the Great War, his attitude towards Zionism remained ambivalent. Despite his reassurances to his Jewish friends, in 1911 Said was a prominent member of a group of Arab parliamentarians who formed an all-Arab anti-Zionist lobby.[41] Yet his activities were insignificant compared with those of Shukri al-Asali, the representative from Damascus and former governor of Nazareth, or of the Egyptian journalist of Syrian origin Ibrahim Salim Najjar, who was beginning to write about Palestine and about 'Israelites in Palestine'.[42] Al-Asali had attracted a good deal of favorable attention in 1911, while he was still governor of Nazareth, when under local pressure he fought against the decision of the Lebanese landowner Elias Sursuq to sell the lands of Marj ibn Amar (Jezreel Valley) to the Zionists.

Said was not the only one to make public his position on Zionism. In 1914 young Jamil al-Husayni was also interviewed in the press, and he may be regarded as a forerunner of the Palestinian resistance movement. He spoke of the need to fight against Zionism because 'it might lead to the expulsion of the Palestinians from their lands'. Zionism was being helped by the government, he warned, and 'ordinary people don't realize what is happening'. He argued that government officials were making it easy for Zionists to acquire lands.[43] Concurrently with his open attacks on Zionism, he took part in attempts by spokesmen of the pan-Arab movement to reach an understanding with the Zionists. The initiative for the contacts with Zionism in which Jamil took part came from the Pan-Arab Decentralization Party, launched in Egypt in 1912, which called for the establishment of an Arab-Ottoman kingdom, on the Austro-Hungarian model, to replace the Ottoman Empire. The plan was for the party leaders to meet Zionist representatives in Broumana near

Beirut in summer 1914. The meeting never took place, but it is significant that Jamil was willing to take part in it.[44]

In 1914 Said also took part in meetings with Zionist leaders, in association with the initiative of Victor Jacobson, the Zionist Federation's representative in Istanbul who invited several prominent Palestinians to dine at his house. On this occasion, Said discovered that the Zionist movement wanted him to promote support for pan-Arab self-determination in Palestine, as opposed to Palestinian self-determination, so as to achieve an enduring understanding between Zionism and the Arab world. For his part, Jacobson learned that the Palestinian leadership would not be willing to accept a Jewish presence in Palestine, mainly because it feared being unable to limit it and that it would eventually take over the whole country. Although this may not have been Jacobson's intention, other Zionist leaders at the time wished the Palestinians to identify themselves as pan-Arabs so as to give up Palestine and move voluntarily to the Arab world around them. When it became clear that this would not happen, a more sinister and coercive plan to move them developed and was finally executed in 1948.[45]

What Ismail, then regarded as the head of the family, thought about Zionism is not certain. Ismail had business dealings with Jews, such as his joint attempt in 1909 to establish the Commercial Bank of Palestine, a project stopped by the Ottomans. It was said in the family that his special regard for Jews was due to the fact that his wet nurse had been Jewish.[46] He himself never said anything definite about it.

It must not be thought that any subject considered essential and discussed at length in the present work preoccupied the Husaynis to a similar degree. When the snow melted, they no doubt turned to other matters. In the spring of 1910 a swarm of locusts arrived and consumed all their crops. Flying in from the east, the insects penetrated the houses and piled up in the streets, and the authorities offered payment for every sackful. Although thousands of sacks were filled, no one actually became richer.

In the midst of this calamity, a son was born to Musa Kazim:

> 'The sun entered the alleys of Jerusalem and lighted its streets, and in that month in 1910, in the neighborhood of the Husaynis, was heard the cry of a newborn baby. It filled the air of the holy city and blended with the ringing of church bells and the muezzins' musical call – it was the voice of the heroic warrior Abd al-Qadir Musa al-Husayni.'[47]

In view of the bad years that followed, not all of which show the family in the best light in the collective Palestinian memory, everything related to Abd al-Qadir, from his birth to his heroic death on top of the Qastel, is treasured in Palestinian history. The fact that his mother, Raqiya, the daughter of Mustafa al-Husayni, died eighteen months after his birth makes his childhood even more mythical, as though it was Palestine itself that nurtured him as her pure son. In reality, he was brought up by his grandmother Nuzha, the daughter of Muhammad Ali al-Husayni, and his nurse Thalija, whom he would later speak of as 'mother'. But memory erases these women and replaces them with the Homeland.

The locusts came from the east, while from the west swarms of pilgrims continued to pour in, and the involvement of the foreign consuls kept growing stronger. Even the Russians, whose standing in the empire had declined since the Crimean War, became prominent. Every day the Russian consul and his wife rode to the crowded *suq*, accompanied by the opulently dressed *qawas* (a consular official who acted as guard of honor to the secular or religious foreign representatives, generally of Balkan or Caucasian origin). Like the others, the Russian consul could intervene in the affairs of the city, since he was not subject to the laws of the empire.[48]

But when they were not troubled by Zionism, locusts or the consuls, the Husaynis went about their daily routine in a world that was changing at an incredible rate. The family's ability to adapt depended largely on the younger generation, its education and preparation for the future. Unlike the reign of Abdul Hamid II, when the family showed some impressive achievements, during the time of the Young Turks it did not manage to occupy any of the new power bases in Jerusalem. For example, it did not have a representative on the General District Council of Jerusalem, a body that was set up in 1911 as an expanded version of the district council that had existed during the Tanzimat. Henceforth, achievements were to be made on individual as well as institutional tracks.

## Between Islam and the West

Izzat Tanus, who studied at St George's and taught there from 1911, recalled that during those years the students were very confused about 'the West'. Their curriculum was European and taught them to appreciate Western literature and philosophy, but at home as well as from some of the teachers they heard criticism and hostility about the West's treatment of Turkey, especially as manifested in Jerusalem. But boys being boys, what really held their attention was football, and the whole city became enthusiastically drawn in. In 1910 some 5,000 spectators attended a football match at St George's School, among them hundreds of veiled women. Not all the Husayni women wore veils, though, as pictures from the period show them wearing lacy Western gowns.

The boys wore three-piece suits and ties. There was one exception: six-year-old Ishaq Musa, Musa's younger son and grandson of the great Umar, who wore the white turban of the Muslim mystic orders. Ishaq Musa's father had destined him and his brother Musa to join an order and devote their lives to the faith. Their father was a member of the Rifa'i sect in Jerusalem, and he introduced his sons into it in a traditional ceremony that included tasting a pinch of sugar – perhaps as a symbolic start of a long and arduous process of religious purification.[49] But Ishaq Musa would not follow this path, nor would his brother. After his father's death in 1911, his mother – a daughter of the reform-minded al-Daudi family in Jerusalem – removed Ishaq Musa's turban and sent him to a local reformist school.[50] Another mother in the family – Zaynab, the mother of Amin al-Husayni – also interrupted her son's paternally directed career, but she diverted it from a secular to a religious track.

To return to the new craze of football – every student dreamed of playing on the school team. In April 1912 the first 'international' match took place, between the Syrian-Anglican College of Beirut and St George's School. The latter won 3–0 to tremendous rejoicing. Even the painful defeat in the return match could not erase the splendid achievement.

Many reports describe al-Hajj Amin – the youngest son of Tahir II and brother of Mufti Kamil – as standing out among the boys of St George's. Even then he was interested in serious matters rather than in boyish activities. His mother, Zaynab, aware of his intellectual curiosity, found him a private tutor, a Miss Hassasin, to broaden his education, chiefly in the Muslim religion. When he wished to go to Istanbul for his higher studies, preliminary to a political career, his mother convinced his brother, Mufti Kamil, to dissuade him from this course and train him to be his heir. This course led al-Hajj Amin to local politics. In 1913 Zaynab made two moves to achieve her aim – she took Amin on the pilgrimage to Mecca and sent him to study at al-Azhar University in Cairo.[51] The young Amin impressed the heads of the university with his scholarship and serious mind, and he was admitted without difficulty – his private tutor had taught him well both in Muslim religious law and the riches of the Arabic language.

Amin al-Husayni went to al-Azhar together with his cousin Yaqub al-Husayni, and studied theology and Arabic. As mentioned, in his second year at the college he became attached to Rashid Rida. Amin al-Husayni, (to whom we will refer from now on as al-Hajj Amin) was so drawn to him that he transferred to his theological seminary, and their warm understanding meant that al-Hajj Amin was often invited to his mentor's house in Cairo. Rashid Rida preached some fairly clear guidelines that became entrenched in al-Hajj Amin's mind: one, that Muslim society everywhere ought to be very cautious in its encounters with Western culture, some of whose aspects constituted an existential danger to Islam; two, to confront this danger it was necessary to return to a distilled form of Islamic precepts, sifting out all vestiges of the negative Western influence; and, three, the religious undertaking must be tied to the political and national struggle. Thus, for example, the British occupation of Egypt was interpreted as a conflict between Islam and the West. Rashid Rida also spoke explicitly about Zionism and the duty of fighting it as part of the overall struggle against the Western political takeover of the Muslim-Arab Middle East. Young al-Hajj Amin reduced these guidelines to an even simpler rule: political Islam was the most efficient way to fight Zionism and the British. From his mentor he learned that it was necessary to combine European technology and Western systems of government and administration with Arab nationalism and Islam in the struggle against the West.

Evening lectures at the Faculty of the Humanities at the Egyptian university provided al-Hajj Amin with a more secular exposure. It was at these lectures that he made friends with a Christian Palestinian whose name is not known, with whom he planned to create in Egypt an association for Palestine and against Zionism. Together with his roommate, Abd al-Rahman al-Alami, he rallied twenty Muslims and Christians to propagate awareness among interested students of the dangers posed by the Zionist presence in Palestine. His friend Kamil al-Dajani stated that in 1913 al-Hajj Amin was the first to perceive that Zionism, rather than the Young Turks, represented the real danger to Palestinians. The association did not last long, but al-Hajj Amin remained committed to this struggle until the end of his life.[52]

Unlike him, al-Hajj Amin's relatives in the Husayni neighborhood received clear indications about Zionism's future plans but did not know how to interpret them. The same year that al-Hajj Amin engaged in his first anti-Zionist activity, the Zionist leader Arthur Ruppin came to Jerusalem and visited Sir John Grey Hill. Hill was a pro-Zionist English aristocrat who in 1875 built himself a summer house on Mount Scopus, not far from the Husaynis. Some of them were present at the meeting and heard about Ruppin's plan to buy the house and turn it into a Hebrew educational institution, but at the time they saw no harm in it. By the time it became the Hebrew University in Jerusalem, it was too late.[53]

To return to al-Hajj Amin – in Cairo he followed two parallel paths, the religious and the secular, and was wavering between them due to his mother's influence. Zaynab realized that in the secular world established by the Young Turks the status of the *muftis* would be quite low. It had in fact been declining before the rise of secular rule. Now it was of less importance than other posts held by the family – mayor, parliamentary representative, senior positions in the Ottoman administration and even in the local chamber of commerce. Al-Hajj Amin's father, Tahir II, had had to struggle to maintain a central position in the family, and his son and successor, Kamil, gave up the attempt. It would be the youngest son, al-Hajj Amin, who would achieve the impossible and not only restore primacy to the Tahiri branch and the centrality of the *mufti*'s post in the family, but also become, if only for a short period, *rais al-a'ala*, the supreme president of the Palestinian political structure under the British Mandate. A number of Palestinian historians would later argue that this achievement came at a very great cost to the Palestinian people.

As al-Hajj Amin set off on a religious career that would sweep him into the maelstrom of national politics, his kinsman Jamal, a scion of the mayoralty sub-branch of the Tahiri Husaynis (and son of Musa Kazim's sister), chose a career none of his family had previously considered: that of medicine. Even in those days it was not easy to get into medical school. Jamal wanted to attend the best faculty of medicine in the Middle East, at the Jesuit college of St Joseph in Beirut, but the language of tuition was French, in which he was not fluent. Then in 1912 a telegram arrived at the house of Musa Kazim's sister and was read aloud to the entire household as soon as the young man's uncle came in. Eighteen-year-old Jamal, newly graduated from St George's School, had been admitted into the Faculty of Medicine of the American University in Beirut.

Jamal arrived in Beirut in the autumn of 1912. His awed impressions of the city's beauty and riches reveal the difference between provincial Jerusalem and the Lebanese metropolis. He was especially impressed by the university campus where he studied – no such large and magnificent architectural complex could be found in Palestine. Built in 1866, it had previously been Beirut's Protestant College and became a pantheon of the new Arab nationalism. The American pastor Daniel Bliss, the first Protestant missionary in the Middle East, had come to the Syrian provinces in 1820 and with his friends began to establish the first private schools. George Antonius ascribes to these schools a major influence on the rise of Arab nationalism, because as well as theological studies the students received a liberal education and heard much about the marvels of American independence and European democracy. The Americans brought the first Arabic printing press to Beirut in 1834, and it served the college students.[54] Butrus al-Bustani and Nasif al-Yazji, two of the early thinkers of Arab nationalism, taught at the college alongside Bliss.

The college was situated in Ras Beirut, on the crest of the mountain overlooking the Mediterranean. On a clear day it was possible to see the snowy mountains to the south, Jabal Kanisa and Jabal Snin, and the plain below the Bay of St George; not far away to the north was the beautiful bay of Junieh. The college was full of students of various backgrounds, including Armenians, some Egyptians and Iranians and a few from Anatolia. Most of the teachers were Canadians and Americans, and the rest were local. The college had six wings or schools – literature and the sciences, commerce, medicine, pharmacology, dentistry and engineering. There was also the international college, attended by all first-year students, including Jamal al-Husayni. It did not take him long to find his way around the place, physically and socially. The college did not differ essentially from St George's School, since both were Protestant missionary establishments. A student's quality of life was determined, as in English public schools, by the students' hierarchy, and perks and privileges were won by passing safely through the first year and into the second. As in the United States, good athletes enjoyed favorable treatment even in their first year, but Jamal was not an athlete. His claim to fame lay elsewhere.

When the First World War broke out, Jamal had been there for two years but had not yet begun medical studies. Like all students of medicine, he had spent the first two years in the College Hall in the Faculty of the Humanities doing general studies. The faculty building was an impressive two-storey edifice, with high windows and a square tower, in the style of Oxford and Cambridge. Jamal should have spent the next four years studying medicine, but this promising career was broken off by the war.[55]

### The Outbreak of World War I

Jamal is our first witness to the outbreak of the war. Early in December 1914, four months after the beginning of the war in Europe, during which the Ottoman Empire maintained its neutrality, the war came to Beirut. It was not only the empire's close relations with Germany that involved it in the war against Britain and France, but primarily the need to resist the relentless territorial ambitions of Russia, which ever since the reign of Peter the Great had been seeking to dominate the Black Sea and its outlets to the Mediterranean, as well as the Slav lands in the Balkans. Two Balkan wars had intensified this struggle, and it was not surprising that the Ottoman entry into the war was triggered by an incident in the Black Sea in December 1914. The Ottoman government used the declaration of war to cancel all the Capitulations – that is, the special agreements between the Ottoman Empire and various foreign governments giving their citizens and subjects exemptions from the laws of the empire. This proclamation won the government some support among the Husaynis.

On the morning of 1 December 1914, the calm of the Beirut university was shattered. Ottoman guards invaded the School of Medicine and arrested every person suspected of belonging to secret nationalist Arab societies. The suspects were brought before Cemal Pasha (his Arabic name, Jamal Pasha, will be used hereafter as this is what the local people called him), the military governor of all the Syrian provinces, nicknamed *al-Safah* ('The Butcher'), who without blinking an eye ordered their execution. Persons whose names appeared in the guest book of the French consulate were marked for death, since the consulate was suspected of aiding the nationalist associations. The terrified consul himself had escaped as soon as war was declared, but the police had a long enough list to satisfy Jamal Pasha. Jamal al-Husayni did not think twice about fleeing to the safety of the Husayni neighborhood in Jerusalem.[56]

But Jamal Pasha had gotten to Jerusalem well before December and the official entry of the Ottomans into the war. In August, after the war broke out in Europe, he had toured the cities of al-Sham – Greater Syria – where, according to Minister of War Enver Pasha, there was nationalist unrest. Driven by his own paranoia, which Enver's warnings had exacerbated, Jamal Pasha started rooting out anyone suspected of nationalist activity or spying for the enemy.[57] He was convinced that the Allies were planning an invasion of Palestine in order to foment an Arab revolt against the Ottoman Empire, and his aides assured him that the landing would be somewhere between Iskenderun and Haifa. Jamal Pasha began systematically crushing all the Arab nationalist associations and every sign of independence in the area under his control. But the massive operation produced few results. There was not nearly as much political activity as his aides believed, and they seized only a few dozen individuals from the regions of Syria, Lebanon and Palestine who may or may not have been involved with independence movements. By mid-August 1915 eleven Arabs had been hanged in Beirut – a mere handful in relation to Jamal Pasha's imaginings. But the action was sufficiently ruthless to instill terror throughout Syria, Lebanon and Palestine, including of course Jerusalem, which Jamal Pasha frequently visited.

Although the Husayni family was lucky enough not to be picked on, it was a time of great anxiety. In fact, war had come to Jerusalem even before it reached Beirut. General conscription was announced in August 1914, and every day patrols scoured the city for likely recruits, or for suspects. Fortunately for the Husaynis, most of them were government officials and so far exempt from military service; nor did they appear on Jamal Pasha's list of suspects. The secretaries of the national associations that had sprung up in reaction to the Turkification policy of the Young Turks – Al-Ahd, Al-Fata and the Decentralization Party – had given advance warning to the young Husaynis to cease their political activities. Later Jamal Pasha would execute people without any sound information, simply at his and his aides' whims.[58]

But at the end of September, things came to a head and conscription reached the Husaynis too. Their friend Khalil al-Sakakini parted from them hastily on a searing hot Hamsin day near the Jaffa Gate. He had been standing beside the road, saying goodbye to some conscripts he knew who were about to be sent to the front, when he spotted among the dusty, sweaty crowd the sons of Musa Salih, nephews of Musa Kazim. Many months would pass before their mothers breathed freely again, but in the end the two returned unharmed from the inferno. Jamal, too, was conscripted, and some time later he was taken captive by the British forces.[59]

The war atmosphere would affect the rest of the inhabitants only from 20 December on. Ten days earlier in Mecca, the Prophet's banner was taken out amid great festivities and carried to Damascus by train, and on the 20th it reached Jerusalem. The banner was received by a huge joyous throng in front of the Dome of the Rock. But it was a strange event. When the loud rejoicing subsided, Jamal Pasha and the *mufti* of his army sat on a raised platform in front of the crowd and began to answer questions concerning the religious aspects of the citizens' duty to help the war effort. Jamal Pasha addressed the crowd in his own name and that of Mehmet Rashad V – the puppet sultan whom the Young Turks had placed on the throne of Abdul Hamid II – proclaiming, 'The Amir of the Faithful has declared the great *jihad*!' This was followed by mass prayers.[60]

Al-Hajj Amin was not one of the conscripts seen off by Sakakini. Bored with his studies, he had joined up just before the war, and when it broke out he began to attend the military academy in Istanbul and was made a junior reserves officer. His brigade was sent to the Black Sea shore, but he never saw action because the Ottomans did not send Arab officers or cadets to the front. He remained in the reserves, but his life was far from easy. The nights were cold, the food was insufficient and so was sleep. In August 1916 he was given a commission in the Forty-sixth Division and his situation improved. At first he served as assistant division commander to the governor of Smyrna, present day Izmir, then as an artillery officer on the Black Sea. But his battle experience did not go beyond exchanges of fire with Russian cannons.[61]

The situation grew worse in 1916. Al-Hajj Amin would later say that he spent most of his time in arguments with the division commander about the rations and quarters given to the Arab soldiers, whom he believed the Ottoman commander was discriminating against. He could have ended up in jail, but in November 1916 he came down with dysentery and was sent to a hospital in Istanbul. Then he was given an exceptional three-month leave and went to Jerusalem. At the end of the three months he stayed home and did not return to his unit. The war had left al-Hajj Amin stronger and tougher.[62]

Despite everything, throughout his military service al-Hajj Amin never considered rebelling against the Ottomans. So long as he served in their army, he remained loyal to Istanbul. In later years he would explain that he thought of the war as a struggle between Muslims and infidels. His diary from the army period was full of longing for Palestine, with such lines as, 'This is my country and the country of my forefathers, I shall defend it with my life for the sake of her children.'[63] And this is probably why he decided to not to support the uprising against the Ottoman Empire, which erupted shortly after his return to Jerusalem.

Most of the Husaynis did not serve in the military and remained in the microcosm of Jerusalem. To use a typical historiographic generalization, it might be said that most of them did not respond to the national Syrian and Arab call. Characteristically, however, neither did they join the opposition movement that Jamal Pasha was trying to organize. For a whole year, between August 1914 and August 1915, Jamal Pasha tried to rally Arab support, and when he failed he began a campaign of unprecedented persecution. The first mass hangings took place on 21 August 1914, the condemned prisoners being members of the Arab national movement. The newspapers published their names – Christians and Muslims were hanged side by side.[64] This was Jamal Pasha's contribution to that essential buttress of the national identity: supra-religious solidarity.

The Husaynis were actively involved in building this buttress, but they did not look only to the Christians. They were willing to regard the Jews, too, as partners in the construction of a new future. While the executioners went about their grisly business, Muslims and Jews met in a gathering which would be unmatched for many years to come.

The inspiration behind the meeting was Zaki Bey, the city's military commander, whom Jamal Pasha's regular visits had left without employment. Zaki Bey was popular with Jews and Muslims alike, thanks to his generous donations to religious institutions and to the citizens' welfare. One day in mid-December 1915, a ceremonious delegation of Husaynis came to call at the Jewish teachers' seminary on Abyssinia Street. Among them were Muhammad Salih al-Husayni, owner of the Rawdat al-Ma'arif ('The Educational Garden'); the headmaster of that school, Abd al-Latif al-Rajab (who took the name Husayni after his appointment to the post); and Fakhri al-Husayni, al-Hajj Amin's younger brother (who would die prematurely in Istanbul soon after this). Eliezer Ben-Yehuda received the guests warmly and opened the meeting with the words, 'The time has come for Muslims and Jews to come together ... We have a common enemy ... We have been slandered ...' and so on. Young Fakhri responded by reading out a letter from Jerusalem mayor Hussein al-Husayni, welcoming the initiative, which he saw as a call to create a joint homeland. Hearing this, the Jews – including David Yellin, Albert Antebi, Yaacov Thon and others – burst into loud applause and were joined by the Husaynis.

The most astonishing appearance was that of Sheikh Abd al-Qadir al-Muzafir, who accompanied the family. In times to come, he would be known as an eloquent orator against the Zionists and a confidant of Amin al-Husayni. He owned a good deal of land in the vicinity of Hulda, some of which he sold to the Jews. He began by saying he was sorry he did not speak Hebrew and advised the Jews to learn Arabic and Turkish, especially at a time when tens of thousands of their brethren had come to the country. Since the first and second wave of Jewish immigration, he said, 'it had become evident that something was happening and taking shape between the two peoples who are racially related, but far apart in their development'. Moreover, the *sheikh* added, 'there is no denying that the Jewish settlers have brought much that is good'.

He was followed by Muhammad Salih al-Husayni, who exclaimed warmly, 'How delightful is this scene, a gathering of the Children of Israel (*Banu Israil*) and Arabs together under the picture of our dear sultan ... This evening ties Muslims and Jews together with love.' David Yellin delighted the Husaynis by speaking the purest Arabic and expressing similar sentiments. A similar meeting was supposed to take place in Jaffa, but the Ottoman authorities prevented it.[65]

Strange are the vagaries of local history. In 1915 the Husaynis led the initiative to create a *watani*, a local patriotic consciousness, under the Ottoman aegis. Most of the leaders of the Jewish community were willing to regard it as a temporary but acceptable solution. Two years later, following the British conquest and the Balfour Declaration, most of the participants on both sides would adopt a sharp nationalistic stance, and hopes for sympathy and cooperation would be dashed.

At the end of December 1915 they met again, this time hosted by Salim al-Husayni. The Jewish group was led by David Ben-Gurion and Yitzhak Ben-Zvi. Dreams of a joint homeland under the Pax Ottomana were still discussed, but by now Jamal Pasha had become alarmed: he dismissed the organizer Zaki Pasha, exiled Ben-Gurion and Ben-Zvi and accused the Husaynis of pro-French sedition.

The family grew very cautious and wondered if they ought not follow the example of the al-Shuqayris. A well-known religious scholar who lived in Acre, Sheikh As'ad al-Shuqayri (the father of Ahmad al-Shuqayri, a future head of the PLO) decided to deal with Jamal Pasha's rage by means of gentle persuasion. He organized a delegation of religious scholars and notables from Syria, Lebanon and Palestine to try to pacify the Ottomans after the executions. To demonstrate their good intentions, the group visited the Ottoman forces in the Dardanelles and distributed gifts. The story was covered extensively in the press, as the group included the *muftis* of Damascus, Homs, Beirut and Haifa, the *naqibs* of Nablus and the Shafi'i *mufti* of Jerusalem – every major city was represented by a *mufti* or *naqib*. The Hanafi *mufti* of Jerusalem, Kamil al-Husayni, had been strongly urged to join, but no one in the family wanted to be unequivocally associated with the Ottomans, who represented secularism, anti-Arabism and above all erratic, unstable policies. The only one willing to consider joining was Shukri al-Husayni, who told the family that he supported the action of Sheikh As'ad, even the latter's willingness to become *mufti* of the Fourth Army – that is, Jamal Pasha's own *mufti*. The newspaper *Filastin* published Shukri's statement in support of al-Shuqayri, mocking those who sought to break away from Ottoman rule: 'The Arab nation must not part from the Ottoman nation, or it may find itself outside Islam.'[66] Kamil, too, realized that he had to pay lip service to this position, and in February 1916, when Jamal Pasha brought Minister of War Enver Pasha by a special train to Jerusalem for a ceremonious dedication of Jamal Pasha Street, Kamil al-Husayni invited the important visitors to the Haram al-Sharif and presented them with valuable gifts.[67]

The Gaza Husaynis, who were vaguely related to the Jerusalem family, were badly hit. Ahmad Arif al-Husayni, the son of Gaza's Hanafi *mufti* and the member of parliament for the city, was put to death by Jamal Pasha in 1916. The Jerusalem Husaynis knew Ahmad Arif's father well, as he was in charge of the connection between Gaza and the Jerusalem representatives in the Ottoman Parliament. Ahmad Arif himself had sat beside many of the Jerusalem Husaynis on Jerusalem's district council. Moreover, in 1913 the Jerusalem family supported his unsuccessful candidacy to the Ottoman Parliament, which he lost to the family that would bedevil the Husaynis – namely, the Nashashibis.

The execution of Ahmad Arif al-Husayni heightened the fear and anxiety in Jerusalem. Jamal 'the Butcher' did not even spare Ahmad Arif's son. The charge against Ahmad Arif was that he had collaborated with the camp of the Hashemite *sharif* Hussein ibn Ali of Mecca, the ruler of the Hijaz region in the Arabian Peninsula. This Hussein – great-grandfather of the future King Hussein of Jordan – openly revolted against the Ottomans in the summer of 1916, and his high religious position as guardian of the holy places in Mecca and Medina made this a serious blow to the empire. At the time nobody knew about the *sharif*'s collusion with the British governor of Egypt, Sir Henry McMahon, and his confidential agent T. E. Lawrence (Lawrence of Arabia). Together they created an alliance that would serve British and Hashemite interests but would split the Arab world. When Albion's perfidy became known, anti-British tendencies in the Middle East intensified. What worried the Husaynis most, however, was that one of the charges against the Gazan's son was desertion, and not all the Jerusalem Husaynis had obeyed the call-up (most of them were exempt in any case).[68]

The year 1916 was a gory one, stained with the blood of Arab notables. On the day the Hijaz revolt was proclaimed, Jamal Pasha put to death another group of activists who had been convicted by a military court in Aley, Lebanon. At least one historian maintains that Jamal Pasha considered executing the most outspoken member of the family, Jamil al-Husayni, but changed his mind at the last moment for unknown reasons.[69]

That year young al-Hajj Amin, aged twenty-one, returned to Jerusalem. Under the tutelage of his famous mentor, Rashid Rida, and after prolonged discussions with his friends Arif al-Arif and Khalil al-Sakakini, he began to seek volunteers to join the *sharif*'s revolt. Thousands put their names down but few would actually fight.[70] Lloyd George, the future Prime Minister of Britain, deplored the fact that the Palestinian Arabs did nothing to help the war effort, and blamed most of them for joining the Ottomans in their fight against his own country. He counted only 150 Palestinians in the forces of the *sharif* of Mecca.[71] Al-Hajj Amin's efforts, which would be recorded in his favor, were conducted with the aid of Captain Brenton, a British military agent active in Palestine, and were much appreciated by the British government. Indeed, it has been argued that this helped his appointment as Grand Mufti of Palestine in 1921. But al-Hajj Amin was finding it difficult to rally actual support – while no one liked the Young Turks, certainly not after Jamal Pasha's depredations, few were willing to betray Istanbul in time of war. The historian Philip Mattar states flatly that the *sharif's* revolt did not arouse enthusiasm in Palestine and that the notable families remained loyal to Istanbul until 1918.[72]

A young intelligence officer in the Arab Bureau in Cairo – set up in 1915 to observe the political developments in the Arab world in preparation for the British takeover – noted al-Hajj Amin's activities in a positive light, and his report described the young Husayni as a pro-British personage. Here is another of history's ironies, as twenty years later al-Hajj Amin would become the bugbear of the British rulers in the Middle East.

Jamal Pasha's continued presence in the region and his frequent visits to Jerusalem – from the summer of 1915, when he was planning his futile 'Operation Lightning' (*yilderim* in Turkish), in which he hoped to conquer Egypt with the German General von Moltke by crossing the Sinai Peninsula, to his equally futile resistance against Allenby's forces in 1917 – hung like a shadow over the family. They were in the position of the knife-thrower's assistant, tied to the target and sensing the whistling of the knives flying past their ears. Even the Husayni children were exposed to the tyrant's violent whims. One day Ottoman soldiers burst into St George's School and ransacked it, having been told that a cannon was hidden there for the pro-British rebels. Though they did not find it, they shut the school down and the boys spent most of the war at home.[73]

The boys probably did not shed tears over this, but they were very reluctant to part from their much-loved teacher, Khalil al-Sakakini, who like other Christian friends of the Husaynis suffered greatly under Jamal Pasha. The latter was not always in the city, but the governor obeyed his orders to the letter. The persecution of Christian inhabitants began two months after the Ottoman Empire joined the war.

Khalil's house was well-known in Jerusalem. It was called the *haririya* – *harir* is Arabic for 'silk', and the house on the little rise beside the railway station had once been a silk-processing workshop. (Today it houses the Khan Theater.) One Tuesday evening Sakakini and Mayor Hussein al-Husayni,

Sakakini's old schoolmate, had just finished supper and were about to settle on the rush mats for coffee, when suddenly they heard a clamor in the street outside. Rifles were fired, shattering the evening calm. Ottoman soldiers were running through the city proclaiming that Jamal Pasha's forces had captured the Suez Canal and taken 8,000 enemy troops prisoner. Khalil did not believe it – 'A war tactic', he said. In fact, Jamal's army had failed to cross the Sinai Peninsula.

Had someone overheard Khalil's heretical statement? No one knows for certain. But some days later, on Saturday, 1 December 1917, the police rounded up Christians and foreign nationals and held them in the police station. The detainees knew from experience that the Ottoman authorities would deport them. Khalil al-Sakakini was one of the detainees, and his sister appealed for help from Hussein al-Husayni – 'my pure-hearted friend', as Sakakini called him in his diary. For a moment she feared she had lost her brother for ever. The respected teacher was sentenced to serve in the Ottoman porters' battalion. Jamal Pasha had decreed that non-Muslims would no longer pay an impost for their exemption from military service – henceforth Jews and Christians would serve in non-combat missions. (Combat service was not considered because in Jamal Pasha's eyes they were all potential spies.) The mayor was moved by the sister's appeal and, despite his usual prudence, pulled the necessary strings to get Khalil released from servitude, which he might not have survived since the non-combat missions were hard labor in the most difficult conditions. Instead, Sakakini was sent to the veterinary service in the town of Bisan (the Jewish development town Beit She'an is built on its ruins). But Hussein persuaded the governor to overrule this sentence too, and eventually got Khalil assigned to work in a Jerusalem hospital.[74]

This did not last, however and the teacher was arrested once again. To begin with, Jamal Pasha regarded Khalil al-Sakakini as a potential asset when he agreed to teach at the reformist al-Salhiyya College founded by Jamal Pasha. But the teacher again fell under suspicion as a supporter of Arab nationalism and possibly even of the British. Khalil tended to be reckless: three days after being released, he gave shelter to an American Jew who was wanted by the authorities. He was sent to prison in Damascus. However, the Husaynis and others of his friends in the empire succeeded in having him freed and smuggled across the lines to British-held territory.[75]

Sakakini spent the rest of the war in the headquarters of Amir Faysal, the son of Sharif Hussein, who had come to Aqaba in early 1917. There he wrote a poem in praise of the Arab commander that would be sung in Jerusalem when the British forces entered the city in December 1917:

Oh, our mighty lord, glory of all Arabia, your reign is as glorious as the reign of the Prophet, your grandfather, to whose rule everyone submitted through the ages, overwhelming all enemies to rescue the homeland.[76]

When Sakakini was in Aqaba writing songs of praise about Commander Faysal, none of the Husaynis expected to support the man who would enthrone himself the following year as the king of 'Greater Syria'. Yet when Faysal entered Damascus, many of the Husaynis agreed to regard Palestine as part of his kingdom.

## CHAPTER 6

# In the Shadow of British Military Rule

## From the Politics of Notables to
## the Politics of Nationalism

On 30 November 1917, a platoon of British soldiers from the Seventy-fourth Division lost its way and ended up behind Ottoman lines near the village of Nabi Samwil. They soon ran into a division of the Ottoman Seventh Army, which had been assigned to defend Jerusalem, and after a brief battle took 450 Ottoman men and officers captive. It was a sign of things to come. Two days later, on 1 December, Ottoman storm troops launched an attack, with the result that an entire Ottoman battalion was destroyed, some of its men taken prisoner and others killed.

Now, for the first time since the start of the fighting for Jerusalem a week earlier, General Allenby could begin to feel more confident. The supply lines of the British forces had been stretched to the limit, and the general feared that they would be unable to complete the conquest. The heavy rains and thick mud prevented reinforcements from reaching the besieging forces; many camels died of cold and others starved to death. On the other hand, the expeditionary force's chief veterinarian wrote, 'The two thousand donkeys which had been brought from Egypt, though they'd never had to tramp through snow in such fierce cold, did very well.' But humans and horses, unlike the donkeys, fell like flies. Since the beginning of the fight for Jerusalem, the British forces had lost 1,667 men and 5,000 horses. Ottoman casualties were heavier, and some 1,800 of their troops were taken captive. The British command believed that they were still facing 15,000 Ottoman troops, and wondered whether they could overcome them.¹ The expeditionary force led by General Allenby was to launch its onslaught on 9 December.

The night before the attack, Hussein al-Husayni awoke to the familiar sound of soldiers marching. 'But where are they going?' his wife asked and opened the shutters. A strange sight met her eyes: the Ottoman army was evacuating the city by the light of oil lamps. Hussein al-Husayni had expected the retreat but not its timing. In the morning the governor of Jerusalem summoned him, as head of the city council, along with other councilors, and gave them a document of surrender to hand to the British commander. A representative of the Anglican bishop, Mikhail Abu Hatoum, was present, and he kept the document for future record. It was written in Turkish, and Hussein wondered whether anyone on the conquering side would be able to read it:

> To the English Commandant [having spent many years with the Prussian general Erich von Volkenheim, the governor imagined that this was also the title of senior officers in the British forces]. Ever since the 6th of December shells have been raining down on Jerusalem, indiscriminately hitting members of all the *millets* [communities] and the sites that are sacred to all. There is no need for it, because the military force that was in the city has retreated. I send this letter with Hussein Bey al-Husayni, representative of the mayor of Jerusalem.²

The final days of secular Ottoman government were strange. After almost a decade, the Ottoman rulers of Jerusalem, as though aware that their names would go down in history for better or worse, began trying to improve their images. The houses they had occupied during the war, as well as the permanent quarters of their officials and officers, were left in impeccable order, property was not looted and no one was hurt. Emile al-Ghuri wrote in his diary: 'The picture of the evacuation is an astounding contrast to the kind of Ottoman despotism that Arabs have suffered under for four hundred years.'³ This was of course a distorted picture of the Arab population's feelings towards the Ottomans, but it fitted well with their emotional response to the Young Turks since 1913.

After the Ottoman flight, the Husayni clan gathered at the house of Ismail Bey, the head of the family. He greeted them with his usual smile spreading over his white goatee. It was only natural that the family would turn to him at such a time – he had never lost his self-possession, least of all in difficult moments. Dressed in the *frangi* (Western) three-piece suit, which had become his trademark and that of other Husayni notables, he managed as usual to calm the family and steer it through the current crisis.

Some twenty members of the family were there, men and boys. The women sat in the women's wing, but there, too, the talk was all about the recent dramatic events. An unexpected guest was the teacher Khalil Baydas, who had not been seen in Jerusalem throughout the war. Like other political activists of the pan-Arab national movement who had evaded capture, after years of living in hiding he was at last able to emerge and breathe fresh air. Ever since the Young Turks' revolution, Baydas had used his newspaper *Al-Nafais* to publish the Arab nationalists' demand that the Ottoman government set the Arab regions free. He published similar articles in the Egyptian journals *Al-Muqatam* and *Al-Ahram*, none of which endeared him to the Ottoman authorities. Baydas was also an ardent supporter of Sharif Hussein of Mecca. When Sharif Hussein called on all the national Arab movements to launch a *jihad* against the government in Istanbul in the summer of 1916, Baydas urged his students to join the revolt, and a company of Ottoman soldiers was sent to arrest him. The Husaynis, who had been careful to avoid being seen as collaborating with enemies of the empire – particularly since some members of the family were actually pro-empire – went out of their way to help him escape. This was due largely to the impassioned urging of young Raja'i, Said's son, whose favorite teacher was Khalil. Thanks to their intervention, Baydas managed to escape to the Orthodox Patriarchate and to the personal protection of Patriarch Damianos, who saved him from the hangman's noose. He remained in the patriarch's house until the eve of Allenby's assault.

But the battle for Jerusalem was not yet over. On 9 December, the Forty-fourth and Sixtieth Divisions of General Allenby's forces were encamped south and east of the city, blocking the roads to Nablus and Jericho. Their intelligence officers were still unaware that the last Ottoman soldier had left the city early in the morning – or, to put it another way, that the last Muslim soldier had quit the city that had been under Muslim rule since Saladin had defeated the crusaders.

But the Christian conquerors returning to the region seven centuries after the Crusaders seemed to be hanging back, and Hussein decided to go look for them. Was he thinking about the historical significance of the event? We do not know, but he probably sensed the fluttering wings of history. However, he was unable to summon a respectable delegation for the great occasion, and there was something ridiculous about the small group that went out to look for the general and offer their submission without a struggle. One of the women offered a white blouse as a flag of surrender, but the mayor thought it would not do to meet the new conquerors with a woman's garment. Better to use sheets, he thought, which were in plentiful supply at the Italian hospital. Two sheets were pulled off an empty bed, hastily stitched together and attached to a wooden plank on a flagpole to be carried by the surrendering delegation. They had never before used this European symbol of surrender – in their society, a white flag marked the residence of a marriageable virgin.

The question was, which way to go? They were afraid to turn east or south, because a heavy cannonade rumbled on those sides. The road to the plains looked peaceful, so they walked out of the Jaffa Gate and went looking for the conquerors. It was boring to wait for the historical moment and unseemly for the notables to wander about with the emblem of surrender, so they commandeered a young idler by the name of Hanna al-Laham, who found himself dragged into the history books through no fault of his own. He was seized by Jawad Ismail, the black sheep of Ismail's sons, a well-known bully who went about even in winter with his collar open to the bitter Jerusalem winds. Almost all the delegates were Husaynis. Two other members of the family joined them, and even little Burhan Tahir al-Husayni (grandson of Tahir II) insisted on coming along. The mayor agreed in the hope that the boy's presence would soften the hearts of the conquerors.

To solve the problem of communicating with the strangers, Hussein also took with him an interpreter of Swedish origin, a member of the Order of St John in the city who was employed by one of the consulates and had attended meetings of the city council. Though he made an important contribution to the occasion, his name was left out of all the reports, while that of the loafer al-Laham remains on record.

The delegates took with them the city's chief of police, Ahmad Sharaf, who in winter dressed like a Cossack in a short Russian coat and high boots, so that he looked like the delegates' bodyguard. Hussein also summoned his cousin Tawfiq (the son of Muhammad Salih al-Husayni) who was now a mustachioed man in his twenties. Tawfiq dressed carefully and in front of the camera put on the haughty expression of the Prince of Morocco, whom he had personified with panache on the stage of St George's School in 1908.

The strange procession was led by the mayor, leaning on his walking stick, his long overcoat billowing behind him, a cigarette in his right hand. He was not a regular smoker, but the solemnity of the occasion made him very tense. Finally, near the neighborhood of Sheikh Badr, on the edge of the village of Lifta (the modern-day main western entrance to the city on Route 1, which connects the city with Tel Aviv), they found what they had been looking for: the troops of His Britannic Majesty.

Sergeant Sidgewick and Sergeant Harcomb, two NCOs leading the scouts of the 219th Battalion of the London Division, which was approaching the city from the west, could not believe their eyes. A group of dignified *sheikhs* was calling to them in Arabic and Turkish, waving a white rag on a stick, while in their midst an elderly grandee held up a small parchment scroll. 'Who are you? What do you want?' Sidgewick shouted, but the answer came in Arabic, which he did not understand. 'Hey, don't any of you Johnnies speak English?' Hussein, who had lived in England and the United States, understood perfectly well but preferred not to reveal this fact. He told the Swedish interpreter to explain their mission. The two NCOs were flabbergasted. 'Good Lord, we can't accept the city's surrender!' they protested. They rejected Hussein's outstretched hand holding a symbolic key to the city, and said, 'You'll have to wait for an officer of His Majesty's forces.'

About midday an officer appeared and obtained Hussein's signature on a letter of surrender written on the back of a crumpled map. Fortunately for future generations, the Swede had a camera and he photographed the occasion. The result was a strange picture of officers and *sheikhs* looking surprised and embarrassed as twelve centuries of Muslim rule (if we discount the Crusaders' eighty years) came to an end.

Young Hanna al-Laham got tired and stuck the flagpole in the ground. Some time later a British officer spotted it and, realizing it was a priceless symbolic souvenir of the war for Palestine, took it for himself. In Jerusalem he met the Swedish interpreter, who persuaded him to hand it over, as he had witnessed the occasion. The Swede kept it for a while but a few weeks later was told to return it to the British forces. When he refused he was arrested. Finally the commander of the London Division persuaded him to give the bed sheets to General Allenby, who delivered them to the Imperial War Museum in London.[4]

British forces took Jerusalem on 9 December, and a few days later General Allenby entered the city. Emile al-Ghuri wrote that the general rode in on horseback, whereas Major Lock, who was present, said that he entered on foot. The commander's gesture of respect for the ancient, war-weary city was also photographed. The conquest of Jerusalem was the climax of the British forces' successful campaign and the beginning of the end of the Ottoman 'Operation Lightning'.

Earlier we noted that few foreign conquerors ever troubled themselves to include Jerusalem in their campaigns because it was strategically marginal.[5] Nor was it a major strategic objective in the Great War, though it was of tactical importance. Its conquest concluded the campaign in the Levant and greatly improved the British position in Iraq. All of the Ottoman reserve forces, which for three years had pinned down the allies in the swamps of southern Iraq, had to be withdrawn and sent to defend Damascus, the last jewel in the Ottoman imperial crown. But the principal value of the conquest of Jerusalem was the moral one: Lloyd George, presented the holy city as the latest acquisition of the British Empire in time for Christmas. A devout Christian, he thought this was the finest gift to the people and armed forces of the empire. But the best news would come almost a year later, when the Ottoman Empire signed the armistice agreement that led to the end of the war.

The conquest of Jerusalem was also of great political importance. A wartime agreement divided the Ottoman Empire's possessions in the eastern Arab world between Britain and France. According to this agreement, known as the Sykes–Picot Pact, the district of Jerusalem (and indeed most of Palestine) was to be an international enclave. But the physical presence of the British expeditionary and other military forces all over the country, including Jerusalem, enabled Britain to claim the entire territory for its own direct rule when discussions on the Sykes-Picot Pact were renewed in 1919.

Immediately after his arrival, Allenby summoned Mufti Kamil al-Husayni, Mayor Hussein al-Husayni, the heads of the Christian churches, the chief rabbi and many of the city's notables to meet him at the foot of the Citadel. Allenby stood on a large podium at the end of the sloping causeway leading to the Citadel gate, while the Jerusalemites were crammed into the three or four meters between the podium and the gate and had to spread along the Citadel wall. The first to speak at this uncomfortable encounter was Allenby's Arabic-language spokesman, General Jibril Pasha Haddad (a Lebanese-born officer who had served with the British forces in Sudan and had become Allenby's aide when the war broke out): 'To the townspeople of blessed Jerusalem and the surrounding inhabitants, the defeat my forces have inflicted on the Turks has led to the conquest of your city by my army ...'[6] These were his opening words. The tall general, his uniform dusty but his boots freshly polished, never moved a muscle throughout his spokesman's speech. Haddad explained that the city would be under martial law but that all religions would be respected. He concluded his short speech with a sentence that sparked the first disagreement with the Arabs: 'This is the end of the Crusaders' wars.'

Mufti Kamil al-Husayni jumped as if stung and took hold of the mayor; the two of them left the scene. They were joined by the Patriarch of the

Greek Orthodox Church and some of the city's notables. Had they been in England when the victory was celebrated, they would have been even more offended. On 12 January, at a thanksgiving service for the Order of St John, the Archbishop of York said, 'If London is the commercial heart of the empire, Jerusalem is its soul.'[7]

The *mufti* was called to a meeting with Haddad, who advised him to cooperate with the British and not to take Allenby's words too seriously, but the *mufti* remained unconvinced. 'Go and find someone else to cooperate with you,' he said. Afterwards he secluded himself at the house of one of his relatives and refused all contact with the British. They, however, kept courting him.

As early as February 1917, the Arab Bureau, a team of British Orientalists in Cairo whose best-known member was T. E. Lawrence, wrote a memorandum stating that the Husayni family 'is one of the oldest and most respected families in Palestine, headed by the Mufti Kamil, who is not a fanatic and is generally friendly to foreigners. He does not have a strong character, but this would make it easier for the British to control him.' However, Kamil was not the head of the family – Ismail and Said were its elders, and Hussein, as mayor, was also one of its heads. Only the death of Hussein in 1918, combined with the importance the British assigned to the post of *mufti*, made Kamil the head of the family.[8] The idea that he could be easily manipulated by the new conquerors was not quite borne out in reality, though by and large Kamil avoided unnecessary friction with the British. Given the position of the family and the posts of *mufti* and mayor that it held, it stood to reason that it would cooperate with the conquerors and even adopt a pro-British stance in public.

The new governor of Jerusalem, Ronald Storrs, spent three rainy days wandering about looking for the *mufti* and the mayor. At night in his room at the Morkos Hotel (which the Americans converted into a military hospital soon after the occupation), Storrs wrote that this walk at least persuaded his Egyptian valet Said that they had indeed arrived in Jerusalem. Until then his servant had been sure that it was Jaffa they had conquered, not Jerusalem.

On 21 December, Storrs located Mayor Hussein al-Husayni, the president of the city council. The dignified Hussein, who was in his fifties, surprised his visitor with his fluent English. He told Storrs that in the final years of Ottoman rule he had lived 'on his suitcases', because the Ottomans, aware of his pro-British sympathies, threatened to exile him.

They talked first about the holy city of Medina in Arabia. 'Has it already been taken?' Hussein asked. Storrs gave him the latest news and said that

T. E. Lawrence was doing his best to complete the task. Then Storrs asked how many Muslim inhabitants there were in Jerusalem. 'Eleven thousand,' said Hussein, adding that the majority belonged to the Hanafi school, which had been predominant in the Ottoman Empire, and a minority to the Shafi'i school, which had been customary before the Ottoman conquest. The Husaynis held the post of Hanafi *mufti*, the only one approved by the Ottoman religious authorities. Storrs made a note of this information and advised his government to declare that this would be the only recognized post of *mufti*.[9]

After this visit, Hussein sent a messenger to his cousin the *mufti* to inform him that Storrs would call on him the following morning. The mayor died a few weeks later, and Storrs was asked to appoint his successor. As we have seen, the Ottomans sometimes appointed the mayor and at other times allowed the city's notables to elect him. The Young Turks were going to institute mayoral elections, but this democratization was halted by the martial law imposed on Palestine by the British authorities. It was simpler to appoint the mayor and so, following the old custom, they appointed a kinsman of the deceased mayor – his older brother, Musa Kazim al-Husayni.

Thus ended Hussein al-Husayni's presence on the stage of Jerusalem's history. He was a remarkable man and was liked by all – the Jews (who had helped elect him), the Christians (whose demands he generally met and whose internal conflicts he arbitrated) and of course the Muslims. Foreigners in the city also enjoyed the company of Hussein, who had been educated in the United States and was broadly conversant with both Arab and Western cultures. But the generation that had reached maturity in the last years of the Ottoman Empire, that had received a mixed Ottoman and Western education and worked in the local and imperial administration, had other prominent representatives, notably the *mufti* of Jerusalem, Kamil al-Husayni.

The day after meeting the mayor, Ronald Storrs went to the Temple Mount to meet Mufti Kamil for the first time. The rain had stopped and the sun warmed the governor and his servant Said as they crossed the great plaza between the magnificent Dome of the Rock and al-Aqsa mosque and entered the *mufti*'s office. They found him sitting in a modest, spotless room behind a long table. The *sheikh* was then forty-five years old, a gentle, soft-spoken man and a pleasant conversationalist. He and Storrs at once found a common interest – Egypt, where Storrs had recently spent several happy years and where Kamil in his youth had studied at al-Azhar for four years. Kamil missed the newspapers of Cairo, above all *Al-Muqatam*. When Storrs promised to obtain for him the previous month's issues, as well as publications in French – Kamil's favorite language – his face lit up.

Now and then as they sat there, messengers came in to receive written *fatwas* on everyday matters. Storrs was impressed by how quietly the *mufti's* subordinates and aides came and went. Finally, the *mufti* complained to the visitor that since the war his budget and that of the religious properties were insufficient for him to pay his staff of seventy. Storrs promised to help out.

And so, after an awkward start, Kamil al-Husayni became a favorite of the British authorities, who came to trust and rely upon him. The family itself was astonished by the number of posts he was granted. First, he was made the Grand Mufti – *al-Mufti al-Akbar*. No longer was he the *mufti* of one school but of all Muslims, and not only of Jerusalem but of all Palestine. This was an idea hatched by the British officials in Egypt. There the religious hierarchy was headed by the Grand *Mufti* of Egypt and had been even when the country was under Ottoman rule. In addition, Kamil was appointed head of the Shari'a court of appeal – which had traditionally been held by a member of the Khalidi clan – and guardian of all Muslim religious properties in the city. These added positions brought Kamil not only greater honor and social standing but also a substantial salary.[10]

The family had grown very powerful in the final years of the Ottoman period and had become one of the country's greatest landowners, possessing over 12,500 acres throughout the country. Rabah was the wealthiest Husayni, owning lands in various villages around Jericho, on Qastel Hill near Jerusalem and even on the inland plains.[11] The new posts given to members of the family assured even greater wealth, and with it a formidable political position *vis-à-vis* the local population and the authorities. Political power entailed social, and perhaps national, responsibility. But the transition to national authority would not always deal kindly with the family or with the society it was supposed to represent. And yet no one offered else better leadership at the time, and were it not for the Zionist presence, history's overall judgment of the family would have been much more favorable.

In his memoirs, Storrs notes that the guiding principle of the British authorities in Jerusalem was to maintain the status quo. They left the existing institutions and their composition untouched. Thus, for example, the municipality remained predominantly Muslim, and the Church of the Holy Sepulchre was left in the care of the Nashashibis. Of course, the occupier was not that passive and eventually took more invasive steps. It began with effecting changes in municipal functions – sanitation, public order, road

maintenance, repair of war damages – putting the city on its feet and ultimately changing the country's identity and politics altogether.

The Husaynis had not enjoyed such economic, social and political power
since the final years of Abdul Hamid II's reign. Storrs acceded to Kamil's
request to look after his younger brother, al-Hajj Amin, and attached him
to the staff of General Jibril Haddad, who was about to be put in charge of
security in Damascus.

Al-Hajj Amin had not been unemployed – he ran the Rawdat al-Ma'arif
(owned by Khalil Sakakini and cofounded in 1906 by another member of
the family, Abd al-Latif III) – but his older brother knew he had greater
things in mind. At this school, and at the secondary school *al-Rashidiya*,
al-Hajj Amin taught the history of Islam in a modern form that fitted the
spirit of national Arab education. In the early days of British rule, he had
the means to purchase the Rawdat al-Ma'arif. Al-Hajj Amin also earned
money writing articles for the journal of his friend and partner in national
dreams, Arif al-Arif, who would later become a leading Palestinian historian.
Together they followed a path from traditional Islamic thought to concrete
political thought.

It was Arif al-Arif who introduced al-Hajj Amin to Syrian politics in the
final stages of the Great War. In late 1918, Faysal, the son of Sharif Hussein
of Mecca, established himself in Damascus. According to Faysal's Hashemi
family, the British had promised them Greater Syria in return for their
uprising against the Ottoman Empire. (This is confirmed by the correspondence between Sharif Hussein and British representatives in late 1915.) T. E.
Lawrence interpreted the agreement between Hussein and McMahon in the
same light, and persuaded General Allenby to install Faysal as military ruler
of Syria on behalf of the Allies. Some historians claim that Lawrence also
stage-managed the conquest of Damascus as a great Hashemi victory, though
it was Australian troops, rather than Faysal's men, who actually conquered
the Syrian capital.[12]

However it was achieved, Faysal's presence was essential to countering the
French claim to Syria. Syria had in fact been promised to the French in the
summer of 1916 under the Sykes-Picot Pact. Faysal hoped to forestall British
compliance with the agreement by establishing an independent kingdom
including Syria, Transjordan, Lebanon and Palestine. Directed by Faysal's
Damascus government – which lasted two years, until 1920 – Arif al-Arif
referred to the three Ottoman districts of Mandatory Palestine as 'Southern
Syria'. This was also the name of his journal, in which al-Hajj Amin published
his early political ideas.

But al-Hajj Amin wanted more. Thanks to his brother's relationship
with Storrs, he realized his great dream of serving in Damascus at the side
of Faysal, who declared himself King of Greater Syria. As noted, Storrs got
al-Hajj Amin appointed as aide to Haddad when he took up his new post as
chief of general security. Amin used his stay in Damascus to establish close
relations with his hero Faysal and his court. In 1919 he helped organize an
all-Syria congress, a conference of representatives from the entire region, to
demonstrate to the world its support for Faysal's rule. Al-Hajj Amin's job
was to organize the delegation from the district of Palestine, which he did
very well.

This was an important stage in the politics of the region and the world.
Faysal was trying to form a new kingdom in the face of local and regional
forces, while preparing for the peace conference that was about to meet in
Versailles to determine political arrangements in all of the countries where the

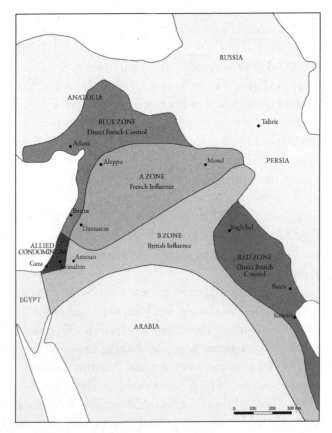

*Sykes–Picot Agreement, 1916*

war had been fought. Keeping with American President Woodrow Wilson's ideas of self-determination, the ten victorious nations, including the Hijaz (the independent kingdom established by Sharif Hussein in 1916), decided that the arrangements should consider the wishes of the local population. Later we shall see how the colonial powers dealt with this difficult principle.

Like any politically aware person in Palestine, al-Hajj Amin realized the importance of sending a Palestinian delegation to the conference. However, to do this in an international forum, it was necessary to create, almost from nothing, a local organization that could claim to represent the wishes of the native population. While it was obvious that only the notable families would take part, it was imperative to achieve a consensus among them regarding the Palestinian position.

Al-Hajj Amin stayed only a short time in Damascus because Haddad was dispatched by Faysal to London and his successor, Ahmad Lahon, did not keep al-Hajj Amin on. The young Husayni returned to Jerusalem and gradually built up his position as head of the family, and the idea of 'Southern Syria' was replaced with that of 'Independent Palestine'.

With his Damascus career at an end, al-Hajj Amin turned his attention to Zionism. In later years, he would claim that the question of how to stop Zionist settlement had preoccupied him since boyhood. But as noted in the previous chapter, it was only in Cairo that he had begun to think of Zionism as an enemy. Al-Hajj Amin's brief stay in Damascus prepared him not only to become an inspiration in the struggle against Zionism, but above all to be the first of the Husaynis to enter the modern politics that developed in the Arab world after the Great War. Although other young Husaynis studied the intricacies of local and regional *siyasa* (politics), al-Hajj Amin was the most skillful, and his talent enabled the family to translate its social standing into modern terms of political parties and organizations.

Many family members did not adjust to the change and chose other modern careers: Ishaq Musa al-Husayni chose literature, Ibrahim Said (brother of Raja'i) chemistry; Abd al-Salam III (great-grandson of Umar) became a journalist and essayist, Salim III an archaeologist and Musa Abdullah (another son of Musa Salih) a historiographer. Thus, despite the temptation to go into modern politics, Hassan's scholarly bent, Tahir's curiosity and Ismail's studiousness were passed on to the family's intellectual branch.[13] But before this division occurred in the family – after centuries of representing the local aristocracy – all the inhabitants of Palestine, Jews and Arabs alike, had to adjust to the new British military occupation (1918–20) that was forced upon them.

Having conquered the country, the British authorities did not assume legislative powers but administered it in accordance with the laws of its previous overlords. There was no civil law or judiciary, only the decision of the military governor (three army generals held this post in those two years: Mooney, Watson and Bowles) or of the local military governor (for example, Ronald Storrs in Jerusalem). The British were chiefly concerned with improving the infrastructure. The homes of the Husaynis and other Jerusalem notables were linked for the first time to modern sewerage and water supply systems. The city's main streets were cleaned once a week, and public sanitation reduced the death rate, which delighted tourists, many of whom had been to Jerusalem in the past and were returning after the war.[14]

Maintaining the status quo was not an easy matter, given the conflicting British promises regarding the future of Palestine. Would it become part of Greater Syria? Or would it become a 'Jewish national home', as implied by the Balfour Declaration of 2 November 1917? A year later a new declaration stirred the anxieties of political activists in Jerusalem and elsewhere about the future of Palestine. On 8 November 1918, the governments of Britain and France proclaimed the right of the peoples of Iraq and Syria to self-determination, but they excluded Palestine, probably because of the Balfour Declaration.[15]

It is important to distinguish between people's preoccupation with the problems of their daily lives and their concerns about the great issues of the day. Palestinian leaders were not always aware of the rapid pace of political developments that would affect their country's future. In this, they were at a clear disadvantage compared to their Zionist opponents who, with an energy and decisiveness that astounded the colonial officials, harnessed every possible act to help fulfill the Zionist dream. Kamil al-Husayni witnessed this himself.

On 27 April 1918, a few months after the British occupation began, Kamil and the leaders of all the other communities of Jerusalem were invited to a garden party at the house of Governor Ronald Storrs. At this time a delegation from the Zionist Congress led by Menahem Ussishkin was permitted by the military authorities to come to Palestine, tour the country and study the prospects of laying the groundwork for the 'Jewish national home'. Ussishkin was the paragon of the new Zionist leader. Unlike some of his colleagues, he openly discussed Zionism as a colonialist project and declared on more than one occasion that any indigenous resistance to the Jewish colonization of Palestine would have to be met with force, coercion and even expulsion. One doubts how much of this Kamil knew, but he did go to Storrs's meeting willingly and was curious to hear what this Jewish leader, whom he had never met, would have to say. To his dismay, the Zionist spokesman expressed support for the united Arab kingdom but without recognizing Palestine as part of it. Rather, he went on at length about Jewish plans for the development of the country and the joy of the people of Zion at the return of the Jews. Kamil stood up and was about to leave.[16] He was persuaded to stay, though, and heard a milder statement from Chaim Weizmann, who said that the Zionists had no intention of taking over the country. In time, Palestinians would prefer the direct approach of the future Ussishkins and find it hard to confront the doubletalk and dishonesty of the future Weizmanns. At the meeting, Kamil responded with a measured, noncommittal statement. Weizmann later wrote in his diary that Kamil had been polite but disbelieving – and for good reason.[17]

Perhaps it was this occasion that prompted the younger Husaynis to organize the struggle against the implementation of the Balfour Declaration. Or it may be that they wished to help Faysal resist the French effort to dislodge him from Syria. These young men were not content with symbolic gestures, and they began to prepare for national action. Yet they tended to occupy themselves with minor matters, unlike the Jews, who were laying the foundation of their state. Al-Hajj Amin, twenty-one years old and with unusually red hair and deep blue eyes, was the spirit of the young Palestinians' movement. When they formed an active organization called 'The Arab Club' – named after the famous club in Damascus where al-Hajj Amin had stayed with Faysal's entourage during the Arab Revolt – they chose al-Hajj Amin as its president. This was not al-Hajj Amin's only occupation. After his return from Damascus, he remained loyal to Faysal's government and obeyed its instruction to join the British administration, which made him an official in the town of Qalqiliyah. Damascus's secret directive was to use this post to recruit young Palestinians for Faysal's army to counter a possible French invasion of Syria.[18]

Al-Hajj Amin's closest friends were his brother Fakhri and his cousins Jamil, Ibrahim, Said, Hilmi and Tawfiq. They were joined by Ishaq Darwish and Muhammad al-Afifi, who were related by marriage to the Husaynis. Tawfiq was known for his community work – he opened and ran an orphanage in Jerusalem, an institution that still symbolizes the Husayni family's social commitment. But the principal activities of the Arab Club were political rather than social, and its members hoped that the British authorities would allow it to function as a literary-political association supporting the union of Palestine and Syria and opposing the expansion of the Jewish presence.

The mentor of the group was Sheikh Abd al-Qadir al-Muzafir, an activist of the Arab national movement during the war who had been deported for his activities. (As mentioned in the previous chapter, al-Muzafir was also an unexpected guest at the first and only collaborative meeting between the Zionists and the Husaynis.)

The young Nashashibis, however, had no use for the Hashemi Amir or Damascus, and they joined the rival Literary Club to demonstrate their different political position. They were a relatively new presence on the Jerusalem stage, and it had taken the earthquake effect of the Young Turks' revolution to translate their economic power into political power. The year 1908 had been especially important for Suleiman al-Nashashibi and his sons Rashid and Uthman, who represented a transition in the family's career as it became an influential social-political factor after the advent of the Young Turks. In later years, however, they would not constitute a substantial political force: at the end of the British Mandate, when the political vacuum offered an opportunity for action, they would have neither the power nor the drive to lead the Palestinian people. But in the period under discussion, the two families were on friendly terms, especially since Jamil al-Husayni was one of the leading members of the rival club, which was named after the famous literary club in Istanbul that he had been part of in 1909. During the course of that year, several Husaynis, including Fakhri, joined both clubs.

In the beginning members of the Arab Club were content to paint the slogans 'Our Land Is Ours' and 'Palestine Is Southern Syria' (that is, part of the Kingdom of Greater Syria to be ruled by King Faysal). Later they organized petitions and even enlisted some of the city's notables to support their activities. The famous six of St George's School – Hilmi, Fakhri, Ibrahim, Tawfiq, Said and Jamal – formed the core of this organization. Those who had got safely through the war, even in the Ottoman army, tended to follow the ideas and activities of the *mufti*'s younger brother al-Hajj Amin and the leadership of Musa Kazim, who became mayor after Hussein's death. In 1918 the older activists included such experienced figures as Bullus Shehadeh, Yusuf Yasin and Hassan Abu al-Saud, whom the younger men described as the leaders of the Arab Club. Some time later they joined the Husaynis, not because of family connections but because they supported the positions taken by Musa Kazim, Jamal and Amin al-Husayni on the future of Palestine. Joining a group for ideological reasons was a novel feature in the lives of Palestinian notables.

Political restlessness was not confined to Jerusalem: young people and notables in other cities and towns sought to help the national movement and even to lead it. On 8 May 1918, a group of prominent Jaffa townsmen, both Christian and Muslim, met in a café to revive the idea of the three teachers who had met at Anaste's café (see the previous chapter) and created Jaffa's Muslim-Christian Association. This was the first time an association was formed on the basis of national rather than religious solidarity. Such ideas had been proposed in the past but never taken shape, and now the Jaffaite al-Hajj Raghib al-Dajani and his Christian friends brought it off. In November 1918, a branch of this association opened in Jerusalem, and before long branches appeared all over Palestine. In January 1919, the first general conference of all the Muslim-Christian Associations was held in Jerusalem. To give it an all-Palestine stature, the organizers invited the associations of the young Jerusalemites, and indeed the event came to be known as 'the first Palestinian Congress' after they decided to hold it every year.

Other political meetings took place in Jaffa in May 1918. At al-Hajj Amin's request, or at least with his approval, some young men from Jaffa formed an underground group that they called 'The Black Hand'. They later chose a new name that would become a national Palestinian label: *al-Fida'iyya* ('The Self-Sacrificers'). It set up branches all over the country and served al-Hajj Amin as the operative arm of the national organization. (It would be disbanded in 1923 and replaced by rather ineffectual attempts to create a more orderly Palestinian fighting body.[19] But at this point, the group's work was principally channeled towards the first conference in Jerusalem.)

The first Palestinian Congress opened in Jerusalem on 27 January 1919 and lasted about a week. Twenty-seven delegates from all over the country attended. Arif al-Dajani, founder of the Muslim-Christian Association in Jaffa, presided over the conference, and the retired judge Hassan Abu al-Saud was his deputy.[20]

Organizing this conference had not been an easy matter. Before it got under way, a sharp dispute broke out between the 'unionists' supporting unification with Syria and those who favored a struggle for independence within British Palestine. The most prominent unionists were the Husaynis – Fakhri and al-Hajj Amin, who benefited from Khalil al-Sakakini's sound advice. Since the attempts to create a unified kingdom with Syria were backed by an orderly political party, and since most of the leading members of the family were part of it, the family became the strongest player in the new political arena delineated by the British authorities and the Zionists in Mandatory Palestine. It was no longer sufficient to be an Ashraf family or to hold a senior religious post – if the Husaynis did not wish to abandon the field to other families or political factors, they needed a modern political organization with national and patriotic platforms.

Al-Hajj Amin was a prominent and active unionist, and he devoted most of his energies to persuading Jerusalem's Muslim-Christian Association to support union with Syria.[21] As we have seen, the first Palestinian Congress was convened not only in response to the Balfour Declaration but as the first political attempt to present the Palestinian position in public. Besides al-Hajj Amin, many others were active behind the scenes – indeed, it is doubtful that al-Hajj Amin was the chief player or even the leading Husayni activist at that first conference. The young Husaynis very skillfully persuaded some of the leading delegates, such as Sheikh Said al-Karmi, Isa al-Isa and Izzat Darwaza, to ensure that the resolutions would conform to the idea of unity with Syria. Al-Hajj Amin proposed allowing the opposition to present its argument, which called for the destiny of Palestine to be separate from that of Greater Syria. He argued that only by hearing both arguments could the participants weigh the two platforms and discover the weakness of the pro-Palestine idea. As we shall see, the time would come when he would adopt his opponents' position.

All the delegates were pleased to see the family's patriarch, the revered Ismail Bey, whose aristocratic presence imparted dignity to the gathering and gave the family a certain influence over the proceedings. The British, too, respected Ismail and acknowledged his fine record by putting him in charge of education in Jerusalem, and he repaid them by adopting a pro-British posture. His attendance at the conference was not wholehearted, and he disapproved of many of the young men's actions. While he did not voice his true opinions at the conference, many of the delegates were aware that he disliked the idea of Greater Syria and was hoping to see the creation of an Arab Palestine. Nor did he support aggressive action against Zionism. Having entertained Chaim Weizmann at his house, Ismail believed it was possible to come to an understanding with the Zionist movement, though he did not dare say so in public.[22]

Despite Ismail's attendance, the family had yet to reach a dominant position in the political arena. The Husaynis were conspicuously absent from the petition sent by the conference to the Paris Peace Conference, though they undoubtedly helped to formulate it. The petition read:

> We, inhabitants of all Palestine, consisting of the Arab districts of Jerusalem, Nablus and Acre, Muslims and Christians alike, have met and chosen our representatives at the conference in Jerusalem ... Before any

discussion takes place on the problem of Palestine, we wish to express
our strong protest against the promise given to the Zionists to establish
a national home in our native land and to migrate to this country and
settle in it.[23]

The petition's authors went on to note that they represented the absolute
majority of the people of Palestine.

The Husaynis took no part in other decisions of the conference. At the
end of the discussions, the conference resolved to send two delegations to
promote the Palestinian cause in world opinion: one to Paris and another
to Damascus. There were no Husaynis in the more important of the two,
the delegation to Paris; in any event, the occupying authorities stopped it
from leaving. But even the lesser mission to Damascus did not include any
of the Husaynis. Mufti Kamil and Mayor Musa Kazim were puzzled by their
younger relatives' frustration that no member of their family was elected
to a representative post. How significant were places in such delegations
compared with an ancient honor like that of *mufti* or the influential post of
mayor? Time would show that al-Hajj Amin was right: a new era had begun,
and the game had new rules.

It was not the military governor's decision to prevent the Palestinians
from presenting their case before the international peace conference that
excluded any significant development in this direction. It was a change in
American posture that froze any genuine attempts to reconsider Palestine's
fate. Had it been up to the American delegation, all the nations and groupings formerly ruled by the Ottoman Empire would have been invited to
address the conference and express their wishes. But the ailing Democratic
US President Wilson was unable to contend with the colonial powers because
the Republican-dominated US Congress was eager to resume America's
prewar isolationism. Thus the two aging colonial empires of Britain and
France, whose time would come before long, were left free to carve up the
defeated Ottoman Empire. Their governments had no intention of allowing
local representatives to appear before the conference and present agendas
different from those decided upon in London and Paris. It was none of the
local people's business, said British Prime Minister Lloyd George; Georges
Clemenceau, who was even less attentive to such wishes from below, readily
agreed. The two powers had divided the region between them as far back as
May 1916, before anyone knew the outcome of the war. Now that they were
in power, they certainly had no intention of letting anyone else have their

say. Zionism, however, being the colonialists' ally, was allowed to appear and make its case before the world.

Nevertheless, there were some in the British Colonial Office and Parliament who viewed the emerging Arab national movement favorably, as a process that might benefit Britain. The famous historian Arnold Toynbee provided them with a metahistorical theory to justify British support for Arab nationalism, which he considered to be a new and youthful phenomenon, rather than for Jewry, which he argued would disappear from history like the colonial empire. But on the whole, support for the Arabs was neither metaphysical, as proposed by Toynbee, nor romantic, *à la* Lawrence of Arabia, but a pragmatic commitment to the interests of the British Empire. In Egypt in 1919, the British refusal to permit local Arab views to be heard by the international forum produced a national revolution and resulted in the creation of the Wafd ('New Delegation') Party – named after the group of Egyptian representatives whom the British barred from traveling to Versailles, as they did in Palestine. The term became synonymous with concepts like 'homeland', 'people' and 'nation'. The Wafd was the dominant party in Egypt until Nasser came to power. It fought against the British presence in Egypt and laid the groundwork for the independent state of Egypt, which would influence the entire Arab world.

Barred from sending a delegation, the Palestinians used the old method of bombarding the participants at the conference with petitions and protests, each town and city sending its own. They had no other choice, given that the Zionists had a very respectable representation at Versailles, led by the skilled diplomat Chaim Weizmann. The brief appearance of King Faysal of Syria in Versailles provided some balance, but only the Americans were moved by such minor spokesmen on the conference floor. The leaders of the old colonial delegations scarcely noticed them and did not give much thought to non-imperial arguments.

Not everyone despaired when the Palestinian delegation was barred from leaving; nor was everyone content with sending petitions. In March 1919, directly after the first Palestinian Congress, the Muslim-Christian Association and the Arab Club decided to act. The dynamic al-Hajj Amin inspired their initiative. He had heard from his brother the *mufti* that the governor of Jerusalem was due to go to Egypt at the end of the month and that before leaving he would advise the Palestinians to hold a protest demonstration against the Zionists. Kamil and Musa Kazim spread a rumor that Storrs had asked that the demonstration be held in his absence, so that he would not be blamed if things got out of hand. Al-Hajj Amin convened the members of his club to discuss the matter and deplored the fact that 'since the Balfour Declaration there has not been a single demonstration against Zionism'.

But not everyone was ready to take such a risk. Al-Hajj Amin's former teacher Khalil al-Sakakini and his cousin Yaqub Faraj poured cold water on the eager young leader and persuaded him that Storrs was playing a dangerous game and could not be counted on to support them if they were charged with organizing a demonstration that turned violent. Sakakini noted in his diary that nobody liked Storrs: because of his close association with the Husaynis, he listened to no one else. This seems somewhat unjust, since at this time Sakakini was in the Husayni camp, but perhaps he was uneasy about the close friendship between Mufti Kamil and the British governor. Sakakini preferred the personality and the interests of Storrs's deputy, Waters-Taylor, and suspected that if there were a demonstration, the governor would blame his deputy and have him dismissed.[24]

The eyes of the world were on the Hall of Mirrors in the Palace of Versailles near Paris. On 18 January 1919, representatives of the ten victorious powers, led by US President Woodrow Wilson, met there to explore ways to avoid another catastrophe like the one that had ravaged Europe, in which 8 million soldiers and some 25 million civilians had lost their lives. But behind the humane concern for peace lurked the old ambitions of the European powers to help themselves to great chunks of the defeated Austro-Hungarian, German and Ottoman Empires. The future of the Middle East was, naturally, among the secondary issues that lay before the conference – the primary ones were the future of Germany, Poland and the Balkans, as well as the economic and military arrangements for running the new world projected by President Wilson. Since Russia quit the war and was caught up in civil strife, Britain and France remained the dominant parties with interests in the Middle Eastern territories of the erstwhile Ottoman Empire. This time the American president demanded that, in contrast to the Sykes–Picot Pact, the future agreement should have international backing; moreover, he wanted to hear the demands of nations in the region or their representatives.

The Zionist movement had prepared well for the dramatic diplomatic show. Its leadership, headed by Chaim Weizmann, had not been carried away with optimism as had the American Zionists, who believed that all the problems would now be resolved and the 'return' of the Jews to their ancient homeland was assured. Weizmann and his associations were pleased by the encouraging developments since the Balfour Declaration but considered the Paris Peace Conference to be the beginning of the struggle rather than its conclusion. The first step was to send a Zionist committee to Jerusalem to accelerate the construction of a 'national home'. But here they ran into the cautious Governor Storrs, whom they regarded as anti-Zionist because he opposed some of their more far-reaching proposals. They had to content themselves with establishing a foothold while getting ready for the peace conference.

Sir Herbert Samuel – later the first British high commissioner in Mandatory Palestine – chaired an advisory committee to help the Zionist leadership prepare for the conference. Together they crafted a demand for the Balfour Declaration to be implemented in every possible way by the British military, and later civil, authority in Palestine. The text of the demand was presented to the conference on 23 February 1919. The Palestinians' demand had been sent to the conference a few days earlier, but no Palestinian Arab was called upon to present their case, and it is not known if anyone at Versailles even read the document. However, Nahum Sokolov, spokesman of the Zionist leadership, was allowed to address the Council of Ten, and it is known that Lord Balfour, Britain's representative on the council, listened most attentively, as did the other council members.

Sokolov outlined the historical reasons for the Jewish demand and stressed that there was no solution to the problems of the Jews of Europe other than the Zionist one. Weizmann later noted that Sokolov had spoken 'as if the suffering of two thousand years of exile rested on his shoulders'. One doubts that this was what impressed Balfour; it was more the option of Britain avoiding the mass immigration of poor Eastern European Jews that delighted him. Balfour himself spoke after Sokolov and suggested that the Jews' economic distress could be resolved only in the framework of a 'national home' in Palestine. They were not the only Jewish spokesmen to address the conference. They were followed by Menahem Ussishkin and André Spire, who upheld the same ideas.

Only one person, a French Jew by name of Sylvain Lévi, was allowed to present an anti-Zionist Jewish position. Lévi's statement put a crimp in the impressive Zionist presentation, but the American foreign secretary broke the rules and gave Chaim Weizmann the floor for the second time to make a resounding conclusion to a most effective Zionist public relations campaign. At this time, Weizmann also persuaded King Faysal of Syria to express some support for Zionism, arguing that this would enable the Jews to use their influence with the Americans and others to pressure the British government to keep its promise to the Hashemites. Faysal soon abandoned his recognition of the Balfour Declaration and his brief cooperation with Weizmann, but his support was sufficient to weaken the Palestinian position in the peace conference even further.

Thus not a single Palestinian representative appeared before this very important international conference, both because of internal dissent and British obstruction. The Husaynis, though still the leading political force in the country, were denied both a place on the international stage and the experience that comes with it. As the struggle continued to rage not only on the ground but also in diplomatic arenas, this inexperience would undermine their effectiveness. Weizmann was able to pilot the Zionist vessel through the rocks of high-level international politics, while the young Husaynis struggled through internal disputes.

Fortunately for the Palestinians, when the Americans realized that they could not persuade their European allies to let the nations of the Middle East present their cases, they decided to send a mission to the region. Once discussions in Jerusalem ended, the Palestinians heard that an American team would tour Greater Syria to investigate the wishes of its inhabitants. (It was first proposed that the mission include British and French experts, but again London and Paris took no interest in the matter.) President Wilson himself appointed the team's leaders: Dr Henry King was President of Oberlin College, and Charles Crane was a trustee at Roberts College in Istanbul (later Boğaziçi University) and a businessman well-connected with many of the regional leaders.

News of the forthcoming visit caused a flurry in Damascus. Amir Faysal, who still governed on behalf of the Allies but was determined to become King of Greater Syria, hoped to convince the visitors that the populations of Lebanon, Syria, Transjordan and Palestine all wished to be united under his rule. He therefore urged all the secret national associations that had proliferated under Ottoman rule in Damascus and other cities to unite into a single party, the Arab Independence Party (Istiqlal), which would take part in parliamentary elections and call for the unity and independence of Greater Syria, if necessary under the overlordship of a mandatory power.[25]

The idea of a mandate was present before the Paris Peace Conference was convened. Several American experts introduced it to President Wilson as the best compromise between independence for the Arab nations, as demanded by their leaders, and colonial rule, as requested by Britain and France. The mandate would be granted by the League of Nations – the supranational organization conceived by Wilson as the principal bulwark against another world war and as means to settle international disputes – for a limited period, during which the mandatory power would guide the state it administered towards full independence. Upon hearing about it for the first time during his visit to Versailles, Faysal found the idea of a mandate acceptable, but only if it were American or British. Under no circumstances would he agree to a French mandate, although according to the terms of the Sykes-Picot Pact, Syria and Lebanon were designated France's sphere of influence. It was this impasse that eventually led to the removal of the Hijazi amir from Damascus and destroyed the prospect of a Greater Syria.[26]

In the middle of 1919, al-Hajj Amin was still the family's leading radical. First he helped set up Palestinian representation in Damascus to support Faysal's peace conference demands, then he worked hard in Jerusalem to achieve a coherent Palestinian stance in favor of unification with Syria. But in this he differed from the rest of the family. His kinsmen Jamal and Said had not yet formed a clear opinion either on Syria or – in contrast to Ismail – on Zionism.

Jamal and Said made efforts to understand Zionism's direction and impact. They met Haim Kalvarisky, a Zionist mystery man and something of a charlatan, who expressed support for a bi-national solution while remaining strongly associated with the Zionist leadership. Unlike other Jewish friends of the family, such as Gad Frumkin, Kalvarisky was widely known as a man of intrigue, and everyone had heard the story of his meetings with Jamal Pasha, the Ottoman governor during the war. 'Kalvarisky,' the governor had said, 'one day I'll see you hanging from the gallows.' 'No doubt, your highness,' Kalvarisky had replied, 'but first I'll sell you the rope.'[27]

Despite his dubious reputation, Kalvarisky's ideas were sometimes surprisingly well received. In mid-May he persuaded Said and Jamal and their close associates Salim Ayub and Bhajat al-Nashashibi to take part in a meeting aimed at creating a permanent apparatus for joint arbitration between the Zionist movement and the traditional Palestinian leadership on inter-communal problems in the Jerusalem area. Kalvarisky was hoping to persuade these families to act against the Muslim-Christian Association, and when young al-Hajj Amin heard this he was furious. Each of the four participants received an anonymous letter signed 'The leading young Arab men in Jerusalem', warning that if they continued to meet Kalvarisky they would be regarded as traitors and collaborators with Zionism. The letter concluded on an ominous note, saying that 'peaceful people might resort to violent actions in the face of such behavior'. Most of the family concluded that the negotiators of the Zionist peace camp were insincere, and those who did not think so, such as Fawzi al-Husayni (about whom more will be said later), would pay with their lives. The national cause demanded obedience to the family leadership, something that had been unheard-of in previous generations. Tradition, Ottoman politics and existential needs had always obliged the family to adopt a joint policy based on internal understanding and consent, not on violence. Nationalism was less tolerant and much more ruthless.[28]

On 7 June 1919, Faysal convened a Greater Syria conference at the Arab Club in Damascus and invited Palestinian representatives. Though the occupying authorities barred Palestinian participation in such pan-Arab gatherings, since they could not prevent individuals from traveling to Damascus certain Palestinians were appointed to key positions in Faysal's administration. Izzat Darwaza was appointed secretary of the congress, Awni Abd al-Hadi personal secretary to the king. The Husaynis were offered a higher post than they had expected: Said was chosen to be the kingdom's foreign minister. But the ailing fifty-nine-year-old Said was unable to leave his house in Jerusalem, and so Abd al-Hadi received this post too. Amin Tamimi was appointed adviser to Faysal's prime minister, and several other Palestinians were placed in senior positions because Faysal appreciated their abilities. There were also many Palestinians in the leadership of Faysal's Istiqlal Party – for example, three of the eight members of the executive committee.[29]

Faysal instructed his people to tell the King-Crane mission they wanted unity, independence and, if possible, an American or British mandate. While Damascus was preparing to receive the mission, the Palestinians had to be ready for it because they were the American observers' first stop. On 4 April 1919, Governor Storrs invited al-Hajj Amin and Khalil al-Sakakini to his office and informed them that the American mission would arrive in the summer. The next week was spent in intense discussions at Sakakini's house about how to present the Palestinian case to the Americans. The sitting room was too small to contain all the individuals who wished to express their views. A group of Nablus notables took part in one of these meetings, and eventually the unelected young leadership of the emergent Palestinian nationalists had to decide how to respond to the international poll on the future of Palestine. Unable to reach an agreement, they decided to consult Ismail al-Husayni. They took a carriage from Sakakini's Silk House to Ismail's residence. The fact that the crucial decision-making meetings took place at the house of the head of their family assured many Husaynis that, despite the dramatic reversals caused by the Great War, they were still center stage, or had returned to it after the upheaval.[30]

Musa Kazim and the heads of other families also attended the consultation, and the presence of these veterans enabled the young men to create a solid Palestinian position. In this house, which later served the Palestinian leadership from the First Intifada in 1987 until the outbreak of the second in 2000, they resolved that the Arabs of Palestine would join the call for an independent Greater Syria while preserving Palestinian autonomy and opposing Jewish immigration.

The declaration presented to the American observers was drafted with the help of Kamil, Said and al-Hajj Amin, and read:

> Syria, from the Taurus Mountains to the Suez Canal, is absolutely independent and part of the overall Arab unity. Palestine, being an integral part of Syria, is independent in domestic matters and will choose its own rulers from among its inhabitants. The people of Palestine are utterly opposed to Zionist immigration and aspirations, but recognize that the Jews who were in the country before the war have the same rights as the local inhabitants.[31]

In view of the preparations for the Greater Syrian Parliament, they decided to hold another nationwide conference of all the Muslim-Christian Associations as a kind of parliament that would give legal validity to the Palestinian position on the country's future. For the second time in a matter of months, a general gathering of these associations met on May 24 and confirmed the above resolutions verbatim.

The King–Crane mission was received warmly when it arrived in the summer. The United States was believed to be the great friend of the Arab cause, and the presence of the president's personal envoys awakened hope that it might still be possible to turn the clock back and undo the Balfour Declaration. Wherever the Americans went they were met by enthusiastic young Palestinians, members of the Arab and Literary Clubs and other organizations. The mission called at thirteen locations, and at each of them delegations from the surrounding villages awaited them.

The fact-finding mission proceeded to Damascus, and in August 1919 it presented its conclusions to the Paris Peace Conference. Its statement must have sounded like *naya* (flute) music to the ears of all who had convened in Ismail's house in the spring: 'As for Palestine we recommend to reject the extreme Zionist scheme of unlimited immigration with the purpose of establishing a Jewish state in Palestine.'[32]

It went on in this vein. The Palestinians themselves could not have drafted a more damning report. However, it soon became clear that the chief players on the Middle Eastern stage, Britain and France, did not intend to consider the report. First they put off all serious discussion about it, and later, after the US Congress did not subscribe to the president's wish to share in all these world-shaping postwar agreements, the report was quietly deposited on a shelf in the American National Archives, where it is still available for historians to peruse. Meanwhile, the statesmen turned their gaze to the holiday resort of Deauville in the north of France, where something they considered more important was taking place.

In Deauville, in September 1919, French prime minister Georges Clemenceau was forced to bow to the infuriating and humiliating dictate of his former ally, British prime minister Lloyd George, and renounce France's claim to some of the territories that had been designated during the war as a French sphere of influence, such as the oil-rich region of Mosul in Iraq. He also had to agree to Palestine being included in Britain's sphere of influence rather than being internationalized, as formerly agreed. Lloyd George's secretary would later report that the future of Palestine was resolved amid loud shouts and bitter protests. As for Greater Syria, France was assured that the British forces backing Faysal would soon withdraw, leaving the amir to face the French forces that had landed on the coast of Lebanon. Clearly Faysal would have no chance at all against a superior army like the French.[33]

In fact, in July 1920 Faysal's army was trounced in a short battle in Maysalun on the Syria–Lebanon border. Less than a year later the British government compensated him by making him king of Iraq, but it was a bitter setback for the supporters of Greater Syria. The dizzying pace of events forced whoever wished to remain politically significant to adapt rapidly to change. Some of the Husaynis, such as al-Hajj Amin, Jamal and Musa Kazim, did so by replacing the idea of Greater Syria with that of independent Palestine, thereby ensuring the family's continuing centrality in the Palestinian national movement.

So the Great Syria option was taken off the Palestinian agenda, and on 20 June 1920 everyone was ready to welcome the British Mandate's High Commissioner for Palestine, Herbert Samuel. The two years of military rule were over, and at least the elder Husaynis, including Ismail, Said and Musa Kazim, hoped to continue conducting the 'politics of notables' – that is to say, maintaining autonomous control of their society's affairs with the blessing of the authorities and of society itself. Unlike the Ottomans, though, the British demanded greater commitment and refused to rule by means of intermediaries, and they greatly reduced the power of the upper class. They appointed officials, some of them Jews, to senior posts that Husaynis or members of other notable families had held during Ottoman times.

The younger men led by al-Hajj Amin were too inexperienced to win the support of all the families and the general populace, and consequently those who were best placed to lead Palestinian society were unable to steer it off the path chosen by external authorities. Such a person was Musa Kazim, who under different circumstances might have changed the course of Palestinian history. He had retired before the end of the Great War, and his appearance in the early days of British rule showed that he was still living in the Ottoman era: he regularly wore his Ottoman medals and traditional headgear, and occasionally the tarbush, as befitted the family's *sharifi* descent. At the time of the Balfour Declaration, he had not yet become interested in national politics. He had been a senior Ottoman official, loyal to his government, and like most of his family had had nothing to do with the Arab revolt.[34] His appointment to the mayoralty in place of his brother looked like a continuation of the Ottoman way of doing things, but the British demand for absolute obedience to London's policy on Zionism drove Musa Kazim, almost against his will, into a position of national leadership. In the next chapter we shall see how Musa Kazim provided the young al-Hajj Amin with the family's backing in the struggle for power, though their alliance lasted too short a time to save Palestine.

Even as they turned their attention to national politics, the Husaynis remained profoundly Jerusalemite. They served in the municipality throughout the British Mandate – even after 1934, when a Jew was appointed mayor – and through it continued to affect the city's character. One of the most dynamic political bodies on the scene was the Association for Jerusalem – an interfaith, inter-communal and bi-national organization that served as an ideal model to anyone in the international community who wished to solve the problem of Jerusalem. However, the nationalization of Jerusalem reduced the association to an obsolete entity that now seems impossible to resurrect. The initiative for this body probably came from Ronald Storrs, who hoped that it would help develop civil services that the military rulers did not tackle. Following the model of similar groups in the English cities of Oxford and Cambridge, the association concerned itself chiefly with the preservation of Jerusalem's religious and cultural heritage.[35]

Two Husaynis were members of the association, Kamil al-Husayni and Musa Kazim. Together with a team of archaeologists, architects and government officials, they supervised the preservation of the holy city. In the final days of military rule, the *mufti* accompanied Storrs when he opened the renovated markets of the Old City. They conducted a strange ceremony reminiscent of guild rituals in Europe, giving each craftsman and apprentice a document obliging him to remain loyal to his craft. Among the recipients were Muslims, Jews and Christians, and no such general ceremony would take place again under the British Mandate or thereafter.

But architectural matters were not all that concerned the family during the first two years of British rule. Following the example of Ismail, some of the Husaynis became pillars of the educational system in the city – notably Ishaq Musa al-Husayni, who was the right-hand man of his old teacher Zurayq Nakhla and who served as deputy director of the English College in Jerusalem. Thanks to Zurayq, Ishaq Musa became a leading authority on the Arabic language and its preservation, and he advanced its research with modern methods adopted from the West. Another of his teachers, Musa Asaaf al-Nashashibi, had introduced him to Arabic literature, and Ishaq Musa regarded him as the person who helped shape his Arab identity during their close association from 1918 to 1920. Ishaq Musa noted in his memoirs that it was thanks to the Arabic foundation he had acquired from this mentor that he was able to preserve his Arabism during the many years he spent in the West.[36]

Although Ishaq Musa occasionally returned to political activity, he was not a central figure in the family's political biography. The Husaynis who led the dual struggle against Zionism and the British rule now took the stage – Musa Kazim, al-Hajj Amin and Jamal.[37]

## CHAPTER 7

# British Betrayal and the
# Rise of the National Aristocracy
## The First Violent Outbreak

At the end of February 1920, after a harsh winter, the people of Jerusalem welcomed the change in the weather. Snow that had piled up to a meter-and-a-half suddenly melted away, and the townspeople strolled outdoors as if it were summer. Spring arrived early and wildflowers bloomed among the rocks. Perhaps it was this early spring, wrote William McCracken in his diary, that prompted the Arabs to resolve to 'do something'. Later he wrote an article to that effect in his newspaper *Jerusalem News*.[1]

But it was not the sudden spring weather that prompted the Arabs to 'do something' – it was the headlong rush of political developments that outsiders like McCracken were unable to perceive. First came worrying news from Damascus: after prolonged negotiations, at the end of which Faysal agreed to a French mandate in Syria, he was informed by the commanders of the French forces in Lebanon that they were not interested in a Hashemite monarchy in their new fiefdom. The French demanded that Faysal remove himself and his entourage from Damascus. In desperation, Faysal decided to declare himself king – which he had not yet officially done – and rally a popular army to fight the French.

So at the end of February, all of the newly crowned king's Jerusalemite supporters met and announced that they would back his effort to prevent the French from driving him out of Syria. One of the main speakers was Sheikh Abd al-Qadir al-Muzafir, who called for 'real action' against the

British and the Zionists. The gathering also reiterated the well-known objection to the Balfour Declaration and the demand for the King-Crane report to be considered.

While the text of the Balfour Declaration remained unpublished, it was the subject of all kinds of rumors. But these were dispelled that February, when the British government made it public. People in the markets and mosques looked to their political and religious spokesmen for guidance and a response. Catholic priests, Orthodox monks and Muslim *imams* cooperated in organizing protests and demonstrations all over the country. While basking in the mild sunshine, Jerusalem, the heart of Palestinian politics, prepared for the first real confrontation with the British authorities.

McCracken hoped that rumors of imminent disturbances were mistaken and that calm would continue to reign in the holy city, to which he and his wife had come on a religious mission the previous winter. His organization, the American Religious Society of Friends (Quakers), had placed him in charge of its welfare and charitable work in Jerusalem, and for good reason. McCracken had managed numerous similar activities all over the world, and his history of the Swiss Confederation was also well-known. In Jerusalem he would become an important eyewitness to a stormy period in Palestine.

He had sensed the tension in the air, and the Arab and Jewish women who worked in the laundry of his social welfare organization spoke about activities in the city. On 27 February, a large crowd gathered outside the laundry. It was the first mass Palestinian demonstration against Zionism. When the women inside heard the roar of the crowd, they panicked and clung together, Jewish and Arab alike. McCracken decided to send for the police to protect and reassure them. Some 4,000 people had gathered outside the building of the British and Foreign Bible Society, shouting and shaking sticks menacingly. The only word McCracken was able to make out was the angrily shouted name of General Bowles, the governor of Palestine.

The laundry occupied the ground floor of the Bible Society's building, beneath its large balcony, from which various people made speeches. Most of the speakers stirred up the crowd, but Mufti Kamil al-Husayni called for calm and urged the demonstrators to disperse. Then Elizabeth McQuin, honorary secretary of the Welfare Enterprises, decided to address the crowd. She found a local man to translate her words into Arabic, climbed the stairs to the balcony and made a speech:

> If you want the world to respect you, you must behave like gentlemen. If the Jews have sinned, they will undoubtedly pay for it. The British saved

you from the Turks. I myself am a citizen of the United States, and have come here to work for social welfare. We are a freedom-loving people, but we know that freedom means proper behavior. The Grand Mufti is your friend; he has love in his eyes, and you had better follow him.

Whether it was her patronizing – but well-intentioned – statement or just the strange sight of the big American woman clutching the parapet, Ms McQuin's speech silenced the clamor.

Kamil, Salim and Said al-Husayni had not been immediately aware that it was a woman. Suddenly an excited onlooker shouted, 'It's a woman, a woman!' – an oddity at an all-male demonstration. Some of the placards – 'Our Country Belongs to Us', 'Death to the Betrayers of the Homeland', 'End Jewish Immigration' – were lowered, and the crowd moved away. A photographer for the *Jerusalem News* captured the unusual occurrence, and the following day the picture of Ms McQuin appeared among photos of the protest.

The protesters proceeded to the Jaffa Gate and then to the American consulate. A delegation led by Said and Salim al-Husayni (son of the late mayor Hussein and brother of Musa Kazim) presented a petition to the American consul, Dr Otis Glazenburg. The Arab population regarded the American consulate as a source of support and hope, both on account of the Palestinian diaspora in the United States and America's neutrality on the subject of the Mandate of Palestine. The consulate received numerous complaints from Jerusalem's notables about Zionism and the British authorities because the consul was widely known as a personal friend and direct appointee of President Wilson. But on this occasion, the demonstrators found an embarrassed diplomat who mumbled some noncommittal phrases about the United States always being on the side of justice. 'But what justice did he mean?' wondered Arif al-Arif, one of the delegates, when he told his friend Amin al-Husayni about the encounter.[2]

From there the protesters went to the French consulate, only to receive a similar reception. Their final destination was the governor's residence, which they reached at five in the afternoon. On their way, they passed a group of Jews singing the Zionist anthem '*Hatikvah*' at the top of their lungs, but they ignored them and walked on. Salim noticed that the police officers sent Jewish policemen out of the ranks to avoid provoking clashes with the protesters. Salim, Said and Arif were allowed to enter the courtyard of the governor's residence. They presented their petition and dispersed the procession.

The following morning, a boy brought the *Jerusalem News* to Salim's house. Arif al-Arif later maintained that McCracken was mistaken in estimating that only 4,000 men took part in the demonstration – he assured Salim that the number was 40,000. Salim was pleased to see that McCracken refuted the Zionists' claims that the procession had been controlled by his guidance and leadership.

A few days later the *mufti* invited the brave Ms McQuin to thank her personally for her action. She had written him a letter explaining that she had presumed to refer to him by name because of her fear for the Jewish washerwomen. On 1 March, the *mufti* wrote to her:

> I was very pleased to receive your letter. I am sorry that the quiet demonstra-
> tion aroused so much anxiety among our poor sisters, the washerwomen,
> and caused you to interrupt your important work with the children. That
> was certainly not our intention, but I am sure you and they understand the
> reason for our demonstration. Your speech was wonderful, full of wisdom
> and insight, and had a good influence on the people ...³

It included further words of praise.

McCracken accompanied Ms McQuin on her visit to the *mufti*. Together they drove to his house, which was up the hill on the way to the Mount of Olives – the future residence of the most renowned Palestinian of the end of the twentieth century, Faysal al-Husayni – and had a beautiful view of the city. On their way, McCracken told Ms McQuin that he had always liked the elderly *mufti*, who reminded him of his father, the Reverend John McCracken. He was not surprised by the *mufti*'s concern for the washerwomen: at their first meeting, when he had called on the *mufti* to obtain his support for welfare programs, the latter had agreed on condition that the organization employ Muslim women. The *mufti* had also asked the American to cooperate with the welfare organization of the women of Jerusalem established by Mrs Jamal al-Husayni in 1919, which had not only helped the needy but also enabled the women of the family to take part in the national effort. McCracken had assured him that most of the women already employed were in fact Muslim.⁴ The *mufti* had no objection to Jewish women being included in the enterprise that received his blessing.

McCracken wondered about the *mufti*'s attitude towards the Zionists. On the one hand, he decried Zionism and headed the demonstrations against it.⁵ On the other hand, in the summer of 1918, he laid one of the cornerstones of the Hebrew University. It seemed that the *mufti* had not yet realized that the era of Ottoman rule had come to an end. Zionists and Britons were new factors in the *mufti*'s life, and he was unable to keep up with the changing times. The younger generation was better able to comprehend the cultural, social and political changes that followed the Great War.

As at their first meeting, the conversation was conducted in French and English. The *mufti* spoke French, which McCracken spoke poorly, and then Musa Kazim, the *mufti*'s cousin and the mayor, who spoke English fluently, came to their aid. Kamil's white robe was bedecked with medals from Turkish times, as well as one from King George V given to him by the British authorities when they appointed him Grand Mufti. The burden always seemed too heavy for his thin frame and middling height. They discussed the Balfour Declaration, and the *mufti*, as always, spoke in moderate and gentle tones about the injustice done to the Arabs of Palestine. Then they passed on to the *mufti*'s favorite subject: the United States of America. He had recently met Colonel Finley, the head of the American Red Cross, and was amazed by the breadth of his knowledge. Now he wanted McCracken to confirm the wonders of the new world power across the ocean.

Ms McQuin had withdrawn to an adjacent room to greet the *mufti*'s wife and daughters before they went out. One other woman was present at their meeting, the girls' English governess. The *mufti*'s son Tahir III was not present, but McCracken knew him from previous visits and, like the British officials, expected him to inherit the *mufti*'s post. (It should be noted that this chapter, like the previous one, refers almost exclusively to members of the Tahiri branch of the family. Though the branches were no longer relevant during this period, it is necessary for the consistency of the family history to keep this in mind.)

The *mufti* liked the American even better than he liked his British friends. He often visited him at home, and even when McCracken in his American way ignored local customs and protocol, Kamil was not offended. At every visit McCracken would present his Egyptian servant Mahmoud, his cook Abdul, and Suleiman, a young African lad, to the *mufti*, as if they were respected members of society, and Kamil responded with understanding and good humor. Had this happened at Storrs's house, he would have seen it as a deliberate insult.

McCracken and Kamil had first met in September 1919, in what had previously been the German Consulate and what was now the quarters of Colonel Popham, senior aide to the chief administrator of Mandatory Palestine, who stood in for Storrs as governor of Jerusalem whenever the latter was out of town. The *mufti* had come to dinner to see the first American automobile in Palestine. (Actually, the first automobile had been brought into the country in 1912 by Aaron Aronson, but it had broken down and then vanished. Another car had been built by a German in Jaffa, but it was merely a carriage with an engine attached.) Popham had brought his car from Egypt. He had invited the *mufti* to take a trip to the north, but feeling that it was inappropriate to his status Kamil had reluctantly declined.

Kamil was feeling like a traveler who had switched abruptly from a horse-drawn carriage to a speeding motor car. He had been swept from a world of measured pace into a frantic race. Something important happened every week. On 8 March, Faysal was declared King of Greater Syria. Said al-Husayni, who had briefly been Foreign Minister in the king's government, attended the occasion, which was as magnificent as it was historically insignificant. Al-Hajj Amin persuaded his brother Kamil and his relative Musa Kazim to mark the event with a demonstration in Jerusalem. They agreed on condition that the poster announcing the demonstration emphasize that it should be peaceful.

And so it was. At the end of the protest, a petition was submitted to the governor of Jerusalem expressing support for an independent Greater Syria and opposing Zionism.[6] Al-Hajj Amin went at once to Damascus to bring the family's congratulations to the new king, and returned on 1 April convinced that the British were willing to give Palestine to Faysal. He had heard as much from Storrs's chief of staff, General Waters-Taylor. 'Best to accelerate the process,' he said to his brother Kamil. The Nabi Musa celebrations, which fell on Easter Sunday that year, would provide the opportunity to pressure the British government.

Not everyone in the family agreed. Al-Hajj Amin's nephew Jamil al-Husayni strongly opposed this tactic. When the six boys were at school they were very close, but during the war they parted ways and their views of the world began to differ greatly. Both Jamil and al-Hajj Amin were members of the Arab Club, but Jamil antagonized al-Hajj Amin by joining the Literary Club of the Nashashibis as well. Now Jamil used Arif al-Arif's paper, *Suriya al-Janubiyya* (Southern Syria), to call on the associations not to use the Nabi Musa celebrations as an occasion for rioting and to respect the holiday's sanctity. Arif al-Arif agreed with this line, though later he was accused of having planned the unauthorized demonstration.[7] He was probably innocent of the charge but was compromised by his friendship with al-Hajj Amin.

At the end of Easter Sunday, 4 April 1920, Ronald Storrs wrote in his diary:

> The Nabi Musa celebrations turned into a riot aimed against the Jews.
> A man by name of al-Hajj Amin al-Husayni, the Mufti's brother, was

responsible for the riot. Like all men who instigate riots, having incited the mob, he himself vanished.[8]

Storrs was convinced that the *mufti* had had a hand in organizing the event from start to finish. Like other British officials, he was ambivalent about Kamil. Though they suspected him of secretly working against them, at the same time they were charmed by his incredible generosity. When they first occupied the city, some hungry soldiers broke into the *mufti*'s house and stole two chickens and some other foodstuffs. General Allenby was furious and asked the *mufti* to make a formal complaint against the marauders. To which the mufti replied in a letter: 'The damage done is insignificant compared to the kindness shown me by your highness, so that the soldiers' actions are no more than children's misbehavior in their father's house.'[9]

Kamil was not blamed directly for the April events, but Storrs had no doubt that he had been the instigator. Yet the family did not consider the event of great importance and did not view it as a crisis with the authorities or even with Zionism. After all, the Nabi Musa celebrations had always occasioned religious riots. The only one who considered the event highly significant was al-Hajj Amin, but even he admitted later that the celebrants had gone too far and that it was necessary to find a way of cooperating with the British.[10]

The Nabi Musa celebration had become especially charged after 1910, when the Orthodox community began to mark its Easter with a procession from the Roman Patriarchate to the Church of the Resurrection. In 1920, it coincided with the Muslim procession. Large numbers of Muslims and Christians thronged the narrow, stepped alley of the Via Dolorosa while many spectators watched from above. The Old City was simply too small to contain such numbers. The crowd was augmented by a group of Jews making their way, though not in a procession, to the Wailing Wall. They were protected by a number of armed supporters, who served to heighten the tension more than they guarded the devout Jews. In 1920 the Orthodox Good Friday coincided not only with the Muslim holiday but also with Passover and, for good measure, with Good Friday on the Western churches' Gregorian calendar.[11]

George Napier Whittingham, an English travel writer, was an eyewitness and could later tell Storrs what really happened. That Friday, on his way to the Church of the Holy Sepulchre, he ran into the traditional Nabi Musa procession in David Street. At its center, he saw a member of the Husayni family doing a dervish dance, which the crowd accompanied with encouraging cries and prayers. Flags and religious banners intermingled, and the procession moved like a tornado capable of swallowing up everything in its path. Whittingham hastily retreated into an open doorway and saved himself. Women on the balconies threw down colorful kerchiefs, which one of the dancing dervishes picked up and tied to the staff of the Prophet's green banner.

Whittingham followed the procession, which advanced towards the Haram al-Sharif forecourt, where speeches were made in Arabic and English. Kamil and al-Hajj Amin addressed the crowd in Arabic, inveighing against the Balfour Declaration and Jewish migration to Palestine. From there the procession turned towards Jericho. Whittingham spent the evening in the Church of the Holy Sepulchre, and Friday passed peacefully for him. But like everyone else, he felt that this would be an unusual Easter.

Meanwhile the Muslim celebrants continued on their way. That year they did not walk all the way to Jericho, but stopped on the last hill before the descent to the Dead Sea, where they waited for the groups from Nablus and Hebron to join them before proceeding together to Nabi Musa's tomb. On their way they passed through the neighborhood of Ras al-Amud, which lies on the way to Abu Dis and the villages east of Jerusalem. The village children watched them from the flat roofs of their houses, some dancing in circles while their parents watched the procession from the roadside. April being a month of sunshine and rain, many carried umbrellas, which is why the Christians dubbed Nabi Musa the umbrella festival. Only men carried umbrellas, and for most of the route the men and women were separated; only in the Bedouin areas did they mingle freely. Peddlers also lined the road and sold their wares, falafel and drinks. Every neighborhood and village flourished its own banners and placards, and the deafening noise was accompanied by the trilling of shepherds' flutes.[12]

The procession was expected to reach the big encampment that had been prepared near Nabi Musa's tomb, where they usually stayed from Friday until the following Thursday. This time they waited until Sunday for the other groups to arrive before going on to the prophet's tomb.

On Easter Sunday, Whittingham again walked to the Church of the Holy Sepulchre, where he encountered a large company of British military police sent there to forestall Christian interdenominational outbreaks. It consisted of almost the entire military police force available in the Jerusalem area, and only later did it become clear that it would have been better deployed to separate Muslims and Jews. A large crowd packed the church's rounded interior, watching the Patriarch hand torches blazing with holy fire to the young priests. By the light of the torches, Whittingham saw that an untraditional circle had formed around Captain Adamson, the commander of the military force, and the image of a British officer illuminated by Latin holy fire made him smile. It was his last smile that day.

After a while, Whittingham left the crush and went out to the Via Dolorosa, where he found himself flanked by the Latin-Catholic procession and that of the Eastern churches. The two circled the tomb in impeccable order, until a pilgrim from the Syrian Church moved a chair belonging by tradition to the Coptic Church. Then, as Whittingham put it, 'all hell broke loose'. Women and children screamed, and amid the blows and curses it was impossible to tell who had the upper hand. Suddenly the church door caught fire, which Captain Adamson succeeded in putting out. Whittingham fled the scene and hurried to the Jaffa Gate, where he ran into the main drama of that Sunday.[13]

When Storrs heard the description he sighed. He had received warnings some days before the Nabi Musa celebration that this time there would be riots. Learning that the procession had not gone on to Jericho heightened his anxiety. General Allenby had ordered him to ensure that the Jewish Passover morning worship did not coincide with the sacred fire ritual at the Church of the Holy Sepulchre, but he had not expected clashes to erupt in connection with the Nabi Musa celebration. Oddly, no one reported to the general what had happened near the church, much less the attempted arson. As far as he was concerned, fights between Jews and Muslims were tolerable, but any attack on Christianity's holy shrines was unforgivable. Adamson, who had kept that information from Allenby, found the courage to tell him about it only in 1922, when he was a guest of the general (by then a field marshal) in Egypt, at the uncovering of Tutankhamun's tomb.

In those days the Nabi Musa celebrations were the only official event on the Palestinian calendar. At its center were the two Husaynis, Mufti Kamil and the mayor of Jerusalem Musa Kazim. Being an official event, it was incumbent on Storrs, as head of the British administration in the city, to help make it a success. Under Ottoman rule, the governor of Jerusalem had the honor of receiving the sacred banners before the procession went to Jericho and was present when the *imam* in the Haram al-Sharif proclaimed the opening of the festivities, usually with a single cannon blast. The British army took over this function and provided the cannon and the band that played during the ceremony. (Storrs's subordinates and superiors alike were opposed to the British army taking such an active part in the festival, but he persuaded them that it would encourage the population to accept the change from Muslim to

European rule.) Storrs kept it up because in 1919 the Nabi Musa celebrations had passed peacefully. The celebrants had spent a week in Jericho, where he had visited them and observed some ceremonies that mixed tradition with modernity (circumcisions alongside a performance by a ventriloquist and a Punch and Judy show). Presumably he expected the carnival atmosphere to prevail again, but it did not.[14]

On Sunday morning, Storrs received a report from the Jerusalem chief of police, an inexperienced young lieutenant, that all was well. The government understood later that too much responsibility had been placed on this officer, given his inexperience and the small number of men at his disposal. Storrs's parents were visiting him that Easter, and together they walked to St George's Cathedral to attend the midday service. He asked to be informed when the Hebronites arrived for the Nabi Musa festivities, because he feared that as usual they would scuffle with the Nablus group. 'Let me know when you see the Hebronites about an hour-and-a-half distance from the Jaffa Gate,' he said to one of his aides. When he was about to leave for the church, his personal servant Kamil told him, in a low voice in Arabic to avoid alarming his parents, that there was trouble at the Jaffa Gate. 'I felt as if Kamil had thrust a sword into my heart,' Storrs later wrote in his diary.[15]

He realized that the forces at his disposal were inadequate and again grew angry with the military commanders, especially Allenby, who had ignored his warning and had not sent a company of soldiers or policemen to accompany the procession from Hebron. The small force was concentrated around the outbreak at the Church of the Holy Sepulchre.

According to Whittingham, the cause of the riot at the Jaffa Gate was the Hebronite group joining the Jerusalem celebrants. They had left Hebron early in the morning and headed for the municipality building outside the city walls, where the Jerusalem and Nablus contingents were waiting. The excited crowd proceeded to the Arab Club near the Jaffa Gate, where they listened to speeches. Musa Kazim and al-Hajj Amin were the main speakers, but the most passionate speech was delivered by Khalil Baydas, who was already known as '*Raid al-Qissa al-Filastiniyya*' – the pioneer of the Palestinian story. He concluded by saying: 'My voice is weakening with emotion, but my national heart will never weaken.'[16] The crowd listened to the speeches and quenched their thirst with lemonade, handed out freely by the young men of the club. Then they went on to the Jaffa Gate to welcome the Hebronites. Reaching the plaza in front of the gate, Musa Kazim addressed the new arrivals, while behind him young al-Hajj Amin held up King Faysal's picture and cried aloud, 'O Arabs! This is your king!'

That day Storrs heard from Khalil al-Sakakini that Kamil al-Husayni had been one of those who incited the Hebronites and instigated their riot. There were several Jewish-owned shops near the municipality, which the mob began to smash and loot. Like an arson fire that is started in a number of places and spreads until the flames engulf the whole building, this outbreak soon converged with the fight between the Hebronites and the Jews that was already raging near the Jaffa Gate.

At the Jaffa Gate, the crowd was inflamed by the sight of the Jewish armed men led by Ze'ev Jabotinsky, the mentor and future founder of the rightwing bloc of Zionist parties, and the fight broke out when a Hebronite attacked a Jewish boy.[17] Before long, troops arrived and put an end to the riot.

What happened afterwards Storrs knew firsthand. He kept the city under martial law for several days, and guards examined every person going in or out of the city. He stationed Indian Muslim troops at the gates of the Muslim Quarter to examine women, claiming this would not cause any offense. Robert Adamson, who was responsible for the Jaffa Gate, reported to Storrs that many of the women were found to be carrying all sorts of weapons. Storrs sent the collection to England, where it remains on display in the Royal Military Police Museum in Chichester. Anyone found carrying a weapon was fined one Egyptian pound. One day the city was shaken when an Indian soldier accidentally shot an old Palestinian woman at the Jaffa Gate. The sound of the shots gave birth to a rumor that the Orthodox Patriarch had been killed, and Adamson had to work hard to persuade the people that there was no truth in it and that the Patriarch was safe inside his church.

Whittingham himself was convinced that Kamil al-Husayni had had no hand in provoking the riots. A few days after these events, he called on the *mufti* at his house below the Mount of Olives and talked about the situation. They sat in the spacious sitting room, where a few months earlier the *mufti* had entertained McCracken and Ms McQuin, and talked in French. After a while, they switched to English with the help of Khalil, the son of Sheikh al-Haram Bashir al-Husayni. (This '*Chef de Mosque*', as Bashir was designated on his visiting card, belonged to the Umari branch of the family, which had lost its wealth and status in the wake of the political upheaval in Palestine.) The timing of the visit was significant: that morning Whittingham had heard at his hotel that the previous day the ten victorious states had confirmed the British Mandate of Palestine, and its terms included the Balfour Declaration.

Kamil listened to the news attentively. He expressed his disappointment but also the hope that it did not mean discrimination against the Muslims.

According to Whittingham, the conversation took an Anglophile turn. The *mufti* spoke of his great admiration for the British Empire and its culture. He also made a point of assuring his guest that he was neither anti-Jewish nor anti-Christian. 'Are you anti-Zionist?' asked Whittingham. 'Yes,' the *mufti* replied, 'emotionally ... The Zionists are preventing us from developing the country,' he complained. 'Without them, we could have made this a prosperous country in fifteen years.' Then he surprised his guest by adding, 'A banking system, that is the key to success. Tell your government, "Let them open banks, and they will finance their own state." If after fifteen years we fail, let others try instead of us.'[18] They talked for about an hour, and on parting the *mufti* was as sanguine as ever. He smiled broadly and said, 'After God, I trust England, which has always stood by the weak and will not let the Palestinians be ruled by a tyranny.'

'Surely such a moderate man could not have provoked the rampage,' Whittingham said to Storrs. He also reported Musa Kazim's version of events, having visited him at his office in the American Colony. It was not the Hebronites who had started the riots but the Jews. It all began with a scuffle between two boys, a Muslim and a Jew. Then the Muslim boy was beaten by a 'Jewish legion' armed with rifles who began to attack the Hebronites as they arrived. Whittingham told Musa Kazim that the same number were killed on either side, but the number of Jewish wounded was far greater. 'That is because we defend ourselves fiercely,' Musa Kazim replied.

That day the American consul sent the following report to Washington: 'Yesterday, while a religious Muslim procession passed through the city, a fight broke out between Muslims and Jews. Both sides suffered casualties, and a state of emergency has been declared.' Zionist public relations strove to contradict the consul's neutral report, which convinced the Husaynis and all Palestinians that he was a trustworthy friend.[19] Indeed it seemed that the Americans present at the time in Palestine related to the events as part of a legitimate and understandable local outrage, although they did not endorse its violent form. The British representatives on the ground, though not necessarily those stationed in London, stuck to the Orientalist theory of a Muslim mass, that can easily be incited one way or another. In any case, the official investigation revealed that seven Jews and five Arabs had been killed on that ill-fated Easter/Passover. No one had been killed in the fight that took place at the same time near the Church of the Holy Sepulchre, where most of the British force had been concentrated.

Storrs also heard about Jabotinsky's armed group and their role in stirring up trouble from Ms Frances Newton, who as an English missionary close to

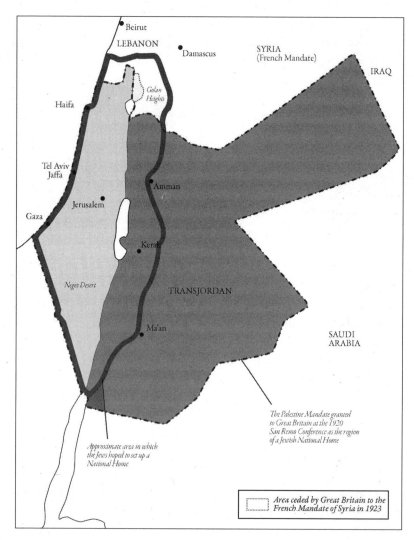

Beirut
LEBANON
Damascus
SYRIA
(French Mandate)
IRAQ
Golan
Heights
Haifa
Tel Aviv
Jaffa
Amman
Jerusalem
Gaza
Kerak
Negev Desert
TRANSJORDAN
Ma'an
SAUDI
ARABIA

*The Palestine Mandate granted to Great Britain at the 1920 San Remo Conference as the region of a Jewish National Home*

*Approximate area in which the Jews hoped to set up a National Home*

> ............ Area ceded by Great Britain to the
> ............ French Mandate of Syria in 1923

*Palestine under the British Mandate, 1923–1948*

the Palestinians normally resided in Haifa. But despite his friendship with the Husaynis, Storrs rejected her version of events just as he rejected the American version. His men told him that Kamil had addressed the crowd on the Temple Mount, repeating a sermon he had delivered the previous week inciting them against the Jews. Storrs also believed that the *mufti* had encouraged al-Hajj Amin and Arif al-Arif to stir up a clamor, and that only when it got out of control had Kamil unsuccessfully tried to stem the riot.

Raghib al-Nashashibi, who had also been present, described a joint action by the three Husaynis: the *mufti*, who incited the crowd with verses from the Qur'an; his brother al-Hajj Amin, who held up a picture of King Faysal, shouting, 'Faysal is our king! Faysal is our king!', which the crowd echoed; and Mayor Musa Kazim, who provided the Hebronites and others with political arguments. Following this report, Musa Kazim was deposed from the mayoralty, and Raghib al-Nashashibi was appointed in his place.[20] The Nashashibis were related to the Husaynis by marriage, but during the British Mandate this connection was forgotten. Their bitter social and political rivalry divided the Palestinians and prevented them from standing united at a crucial historical crossroads when they needed solidarity above all. When Storrs informed Musa Kazim of his intention to dismiss him, the mayor said that none of the city's notables would presume to replace him. Raghib's willingness to do so hurt him and his family deeply. When Raghib tried to prevent al-Hajj Amin's appointment to the Supreme Muslim Council in December 1921, it further inflamed the enmity between the two clans.

It is worth noting that not even Chaim Weizmann and the other Jewish leaders suspected Kamil of provoking the outbreak. Nevertheless, Storrs convened a court martial, which decided that al-Hajj Amin and Arif al-Arif had instigated the riots. They were sentenced *in absentia* to ten years' imprisonment with hard labor, but they had escaped and could not be found. Al-Hajj Amin found refuge in Dira, the grazing lands of a Bedouin tribe that lived permanently in Ayn al-Hawari, a desert region between the Jordan River and Amman. A company of soldiers searched the *mufti's* house and fired warning shots at his son, mistaking him for al-Hajj Amin. The furious and agitated *mufti* complained to the occupying authorities about the humiliating conduct of the soldiers, and demonstratively returned the medal and decoration he had received from King George V. The following day, Storrs was incensed to learn that Allenby had written the *mufti* a letter of apology. 'The main casualty', he said to his aide Said, 'is the empire.'[21]

But the conflicting versions of the incidents called for resolution, and London appointed a court of inquiry. (Mandatory Palestine would find that this was a favorite British device.) The Palin Commission, as it was known, reported that the Jewish presence in the country was provoking the Arab population and was the cause of the riots. Everyone knew this, of course; nevertheless the conclusions were kept secret. The commission also expressed the hope that the flames of inter-communal hatred that had erupted in 1920 would draw the world's attention to the underlying volcano. But the world, or at any rate London, was not upset by the events – after all, in the empire on which the sun did not set such occurrences were not uncommon in 1920. Shi'i tribes were rebelling in southern Iraq, Egyptian nationalists were defying the British authorities, Hindus were showing signs of resistance in India and Ireland was beginning to tear itself apart.[22]

Ze'ev Jabotinsky, too, was found guilty of incitement and sentenced to fifteen years' imprisonment with hard labor. (He was also convicted of carrying an unlicensed firearm.) But the sentence was immediately reduced to two years, and he was freed before the term was up. The veteran teacher Khalil Baydas was also arrested that night and taken away in pajamas; he was sentenced to fifteen years in the Acre prison.

Mayor Musa Kazim was likewise sent to the Acre prison. Though promptly released, he was, as mentioned, dismissed from his post. In prison he met Baydas, who would write *Hadith al-Sajun* (The Story of the Prisoners), a bitter denunciation of British prisons. Several sources argue that it was Baydas who persuaded Musa Kazim to refuse to cooperate any longer with the British authorities.[23]

As if the imprisonment of some of its leading figures and the flight of others was not enough, the San Remo Conference deepened the despair of the Palestinian public. In the little Italian resort, the ten allies of the Paris Peace Conference confirmed that Palestine would come under a British Mandate that incorporated the Balfour Declaration (which could be understood to apply to Transjordan as well). The British also received the mandate over Iraq, and the French over Syria and Lebanon.

The Husaynis had succeeded in rallying a significant number of Christians to take part in the Nabi Musa procession, which could be seen as an impressive demonstration of Muslim-Christian power. Christian Palestinians were beginning to regard the festival as a national event. But this was a meager comfort, and there was little for Palestinians to rejoice about in the summer of 1920.[24]

The second Palestinian Congress took place amid this gloom. Its main purpose was to lift people's spirits, or at least to encourage those who were politically active and anxious about recent developments. It was also necessary to decide how to respond to those developments. As in the days of Abdul Hamid II, the participants had to work in secret, because the military authorities banned all Arab political gatherings. The British authorities were especially wary of any support for Faysal since it seemed impossible to forestall a clash between him and the French in Syria, which the British government had promised (explicitly or by implication) to both camps.[25]

On 31 May 1920, in the absence of Arif al-Arif and al-Hajj Amin, their followers and friends decided to carry out an old idea the two had advanced: they created the organization that would become the first Palestinian political party in history – the Palestine Arab League. The two exiles were chosen as its leaders, together with Rafiq al-Tamimi, Izzat Darwaza and others. The choice of al-Hajj Amin as the secretary of the league illustrated the high regard in which many held him even though he was only in his early twenties. The conference published a demand to bring back the deportees as well as a strong protest against the decision of the San Remo Conference to include the Balfour Declaration in the text of the mandate.

Not all the Husaynis directly confronted the British authorities. During May and June, Kamil and Storrs revived their former friendship. The *mufti's* medals were formally returned to him, and he, for his part – possibly in gratitude – gave a sermon at al-Aqsa in June 1920 calling for moderation, calm and the preservation of public order. He even expressed confidence that the British government would fulfill its promises to the Muslim community in Jerusalem.[26]

But the situation was volatile and uncertain, and the Husaynis did not take a clear-cut position. Even after the events in April, some of them were unsure about what was happening in Palestine. Their public activities and speeches appeared to be plainly anti-Zionist, but in June 1920 even al-Hajj Amin was still examining various ways of opposing Zionism (as he continued to do until 1948). He took part in the political activities of the Syrian Congress, which included contact with Zionist leaders, notably Chaim Weizmann. In June 1920, al-Hajj Amin and two other members of the Palestine committee of the Syrian Congress met with a Zionist delegation at the Victoria Hotel in Damascus. They discussed the Weizmann-Faysal agreement, signed in January 1919, which secured Zionist support for Greater Syria in exchange for an all-Syrian acceptance of some implementation of the Balfour Declaration. Al-Hajj Amin would later claim that he had attended the meeting in order to get to know the enemy better, but it is possible that he went because he was ambivalent about the Zionists.[27]

## Under the High Commissioner Herbert Samuel

On 20 June 1920, a boat brought Sir Herbert Samuel from the SS *Senator* to the quay at the Port of Jaffa. Eight young Muslim men dressed, despite the heat, in jumpers bearing the text 'OETA Property' (that is, property of the occupation administration) helped him ashore. Samuel had been appointed High Commissioner of Palestine following the San Remo confirmation of the British Mandate of Palestine. Then in his fifties, the Englishman had previously been Chancellor of the Duchy of Lancaster. His Jewish origin immediately aroused Palestinian suspicions, and perhaps they also held his assistance to the Zionist delegation at the Paris Peace Conference against him, though it is not certain that the Palestinians were aware of it. Yet for some time there were no indications that he was in any way hostile to the Palestinians.[28]

The new High Commissioner was received with a seventeen-gun salute, after which he was rushed away in a car to Jerusalem, for fear that some local person would make an attempt on his life. Two days after the High Commissioner's arrival in Jerusalem, General Bowles threw a formal reception in his honor at a government house on Mount Scopus, marking the end of his role as military governor and the start of Sir Herbert's civilian rule.

Bowles may have felt that he had not done enough or wished to erase the bitter memory of the recent events. At any rate he made an effort to reconcile the Jewish and Muslim leaders, if only superficially. Menahem Ussishkin, head of the Zionist Commission, and Grand Mufti Kamil al-Husayni were the two leading local figures, and Bowles seized their arms, one on each side. A man of eloquent gestures, Kamil was willing to shake Ussishkin's hand, but the latter declined.

Judge Gad Frumkin witnessed the scene and was appalled. He ran after Ussishkin and asked him why he had refused to shake the *mufti*'s hand. 'How could I offer my hand to the head of a religion whose sons raped daughters of Israel?' was the answer. However, Ussishkin could not have thought of any particular case, nor was there evidence of any such atrocities. Frumkin later noted in his memoir that this incident, like many others, typified the insolence of the Zionist leaders.[29]

Deeply offended, Kamil gathered his family and told them about the incident. His brother Amin al-Husayni listened attentively and would often repeat the story. When Kamil died in March 1921 and al-Hajj Amin succeeded him as Grand Mufti, one of the first people to visit and congratulate him was M. D. Eder, the member of the Zionist Commission in charge of political affairs. Afterwards Dr Eder waited in vain for the *mufti* to pay him a return visit. Frumkin found out about this when he tried to persuade Eder's successor, Colonel Kisch, to meet 'the head of the Muslim religion' in Palestine, and heard that since the *mufti* had not repaid his predecessor's courtesy visit, Kisch saw no point in meeting.

All this happened during the fasting month of Ramadan. Frumkin was a regular visitor at the Husaynis' on the sociable nights when the fast was broken. After talking to Kisch, he hurried to visit al-Hajj Amin. Not finding him at home, he looked for him among the many diners who crowded the big hall. At his request, someone called the new *mufti*, and the two talked privately in another room.

'Why did I not return Eder's visit?' al-Hajj Amin said, agitated. 'Because his predecessor, Ussishkin, insulted my late brother publicly and unforgivably!' Nevertheless, Frumkin persuaded al-Hajj Amin to meet Kisch at a dinner at his, Frumkin's, house. But Kisch again behaved rudely and rejected the invitation. This time he had a different excuse: Dr Ticho, the commissioner's private physician, had invited both him and al-Hajj Amin to his house, but when the latter had heard that Kisch was going to be there, he refused to come. Frumkin had no doubt that the problem lay in Kisch's reluctance to have anything to do with the Arabs. At first glance, these encounters may seem to be quarrels between gangs of overgrown children – this was how the British perceived them – but they were more than that. Gestures counted for a great deal in Palestine, as they often revealed the raw and authentic attitude, which at times could be covered with doubletalk and insincerity.[30]

But we are anticipating – in 1920 Kamil was still alive and al-Hajj Amin had not yet succeeded him. That June, Kamil's family and the rest of the Husaynis worried that the pro-Zionist Jewish High Commissioner would encourage the leaders of the Jewish community to continue behaving in an arrogant and overbearing way. Kamil was hoping that Chaim Weizmann would head the Zionist camp, because he had been impressed by him and believed he did not wish to dispossess the Palestinians. He was more suspicious of the High Commissioner, and a meeting held on 7 July between Sir Herbert and a number of Palestinian notables including Kamil did not help. However, in August a minor gesture made by the High Commissioner placed him on the positive side of the ledger in Kamil's book, if not in Palestinian history.

On 20 August, the tired Sir Herbert came to al-Salt in Transjordan to reassure the Bedouin *sheikhs* that Faysal's departure from Damascus did not mean Britain's withdrawal from Transjordan; as the chief representative of the British Mandate, he was also responsible for this region. He was sitting on a chair inside the great tent, facing the *sheikhs*, who sat cross-legged on rugs, when an eager young officer broke into the conversation: 'Al-Hajj Amin and Arif al-Arif are here. Let's grab them and take them back to Jerusalem!' Sir Herbert turned questioningly to a *sheikh* who had impressed him as wise and moderate. 'That would not be wise,' the *sheikh* replied. 'Your forces are small, and al-Hajj Amin and Arif are the guests of a tribe armed with thousands of rifles. You're camped down in a deep *wadi*, while they are on the surrounding hillsides, and they will protect their guests to the last drop of blood, because that is the custom here.' The decision was made immediately not to try to capture the two.[31]

The following day, Sir Herbert presented himself before the *sheikhs* wearing his medals and a fresh white suit. Before he could say anything, some of the *sheikhs* appealed to him to pardon the two young Palestinians. The High Commissioner had considered the matter during the night and made up his mind; to general surprise, he pardoned the two then and there. Almost by magic, Arif al-Arif appeared, borne on the shoulders of local young men. The cautious al-Hajj Amin stayed out of sight, perhaps because he did not trust the British official. He wrote to his brother that he did not care to be pardoned because he was not a criminal. But when Kamil fell ill, he accepted the pardon and returned to Jerusalem in December 1920.

Sir Herbert must have hoped to indicate by his gesture that he was not pro-Zionist but had the welfare of the entire population at heart. When Izzat Darwaza heard about the pardon, he told the Husaynis that Sir Herbert must have been concerned that, with al-Hajj Amin absent, their rivals the Nashashibis, who had already obtained the post of mayor, would grow too strong, thus depriving the British of the old colonial ploy of 'divide and rule'. But Kamil did not accept this explanation. He believed that the High Commissioner's kindness and his desire to begin his tenure in an atmosphere of goodwill had prompted him to issue the pardon.

That summer the Husaynis had to change their position on the future of Palestine. On 23 July, Faysal was defeated by the French forces in Maysalun. He then came to Haifa and waited for a new position in one of Britain's territories. Since Greater Syria was no more, what would happen to Palestine? The Literary Club – composed mostly of Nashashibis and some Husaynis – had been right not to support the union of Syria and Palestine. At the end of the month, Musa Kazim addressed the activists of the Palestinian organizations: 'Now, after the recent events in Damascus, we must change our plans entirely. Southern Syria is no more. We must defend Palestine.'[32]

Aided by Jamil al-Husayni, Musa Kazim accepted the leadership; al-Hajj Amin was still in exile. Jamil, the only scion of the Umari branch who was still active in politics, had thought of himself as a candidate, but Musa Kazim was more prominent. When the members of the organizations asked Musa Kazim to lead them in preparation for the third Palestinian Congress, he agreed. The conference convened in Haifa in December 1920, and Musa Kazim was elected its president.

But before the Haifa conference, the fourth anniversary of the Balfour Declaration came around. The population was becoming accustomed to national anniversaries being marked alongside the saints' days and pilgrim-ages. As time went on, the number of commemorated injustices and catas-trophes in Palestinian history grew so much that by the end of the twentieth century there was hardly a free day left on the calendar. In November 1920, the protests in Jerusalem were fairly limited and confined to the Old City. The turmoil lasted only a few hours. The American consul described it in his report to Washington in the dry language of a diplomat: 'All the Arab shops in Palestine were shut today, in protest against the Balfour Declaration. The Jews threw a hand-grenade and wounded Arabs; in retaliation, the Arabs killed four Jews. Martial law has been re-imposed.'[33]

It all began when the demonstrators tried to pass through the Jewish Quarter. As in April 1920, the Jews, feeling threatened, again responded with firearms, leaving one Arab dead. The Arabs, who were more numerous, used knives and other weapons, hence the large number of Jewish wounded. By the end of the month, everyone was busy with preparations for the Haifa conference, and the agitation died down for a time.

On 13 December, three Husaynis went to Haifa to take part in the seven-day conference. Their attendance signaled the family's continued presence (but not yet their prominence) in the political arena, not only in Jerusalem but throughout Palestine. Musa Kazim, al-Hajj Amin and Muhammad Salah had come to Haifa a few days earlier after celebrating al-Hajj Amin's pardon and return. Only al-Hajj Amin, with his relentless energy, had the necessary qualities to dominate events; only he was capable of compelling Palestinians with senior posts in the mandatory government to donate two months' salary to finance the conference. Not that the notables were short of funds, but this was their way of showing real commitment to the national cause. Preparations for the conference had to take place in secret. Having been forbidden to engage in political activity, al-Hajj Amin was back in his former post of teacher at the Rawdat al-Ma'arif school – which was actually his private property. For this reason, the conference was convened in Haifa under the aegis of the Haifa Muslim-Christian Association, a local organiza-tion regarded favorably by the British authorities.

The need for secrecy made organizing the conference problematic. Nev-ertheless, the towns and villages were represented as fairly as possible under the circumstances. Thirty-six delegates took part. Having each talked to his community about the need for religious and national cooperation, the great religious leader Sheikh Suleiman al-Taji al-Faruqi and the head of the Catholic community, Bullus Shehadeh, together prepared the groundwork for a demonstration of Muslim-Christian solidarity.[34]

Backed by slogans proclaiming the sanctity of Palestine for Christians and Muslims, Haifa's *mufti*, Muhammad Murad, opened the conference and welcomed the honorable delegates and guests who had come from all over the country. He gave special thanks to the Haifa Muslim-Christian Association, which had convened the conference on behalf of the people of Palestine to protest the decision of the League of Nations to grant Britain a mandate that incorporated the Balfour Declaration.

The slogan of the conference was 'Equality with the Mandate of Iraq'. The text of Iraq's mandate stipulated that it would have a parliament elected on the democratic principle of one citizen, one vote. It acknowledged Iraq as a *watani* (national entity) that would eventually become independent. The *sheikh* explained to those gathered that these were the most elementary demands, yet they had been denied to the Palestinians because of the Balfour Declaration.

The conference also discussed issues of lesser magnitude concerning the participants and the public they represented. Since there was a shortage of grain in Palestine, the British authorities forbade exporting grain to neighboring countries, and the merchants were asking to be allowed to renew trade with Arab countries. Musa Kazim, who had spent time in a British jail, talked about the harsh conditions inside, and it was resolved to demand that the authorities improve the prison system.

This was Musa Kazim's hour of greatness. Since having been deposed as mayor of Jerusalem, he had not found his place in Palestinian politics. Now he began to fight for his role as leader of the national movement. He was chosen to head the executive committee of the conference, a nine-member body that soon became the Palestinians' unofficial government under mandatory rule. Musa Kazim's speech showed that he felt like the prophet of a new national movement:

> This is the story of Palestine, the land of miracles and the supernatural, and the cradle of religions ... And this is the congress which was born from the suffering of Palestine. It is Palestine's representative and spokesman.

He went on to speak about Zionism as an organization that sought to separate Palestine from her friend Britain, and described the practical assistance the Palestinians had given the British during the battle for the country. The conference resolutions were phrased in the same spirit.

Needless to say, since Faysal had been driven from Damascus, Palestine was never again referred to as part of Greater Syria. However, Musa Kazim also introduced in his speech various imaginary elements that would do more harm than good once they were adopted by Palestinian public relations. He mixed morally and politically persuasive concrete arguments with foolish statements like, 'Wherever the Jews lived they engaged in destruction, which is why they invented Marxism,' undermining rational arguments against the Jewish claim to Palestine. This confusion persisted at the heart of the Palestinian national discourse – to some extent because of the Husaynis.

In all of the photographs from the conference, a mustached young man dressed in the modern suit preferred by his generation is standing on Musa Kazim's right. Before long this young man, al-Hajj Amin, would grow a beard and put on a tarbush and become the Grand Mufti of Palestine. At this time, his position was not yet established in Haifa.

In the fourth session, the delegates held a secret ballot to elect the executive committee, choosing the nine candidates with the largest number of votes. Al-Hajj Amin was not among the winners. Thirty-three delegates (all but the three Husaynis) chose Arif al-Dajani. Musa Kazim received only twenty-six votes but was elected, as noted, as a chairman as a tribute to his seniority. The three Husaynis did not play a prominent part in the debates, and only in one of the sessions (when the venue of future conferences was discussed) did their voices predominate. Haifa and four other centers were proposed, but al-Hajj Amin pressed for Jerusalem and won.

The third conference also signaled the end of Kamil al-Husayni's role in this story. He was to be replaced by Musa Kazim, al-Hajj Amin and Jamal, who became the leading figures in the Husayni clan during the British Mandate. Kamil made his last appearance in this history when he met with McCracken, Whittingham and Storrs at a reception held in the garden of the municipality in honor of the king's birthday. It was a pleasant occasion, and the conversation was not about politics. Whittingham recalled that they talked about a custom that surprised foreign visitors – namely, Palestinian monogamy. Musa Kazim noted that most Muslims in Palestine were content to marry one woman, and suddenly the Europeans, Americans and Palestinians shared a sense of closeness.

Kamil al-Husayni died in March 1921. It is not surprising that the Jewish High Commissioner, Sir Herbert Samuel, would describe Kamil as a symbol of Palestinian cooperation with the British. Even Storrs had to admit that with Kamil's passing the British authorities lost the one Husayni who showed understanding for Britain's problems, even though towards the end of his life he spearheaded the struggle against the Balfour Declaration.

That March two very important persons visited Jerusalem: Winston

Churchill, then Colonial Secretary, and Amir Abdullah, the brother of Faysal. They would nail down decisions about the future of Palestine that the Palestinians would be unable to alter or to accept.

Until 1920 Abdullah had been the foreign minister in his father's government in the Hijaz and had considered himself a candidate for the throne of Iraq under a British mandate. Seeing that his father's family was greatly weakened by the rise of the rival house of Saud and that the British government was about to install his brother Faysal in Iraq, he made an extremely shrewd move. Leaving his father's kingdom, he advanced towards Transjordan and declared he was going to wrest Damascus from the French. In reality he settled for much less. He reached a small Circassian town called Amman and forced the British government to accept him as the ruler of the territory, which also came under the British Mandate.

Winston Churchill was only too pleased. He separated Mandatory Palestine and Transjordan into two entities (as they had been during the Ottoman period) and accepted Abdullah as ruler of the latter. The question arose of what to do about the Balfour Declaration, which had included Transjordan, and Churchill and Abdullah discussed the matter in Jerusalem in March 1921.

They met Musa Kazim on the steps of the Augusta Victoria Church and informed him that the Balfour Declaration would remain in force but that Transjordan would be a separate political entity under British protection. Both decisions were equally damaging and frustrating. Musa Kazim represented the Palestinians who believed that it was imperative to fight against Churchill and his schemes, by force if necessary. Overnight, Churchill became an enemy of the Palestinian people: 'I always regarded him as a venomous and ruthless enemy,' al-Hajj Amin would say towards the end of his life.[35]

When Churchill's car passed through Jaffa, the streets emptied and the shops and offices closed in protest against his policy. Churchill tried to draw Musa Kazim's attention to the second part of the Balfour Declaration, which promised that 'nothing shall be done which may prejudice the civil and religious rights of existing non-Jewish communities in Palestine'. British politician and historian Mark Sykes writes that 'al-Husayni did not understand politics when he rejected the second part'.[36] Did he not? The second part was subsidiary and vague. It is possible that had the Palestinians accepted the Balfour Declaration *in toto*, they might have embarrassed Britain and caused it to reappraise the situation. But this did not happen, and it is doubtful whether in the years come, when the Zionist lobby became stronger, the obfuscating and uncommitted British attitude would have changed.

The meeting with Churchill depressed not only Musa Kazim. Many of the politically active people in Jerusalem and all of Palestine felt helpless and despairing in the face of the new force that had arisen in their world – namely, Zionism. Had this feeling impelled them to act, they might have succeeded. But their low spirits only deepened the dissension, and especially the inter-clan rivalries, amongst them.

## CHAPTER 8

# The Grand Mufti and His Family
## Al-Hajj Amin Elected *Mufti*

Not all the heads of the family were shaken by the fall of Faysal's rule in Damascus. But those who had cast their lot with Greater Syria were stunned to hear about the French army's swift advance to the plain of Maysalun, northwest of Damascus, and the crushing defeat inflicted on Faysal's small army. Now their political energy had to be diverted to building up a Palestinian national movement. The Arab Club preferred by the Husaynis and the Nashashibis' favorite, the Literary Club, were replaced by the Muslim-Christian Association.[1]

The fall of Faysal was not the worst setback to contend with – harder still was the British government's hostility to the demands of the new national association. The government refused to recognize the executive committee of the third Palestinian Congress as a representative body. Yet it treated the Jewish leadership with sympathy, and the pro-Zionist High Commissioner Sir Herbert Samuel dealt with it as though it were a quasi-government. Though the High Commissioner's advisers persuaded him to maintain working relations with the Palestinian executive, this was not enough to bridge the gap, which would grow wider through the years of the mandate.

Despite the drama of the British conquest, the family had a sense of unity and continuity. Most of the family lived in the same neighborhood, known as the Husayniyya. Half of its twenty-two houses were occupied by the family. When they did not discuss the major issues of the day, the politicians of the family gave much thought to the *mufti*'s successor as Kamil's health deteriorated during the winter of 1920–1. Hearing that he was ailing, several members of the family returned from other parts of the Arab world. Kamil's brother al-Hajj Amin and his son Tahir III were the main contenders for the post. Kamil himself had hinted more than once that he regarded al-Hajj Amin as his successor, but since Tahir also wanted the post the family had to choose between them.[2]

However, new conditions called for unprecedented political and social efforts – this time the *mufti* had to be elected. In Ottoman times, the *sheikh al-islam*, the Grand Mufti of the empire, would generally choose the *mufti* of Jerusalem from among the family dynasties that had held the post, so that it passed from father to son or another heir. In any case, Ottoman law required that the *mufti* be chosen from among the notables. The British rulers did not wish to change local customs, believing that international law demanded they follow the Ottoman law that laid down the procedure for choosing a new *mufti*.

Had the Ottomans been in power, they might also have chosen al-Hajj Amin. In any event the Husaynis would have retained the post, since very few families could boast a lineage as grand as theirs. A typical product of the age of nationalism, al-Hajj Amin was a natural for the post, having served in Faysal's entourage and shown leadership qualities during the events of April 1920. But the Ottomans were gone, and Kamil died in March 1921. Not long before his death, the British rulers weakened his position by making Sheikh Khalil al-Khalidi president of the Shari'a Court of Appeal, a post that had been Kamil's.[3]

Ottoman law required a special gathering of the *ulama* and members of the district and city councils to propose three candidates, one of whom would be chosen by the *sheikh al-islam* as the next *mufti*. This time it was decided that an *ad hoc* council of religious scholars would select four candidates and then vote on the final choice. Al-Hajj Amin was the Husaynis' candidate, while the rival Nashashibis wanted to put forward a candidate of their own, hoping to deprive the Husaynis of this power base. The sharp break between the families was probably occasioned by the appointment of Raghib al-Nashashibi as mayor in place of the deposed Musa Kazim, as described in the previous chapter.

But the Nashashibis had no suitable candidate of their own, and so they turned to the Jarallahs. During the eighteenth century, before the Ghuddayas had become the Husaynis, the Jarallahs competed with them for the posts of *mufti* and *naqib*. Two centuries later, in 1948, when East Jerusalem was annexed by the Hashemite kingdom, the post of *mufti* was given to the Jarallahs, in keeping with Jordan's policy of sidelining the Husaynis.[4] In the past, the Jarallahs had twice been defeated in contests for senior posts in Jerusalem. The first time was in 1720, but it is doubtful that they were impelled by such a distant memory. The second time was in 1856, when the post of *mufti* went to the Husaynis, which may well have been sufficient cause for the Jarallahs to support the Nashashibi bid.

They chose Husam Jarallah, partly because he was a graduate of al-Azhar. While his diploma did not represent a serious advantage, it became central to the Nashashibis' campaign simply because al-Hajj Amin had failed to graduate from that august institution. Husam was also the superintendent of the Shari'a courts, and most important, he was an older man, as were the other two candidates. Since the electors among the *ulama* were also older men, it was reasonable to assume that young al-Hajj Amin would strike them as unsuitable.[5]

To Tahir's dismay, the family decided that, young as he was, al-Hajj Amin was the right man for the post and began to campaign for him. Since the creation of the municipality, the main method of campaigning had been to circulate a petition. The young members of the family wrote the petition proclaiming that al-Hajj Amin was 'the people's choice', and distributed and pasted it up all over the city. Some of the flyers had been written in advance, others were actually penned by supporters. The ones signed 'the common people' were probably written by a member of the family.

Among the signatories in the Haifa area was Izz al-Din al-Qassam, a Syrian Muslim cleric. After having taken part in the national revolt against the French, he had been captured and sentenced to death but managed to escape to Haifa. This man, who would have considerable influence over al-Hajj Amin's future, contributed to the latter's election as leader of the Muslim community in Palestine.[6] His name is as familiar to students of Palestine at the beginning of the twenty-first century as it was during the mandatory period.

One reason the family believed that al-Hajj Amin would win despite his youth was that he had the support of Muhammad Abu Saud al-Ghori, the *qadi* of Jerusalem. Immediately after Kamil's death, al-Ghori wrote Governor Storrs that 'his brother, al-Hajj Amin Effendi, is his heir'.[7] This greatly impressed the family, who saw it as approval from on high. Directly after his older brother's death, al-Hajj Amin put on the *hamama* (the Hajj's white hat) and began to grow a beard as though he were already the *mufti*. That day he discarded his European suit for ever.

Elections were held on 12 April 1921. Husam Jarallah received most of the votes while al-Hajj Amin only made it to fourth place.[8] Shocked, the family gathered in Ismail's house and railed against the results. Ismail and Jamil had conducted the campaign for al-Hajj Amin, and though he was not their favorite, they all felt that the family's prestige hung in the balance. Now they all assembled to launch an intensive second campaign to change the outcome. Helped by his friends in the Arab Club, Jamil invited *ulama* and notables from all over Palestine to his house and asked them in the name of the people to organize an opposition in the towns and villages. The result was hugely successful: hundreds of petitions arrived from all over the country along with the especially heartening support of the heads of the Christian communities. Faysal, the exiled King of Syria, and his brother Abdullah also sent letters of support. In later years, Abdullah would become al-Hajj Amin's nemesis, but such are the vagaries of history – today an ally, tomorrow an enemy.[9]

The petitions advanced two arguments – one, that the choice of *mufti* concerned all Palestine; two, that the post should be held by the descendant of a family of *muftis* – combining older concepts with contemporary national realities and illustrating the transition of Palestinian society from a tradition-bound community to a national society.

Typical of the gossipy nature of politics at that time, other petitions circulating sought to convince the Palestinian public that a Nashashibi-Zionist conspiracy was afoot. On the night of 19 April 1921, a week after the vote, young Husaynis pasted five posters on the walls of the Old City warning the public that the Jews were trying to install a traitor as *mufti*, one who would accept Zionism and try to kill the Palestinian national spirit. This traitor would sell the religious property known as Abu Maidan – which included the area of the Wailing Wall – to the Zionists, who were trying to take over the Haram al-Sharif in order to build the third Jewish temple upon its ruins. The poster quoted Zionist leaders who spoke of building the Temple of Solomon anew on the Temple Mount. It is doubtful that anyone actually read those posters, because they were removed the following morning, but this message was transmitted by other means and served al-Hajj Amin's campaign.[10] The Husaynis were gathering sympathy for their cause.

Some Husaynis did not fight on the anti-Nashashibi front. Shaker al-Husayni (grandson of Mayor Hussein) of the Umari branch not only sided with the Nashashibis, he also headed their efforts to reach an understanding with the Jewish Agency. In February 1923, Shaker met with Colonel Kisch, an Anglo Jew enlisted by Weizmann to head the Zionist executive in Palestine. Shaker told Kisch about his attempt to persuade the Husaynis to support the idea of an advisory council, a kind of joint Palestinian-Zionist parliament with an equal number of representatives for each group (though the ratio in the country was nine Palestinians to one Jew). The formation of such a body would have implied Palestinian acceptance of the Jewish claim to at least a part of the country. The idea had been worked out with Raghib al-Nashashibi and Arif al-Dajani. Kisch worked hard to unify these Palestinian forces and was successful to some extent.[11]

The British government was now under pressure. On the one hand, there were the results of the preliminary vote for the *mufti*, while on the other, there was clear popular support for al-Hajj Amin's candidacy. The High Commissioner was faced with a dilemma: al-Hajj Amin was inexperienced and had taken part in anti-British activities, but there was no denying his family's prominent position in local politics. Sir Herbert Samuel had little sympathy for al-Hajj Amin. This was due not only to Samuel's pro-Zionist inclination but also to the influence of al-Hajj Amin's chief opponent in the British administration, Sir Wyndham Deedes.

Al-Hajj Amin won this contest of wills: the vote was canceled, and he was appointed *mufti* by the mandatory government. The day after he became *mufti*, Deedes resigned his post. Samuel met with al-Hajj Amin the day before the preliminary vote and was favorably impressed, believing that the young man would use his own and his family's influence to bring calm to Jerusalem and the entire country.[12] Later that month they met again, and according to Norman Bentwich, a future public prosecutor in the mandatory government, al-Hajj Amin promised to cooperate with the government and even expressed regret over his part in organizing the events of April 1920.[13] He also maintained that the violent demonstrations that occurred at the time had been spontaneous and unplanned. Bentwich, who would come to regard al-Hajj Amin as a very dangerous man, believed that he was sincere in his promises to appease the country, as shown by the fact that it was quiet between 1922 and 1929. The public never knew the details of these talks, but many suspected that Samuel's support had been won by al-Hajj Amin's moderation – an assumption that would become a central argument of the Palestinian opposition in years to come. Both his Palestinian opponents and the Zionists described him as an opportunist because he cooperated with the British to secure his position. At any rate, he obtained the government's support. Just before leaving the High Commissioner, al-Hajj Amin asked him directly, 'Which do you prefer – an avowed opponent or an unsound friend?' 'An avowed opponent,' Sir Herbert replied.[14] Perhaps this final exchange convinced the High Commissioner that he had chosen well.

The government vacillated throughout April, which ended with the Nabi Musa celebrations. The festival was peaceful and orderly that year. Al-Hajj

Amin conspicuously worked hard to keep them quiet, and his impressive conduct as a man of religion, rather than of politics, impressed the British authorities. Astutely, he took the *mufti*'s place at the head of the procession to Nabi Musa, where he made a conciliatory speech, and everything passed off calmly. To reinforce the impression that a peaceful new era had begun, he invited Sir Herbert to a kosher dinner at his house, which marked a real rapprochement between him and the British authorities.[15] The High Commissioner felt that al-Hajj Amin had matured and meant to follow his late brother's cooperative ways.

Ernest Richmond, a political adviser to the city governor, was instrumental in persuading the High Commissioner to cancel the final vote and appoint al-Hajj Amin. Richmond was an architect who had served in the Public Works Department in Egypt before the Great War. His close friend Storrs had rescued him from a gloomy job at the Imperial Internment Department in Cairo and brought him to Jerusalem. There Storrs made Richmond supervisor of the restoration of the Dome of the Rock on the Haram al-Sharif, a position that brought him into close contact with the Husaynis and their world. As *mufti*, al-Hajj Amin devoted himself to the restoration of the two shrines, enlisting the help of his adored teacher Rashid al-Rida and Prince Muhammad Ali, the uncle of King Fuad of Egypt. As a consequence of his work on the shrines, Richmond became an informal adviser to Storrs, in whose house he stayed (as he had done in Egypt before the war), and in 1918 he was made an official adviser. His unreserved support for the Palestinians, notably the Husaynis, won him a place of honor in the family history. However, his career in Jerusalem came to an end in 1924 when a pro-Zionist British administration drove him out of the city.[16]

Richmond was very active on al-Hajj Amin's behalf. He translated petitions from Arabic into English for Storrs and enlisted him in the campaign, and so a pro-al-Hajj Amin lobby came into being.[17] Storrs considered himself an expert on native affairs, and in this capacity advised the High Commissioner that petitions were a clear indication of a man's popularity. Storrs was even persuaded to cancel the vote and accepted Richmond's advice to consider raising al-Hajj Amin's salary when he became *mufti* and to let him keep the title of Grand Mufti, which the government had granted to Kamil. Perhaps he hoped to restore the balance between the Husaynis and the Nashashibis, which had been disturbed by the dismissal of Musa Kazim from the mayoralty.

However, the High Commissioner ultimately rejected proposals to make al-Hajj Amin the Grand Mufti, to give him an official letter of accreditation and even to announce his appointment in the *Palestine Gazette*. But he did concede on the most important demand – to cancel the vote and appoint al-Hajj Amin as *mufti*. And so, although he had not completed his academic studies and had not been elected, and despite the possible availability of better candidates in his family, al-Hajj Amin became the *mufti* of Palestine at the age of twenty-six. There can be no doubt that the main reason for his success was the family's campaign on his behalf.[18]

Now it was up to Storrs to resolve the legal problem of the disregarded vote. He persuaded Raghib al-Nashashibi to withdraw his candidacy, at the cost of a fierce argument with his family.[19] Raghib even agreed to help Storrs get Husam Jarallah and Ali Jarallah (the other Nashashibi candidates) to withdraw their names. The problem was solved.

Samuel had reconciled the families, but he failed to reconcile Palestinian society, which by and large continued to regard him as the emissary of the Zionists. Wherever young urban and country men were frustrated in their search for employment and housing, political bitterness came to the fore. In Nablus and Jaffa groups of young men vented their desperation and their violent opposition to the Jews and the British.

On 1 May 1921, a few days after the Nabi Musa celebrations, clashes broke out between Jews and Palestinians in Jaffa. Oddly, the trouble began among the Jewish settlers when communist activists calling for a Soviet Palestine clashed with members of Poale Zion, a party that wanted a Zionist Palestine. The Zionist May Day procession entered a Muslim neighborhood, where a violent scuffle broke out. Young Palestinians gathered from all around to demonstrate, some confronting the army while others battled with young Jews. This pattern of escalation was repeated in several places, the worst being in the area of Tulkarem. As in 1920, the number of fatalities was almost equal on both sides – forty-eight Arabs, forty-seven Jews.[20] The experienced British authorities appointed a court of inquiry known as the Hycraft Commission, which concluded that the riots had not been organized but had erupted spontaneously.

An outside observer would have noticed that in 1921 al-Hajj Amin was not yet the head of the family or of the national leadership. Musa Kazim and Jamal al-Husayni were regarded not only as the heads of the Husayni clan but also as the foremost representatives of the Palestinian community. Moreover, they had become its pro-British indicators. Fulfilling the promises he had made to the High Commissioner when they met immediately after the clashes, Jamal called on the inhabitants of Jaffa and Jerusalem not to be drawn into confrontations with the Jews and the authorities. The Hycraft

Commission was particularly impressed by Musa Kazim, who had addressed the Palestinian community in the same spirit even before the skirmishes in Jaffa. He had publicly appealed to the Palestinians to place their trust in the British government,

> 'which is famous for its justice, its concern for the welfare of the inhabitants, its protection of their rights and its response to their just demands. It will not fail the people's hopes, because the voice of the mass is like God's voice.'[21]

Others condemned the outbursts of rage, including the journal *Al-Karmil*, which was associated with the Palestinian executive.

Al-Hajj Amin's temporary disappearance from center stage may have been due to his uncertain political position. It is difficult to pinpoint where he stood at that time with regard to current events. There is some evidence that the outbreak of violence in Jaffa was linked to the group known as the Black Hand, later called the *Fida'iyya*. As mentioned before, in 1919 al-Hajj Amin had created this group, which sprouted offshoots all over Palestine, and its members, who were his contemporaries, remained loyal to him throughout his life.[22] A good number of the Tahiri Husaynis thought al-Hajj Amin was endangering the family – notably his nephew Tahir III, who accused him of incitement and of having organized the 'riots'. The rest of the family referred to those events as an uprising or revolt; only people who adopted the Zionist or government terminology called them riots.[23] Tahir's animosity was not surprising. He had hoped to succeed his father as *mufti* and regarded his uncle al-Hajj Amin as a usurper. Yet at that time, the British authorities described al-Hajj Amin as a trustworthy and moderating leader.

Al-Hajj Amin returned to center stage, not to replace Musa Kazim or Jamal but to join them. The three became the family leaders – al-Hajj Amin at its head, flanked by the aged Musa Kazim, who sometimes acted as his firm supporter but who gradually began to undermine his leadership, and Jamal, who would remain loyal to al-Hajj Amin until the end of the British Mandate. All three belonged to the Tahiri branch of the family, but as we have pointed out, the different branches no longer had any significance in local politics. Nevertheless, the Husayni women say that marriages were kept within each branch.[24] The reason for this was entirely material: Muslim laws of inheritance stipulated that in most cases the family's estate did not pass to the eldest son or to a chosen heir but rather was divided among the men of the family branch. Clearly, it would have been imprudent not to enlarge the branch by adding new members.

Politically, the Husaynis in the 1920s were a unified clan, and everything the Palestinians did was associated with it. Thus during the sitting of the Hycraft Commission, it seemed as if the British government would again charge al-Hajj Amin, and implicitly his family, with being responsible for the outbreaks. A wave of arrests and speedy trials of suspected participants followed the events, but surprisingly the Husaynis were cleared of all suspicion. Sir Herbert expressed sympathy for al-Hajj Amin and his family, and the mandatory government announced that it would halt Jewish immigration as a gesture of goodwill towards the Palestinians. This decision was made public together with the announcement of al-Hajj Amin's appointment as *mufti* – perhaps the first British attempt to conciliate the Palestinians. Al-Hajj Amin had obtained his position thanks to his family's history, the weakness of other Husayni candidates and his having won the support of the new government. It is not correct to say that the British enthroned al-Hajj Amin, as certain history books maintain. Rather, they decided to accept the social and religious hierarchy that had existed in Muslim Jerusalem in the Ottoman period and to apply it to the country as a whole.

In the following months, the authorities made a few more moves to please the Palestinian population. However, these were very small compared with their basic policy, which remained principally to support the Jewish claim to a 'national home' in Palestine. In the name of this claim, they reopened the gates to Jewish immigration and enabled the immigrants to purchase land and establish independent institutions. Before long this led to outbursts of rage and protests by irate young Palestinians, and the sympathies of certain pro-Arab officials could not sweeten the pill. The policy as a whole was perceived as anti-Palestinian.

The Palestinians' hopes for change were soon dispelled. On 29 May 1921, the fourth Palestinian Congress met in Jerusalem and resolved to send a delegation to London to demand an independent Arab Palestine. This was a necessary move: many Palestinians had supported the idea of a Greater Syria until the bitter end, and now it was time to demand independence. The idea of sending such a delegation was encouraged by certain pro-Palestinian British figures, such as Lord Sydenham and Lord Leamington, the owners of the daily *Morning Post*. The delegates were chosen by a vote – another opportunity for the family to test its standing amid the dramatic upheavals in the country. Musa Kazim received the most votes but was the only Husayni in the delegation. The opposition had not relented, and the journal *Al-Karmil* maintained that the composition of the delegation was unsatisfactory, despite its being widely supported.[25] The High Commissioner tried to dissuade them from going to London but acquiesced when they assured him that they would not conduct negotiations but only present their views.

Five men went to London in the autumn of 1921. For most of them this was a first foray outside the Middle East. They made several stops in Europe. In Rome, they were received by the Pope, who, they were relieved to discover, was a warm supporter of the Palestinian cause. From Rome they went on to Geneva, the seat of the League of Nations, which had that year begun its debates – as it would go on doing until 1924 – on the nature and substance of the mandatory regimes in the Middle East. It seemed for a moment to Musa Kazim that it might be possible to stop the wheels of history and prevent the ratification of the British Mandate of Palestine and the French Mandate of Syria and Lebanon. This unrealistic notion was put to him by Michel Latifallah and Riad al-Sulh, leading figures in the Lebanese national movement who proposed holding a pan-Syrian gathering in Geneva and presenting a unified protest to the League of Nations. But after the United States had withdrawn into its 'splendid isolation', the international body fell under the unfettered control of the two colonial powers. There was no chance whatsoever that the Palestinians, Syrians and Lebanese could change the colonial map of the Middle East without resorting to forcible struggles for national liberation. Such struggles would indeed take place before World War II and grow fiercer afterwards.[26]

After these frustrating meetings in Switzerland, the first-ever Palestinian delegation finally arrived in London at the end of September 1921. Five notables, all born into the Ottoman world and shaped by it, were confronted by the smoothly functioning British political establishment. They also faced the new but highly efficient Zionist lobby, which had already scored some major achievements.

On 2 November 1921, four years after the Balfour Declaration, Musa Kazim sat in his room in the Cecil Hotel on the Strand, writing gloomy letters to fellow notables in Jaffa, Nablus, Hebron and Jenin. He was feeling alone and helpless in the face of the supercilious Britons and the efficient Zionists, but above all he felt the humiliation of a Husayni having to cope with the minutiae of conducting such a diplomatic mission without a proper organization to help him. In his letters, he begged his associates to send him additional funds, not for public relations for the Palestinian cause but simply to finance his and his friends' stay in London. The small amount that had been raised in Palestine before their departure was running out.[27]

Despite this awkwardness, Musa Kazim tried to hold serious talks with the persons in charge of the Middle East at the Colonial Office. His primary request was for the Balfour Declaration to be reconsidered, but in this matter he and his fellow delegates ran into a brick wall. None of the officials would consider the slightest change of policy. The delegates also demanded the revocation of the Jewish 'national home', an end to immigration and for Palestine not to be severed from its neighbors. These three demands were raised in three meetings with Colonial Secretary Winston Churchill and were rejected outright.

Despite this disappointment, the British government managed to pacify the country for a considerable length of time. Unwittingly, while they themselves attempted with little success to create a unified national movement, the Palestinian leaders provided the Zionist movement with a period of calm during which to lay the foundations of the future state. Between November 1921 and August 1929 there were almost no violent clashes between Jews and Palestinians or between Palestinians and the British authorities. The calm was achieved thanks mainly to the creation of the Supreme Muslim Council.

### At the Peak of Power: The Creation of the Supreme Muslim Council

At the end of 1920, Samuel asked a committee of Muslim religious leaders in Palestine led by Kamil al-Husayni to consult with government officials on how to transfer the administration of their religious affairs to the Muslim notables. In March 1921, the committee submitted its proposal to create a Supreme Muslim Council. The demand for the council grew even greater when Norman Bentwich, a pro-Zionist Anglo Jew, was put in charge of the judiciary in Palestine, including the Shari'a courts.[28]

Having considered the matter for several months, the *ulama* proposed replacing the old Ottoman structure that oversaw the religious properties and the religious law with an autonomous council. Departing from its usual policy of preserving existing customs, the British government agreed, perhaps to placate Palestinian anger about the Balfour Declaration. The electors of the Ottoman Parliament – that is, the persons who elected candidates from the district of Jerusalem to the parliament – were asked to elect the council, which in turn would choose its president, the *rais al-ulama*.

It was a foregone conclusion that al-Hajj Amin would be chosen, and so he was in March 1922. Once again the Nashashibis tried to block the Husaynis' growing power. Raghib al-Nashashibi called for a boycott of the election, but to no avail. The significance of this new institution was very vague. The prerogatives seemed so extensive that the British officials feared they would supersede the local administration. For a moment, it looked as if the young national movement was coming into its own, and everyone echoed Jamal al-Husayni, who declared that the council's creation was 'a triumph of the national movement', since even opponents regarded the council's head as the national leader.[29]

The council's chief importance lay in its combination of political and financial power. With an annual budget of 50,000 to 65,000 Palestine pounds (drawn mainly from the religious properties), al-Hajj Amin was able to increase his influence throughout Palestine. He could give favored areas preferential treatment in development and welfare and neglect others where his standing was weaker, such as Hebron, Acre and Haifa. He also had the authority to hire and dismiss staff in the Shari'a courts.

Twenty-eight members of the Husayni clan received handsome incomes thanks to the council. Al-Hajj Amin was well aware of the value of this new post. Immediately after his appointment he made sure to inform all and sundry that it was a lifetime position, though this had probably not been the intention.

Future Israeli scholars would describe the new appointment as trickery, because the man chosen to fill the religious post was in fact a politician.[30] But of course religion and politics have been intertwined since the dawn of history, and Mandatory Palestine was no exception. In fact, al-Hajj Amin erred in not expanding his political activity. Though he did bring in some members of rival families, he failed to recruit talented individuals into the system he ruled over, probably because his dominant personality could not tolerate disagreement or disobedience.

But politics was not the *mufti*'s only sphere of activity. As head of the council, he established an orphanage for 160 boys and girls, supported schools, renovated the school in the Haram and established a museum and library in the sacred precinct. He was probably inspired by Ismail's extensive activity as head of the Board of Education in the late nineteenth century. On al-Hajj Amin's initiative, 50,000 trees were planted on religious property, and the system of public clinics and other welfare institutions were expanded. To cap it all off, he renovated the shrines on the Haram al-Sharif.[31] Though community welfare was not his main occupation, it should be included in the ledger of his career.

The creation of the council also enabled him to extend his influence over the educational system and to turn the Rawdat al-Ma'arif into a national college, an alternative to the system offered by the government and the missionary secondary schools. One of its first students was Abd al-Qadir al-Husayni, the son of Musa Kazim, and the father would later praise the new college for undoing the bad influence of the missionary Sahayun School on his son's personality.

Nonetheless politics were the *mufti*'s main occupation. The Palestinian delegation led by Musa Kazim returned empty-handed from London. In July 1922, the mandate was ratified and renewed, and a month later an 'Order in Council' (an official government announcement) was published in London. Colonial Secretary Winston Churchill placed before Parliament a proposed constitution for Mandatory Palestine predicated on the Balfour Declaration. The only local body it proposed was a Zionist-Palestinian (or in the lingo of those days, 'Arab-Jewish') legislative council that would help the High Commissioner to administer the country. Palestinian disappointment ran high, and it was against this background that the fifth Palestinian Congress was convened in Nablus on 22 August 1922.[32]

Angry and frustrated, the conference resolved to boycott the elections to the legislative council, using the *imams* in the mosques and the village heads to spread the word. Among the Husaynis, the divisions once more came to the surface. Musa Kazim feared aggravating relations with Britain. Nor did he care to fight against the Zionists, whereas al-Hajj Amin was more determined than ever to resist the British government's policy.

Throughout these years, Musa Kazim sought channels of communication and even reconciliation with Zionism. Still, he refused to meet Chaim Weizmann, because such a high-level meeting, especially if held publicly, would have been viewed as complete Palestinian submission to Zionist demands. It seems that Musa Kazim came to dislike Weizmann personally, though he had never met him. However, he maintained close relations with Haim Kalvarisky, who became head of the Zionist Federation's Arab Department after the British occupation.

As noted before, Kalvarisky continued to believe that eventually Zionism would win over many Palestinians, and he persuaded Musa Kazim to regard him as a major figure in the Zionist movement. Musa Kazim promised him that there would be no anti-Zionist action. One historian argues that the understanding between the two was so good that Kalvarisky succeeded in turning Musa Kazim's sympathies towards Zionism and sometimes even persuaded him to take certain actions.

Their understanding was at its peak in late 1922, when Musa Kazim and his

The Grand New Hotel, one of many Western buildings constructed as the foreign consulates in Jerusalem gained power. Pictured is Bertha Spafford Vester, who was chosen by Ismail al-Husayni at the turn of the twentieth century to run the only Muslim girls' school in Jerusalem.

Ismail al-Husayni's home, one of the few properties commissioned by the wealthy class in the late nineteenth century displaying classical Islamic architectural features. It was later turned into the Orient House Hotel.

Sharif Husayn with Kamal al-Husayni in 1914, bringing the holy carpet of the Prophet Muhammad from Mecca to celebrate the Nabi Musa pilgrimage.

Salim al-Husayni, Mayor of Jerusalem, circa 1909.

Salim al-Husayni with a Turkish general in 1914.

The military governor of Syria, Jamal Pasha, visits Jerusalem in 1915.

Musa Kazim and Ronald Storrs, the new mayor and governor of Jerusalem respectively, celebrating Armistice Day in 1919.

Mufti Kamil al-Husayni in 1919.

A delegation led by Hussein al-Husayni meets the
British army in 1917 with an official document of
surrender.

Al-Hajj Amin in the mid-1920s, in front of the Dome of the Rock.

Amir Abdullah, Winston Churchill and
Musa Kazim in March 1921.

Winston Churchill and Herbert Samuel in Jerusalem, March 1921.

Nabi Musa festival procession in the mid-1920s, likely one of the last.

Al-Hajj Amin and Musa Kazim, at the head of the 1929 Palestinian delegation to London.

The Shaw Commission.

Al-Hajj Amin greets the 1931 Islamic Conference.

The British District Commissioner and assorted notables address the public in 1941 near the Jaffa Gate in the Old City of Jerusalem.

fellow delegates were staying in Lausanne. The following year, Musa Kazim's speeches revealed the influence of Kalvarisky, as he repeatedly called for cooperation between Jews and Muslims. Under the same influence, he was even willing to postpone the sixth Palestinian Congress.[33] But even if there was a 'Zionist' phase in Musa Kazim's life, it would pass without a trace, and later he was willing to act openly against Zionism.

Or at least this is how his son Abd al-Qadir remembered it. From his twelfth birthday on, Abd al-Qadir accompanied his father to almost every political activity in which he took part. This contrasted with Abd al-Qadir's formal education, first in the Ottoman school, then at Bishop Gobat's Sahayun on Mount Zion and even during his spell at Rawdat al-Ma'arif. But despite his generally Westernized education – which he continued at the American Universities in Beirut and Cairo – Abd al-Qadir was never ambivalent about Zionism like Musa Kazim and his contemporaries in the family who were politically active until 1929. Led by al-Hajj Amin, the younger Husaynis continued to 'nationalize' the family, and their objection to Zionism was unequivocal.

Jamal straddled the fence. In the summer of 1923, he was willing to accept the British proposal of a legislative council provided all its members were elected and it had genuine prerogatives, especially on immigration. British documents show that the local authorities suspected Jamal of duplicity: while he called on the people to obey the government, he secretly conducted a campaign of intimidation against Palestinian participation in elections for the legislative council. In the end, however, they concluded that he was a reasonable and pragmatic representative of the Palestinian leadership. In 1923 Jamal won an important concession from the British government: recognition of the legitimacy of a representative Palestinian body – namely, the Executive of the Palestinian Congress – alongside the Jewish leadership and the British authorities.

'It was not a representative body,' argues Orientalist Elie Kedourie in a book listing the mistakes made by the British government in the Middle East between the two world wars.[34] But his argument is flawed, because the Jewish leadership was not a true representative body either – in fact neither community was especially democratic. With regard to the Husaynis, it may be said that although they were not democratic, they were certainly not antiparliamentary. Like all urban notables in the Arab world, the Husaynis welcomed the institution of a parliament, since for the past century and a half they had taken part in representative bodies and for the past fifty years in elected ones.

Kedourie's comment is important not because it is correct but because it points to the Palestinians' failure to create a more enduring institution. In October 1923, Sir Herbert Samuel informed a delegation of Palestinian leaders of the government's proposal to set up an Arab Agency alongside the Jewish Agency. The delegation was headed by Musa Kazim, who rejected the proposal outright, saying that 'it did not meet the aspirations of the Arab nation'. He suspected that if he consented, the Palestinian community would be expected to extend formal recognition to the Jewish Agency.[35]

An uncharacteristic remark from al-Hajj Amin stands out amongst the statements made during this period. He said that if it had not been for the Balfour Declaration, he would have consented to Jewish immigration and settlement. This idea was echoed in Musa Kazim's speeches at the time, and it indicates that they were still uncertain then about their attitude towards Zionism. But this uncertainty vanished in the 1930s.

### *Zionist Buildup and Palestinian Distress: The Quiet Years*

The first seven years of Mandatory Palestine have been dubbed by many historians 'the quiet years'. In fact, between the bloody outbreaks in 1920 and in 1929 there was some prosperity and growth. In the early days of this period, the British government made unavailing efforts to provide a legal and political foundation for a kind of mandatory state. But as the Jewish presence in the country increased, the Zionists became less willing to accept any arrangement that could have been acceptable to the Palestinians. The Palestinian leadership, though troubled by internal dissent, was willing to compromise; it wanted to enter into a genuine dialogue on the British proposal to create a state with a legislative council granting equal representation to Jews and Palestinians and with making joint resolutions on immigration and land purchases. But the Zionist leadership rejected it, and so did the British government.

The first fruitless British attempt to create such a quasi-state was made in the autumn of 1922, when the government announced the forthcoming elections to the legislative council. Wisely, it decided not to force the issue, and thus avoided an outright confrontation. Palestine was still very much the country of the Palestinians in 1922, and it was difficult to see why the local leadership should agree to partake in its Zionization. According to the British census taken in 1922 in preparation for the failed 1923 elections, there were 666,000 Arabs and 84,000 Jews in the country.

On the day of the elections, the Palestinian boycott succeeded beyond expectations. Whether correctly or not, the family members attributed some of its success to the tireless and eloquent preacher Sheikh Abd al-Qadir al-Muzafir.

By the time the sixth Palestinian Congress was convened in June 1923, all hope of persuading the British government to change its policy had evaporated. It was briefly thought that Sharif Hussein of Mecca would demand the abrogation of the Balfour Declaration in return for his endorsement of the peace accords concluding the Great War, but the aged *sharif* was under attack from his Saudi and Yemeni neighbors and could not alter the rules of the game dictated by the Great Powers.

In 1923 al-Hajj Amin sought to enlist the support of an active opponent of British rule, Ahmad al-Sharif al-Sanusi, leader of the Sanusi movement. He invited al-Sanusi as his first guest in his role as *mufti*. Wearing a curved dagger in his sash, the visitor toured the Haram and noted its rundown state. This was the first of a series of visits designed to raise awareness of the Muslim and Arab situation in Jerusalem.

Amid widespread disillusion with the British, Jamal al-Husayni became publicly prominent. In 1922 Arif al-Dajani was dismissed from his chairmanship of the fifth congress's executive. Jamal, the executive secretary, became acting chairman, with Ishaq Musa al-Husayni as his deputy.

As noted before, Ishaq Musa did not persevere in politics. In 1923 he moved to Cairo, where he took up an academic career, first at the American University and then at the Egyptian University. His contemporary Tahiri kinsman Muhammad Yunis also stayed out of politics. He studied economics and law, switched from the American University in Beirut to the Hebrew University in Jerusalem and in the 1930s moved to London. In those years, three of Musa Kazim's sons also took up various professions (except during the uprising). Fuad engaged in agriculture, Rafiq became an engineer and Sami taught at the Rawdat al-Ma'arif. Only Abd al-Qadir followed his father to the front rank of the Palestinian national movement.

But they were the exceptions. Most of their generation was deeply involved in local politics. Young Muhammad Yunis, for example, was deputized whenever Jamal was out of the country. (In 1923 Jamal spent a long time in India, where he formed close ties with the Muslim elite that would serve the Husaynis during the 1930s.)

At that time Jamal gave an interview in the journal *Mirat al-Sharq* in which he stated that the main lesson to be learned from the British treatment of Sharif Hussein was that perfidious Albion could not be trusted. The fact that a considerable number of Arab leaders outside Palestine were willing to negotiate with the Zionist leadership deepened Palestinian frustration, and the sixth congress condemned all such attempts.[36]

In some ways, Jamal himself was 'guilty' of such contacts. Towards the end of 1924, Jamal met Kalvarisky and suggested that the Palestinians would give up their demand for an independent national state in Palestine in return for an Arab-Jewish agreement to create a two-tiered legislative assembly. The lower house would be based on proportional representation and the upper chamber was to be composed – as the British had suggested – on a communal basis, with the Jews having two out of ten representatives. Jamal also suggested a joint immigration commission and, to calm the Zionists' fears, proposed that the High Commissioner have the right to veto any resolution of the lower legislative assembly. Jamal's proposal was rejected out of hand, not only by Zionist leaders but also by the pro-Zionist Sir Herbert.[37] Contrary to a view commonly held in Israel, the history of the conflict is not made up simply of peaceful Jewish proposals met by Palestinian rejection; quite often it was the other way around. Jamal seems to have been unable to decide on the best way to deal with Zionism.

Perhaps it was this vacillation that made it difficult for Jamal and al-Hajj Amin to organize Palestinian resistance to the frustrating British stance. The opposition began to take shape in the winter of 1923. The Nashashibis rallied around Raghib, a member of parliament, Jerusalem's chief engineer and a former candidate for the post of *mufti*. They enlisted the support of such figures as Taji Faruqi, Bullus Shehadeh (the editor of *Mirat al-Sharq*) and the Jaffaite Arif al-Dajani. Together they resigned from the Executive Committee and created the National Muslim Association, a move applauded by Kalvarisky. This body soon collapsed after the financial support from the Zionist Federation its members had hoped to receive did not materialize. In November 1923, they decided to create another organization, the National Palestinian Arab Association, which adopted a strident attitude but followed a moderate program for dealing with both the British and Zionism.[38]

The new association's program dismayed al-Hajj Amin, Jamal and Jamil when they read it at Ismail's house. Until that day, the call for an Arab Palestine (the first issue of the program) and the non-recognition of the Balfour Declaration (the second issue) had been associated with Husayni positions. The declaration that 'the peasant is the nation's body [*mada*]' made no impression on them.[39] Neither then nor in later years did al-Hajj Amin take any interest in the life of the *fellahin*, and he missed the opportunity to win mass support for his national movement. When the British Peel Commission described al-Hajj Amin as 'the leader of the Palestinian peasantry', it was a mistaken and misleading epithet. The rival party, by contrast, cultivated close contacts with the rural *sheikhs* and through them was more connected to the world of the farmers. In the early 1930s, the Nashashibis created an offshoot organization called the Farmers' Party, and the Husaynis made no attempt to counter it in any way.[40]

Nor did the Husaynis respond by reactivating their own party, which was well-established but had ceased to function once al-Hajj Amin had become Grand Mufti. After all, they were the establishment, and they dominated two bodies – the Supreme Muslim Council and the executive of the Palestinian Congresses. (There were eight such congresses between 1920 and 1928, with an Executive Committee elected to administer Palestinian affairs between one and the next.)

The Nashashibi opposition conducted its propaganda campaign mainly against the Supreme Muslim Council, attacking it with constitutional, administrative and ethical arguments. But it failed utterly, as the British government was not persuaded by such accusations. Still, the opposition damaged the Supreme Muslim Council's ability to build up the social strength needed for the struggle. Al-Hajj Amin was especially incensed when the opposition persuaded the people of Nablus to stay out of the Nabi Musa celebrations in 1924. The Nablusites held their own procession, charging that the Husayni family was using the festival to its own political ends.[41]

People adjust to enforced changes with astonishing speed. Before the British legal system had taken root in Palestine, Amin was the first local leader to use a British concept in his battle with the Nashashibis. In 1924 the *mufti* sued the editor of *Mirat al-Sharq* for libel because of a long article that accused him of misusing the Muslim religious properties. However, the suit failed.[42] The journal *Al-Karmil* also attacked the Husaynis and blamed Musa Kazim for the divisions in the Palestinian camp.[43]

In 1924 the weakness of the Palestinian national movement became obvious to everyone. In January, a Labour government was installed in Westminster and soon showed that no matter which party ruled Britain, the policies remained the same. Even the appointment of a new High Commissioner in 1925 would make no difference. In 1924 the seventh Palestinian Congress was supposed to convene, this time based on real elections, but the opposition refused to take part in the democratic exercise. The conference was postponed, to no one's disappointment.

The congress took place some time later, after the Palestinians were encouraged by the sharp decline in Jewish immigration following an economic crisis and recession in 1925–6. The Palestinians associated the appearance of Brit Shalom – a Jewish group with a very different Zionist outlook than that of the mainstream leadership – as a sign of the weakness of mainstream Zionist convictions. This sense was strengthened by unexpected moderation from the principal Zionist leaders and a new round of negotiations. The Palestinians both in the sixth congress's executive and in the opposition began to view the idea of a legislative council in a more favorable light. Had the British authorities made an effort at that time to push the two sides together, there might have been a breakthrough. But the British authorities hesitated and demanded a democratic mandate for this move, especially from the Palestinians. It was against this background that another attempt was made to convene the seventh congress.

Once again the Husaynis were the aristocracy of the land and its foremost family. The poet Fadwa Tuqan recalled how, as a little girl sitting next to her uncle Hafiz Tuqan, she was impressed by the respect he received simply because he was associated through family connections and politics with al-Hajj Amin. Hafiz headed the Nablus branch of the Husaynis' National Party and organized support in Nablus for the annual elections of the Supreme Muslim Council. Sitting in the family's drawing room, he would receive the city's leading figures, who came in to greet him or to ask his advice.[44]

Further clashes with the opposition before the seventh congress upset the family. In January 1926, there were new elections for the chairmanship of the Supreme Muslim Council, and the opposition looked set to win them. But the British authorities suspended the elections on suspicion of corruption. The government moved in and created a new, more genuinely representative Supreme Muslim Council whose composition in some ways restricted al-Hajj Amin's freedom.

In 1926 the factions fought it out in the Supreme Muslim Council, and the following year in the Jerusalem municipality. Municipal elections were held in the spring and summer of 1927. In cities with mixed populations, it looked as if the bloody 1920 conflict between the Zionists and the Palestinians had been forgotten, as Palestinians appealed to the Jewish voters to support them. Perhaps this meant that the majority of the inhabitants, both Palestinians and Jews, were not still caught up in the conflict like the political elites.

In Jerusalem the Jews were asked to support the Husaynis' candidate, Arif al-Dajani, and certain members of the family, notably Jamal, who were running for the city council. Perhaps the fact that Zionism was in crisis and looked less threatening made this possible. Jamal and Jamil al-Husayni asked Colonel Kisch to try to persuade the Jewish voters in Jerusalem not to support Raghib al-Nashashibi. In return they promised not to vote for the anti-Zionist Jewish Orthodox party Agudat Israel. Many Zionist leaders in the city believed that Musa Kazim was Jerusalem's strongman and should be cultivated since he desired better relations with the Jews.[45] Al-Hajj Amin himself took part in these moves and even invited Colonel Kisch to his house. But Kisch declined and later met Jamil and Jamal at the house of Dr Ticho, Jerusalem's well-known ophthalmologist.

The meeting at the doctor's handsome residence surrounded by cypresses was also attended by the family's friend Gad Frumkin, the only Jewish judge in the Mandatory Supreme Court. They talked until the small hours of the night, and the Husaynis, speaking on the *mufti*'s behalf, proposed a fair division of posts, expenses and budgets between Jerusalem's Jews and Arabs. The Husaynis' proposal was leaked to both the Arabic and Hebrew press and damaged their standing in Palestinian society. Indirectly, it led to their failure in the municipal elections in Jerusalem: 'Palestine is being auctioned off; the Zionist Federation is buying. The auctioneer is the Arab Executive!'[46]

The family even tried to enlist the support of the Palestine Communist Party. Its usual attitude towards the PCP was suspicious and disapproving. It was perceived as a Jewish party, and its platform was inimical to the family's interests. Jamal al-Husayni was probably the only one who understood the connection between the communist position and the struggle against Zionism. In 1924 he made contact with one of its leaders, Yosef Barzillai, who tried to get Jamal's support for its anti-imperialist campaign against both Britain and France. Barzillai gave Jamal 100 Palestinian pounds to buy arms for the struggle, but this financial connection went no further. Jamal did not buy arms but donated the money to the Husaynis' party. He continued to vacillate between sympathy and hostility towards the PCP, but being a pragmatist, he renewed contact before the elections. He actually obtained a PCP contribution to the Husayni campaign in the form of the hire of a motorcar – not a trivial matter in those days – which drove around the city with a loudspeaker on the roof, vociferously attacking the Husaynis' opponents.[47]

In the end, most of the Jews in Jerusalem voted for Raghib al-Nashashibi. The Husaynis' attempt to reach an understanding with the Jews confused most of the voters and certainly damaged the Husayni camp. Nashashibi won by a landslide. Yitzhak Ben-Zvi had the foresight to deplore the choice, arguing that the Zionist leadership had lost an important opportunity to build stronger ties with the dominant force in the Palestinian community.[48] Moreover, the corrupt and nationalistic Nashashibi turned out to be a bad mayor for the Jewish inhabitants.

The bitterest loss was in Jaffa. Not only did the municipality fall to the opposition but the newspaper *Filastin* also transferred its allegiance to the Nashashibis. Mayor Isam al-Said, who had joined the Nashashibi camp, had already fallen out with the Husaynis in 1923 when he agreed to connect his city to Pinhas Rutenberg's electrical grid. By doing so, he had linked Jaffa with an exclusively Zionist concession that was in the hands of a highly placed Zionist leader. Since they were dominated by neither camp and were more localized and autonomous, Haifa and Nablus remained relatively neutral. Tiberias and Safad, like other peripheral towns, remained loyal to the Husaynis.

But the outcome was unexpectedly favorable. Elated by its victories, the opposition wanted to present a unified front against Britain and Zionism at the seventh congress. The first sign of bridging the inter-clan divide was a tour taken by a broad Palestinian delegation through the Arab world during 1927, with al-Hajj Amin at its head. Their first destination was Syria, where al-Hajj Amin hoped to get help from the Syrian national movement, especially from its leader Shuqri al-Quwatli. Al-Hajj Amin had been in touch with him two years before when a revolt had broken out in Syria against the French Mandate and al-Hajj Amin had headed a Palestinian committee to raise funds for the uprising.[49]

From Syria the delegation turned southwards to Egypt. An Egyptian photographer took a picture of the *mufti* in the company of many opposition figures, sailing on the Nile on the occasion of the birthday of Egyptian poet Ahmad Shawqi.[50] The group returned to Jerusalem to take part in the festivities celebrating the new golden dome on the shrine of the Dome of the Rock, which also attracted many visitors from abroad. Everything was set for the congress, which would turn out to be the first and last to host a unified national movement.

The congress met on 20 June 1928 at Rawdat al-Ma'arif, a Husayni stronghold in Jerusalem. It ended with a unified Palestinian call for a legislative body, and for the first time the final resolutions did not include explicit attacks on the mandate and the Balfour Declaration. The congress elected a new executive to represent all the constituent groups fairly, thereby meeting the British demand for a truly representative government. The family was gratified – though al-Hajj Amin may have been disappointed – that Musa Kazim was chosen president of the congress. It is not known to what extent al-Hajj Amin was still a man of the family. Perhaps he preferred Musa Kazim over any candidate from a different family, but he might have hoped that another Husayni would be president instead of Musa Kazim, who now and then expressed his displeasure at al-Hajj Amin's leadership.

Following this congress, in the summer of 1928, the Palestinians presented the government with a memorandum signed by Raghib al-Nashashibi and Musa Kazim al-Husayni. For the Palestinian camp this was a moment of elation, unity and firm determination. It also offered a solution to the conflict, one of many openings that would be available to the contending sides. (All of these openings were slammed shut either because the Palestinian unity was so short-lived or – in most cases, including this one – because of Zionism's uncompromising attitude and British ineptness.) The leadership of the Jewish community was alarmed by the Palestinians' moderation, and they launched a diplomatic campaign to counter it. The Zionist leaders wished to be seen as peace seekers and at the same time undermine the Palestinian willingness to reach an agreement, which struck them as a danger to Zionism.[51]

Behind every peak of hope lurked a trough of despair. In August 1929, many Palestinians, led by al-Hajj Amin al-Husayni, fell into such a trough. Al-Hajj Amin had acquiesced to the moderation and unity of the Husaynis and Nashashibis, but he did not believe in them. The thwarted hope of reaching an understanding with the government not only drove al-Hajj Amin to adopt a more extreme position, it also aroused in him strong anti-Christian feelings that did not fit with the family's traditional attitude throughout the past two centuries. Early in 1928, he initiated the creation of the Young Muslim Association, which undermined Palestinian Muslim-Christian solidarity. The new association was inspired by Egypt's Muslim Brotherhood, launched that year by Hassan al-Bana. Yet al-Hajj Amin's renewed Muslim religiosity was not nearly as potent as the powerful blend of nationalism and Islam introduced into the Palestinian struggle by Izz al-Din al-Qassam that would ignite the fires of revolt in Palestine.

## The 'al-Buraq Revolution' of 1929

Even before the first spark that ignited Arab revolt throughout Palestine, a smaller uprising erupted in Jerusalem and other places in 1929. The ancient city had experienced all kinds of religious strife up to the late Ottoman period, most of which occurred between the diverse Christian sects and occasionally between Muslims and Christians. Very rarely were Jews involved as a religious sect in such embroilments. As far as they were concerned, the Muslims ruled all aspects of life in the city, and all religious disputes – including those concerning the status of the Western Wall (as the Jews call it), or *Waqf Maidian* (its Muslim name) – were resolved by the Ottoman government. If the new Zionist arrivals shared a common ground with the Ottoman Jews, who generally disliked them, it was the sense that the Ottomans throughout the years had ruled unfairly on the question of Jewish prayers at the Western Wall.

The wall in question was the western outer wall of the Herodian Temple, which the Jews believed had been built on the ruins of the Temple of Solomon. Since the Middle Ages it had been a place of prayer and lamentation for the fallen glory of Ancient Israel (hence its popular name, the Wailing Wall).[52] But the wall is also the western wall of the Haram al-Sharif, and the Muslims call it '*al-Buraq*', after the Prophet's famous horse. It abuts on what was known as the neighborhood of the Mughrabis (North Africans), and throughout the Ottoman period, until the Great War, it was part of a religious property named after Abu Maidian.

Throughout the Ottoman period, Jews had to obtain permission from the Muslim authorities to visit the site, which they were not allowed to treat as a place of pilgrimage and regular worship. Sometimes the Jews appealed to the Ottoman authorities, but these generally ruled in favour of the Muslims. The British authorities eased conditions for Jewish worshippers to some degree while agreeing with both sides to preserve the status quo with regard to all the holy places. But after the First World War, the Jewish community was the second largest in Jerusalem. Since the new government tended to be pro-Zionist, it was natural that the status of the Jewish holy places would be affected. Muslim anger about these changes contributed to the bloody events of 1929, especially in the Jerusalem area. (As we shall see towards the end of this chapter, the deteriorating socio-economic conditions in other parts of Palestine caused partly by the pro-Zionist British policy were far more important factors than the religious strife.)

As mentioned earlier, the Zionist movement attempted to purchase the space in front of the Western Wall, which the Muslim authorities allowed Jews to use only in restricted ways. The British conquest of Jerusalem made the Jews feel more confident, and they broke some of the restrictions to which they had been subjected under the Ottomans. The mandatory government enabled the Zionist movement to increase their presence on the site by small increments. Chaim Weizmann was actively engaged in the matter and immediately after Allenby's conquest of Jerusalem proposed to Storrs to purchase the Wall. The Mughrabi community, which had lived in the area ever since they came to Jerusalem as pilgrims, was interested in Weizmann's offer of some 70,000 Palestinian pounds if they evacuated the site, but the Palestinian leaders prevented the deal.[53]

While Kamil al-Husayni was *mufti*, the Muslim authorities reacted mildly to the Jewish breaches of the status quo at the Wall. But once the Supreme Muslim Council was launched, and the Jews' confidence grew even more, clashes at the site intensified. Increasingly the Jews brought chairs and benches into the area, and the Palestinians connected this behavior to statements made by Jewish and Zionist leaders about the need to build the 'Third Temple'. Testifying before the government commission that investigated the events of 1929, al-Hajj Amin referred to those statements as one the main causes for the violent wave that swamped Palestine in 1929.[54]

After the establishment of the Supreme Muslim Council, al-Hajj Amin kept calling the government's attention to the fact that the Jews were bringing more objects and religious appurtenances into the area in front of the Wall. The council also presented the government with retouched photographs showing the Jewish Temple standing on the Haram al-Sharif – pictures that were sent out to potential Zionist donors overseas. Throughout the 1920s the Palestinian Executive and the Supreme Muslim Council dispatched delegates and appeals to all parts of the Muslim world, asking for assistance in fighting the threat of a Jewish takeover of the Haram.[55]

One of the *mufti*'s most effective ways of enhancing local and regional interest in Jerusalem was to restore the shrines of the Haram al-Sharif. They had already been in need of such work in Ottoman times, but now the main impetus for the enterprise was political. From 1923 to 1924, al-Hajj Amin managed to raise substantial contributions from all over the Muslim world and started the renovation, whose climax was the gold-plating of the Dome of the Rock.

The atmosphere was growing increasingly tense. In 1925 there was a flare-up near the Western Wall, in the wake of which the Jewish Agency demanded that the British government compel the Muslim religious authorities to sell the Wall. The following year the Agency proposed purchasing fifty meters of the Haram al-Sharif, including the Wall, and began to negotiate with the government, but the deal fell through. At the end of 1928, Weizmann wished to offer 61,000 Palestinian pounds for the property, but he took the advice of High Commissioner John Chancellor to wait for a more opportune moment.[56] The Husayni family could take pride in al-Hajj Amin, who guarded the Haram as though the Ottoman sultan at the end of the eighteenth century had foreseen the future when he entrusted the guardianship of the holy places in Jerusalem to Abd al-Latif al-Husayni and his progeny.

Early on 23 September 1928, the eve of Yom Kippur (the Day of Atonement), the janitor of the Sephardi congregation came to al-Hajj Amin's office to report that he had just seen the janitor of the Ashkenazi congregation in front of the Western Wall setting up an arch, from which he suspended a large curtain, as well as pallets and oil lamps. The curtain was an unusually large screen, and it angered the *mufti* when he saw it for himself. It was a provocation not only for the Muslims but also for the Sephardi janitor, who would not receive the traditional fee for the job. The Muslim leadership immediately complained to Edward Keith-Roach, deputy governor of the Jerusalem district, who ordered the janitor to remove the architectural addition from the Wall's forecourt. But the following day, the screen was still standing – the Orthodox Jews would not do any work on the holy day, nor would they allow anyone else to do it for them. The installation of this screen separating men and women on the eve of the Day of Atonement in 1928 set off the first clash. In response, the Supreme Muslim Council created a committee 'For the Defense of *al-Buraq*'.[57]

How did this incident set off a violent clash, the bloodiest since the start of the British Mandate, between the Palestinians and the Jewish settlement? Palestinian historians have praised the *mufti* for turning a marginal event into a national one, thus establishing his leadership, while Israeli historians have accused the *mufti* of exploiting trivial discord to incite Muslims to 'murder Jews'. However, the *mufti* was the not the first to drag the opponents onto a battlefield. It was the World Zionist Federation, shaken by the incident, that charged the British police with aggression against the Jewish worshippers who refused to dismantle the arch and the screen they had set up. Four days later a big Jewish demonstration took place in Jerusalem. The more extreme elements threatened to seize the policeman who had dismantled the screen and tear him limb from limb. Then a general strike was declared. The Hebrew papers poured fire and brimstone on the 'Gentiles' – specifically the Muslims – and the national poet H. N. Bialik bemoaned the desolate Western Wall. Subsequently, Harry Lock of the government secretariat stated that 'Jewish public opinion has turned what was essentially a religious matter into a political-racial one'.[58]

Among historians, the Palestinian Philip Mattar and the Israeli Zvi Al-Peleg have questioned the thesis upheld by a good many Palestinian scholars and adopted by the Israeli Yehoshua Porath – namely, that the *mufti* consciously turned a minor incident into a violent clash. Mattar states that al-Hajj Amin said nothing for six days after the incident at the Wall and that even his publication *Al-Jamaa' al-Arabiyya* did not print any hateful or inciting material because the mufti did not wish to do anything that might affect the mandatory government's growing sympathy for the Palestinian position.[59] But when a week passed and the government had done nothing, he decided to act.

Throughout that week the Jewish reactions were fierce, and the atmosphere grew heated. Bialik, the Hebrew newspapers and Zionists spokesmen overseas all communicated a clear message: the Western Wall was in danger and needed to be protected. The Hebrew daily *Doar Ha-Yom* described those who threatened the Wall as 'hooligans, like the Russian pogromists'.[60]

On 30 September, the Supreme Muslim Council rallied thousands of Muslims from Jerusalem and its environs to the al-Aqsa mosque, where three of al-Hajj Amin's loyalists, Sheikh Abd al-Ghani Kamla, Izzat Darwaza and Sheikh Abu al-Saud, made speeches denouncing the Jewish aspiration to take over the Western Wall.

Now the Jewish National Executive realized the danger and tried to defuse the situation. On 10 October, it published an open letter stating categorically that there was no Jewish intention to seize the Temple Mount. But at the same time various Jewish leaders, led by Chaim Weizmann, continued to address the Jewish public, at home and abroad, about the need to resist Muslim intentions. Such statements could not be kept hidden from the public in Palestine.[61]

All through September 1928, al-Hajj Amin resisted the idea of acting in opposition to the laws of the mandatory government. When he was approached that month by the Syrian nationalist Shakib Wahab with a proposal to organize guerrilla groups to fight the government, al-Hajj Amin rejected it outright. A month later, however, he decided to take stronger measures. His role as head of the council and guardian of the Muslim religious properties, his ambition to lead the Palestinian people, the opposition's carping about his feeble reactions and the inflammatory Zionist propaganda all impelled him to take action. He launched the campaign of *al-Buraq*, which is still considered the finest passage in his career and one of the few to become part of the Palestinian mythos.

As he saw it, he was faced with a triple alliance – the British government, the local Jewish leadership and the Jews of the United States – against which he hoped to rally the Muslim and Arab world. On 1 November, he conducted a conference on Arab solidarity with Palestine that included 700 delegates from several Arab countries. The conference appointed a 'committee for the defense of the holy Muslim places in Jerusalem' and sent a delegation to the Chief Government Secretary Sir Harry Charles Lock (the deputy for High Commissioner Chancellor, then on home leave). Among other things, the delegation demanded the dismissal of the pro-Zionist Jewish prosecutor

Norman Bentwich, whose position enabled him to influence decisions concerning the Western Wall.[62]

Al-Hajj Amin also wrote Lock a personal letter arguing that the reactions of the Jews proved not only that they sought to deprive the Muslims of the religious property of Abu Maidian but also that they were plotting to take over the entire Haram al-Sharif. Early in October, al-Hajj Amin's paper *Al-Jamaa' al-Arabiyya* published articles about the Muslim right to the Abu Maidian. Though in October and November 1928 the Jewish leadership in Palestine tried to respond moderately and defuse the tension, as usual its overseas representatives took a more radical stance and suggested that the British government force the sale of the Western Wall to the Jews.[63]

In the winter of 1928, the British authorities in Palestine decided to intervene, and as a first step they published a White Paper. Considering the mounting confrontation as part of the conflict surrounding the future of the country as a whole, the White Paper linked the issue of the Wall with that of the legislative assembly. The Colonial Office backed the *mufti's* positions both on the legislative assembly (he held that its membership should reflect the demographic ratio in the land) and on the ownership of the Wall. On the ground, however, the Jewish presence at the Western Wall continued to increase, and practical talks about creating a parliament in Palestine were not renewed.[64]

Al-Hajj Amin felt frustrated by the government's attitude and launched what he called a holy war for the Haram. At first the war was vocal: he stationed a *muezzin* above the Wall who called on the Muslims to come and defend the Wall five times a day, disturbing the Jewish prayers below. To the same end, the Muslims also revived the loud *zikr* rites commonly practiced by Sufi sects. Gathering near the little garden close to the Wall, they filled the air with a deafening noise. 'We promised our Mughrabi brothers, who are attached to the Sufi tradition, to reinstate these rites as in past times,' the *mufti* explained to the Shaw Commission, which was appointed to investigate the violent outbreaks.[65] He also ordered an additional wing to be added to the Shari'a court building, and the stonemasons' hammering and shouting made things harder still for the Jewish worshippers.

In the 1950s, the *mufti* would argue that the struggle had been directed against the British too, but this does not seem to have been the case. Though many Palestinian historians have accepted this argument, others such as Philip Mattar have not. After all, during that time al-Hajj Amin was trying to cooperate with the British authorities and urge them to adopt a pro-Palestinian position. He was suspicious about the British government in London but tended to trust many persons among the mandatory authorities.[66]

The year 1928 passed without a violent outbreak, but the war of words intensified and tensions kept mounting. In April 1929, High Commissioner John Chancellor suggested the *mufti* sell the religious property and allow the Jews to build a courtyard in front of the Western Wall. The *mufti* responded mildly, saying he could understand that the Jews needed to pray but such a concession would endanger Muslim standing throughout the Haram al-Sharif. Palestinian historiography, including recent work that draws on newly revealed materials, suggests that the *mufti*'s concern was not baseless and that there really was a Jewish plan to seize the entire Haram.[67] But this does not correspond to the pragmatic Zionism of the time, which would have been satisfied with the Western Wall and would have regarded its possession as a major step forward for Zionism.

The 1929 outbreak was caused not only by the events in Jerusalem but also by larger circumstances. Some 90,000 Jews immigrated to Palestine between 1921 and 1929. Though the influx ebbed from 1926 to 1928, the presence of so many new immigrants in the labor market and the efforts of the Zionist organizations to purchase land for them made Zionism into a tangible factor in the lives of many ordinary Palestinians. While in 1920 Jews bought a total of 262 acres, in 1925 they bought 44,000 acres. During those 'quiet years', the Jews purchased a third of all the land they would acquire throughout the British Mandate, though never at such a fast rate as in 1925. By the end of 1928, there were about 100 Jewish settlements in the country, the leading commercial concessions were in Jewish hands and the percentage of Jews in trade and industry kept growing. At the same time, rural Palestine was experiencing an economic decline, giving rise to internal migration to the growing cities, a process that would accelerate in the 1930s. Shanties began to surround the growing towns and cities, providing cheap labor for the urban population, both Jewish and Arab, and their misery could be used to achieve political objectives. Long working hours in inhuman conditions intensified the bitterness and produced pockets of wretchedness that in 1929 could explode into violent action. It was easy to persuade the populace that their misery was caused by Zionism, since the internal migration, the loss of land and employment, were connected to the growth of the Jewish community. This volatile situation was made worse by the activities of the Zionist rightwing movement Beitar, which launched a series of provocations that made the outbreak of violence unavoidable.

Yet the first half of 1929 passed relatively peacefully. Despite the tension in the city, al-Hajj Amin had the leisure to cooperate with an urban project that had been close to his heart for some time: the construction of a hotel to accommodate the leaders of the Arab and Muslim world. Appropriately enough, he named it 'The Palace Hotel'. This not only advanced the development of Jerusalem, it also answered the demands of the Palestinian tourist industry, which watched anxiously as Jews became the principal hoteliers in the city. To pay for the construction of the new hotel, al-Hajj Amin used funds from the Muslim religious properties. The site chosen was in the heart of the Mamilla neighborhood. This fact provoked a response that is only too familiar in our time: Muslim religious scholars protested that it would be built on top of Muslim graves (as though there were any site in Jerusalem that does not contain tombs!).

At long last, the objections were dropped and the building rose up. Designed by an imaginative and experienced Turkish architect, it elegantly blended Arab and Western elements. The contractors were Jewish. Engineer Baruch Katinka and his colleague Tuviah Dunya, a well-known figure in the Jewish community, owned a construction company that operated in Haifa and Jerusalem during the 1920s.

Early in 1927, Katinka heard from a Palestinian acquaintance that the Supreme Muslim Council had published a tender for the construction of a hotel, which the acquaintance thought would be a suitable project for Katinka and Dunya. Moreover, he suggested that they add his name – Oud – to the bid, so that it could appear to be a Jewish-Arab enterprise. To their surprise, the contractors won the tender. As Katinka recalled, they continued to be surprised during their meeting with al-Hajj Amin and Hilmi Pasha: 'They received us courteously, and got down directly to drafting the contract.' Other preconceived ideas were dispelled in the course of the negotiations. Al-Hajj Amin demanded that the contractors meet the stiff timetable he had set for the project.

An elaborate Arabic inscription was painstakingly carved and placed high on the hotel's façade. The entire building was designed in arabesque style, expressing the taste of the Turkish architect Nihas Bey. Al-Hajj Amin demanded that the contractors give priority to Arab workers, which they did. As often happens in Jerusalem, on the second day of the project Katinka came across ancient burials. The worried *mufti* asked him to keep it secret, fearing that the work would be stopped. He knew only too well that Raghib al-Nashashibi would not hesitate to turn the 'desecration' to his own political ends. 'And so I became the Mufti's confidant,' wrote Katinka in his memoirs. He found al-Hajj Amin 'a fairly easy person, intelligent, sharp and polite'.

This was probably the last favorable comment made by a Zionist about al-Hajj Amin.

Al-Hajj Amin came to the site every day to observe the progress and often expressed his satisfaction with the work of the Jewish contractors. He was so pleased with them that he hired them to build his new house in Sheikh Jarrah. 'It was 1929,' Katinka recalled, 'and the tension between Jews and Arabs was mounting day by day. But my association with the Mufti had reached the stage of warm personal conversations.' Al-Hajj Amin revealed to Katinka that his financial situation did not allow him to finish his house: 'The foundations have been laid, but the rest is stuck.' After studying the plans, Katinka offered to build the house cheaply and complete it in two years.

Al-Hajj Amin's house rose up, as did the hotel – both built by the Jewish contractors. This was not a trivial matter. Dunya was Chaim Weizmann's brother-in-law and friend, and al-Hajj Amin knew it. Dunya recalled that al-Hajj Amin tried to send political messages through him, but he politely declined. One message, however, that al-Hajj Amin communicated to Dunya (though not to Weizmann) was that his opposition to the partition of the country was not personal but political, because it would not be accepted by the majority of the Palestinians. 'When I stand before the Arab people and announce that I have come to an agreement with the Jews, based on concessions I made them, the entire Arab people would ostracize me and denounce me as a traitor who sold his homeland.'

At the hotel's opening ceremony, al-Hajj Amin publicly praised Katinka and Dunya, and thereafter always invited them to the Nabi Musa celebrations. He also sent them platters with warm dishes at the end of Passover, so they could enjoy fresh risen bread as soon as possible. Dunya and Katinka 'repaid' him by using the hotel to hide two arms caches for the Hagana.[68]

But this kind of local and personal cooperation did not extend to the political arena. Tensions rose from day to day leading up to the eruption of 1929. (The Palace Hotel, incidentally, lasted for five years, then closed when the new King David Hotel eclipsed it as Jerusalem's most palatial hostelry.)

The *mufti* continued to cooperate with the British authorities through the spring and summer of 1929 in the hope of stopping the escalation, and he was bitterly disappointed when it turned out to have been in vain. In the summer of 1929, a new government came to power in London – a Labour government led by the vacillating Ramsay MacDonald. Colonial Secretary Sidney Webb had yet to acquaint himself with the issues. Between them they suspended all British action and initiatives in Palestine, and in the absence of clear directives, the mandatory government dealt only with the symptoms.

The *mufti* was pressured to stop the Sufi performances near the Western Wall, and when he gave in, he was accused by his opponents, notably the Nashashibis, of surrendering to the British. Seeking to counteract these charges, he started a restoration of the Wall near the section where the Jews prayed. Young Beitar men stopped the work and were praised by the chief rabbi, Abraham Kook. However, the leaders of the sixteenth Zionist Congress in Zurich were less impressed. They asked Jabotinsky to moderate his followers' aggressive behavior, but it only grew worse. Two thousand young Beitar men led by Yosef Klausner circled the city walls, proclaiming that they were the 'Western Wall Defense Committee'.[69]

In the summer of 1929, al-Hajj Amin began to feel the ground rumbling beneath his feet. He was less occupied with the Western Wall, but the young men and many other Palestinians anxiously followed the developments there, waiting for the *mufti* and other leaders to take firm action. Just before the outbreak, al-Hajj Amin met again with John Chancellor, who expressed the hope that the *mufti* was satisfied with the government's position. Al-Hajj Amin responded that he was loyal to the government but added that if the Muslim community did not receive any substantive proposals, he could not vouch for continuing law and order. At this point Chancellor, who had hitherto been pleasant, frowned and said sharply, 'You need not worry about law and order. These matters are my responsibility.' This arrogance was one of the reasons the British were taken by surprise in the summer when, for the first time since they had occupied the country in 1917, violence erupted on a large scale.[70]

In August 1929, the seeds of disaffection sown the previous winter sprouted a venomous crop. On a Thursday in the middle of the month, a group of young Beitar men gathered in front of Government House and began to march towards the Western Wall. Facing the Haram al-Sharif, they raised the Zionist flag, sang '*Hatikvah*' and shouted, 'The Wall is ours!' Rumors about the Zionist demonstration in the Mughrabi neighborhood spread quickly, inflated with a claim that Muslims had been beaten up. Tensions grew higher.

The following day, during Friday prayers, they reached an intolerable point. Muslims held an anti-Jewish demonstration, and a Jewish boy who had kicked a ball into his neighbor's tomato patch was murdered. The next day, a Muslim boy was stabbed. The funeral of the Jewish boy was large and forceful. It was organized by the Jewish Agency, which the Arabs of Jerusalem regarded as a particularly intimidating, rich and powerful body.[71] The following week, Beitar held another demonstration, which was met with a mass counterdemonstration by villagers from the vicinity of Jerusalem, to whom al-Hajj Amin addressed a fiery speech. Unable to contain their rage, the crowd broke into the area in front of the Western Wall. In the following few hours, they also burst into most streets in the Jewish Quarter of the Old City.

That Thursday the *mufti* consulted with his associates about the developments. He had not forgotten the British persecution of him in 1920 and tried to obtain a visa to go to Syria, but the local consul refused to give him one. In any event, he did not have to confront the British authorities. Testifying before the commission of inquiry that would investigate the events of 1929, al-Hajj Amin stated that he had not asked for a visa to flee the scene but for his regular summer vacation. He had been accustomed to go to Turkey every August, but since he suffered from seasickness, he had decided on an overland holiday.[72]

That Thursday Jamal called on Harry Lock, the government secretary, who was trying to arrange a Jewish-Palestinian meeting to cool the atmosphere. But the two sides could not agree, and they decided to hold another meeting the following Monday. By then, however, scores of Jews and Palestinians had paid with their lives for the aborted reconciliation.

That Friday a wave of violent unrest swept over the country, lasting a whole week. Al-Hajj Amin was urgently summoned from home by Alan Saunders, the acting commander of the Jerusalem police and deputy commander of the mandatory police. Thousands of Muslims armed with clubs and knives and a few rifles had gathered on the Haram al-Sharif, claiming that the *mufti* had told them to wreak vengeance on the Jews. In reality, the *mufti* was not responsible for this rumor. When he reached the plaza, he heard the cry *'Sayf al-din, al-Hajj Amin!'* ('The Sword of the Religion, al-Hajj Amin!'). He and Said al-Khatib, the *imam* who conducted the Friday worship, agreed that the sermon that day would be a moderate one, to calm the atmosphere.

On Saturday al-Hajj Amin and Musa Kazim were summoned to the house of the High Commissioner, who demanded that the *mufti* do more to defuse the tension. Al-Hajj Amin replied that there would be no point in his issuing such a call unless the Jewish leaders did the same. 'It's Saturday, the Jewish Sabbath,' Deputy Governor Keith-Roach said. 'They can't be reached by telephone.'

That day al-Hajj Amin invited the headmen of the surrounding villages and asked them to calm their people. 'The government is looking after the interests of the Arabs,' he assured them. But neither there nor on the Haram, nor later at the Nablus Gate, was the *mufti* able to stem the irate human tide.

Jewish attacks on Sur Baher and an attack on the Nashashibi house at Bab al-Sahra ignited an all-out Arab assault. A baseless rumor that a Palestinian had been lynched in the Orthodox Jewish neighborhood of Meah Shearim made it into the arena. Thus the first casualties were non-Zionist Jews of that neighborhood, and later of Yemin Moshe, who had always been on good terms with their Arab neighbors.

The *mufti*'s call, 'Arm yourselves with compassion, wisdom and tolerance, because Allah is always with the tolerant!' fell on deaf ears. Together with his friend George Antonius, he addressed the crowd:

> Calm yourselves, go home and leave me to do all I can. The government is not against you, nor the police. It is the duty of the government to maintain order. You know my feelings and views – I have always advised you to trust your leaders.

But his voice was drowned out by the roar of the crowd. Antonius saw that the *mufti*'s presence stirred the people rather than calmed them, and at his urging al-Hajj Amin went home.[73]

Al-Hajj Amin held talks with the leaders of Nablus and Hebron, but failed to pacify them. This was especially true where the Hebronites were concerned, since al-Hajj Amin's standing in that town was shaky and they would not listen to him.[74] There the Nashashibis were better entrenched, a fact that contradicts Israeli historiography's dichotomous depiction of the Husaynis as 'militants' and the Nashashibis as 'moderates'. They incited the mob against the Jewish community, with the result that sixty-four Hebronite Jews were massacred.

The same thing happened in Safad, where twenty-six Jews were murdered. The opposite camp, Zionist and British, was no less ruthless. In Jaffa a Jewish mob murdered seven Palestinians, and all in all 133 Jews and 116 Muslims perished during that bloody week.

Most of the Palestinians were shot by British policemen and soldiers. By 24 August, the government had decided to arm 500 Jews, and this contributed to the deadly score. Three days after this decision, a furious crowd surrounded al-Hajj Amin's house demanding weapons. Al-Hajj Amin lost his head for the first time. He telephoned Harry Lock and asked him to receive a delegation led by Musa Kazim. Al-Hajj Amin sent Musa Kazim reluctantly, but he felt he was under pressure and in grave danger. At the urging of the delegation, the authorities agreed to disarm forty Jewish policemen as a countermeasure to the arming of 500 Jewish civilians.

As soon as the violence subsided, the mandatory government took harsh measures, blaming the *mufti* and the Palestinians for what had occurred. High Commissioner John Chancellor had returned from home leave the day before the bloodshed in Safad. It was 1 September 1929.[75] He published an announcement placing all the blame on the leaders of the Muslim community. Later the Commission of Inquiry would exonerate the *mufti* and place the blame on both sides, but by then a gulf had opened up between the Palestinians and the British. Thereafter the Palestinian population would judge al-Hajj Amin by his anti-British as much as by his anti-Zionist position.

By November 1929, there were indications that the violent eruptions were due to a mistaken British policy rather than 'inherent Muslim aggression', as the Israeli and pro-Israeli historiography would have it. The High Commissioner thought as much, and so did the government in London. On 19 November the Colonial Secretary issued a statement promising the Palestinians that the Haram al-Sharif would be restored to its former situation. But this was no longer sufficient: the Palestinians, or at least their political elite, expected a more substantive change in Britain's Palestine policy.[76]

## CHAPTER 9

# The Great Revolt
## The Family as Revolutionary Aristocracy

*Family Statesmanship: The First Chapter*

The events of 1929 strengthened the standing of al-Hajj Amin al-Husayni and opened the way to his becoming the leader of the entire Palestinian nation. A British poll published in 1931 showed him to be the leader of nearly a million Palestinians. He was depicted as the captain of the 1929 Intifada and the one who had successfully defended the Haram al-Sharif and its shrines.[1] The large number of Muslim casualties obliged the Supreme Muslim Council to organize aid for the victims, and al-Hajj Amin administered the welfare program. The opposition claimed that he did not do enough with the funds at his disposal, and later historians, albeit Israelis, found disorder and forgeries in the council's bookkeeping. The old pattern of mixing private and public finances apparently persisted.[2]

Looking back on this period in the 1950s, al-Hajj Amin described himself as a fearless opponent of the British, but in reality he was happiest when he did not have to confront them head-on. Even after the outbreaks, he continued to regard them as allies. They might have been at fault, but they were indispensable. This was very different from Ben-Gurion's outlook, which was beginning to take shape at that time: if it became necessary, as it probably would, the Zionist enterprise would succeed even at the expense of a struggle against Britain.

Having become a political leader in the mandatory regime, al-Hajj Amin had two tasks before him. Besides material concerns, he had to represent the interests of the Palestinians before the Commission of Inquiry chaired by Sir Walter Shaw, which began its work in March 1930. Now al-Hajj Amin discovered the value of having Jamal at his side as a kind of Palestinian foreign minister when dealing with such British forums.

The four members of the Shaw Commission arrived by train from El-Qantara on 24 October 1929 and were whisked off unceremoniously to the Fast Hotel in Jerusalem. Prisoners, Jews and Palestinians were at once sent to repair the road leading to the court, where the judge Muhammad Yusuf al-Khalidi presided. A company of armed British policemen guarded the entrance to the court, but there were no demonstrations. The only people who gathered in front of the judge's office were journalists, both local and foreign. Four chairs were placed on the dais for the members of the commission and a secretary, and representatives of the Zionists and the Palestinians were ushered into the court. Al-Hajj Amin made sure that most members of the Supreme Muslim Council were present at his first public diplomatic confrontation with the Zionists and the British.

Later sessions were held in the Customs House in Jerusalem, where the future of Palestine was debated in a small office. Each side had hired expensive and well-known British lawyers to advise them. That was the way of the world in those days: command of British law became a major weapon in the national struggle. Having toured the country, the members of the commission began to realize the magnitude of their task and had the walls of the stuffy little office knocked down to create a proper hall.

The *mufti* was invited to testify at the forty-sixth session. In fact, the commission met in his office, and his testimony went on for five sessions. Al-Hajj Amin replaced the Christian interpreter Khalil al-Sakakini with the Muslim Musa al-Alami – not because of any doubt about the trustworthiness of the family's great teacher and loyal friend but to indicate that the central issue, the fate of the Haram, was a purely Muslim matter.[3]

Al-Hajj Amin used these sessions to conduct a historical review of the injustice done to the Palestinian people by the discriminatory British policy. For example, he noted that the mandatory government paved roads leading to Jewish settlements but refused his request to pave a two-kilometer road to Nabi Musa. But his main complaint was that the government regularly broke its promises – first the pledges made in the Hussein–McMahon correspondence, then the government announcements made during the 1920s. The lawyers for the Jewish side questioned his claim that there was a Jewish plot to seize the Haram.

The *mufti*'s British lawyer was Henry Stalker. A corpulent man who sported a monocle in his right eye, Stalker was over seventy but looked ten years younger. Stalker got al-Hajj Amin entangled with *The Protocols of the Elders of Zion*, which did him no good. He had brought a copy of the book in Arabic and French with him, and the *mufti* was seen reading it during the sessions. The lawyers for the Jewish side made the most of the apparent connection between the book and the Palestinian claims that the Jews were conspiring to seize the Temple Mount.[4]

Nevertheless, the commission ended up vindicating al-Hajj Amin, though it is uncertain whether this was thanks to his efforts or because the commissioners retained their independence. The Shaw Commission published its report at the end of March 1930, in which it upheld the basic Arab claim that Jewish provocations had caused the violent outbreak. 'The principal cause', Shaw wrote after leaving the country, 'was twelve years of pro-Zionist policy.' Now it seemed that the scales had tipped in favor of the Palestinians – and under the leadership of a Husayni.[5]

Furthermore, the Shaw Commission did not blame the *mufti* for the violent outbreak. Whether this made al-Hajj Amin feel better is unclear, as a British declaration of his innocence did not enhance his national standing. Perhaps that was why he did not express his approval of the report when it was adopted as the British government's official policy and published as a White Paper. The new policy determined that Jewish immigration and settlement in Palestine were to be curbed – which was, in effect, a repeal of the Balfour Declaration.

All these developments, before and after the crisis, disrupted solidarity among the Husaynis. Jamal rallied the younger generation, his contemporaries, to support al-Hajj Amin, while the older relatives considered Musa Kazim's conciliatory approach to be the best policy.

Musa Kazim had managed to maintain good relations with the Nashashibis throughout the crisis, and together they evolved a compromise position in Palestinian politics focusing on support for a Palestinian-Zionist legislative council. The British authorities certainly regarded Musa Kazim's stance as the embodiment of Palestinian moderation, but several of the Husaynis, notably al-Hajj Amin, thought it betrayed the cause. However, Musa Kazim's position was strong enough to withstand heated criticism in the family. During the 1930s, he and Raghib al-Nashashibi cooperated closely. Perhaps in different circumstances the Palestinians might have benefited from such a dual leadership. It might have helped the families overcome the tension and hostility between them.[6]

Though the Shaw Report appeared to vindicate al-Hajj Amin, if one examines British policies in the 1930s, al-Hajj Amin's position became increasingly insignificant in the eyes of those who formulated Britain's policy in Palestine. Neither moderation nor fanaticism would have enabled the Palestinians to persuade the British to turn against Zionism – certainly not in view of the dramatic and tragic developments in Central Europe during the 1930s and 1940s.

Musa Kazim remained in the picture and was still the most popular of the Husaynis among the social elite behind the political leadership. In the spring of 1930, he was again chosen to lead a Palestinian delegation to London to discuss the country's future. This time he was elected democratically. All al-Hajj Amin could do was ask that his kinsman and confidant Mustafa Kamal al-Husayni be included in the delegation as a representative of the paper *Al-Jamaa' al-Arabiyya*. Plump, jovial Mustafa Kamal did not have to act against Musa Kazim because the delegation returned empty-handed.

On this visit to London, Musa Kazim saw for himself how paltry the *mufti*'s achievements were. A crushing proof of the Palestinian leadership's insignificance in British eyes was the reception which met the delegation when they arrived at Victoria Station. Instead of an official representative, three elderly English ladies met them waving a Palestinian flag enthusiastically. They were the only supporters of the Palestine cause during the talks in the British capital.[7]

Sitting around a big square table under a dim ceiling lamp in a government office in Westminster, the delegates recapitulated the Palestinians' demands. The British officials hardly referred to the Shaw Report but put forward a private proposal made by the British Arabist and best-known agent on the Arabian Peninsula, St John Philby. It was an anachronistic compromise solution based on most of the former British government proposals that both sides had already rejected. Inevitably, it would suffer the same fate.[8]

Musa Kazim returned to Jerusalem immoderate and impatient: the British attitude had left him angry and frustrated. He decided to act more decisively in warning the Palestinian public of the Zionists' plans. Together with Munif al-Husayni, editor of the family-owned newspaper *Al-Jamaa' al-Arabiyya*, he launched a campaign in 1931 to convince the Arab public that the Zionist objective was the same as what it had been in 1929 – namely, to take over the Haram al-Sharif. Musa Kazim went to Gaza to get the local newspaper to publish his article on this subject, 'A Call to Palestine'.[9]

Any biography of the Husayni family covering the 1930s as well as the 1920s must focus on the political presence of the three leading figures in the family: al-Hajj Amin, Musa Kazim and Jamal (in this order). Yet Jamal really came to prominence only in the 1930s. Palestinian historians would agree that his contributions ought to be included in the finest chapters of Palestinian history, because there were few to match them at the time.

Jamal was above all a gifted diplomat. During the later stages of the British Mandate, the diplomatic skills of both sides were decisive in the struggle to win the country. Jamal was the most eloquent spokesman of the Palestinian cause and one of the few who tried to counteract the endless stream of reports and articles published by Zionists in the popular and even the academic press from 1929 on.

Jamal's first article appeared in November of that year.[10] Written in response to Zionism's most eloquent spokesman, Chaim Weizmann, it opened by drawing a clear distinction between Palestinian attitudes towards Judaism and Zionism. The Palestinians, Jamal wrote, were not opposed to the Jewish people but to Zionist aggression. Moreover, he went on, the struggle against Zionism did not mean a struggle against the British. Though the Palestinians were unhappy about Britain's policy, especially failure to keep promises to the whole of its Arab nation, they nevertheless considered themselves the British Empire's allies.

Jamal was one of the first Palestinians to recapitulate the history of Palestinian nationalism. One of his articles stated that 1908 was the year when Palestine emerged as a distinct territorial entity within the Ottoman framework. Had it not been for the Great War, this geopolitical entity would have become a democracy within the Ottoman Empire and later, like Greece, an independent state. This was an important argument, because it countered the Zionist claim that it was the Jewish demand for a national home in Palestine that made the country a distinct geopolitical entity. This was a direct answer to Weizmann's claim that but for Zionism the country would have been divided amongst its neighbors.

Jamal was also the first to try to systematically undermine Zionist claims by juxtaposing the demographic reality in Palestine with its political structure. Ever since the 1920s, he argued, 93 percent of the population had had no share in determining the country's future, while the Jewish population was over-represented in the political structure. Their representation was buttressed by the appointment of pro-Zionist individuals to senior positions, among them the general prosecutor, the legal secretary of the government, the administrator of the immigration department and the head of the Land Registry Office. The article also noted that even before the country's future was determined, the Palestinians had already paid with their taxes for the Jewish 'national home'. They paid for the entrenchment of an alien and hostile presence – the revival of the Hebrew language, a separate educational system and the salaries of the immigration department intended for the Jews.

The article was a carefully constructed vindication of the Palestinian national ideology, and Chaim Weizmann hastened, the same year and in the same publication, to refute its arguments with ideological justifications of Zionism.

It should be noted that Jamal's article, and the arguments he presented in other forums about the economic cost that Jewish immigration imposed on the local population, did have some impact in Britain. While in London, he managed to persuade his British interlocutors that his arguments were factually sound, and apparently he sowed some serious doubts in the minds of policymakers regarding the meaning of the Balfour Declaration and its repercussions for the local population.

An indication of such fresh thinking was seen in the work of the Hope Simpson Commission, appointed in October 1930 to reexamine the vague promises made to the Jews over the years, above all the promise to allow mass immigration into Palestine. It was also directed to find out if the country was economically capable of becoming a Jewish safe haven without harming the local population. High Commissioner John Chancellor hoped that the commission would leave out the political aspects, but this could not be done.

Sir John Hope Simpson was the vice chairman of the League of Nations Refugee Settlement Commission in Greece. Having experienced firsthand the human price of ethnic conflict, he was determined to avert it in Palestine. He came back from Palestine convinced that the Palestinian population had been harmed, and suggested measures to alleviate their plight. He proposed curtailing the sale of land to Jews for five years and reducing immigration to such numbers as could be settled on unoccupied Jewish-owned land. The commission also proposed a new law granting Palestinian sharecroppers the right to lease their land and to develop lands for the settlement of Palestinians dispossessed by land transactions. The commission's report was warmly approved by Colonial Secretary Sidney Webb (Lord Passfield), who saw it as a blueprint for a resolution to the conflict. It was published as a government White Paper in 1930.

Although *Al-Jamaa' al-Arabiyya* disapproved of the commission's report, al-Hajj Amin was generally pleased with the change in Britain's policy. Perhaps he thought that it was tactically useful to express disapproval, but it is more likely that, given their national outlook, al-Hajj Amin and Jamal expected and demanded much more than a tactical change in Britain's policies. Be that as it may, the commission's report became one more document of an alternative that could have directed the Palestinians towards a better future.

Chaim Weizmann's personal efforts and his influence with British Prime Minister Ramsay MacDonald caused Lord Passfield's White Paper to be effectively disregarded. In February 1931, MacDonald sent Weizmann a letter spelling out the government's interpretation of the White Paper: it did not repeal the restrictions placed on the Zionist movement but implied that Britain would not take action to implement them. Lord Passfield's views notwithstanding, the British government did not feel the need to retract the principle embodied in the Balfour Declaration. It also became known that the government regarded the Jewish Agency as the official representative of the Jewish community in Palestine. It seemed that all the Palestinian gains of 1930 had gone up in smoke.

At about this time, al-Hajj Amin paid a secret visit to London. According to his companion in England, Izz al-Din al-Shawa of Gaza, it was a complete failure. Ostensibly he was shown all the important sights in the city: he was taken to Piccadilly and Oxford Street, and then the car stopped on Regent Street in front of the Café Royal. The *mufti* was led down into the hall, which was full of cheerful music and couples on the dance floor. 'What is this place?' the *mufti* asked, and the guide assigned to him by the Colonial Office replied seriously, 'This is one of the most important places in London. We want you to see it, to give you an idea of our culture and way of life.' The *mufti* wanted to leave but politely went on listening to the learned guide. 'Some of the most important people frequented this place. Oscar Wilde used to come here for tea, and people from all walks of life, young and old. Here class distinctions don't matter.' The guide spoke as though al-Hajj Amin were an emissary of the Palestine Communist Party rather than a member of Jerusalem's aristocracy. At which point the *mufti* lost his patience and asked to return to his hotel.

At every point during his visit, his British hosts made him feel that he was not the equal of the Zionist leaders and that in their eyes he was a primitive colonial native who should be impressed by crystal chandeliers and thrilled by a lively dance floor. Al-Hajj Amin had hoped for understanding and support, but he was shown superciliousness and disdain. It is worth remembering this episode, as Chapter Eleven will deal with al-Hajj Amin's visits to Mussolini and Hitler. These visits were equally ineffectual, but he was treated respectfully and ceremoniously as a national leader. This may help to explain why he chose to associate himself with those who would become the enemies of humanity.

The vexation was not only personal, it was national, and for a brief moment it unified the factions in the Palestinian camp. MacDonald's letter caused the Palestinians to overcome past resentments and brought together the two great families, the Husaynis and the Nashashibis. Early in March 1931, the public was treated to a rare example of solidarity: both Raghib al-Nashashibi and al-Hajj Amin al-Husayni attended a special meeting of the Palestinian Executive in Jerusalem, another significant milestone in the history of a people confronted with fateful decisions almost every year. The situation was clear, as the British rulers had made it known exactly how far they were willing to adjust their policies. Even the Nashashibis could not accept the idea that the Jews (who constituted 17 percent of the total population and most of whom were recent arrivals) would determine the character of the country, let alone the prospect that many more immigrants would arrive.

On his way to the meeting, the *mufti* consulted with his relative Ishaq Darwish. As president of the Supreme Muslim Council, al-Hajj Amin was an official of the mandatory government, and if he wished to keep his post he had to respect certain limits. He believed that the proper response to Britain was a general strike throughout Palestine, but he feared that if he called for it he would lose his position. So it was agreed that Darwish would call for the strike. Perhaps, as some historians suggest, al-Hajj Amin also knew that the Nashashibis would not wish to go so far and that a resolution that worsened his relations with the British would fail. Finally, after prolonged debates, the council adopted Raghib al-Nashashibi's moderate proposal to call on the Palestinians to boycott Jewish goods and buy Palestinian products.[11] Consequently, in 1931 al-Hajj Amin al-Husayni seemed to be trying to avoid at all costs a head-on collision with the British or the Jews.

But as in 1928, the Palestinian camp was not so easily mollified. John Chancellor made hostile public statements, the British police continued to treat Palestinian suspects brutally long after the events of 1929 and, to add insult to injury, the pro-Zionist Jewish general prosecutor Norman Bentwich retained his post. The mood grew uglier still when three Palestinians who had been charged with inciting riots were hanged, while not a single Jew was sentenced to death. The sentence looked like a deliberate perversion of justice and part of a hostile policy.[12] Now whenever al-Hajj Amin addressed a large angry crowd, he had to revert to the role of the aggressive, demagogic *sheikh* pouring fire and brimstone on Zionism and British policies.

His public utterances were also fueled by the fact that the Haram al-Sharif, particularly the Western Wall, was still threatened by a Jewish takeover. High

Commissioner Chancellor suggested to the *mufti* that the mandatory government, together with the Palestinian leadership, come up with a compromise. Otherwise the government would put the issue of the ownership of the Wall to an international forum, which would probably rule in favor of the Jews. The *mufti* replied that he would prefer an imposition by an international forum to voluntary surrender. Chancellor replied, 'But this way you'll show yourself a statesman.' 'But I'm not a statesman,' replied the *mufti*. 'I am a cleric.'[13] Disregarding the *mufti*, the British authorities appointed a special committee headed by a Swede named Lufgren to examine the question of the Western Wall. The committee tended to favor the Muslim side but nevertheless called for considerable changes in the status quo.

In the meantime, al-Hajj Amin went on rallying the Muslim world to help save Jerusalem. In October 1930, he spent a few days in Cairo to meet with a delegation of Muslims from India led by Shawqat Ali, one of the leaders of the Muslim minority in the subcontinent and the brother of its greatest religious scholar, Sayyid Muhammad Ali. In December of that year, al-Hajj Amin sent Jamal to follow the delegation to London and strengthen their association with this important ally.[14] When Muhammad Ali died early in 1931, he was buried in Jerusalem in accordance with his will. His funeral became a great Muslim demonstration.

It was a very cold day in January when Muhammad Ali's coffin, draped in a green flag embroidered with verses from the Qur'an, was carried to his grave. Long consultations before and after the funeral prepared the groundwork for the Pan Islamic Congress that took place in Jerusalem later that year. It was not the only important funeral that year. Sharif Hussein, a sincere friend of the Palestinian movement, though he lacked power or political influence, died that summer. A vast throng surrounded the Dome of the Rock to pay homage to the man who at the end of his life sought in vain to claim Palestine for the Arabs. Towards the end of the mandate and immediately after, his son King Abdullah of Jordan would use the tomb as a pretext for claiming Jerusalem.

Muhammad Ali and the *sharif* were buried in the same mausoleum in Dar al-Khatib, behind the eastern wall of the Haram.[15] This mausoleum had originally been a religious school – an Anatolian noblewoman had donated it to the religious authorities in the fourteenth century. Later both Musa Kazim and his son Abd al-Qadir would also be buried in its chambers. But the amicable coexistence of the deceased contrasted with the conflicting political aspirations of the Hashemites and Husaynis in Jerusalem. During the Jordanian rule, a visitor might have guessed that only Sharif Hussein was buried there, as the entrance bore his emblem flanked by Jordanian flags. Today it is once more the burial place of the Palestinian aristocracy.

As soon as the mourning period was over, al-Hajj Amin was eager to hold the first Pan Islamic Congress in Palestine. Such congresses had already taken place, but never in Jerusalem. Al-Hajj Amin had tried to organize one in 1922 and failed, but in June 1931 he succeeded. First he had to secure the High Commissioner's support, which he obtained by promising that the congress would not discuss any issues that might embarrass the British authorities.[16] Chancellor was about to be succeeded in October by Sir Arthur Wauchope and was therefore fairly sympathetic. The *mufti* did not, however, try to conciliate the opposition. Nor did he cooperate with the later attempts of the visitors from India and Egypt to unify the Palestinian camp.

Al-Hajj Amin wished to give the event an air of spontaneity. During Friday prayers at the al-Aqsa mosque on 4 September 1931, Shawqat Ali announced, probably by agreement, that a Pan Islamic Congress would open in Jerusalem on 31 December that year. A letter of invitation that still survives today indicates that the *mufti* was indeed careful not to make any reference to the political struggle in Palestine. The honored addressee is invited to take part in a congress whose purpose is to prevent divisions in the Arab world. There could not have been a more appropriate place for such a gathering than the mosque of al-Aqsa.[17]

Twenty-two Muslim countries, both Shi'i and Sunni – all the Muslim states at that time with the exception of secular Turkey – were represented at the congress.[18] Most delegates were not official representatives, since the governments of the states concerned were being very circumspect about Jerusalem and Palestine. The Turks did not come because Shawqat Ali, who considered himself a potential caliph, had sent an invitation to a member of the Ottoman family known as Abdul Majid III.

At the time, there were rumors all over the Middle East that the caliphate might be revived, an idea that Ataturk's Turkey resisted with all its might. The gathering was pulled in two different directions: the Indian representatives wanted to use it to promote the idea of the caliphate, while al-Hajj Amin wanted it to strengthen Muslim support for the Palestinians. He received the blessing of his old mentor, Sheikh Rashid al-Rida, which carried much weight. Rida was one of the promoters of the caliphate, and his willingness to place the issue of Palestine at the top of the agenda testified to the strong link between him and his former disciple.

During the congress, al-Hajj Amin also had to struggle against hostility towards Christians, expressed in particular by al-Tabatabai, the former prime minister of Iran. Aware of the standing of Christian Palestinians in local politics, and perhaps loyal to the tradition of his branch of the family, which had coexisted peacefully with Jerusalem's Christian elite, al-Hajj Amin fought against this sentiment.[19] When he had gone to Egypt in person to seek official support, he had run into an advance campaign by the Jewish Agency to dissuade the Egyptian government from sending representatives to the congress. The government was worried by the idea of the caliphate and sent no delegates, but the Wafd, the largest political party in Egypt, did.[20] Another proposal on the congress's agenda that worried the Egyptians was the establishment of a Muslim university in Jerusalem, which the scholars of al-Azhar feared would eclipse their own institution. Rashid al-Rida succeeded in dispelling their anxiety, as perhaps did al-Hajj Amin's letter to King Fuad I and to Egypt's prime minister, Sidqi Pasha, explaining the modest aspirations of the projected university. It was mainly intended to provide a Palestinian counterbalance to the Hebrew University.[21]

Al-Hajj Amin did not fare much better in Damascus, where the leaders of the national camp declined his invitation. They were in the midst of delicate negotiations with the French and did not wish to be identified with an Arab anti-colonialist front. Some of the Syrian leaders also suspected that the congress was intended to attack the Palestinian opposition, and so when al-Hajj Amin arrived in Damascus in June 1931 he found them unresponsive.[22] Those who turned al-Hajj Amin down had been helped by him during the Syrian revolt in 1925, but they would help him in the 1930s when he found refuge there as a political exile.

Despite these setbacks the list of participants was quite impressive, and al-Hajj Amin managed to steer the congress through conflicting agendas and interests. One of the foremost thinkers of Shi'i Islam, Sheikh al-Ghaita, making his first appearance in such a gathering, was persuaded to become a spokesman for the Palestinian cause. He delivered the important message that Palestine was greater than the factions of Islam and united its two main currents.[23]

The congress opened on 7 December, the morning after an evening ceremony at al-Aqsa mosque described by the British as al-Hajj Amin's 'one man show' and recorded on film by an Egyptian production company. (This was the movement's first political film, to be followed by many more. It is a vivid document of the congress opening.) Photographs were taken outdoors, then the delegates went into the mosque, sat down on its rush mats and listened to al-Hajj Amin exhorting them to help save Jerusalem.[24]

Al-Hajj Amin's friends had not seen him so active and dynamic for a long time. He pushed resolutions in the plenary sessions and fought to neutralize opponents in the subcommittees. The success of the congress was clearly due to him, and he was chosen to head a pan-Islamic body, giving him one more title to add to Grand Mufti and President of the Supreme Muslim Council.

The opposition ran interference through its newspaper *Mirat al-Sharq* and with a parallel gathering at the King David Hotel titled 'The Conference of the Islamic Nation', which drew representatives from all over Palestine.[25] But as the High Commissioner reported, 'The congress strengthened the standing of al-Hajj Amin al-Husayni.'[26] Al-Hajj Amin was convinced that Fakhri al-Nashashibi, who led the opposition to the congress, was in the service of Zionism. This was not so far-fetched, given Fakhri's strong ties to the Jewish Agency. At least one Israeli scholar has found a hint to that effect in a letter from Chaim Arlosoroff to the Jewish Agency in London.[27]

Yet al-Hajj Amin's inability to compromise with the opposition did harm the congress and its goals. His close associate Shawqat Ali wrote to a friend, 'The *mufti* and his party are unwilling to let others take part in preparing and directing the conference. The opposition behaved chivalrously, announcing that it supported the idea of a Muslim university and the congress, but could not accept a situation wherein the *mufti* alone makes all the decisions ... Had the *mufti* taken my advice, the results would have been much better,' he concluded sadly. (He had advised al-Hajj Amin to advance the idea of a new Islamic caliphate.) Indeed, he was so disappointed that the issue of the caliphate was left out of the agenda that he resigned. His resignation did not hurt al-Hajj Amin – on the contrary, it reassured the Arab delegates, who were unenthusiastic, to say the least, about the idea of the caliphate. Though al-Hajj Amin's inability to unify the ranks was ominous and militated against his success, on the whole the congress left him stronger than before.[28]

In 1932 the festival of Nabi Musa also became a battlefield between the rival camps, each of which tried to organize a bigger delegation to the festivities.[29] Though for hundreds of years the Husayni, or Prophet's, banner had led the procession, the Nashashibis announced that their procession would raise a different banner. Al-Hajj Amin did not scruple to get the British authorities to make sure that the Husayni procession, rather than the Nashashibi one, would take place – and so it did.

In the final analysis, the achievement of the Pan Islamic Congress was personal rather than national. The pro-Palestinian tendency which the Hope Simpson Report seemed to indicate was eroding. The new High Commissioner, Sir Arthur Wauchope, was friendly to al-Hajj Amin but not necessarily to the Palestinian cause. Wauchope maintained strong personal ties with al-Hajj Amin and helped him to thwart attempts at reforming the Supreme Muslim Council that might have damaged his standing.[30] But Wauchope represented the British government, whose policies in 1932 provoked increasing anti-British feelings among the local population.

In April 1932, a British official by name of Lewis French was appointed to study what could be done to develop the country and help those who had been hurt by the sale of land to Jews. He did not find many such cases and was not persuaded that there was strong resistance among Palestinian landowners to these sales. But he deplored the lack of development plans for rural Palestine and demanded that the economic discrimination in favor of the Jews be stopped. French's report stunned the Palestinian leadership, historian Yehoshua Porath asserts in hindsight. If that was so, then the leadership overlooked the most significant passages in the report. French was supportive of the Palestinian cause and tried to awaken the leadership to the realities it ignored. But instead of rousing and stopping the sale of land, the leadership was paralyzed, and the executive was not convened until October 1933. When it did, it was dominated by unprecedented hostility towards Britain.[31]

The public at large may not have been aware that the Husaynis, too, sold land, though it was an open secret to the family. Even Musa Kazim sold the land of Dalab (on which the kibbutz Kfar Anavim would later be built). Jamal's brother Tawfiq sold the Jews whole orange groves in Nes Ziona.[32] But this practice ended in 1929 and was not revived.

It took the *mufti* three years to acknowledge that the 1929 revolt had not made a noticeable difference in the plight of the Palestinians: the Zionist presence in Palestine kept expanding and the British policies remained unchanged. In the 1930s, al-Hajj Amin was not only a social and religious leader but also the head of an important political movement. He became a nationalist politician motivated by considerations of political survival as much as by his commitment to the national cause. It is possible that at this time a kind of Husayni nationalism was developing that guided not only al-Hajj Amin but Jamal and other members of the family as well.

The hardening attitude of many members of the family was mainly a reflection of the dramatic changes in the character of the country and that of its Arab population rather than any private initiative. In the early 1930s, Jewish immigration became an oppressive reality, and the lack of appropriate action by the British government heightened the feeling of the Palestinian leadership that Palestine could be saved only by extreme measures. But the growing extremism was also indicative of the internal conflicts in the Palestinian camp, which intensified due to the financial straits of the political structure.

None of the political players could raise sufficient funds to act independently. And even the Husaynis were struggling to raise the necessary budget for the new all-Palestinian conference they wished to convene in the early 1930s. The attempt to revive the annual conferences that had taken place before 1920 was largely a failure.

### Leading the Resistance: Musa Kazim and His Son Abd al-Qadir

For the first time since the family had become a social and political force in the age of nationalism, or perhaps even since the eighteenth century, its members were challenged by popular leadership. The encounter between the high and the low did not go well, and the historians of the Palestinian Left would later denounce the family for its alleged haughty and heartless treatment of the lower strata of Palestinian society.

The first signs of political organization from below could be discerned in 1932, when Palestinian merchants refused to take part in a government-organized regional trade fair, the Levant Fair, held in Tel Aviv. Employees in the Departments of Education and Transportation resigned their posts. These were sporadic and spontaneous actions, and to some extent the revived activity at the popular level reflected changes in Palestinian political life.

The Husaynis, Nashashibis and other leading families launched political parties. Some of these took on an independent dynamic that did not always harmonize with family interests, though their agendas were usually factional rather than national. But this was not true for all of the parties. For example, Istiqlal, which came into being in 1932, rose above the clans, calling for unity in the Arab world and protesting its breakup into small states that it regarded as colonialist creations. Perhaps this is why Istiqlal soon fell apart.

The Husaynis supported the National Youth Party inspired by the Muslim Brotherhood of Egypt, both of which came into being in 1932. In 1934 the opposition, led by the Nashashibis, launched the National Defense Party, while the Husaynis launched a party of their own in March 1935 that will be discussed later. Palestinian society was beginning to develop forms and organizations that might have led it, like other Arab peoples in the region, to political independence but for the presence of a settler movement that coveted their homeland. Such a reality required unity, not pluralism – a solid national movement, not a national society in its infancy.

The opposition built itself power bases among the rural population and launched an affiliated village party. Many village headmen wrote al-Hajj Amin begging him to honor them with a visit and to involve them in his activities, but the replies sent back in his name offered various excuses (including a broken leg and a sudden illness). He and his family thus failed to acquire a popular power base.[33]

In addition to the formation of political parties, there were numerous unofficial conferences, beginning in Nablus. Jamal and his cousin Munif observed the developments and concluded that such spontaneity might eventually restrict al-Hajj Amin's control over Palestinian politics.

Jamal set out to channel the radical dynamism of the young men of Nablus. Early in January 1933, he held the first conference of young Palestinians in Jaffa. This meeting was marked by anti-Christian fervor that cooled only after strenuous efforts by Musa Kazim's young son Abd al-Qadir, at his father's urging. After all, the Husaynis had traditionally cooperated with the Christians and his father's nationalism was based on secular Muslim-Christian cooperation.[34]

This was an uncharacteristic action for Abd al-Qadir, who represented radicalism in the family – though he never acted against them. Only in 1933 did he appear on the scene as a distinct political figure, and he very quickly made his mark on the Palestinian struggle. In that year, he returned from Cairo, where he had won his spurs in a national struggle alongside the young Egyptians.

His first political activity had been in 1932, when he helped to organize a boycott against Fuad University in Cairo, which was believed to have been collaborating with the British. Abd al-Qadir himself had been sent to the American University in Cairo, and though the Americans were not viewed as colonialists, it was a Western institution and thus in his eyes a foreign presence on Arab soil. Abd al-Qadir's protest became progressively radical. At first he was content to design an individual course of studies with the emphasis on Islamic subjects. His favorite subject – 'Sport and Religion in Arab History' – foreshadowed his destiny, but he also read extensively about armed struggle in history and religion. Most of his tutors were Western 'Orientalists' who believed they had cracked the Islamic code and were now teaching Islam to the Egyptians. When the university diplomas were given out, young Abd al-Qadir's piercing eyes did not betray his animosity or his intention to embarrass the alien establishment at its most ceremonial.

The official graduation ceremonies in the summer of 1932 on the university's splendid campus were expected to run their usual course. The heads of the university, with leading figures in the expatriate community and the Egyptian administration, were all in attendance as the graduates were called one by one to come to the stage and receive their diplomas. Leading the ceremonies was the president of the university, Charles Watson, flanked by heads of departments, including the head of the Department of Oriental Languages, unwittingly destined to become the hero of the day. When Abd al-Qadir al-Husayni was called to the dais, he asked to say a few words to the audience.

To general astonishment, he launched into a fiery speech against Western policies in the Middle East and against the part played by the American University in implementing them. He accused the institution in which he had studied of consciously and deliberately undermining the Muslim religion and its traditions and supporting the Christian mission. The aim of the Christian mission, he said, was to sow dissent between Christians and Muslims, whereas the Muslims aspired to pan-Arab solidarity. He stopped, raised the diploma he had just been given and declared, 'This is your diploma. Take it away. It's nothing to do with me!' Then he tore the thick document before all the dignitaries, local and foreign, sitting on the terrace.

The university was all agog, and its administrators appealed to the local authorities as well as to the American and British embassies. That evening they resolved to expel Abd al-Qadir from Egypt within twenty-four hours. During that time, the young man managed to tell his version of the event to the Egyptian press, preventing the university from denying the occurrence, as its directors were naturally inclined to do.[35]

Abd al-Qadir returned to Palestine a national hero, and the young revolutionary became a journalist. At first he joined the newspaper of the Muslim Brotherhood, *Al-Jamaa' al-Islamiyya*. Before long he realized that his articles were not published, and he suspected that the paper was succumbing to British pressure. He then began writing for the family-owned newspaper, *Al-Jamaa' al-Arabiyya*. Every day he made his way to the editorial offices, located in what is today the Clark Building on Mamoun Allah Street, to hand in a fervent column that would stir the young nationalists of Jerusalem. Often it was not published but rather distributed in secret to the young people. When he felt that here he was being thwarted again, he made one final attempt to work through the press by joining the board of the newspaper *Al-Liwa*, edited by Jamal al-Husayni, whose offices adjoined those of *Al-Jamaa' al-Arabiyya*. The latter publication represented the Supreme Muslim Council, and the former the Husayni party. But Abd al-Qadir soon realized that here, too, most of his columns were not printed, for fear of British reprisals.

Thus ended his short career as a journalist. Helped by his family connections, he obtained a post in the Government Lands Office. One of his biographers, Muhsin, describes this as an impressive achievement. First he agitated against the government's practice of preferring to hire Christians rather than Muslims, then he formed an organization named the Association of Educated Young Muslims, which pressured the High Commissioner Wauchope to give twenty-five Muslims jobs in the administration. The twenty-sixth post, with a handsome monthly salary of 25 Palestinian pounds, went to Abd al-Qadir.

At first he was satisfied with the clerical post in Jaffa, but he advanced quickly and became chief of the Land Registry in the district of Ramleh. Here he became aware of the extent of Jewish land acquisition and the growing Palestinian distress, and he wrote to his friends in Egypt that he was using his post to tackle these issues. He claimed to have stopped the sale of many tracts in the center of the country and to have increased the number of Palestinians in high government posts. There is no external evidence for these claims, but this may well be the case. His committed biographer highlights these achievements in order to justify Abd al-Qadir's willingness to work in the very government department that enabled the Zionists to buy more land (that is, he wished to work from within the system to curb the Zionist enterprise).[36]

His energy and working pace were noted by the family. Not content with his newspaper and government work, he labored indefatigably to organize support for the family and opposition to the British and the Zionists. We have mentioned his creation of a group dedicated to fighting the growing unemployment among educated Muslims. Only a few months after his return from Egypt, he convened in Jaffa a conference on unemployment that called on the government to sack its British and foreign staff and to pass a law requiring companies to hire Muslims in proportion to their profits from the Muslim community. If these demands were not met, the conference threatened to call on Muslims to boycott those companies.

But the government did not meet the demands. Abd al-Qadir failed to rouse the public to tackle this issue, since the breach with the opposition prevented large-scale action. Moreover, the opposition newspaper *Mirat al-Sharq* charged that Abd al-Qadir always acted in a Muslim context and was therefore anti-Christian. It was a difficult charge to refute, but a search through the opposition's leaflets and publications has produced no tangible evidence of such discrimination on Abd al-Qadir's part.

Like other members of the Husayni family, Abd al-Qadir needed a government post in order to survive economically and to maintain a strong political stance in society. This created a dilemma similar to the one faced by the notables under the Young Turks – except that they had not been strongly opposed to the government and certainly did not aspire to replace it with an independent national entity. In the 1930s, the family was troubled by the question of whether to resign from or remain in government posts. Abd al-Qadir was the first to resolve it, and his determination spearheaded the Husaynis' clash with the British and the Zionists. For this he eventually paid with his life. In 1934 he proclaimed that he was resigning his post in the mandatory government's land registry because it was helping the Jews to take over the land.[37]

The bravest of the family, however, was the aged Musa Kazim. He accepted the invitation of young Jaffaites to lead a demonstration they were organizing. The eighty-year-old Husayni thrilled the young men as he faced the mounted police and was knocked down by the horses. The newspaper *Filastin* reported that the old man was miraculously spared when a bullet fired at him struck one of the other demonstrators.[38]

Abd al-Qadir's action, and possibly Musa Kazim's bravery as well, prompted al-Hajj Amin to act more decisively. But his decision to take stronger action against the British and Zionists might have been made at the start of 1933. This led to another attempt to unify the Palestinian camp – though, as before, the union was too brief to change the course of history.

At the end of March 1933, after months in Jerusalem, the *mufti* took the train to Jaffa to attend a rare gathering of representatives from all the Palestinian political factions. Five hundred men listened to speeches calling for a boycott of Zionist and British goods and the rejection of the legitimacy of the mandatory government. Inspired by al-Hajj Amin, they publicly denounced Arabs who sold land to the Jews and delivered an unprecedented attack on the government's pro-Zionist policy.[39] The anti-Zionist utterances were clearer and more uncompromising than ever: 'It is the overall plan of the Jews to seize the soil of this holy land, and by arriving here in hundreds and thousands, legally and illegally, they are spreading fear and terror through the country,' stated a proclamation issued by the Jaffa conference.[40]

Upon his return to Jerusalem on 31 March 1933, al-Hajj Amin visited the residence of Dr Heinrich Wolf, the German Consul General in Jerusalem appointed by the new Nazi government two months earlier. To Israeli historiographers, this visit made him one of the worst enemies not only of Zionism but of Jewry as a whole.

The consul was unimpressed by al-Hajj Amin and wrote to his superiors that the *mufti* boasted he could rally Muslims, not only in Palestine but throughout the Arab world, to support Nazi Germany. The consul had the impression that it would not be easy to build up pro-Nazi sentiment among the Muslims of Palestine, in part because it would be difficult to convince them that Judaism was the source of all evil and responsible for the hardships they suffered as merchants and farmers. In reality, the strength of Palestinian nationalism lay in the widespread belief that Zionism, rather than Judaism, was the source of the trouble.

Most of the Consul General's report seems very dubious. According to Wolf, al-Hajj Amin urged Hitler to impose a boycott on the Jews of Germany, but not the kind that would drive them to migrate to Palestine. In reality, it is doubtful that al-Hajj Amin would have proposed such a thing, since he was concerned with boycotting the Jewish community in Palestine and preventing any situation in Europe that would impel more Jews to immigrate there. Nevertheless, this meeting would be viewed by a good many Israeli researchers as proof that al-Hajj Amin was a dyed-in-the-wool Nazi.[41]

While in Jaffa, al-Hajj Amin also dealt with some family interests, mainly to strengthen his relations with the non-clannish Istiqlal Party, which was in decline after having become a stronghold of the al-Hadi family of Nablus. Eighty years earlier, the Husaynis and al-Hadis had found themselves in opposing camps when the Husaynis formed marriage ties with the al-Hadis' Nablus rivals, the Tuqans. But times had changed, and now the ideological element had come into play. Awni Abd al-Hadi was promoting a pan-Arab national program, according to which Palestine could only survive in the framework of a pan-Arab republic. Given the hardships of the 1930s, al-Hajj Amin al-Husayni felt he could live with such a platform, particularly if it caused a rift in the opposition camp. After all, he himself had once supported the idea of Palestine as a part of Syria. This duality between local nationalism (*wataniya*) and pan-Arab nationalism (*qawmiya*) would haunt the Palestinian national movement until the death of Gamal Abd al-Nasser in 1970. Pan-Arab solidarity would remain a major cultural-social component in the identity of the diverse Arab nations, and its remarkable persistence testifies to its vitality in the culture of the Middle East. However, it was not sufficient to rally the Arab world to Palestine's aid.

Relations with the Abd al-Hadi family improved, and ties with the Khalidis were at their best. Relations with the Nashashibis, however, were worsening. Al-Hajj Amin's main purpose in holding the conference in Jaffa was to prevent Fakhri al-Nashashibi, the most dynamic figure of his family, from standing between the Husaynis and the Istiqlal Party. There was no pressing reason for Awni Abd al-Hadi to declare his support for one camp or the other. He enjoyed being courted by both and wished the state of affairs to continue.

Al-Hajj Amin also had some satisfying moments while in Jaffa meeting the young men who ran his Young Muslim Associations. He was particularly impressed by Izz al-Din al-Qassam, whom he had already met when the Supreme Muslim Council appointed him registrar of marriages at the Shari'a court in Haifa. At the time, al-Hajj Amin had considered this appointment very carefully, because the Syrian al-Qassam had been famous in the 1920s as an eloquent and passionate preacher at the al-Istiqlal mosque in Haifa.

When they met in Jaffa, al-Hajj Amin knew that al-Qassam had been active for three years in the Black Hand.[42] This group trained young men in guerrilla warfare against the British in the Carmel Mountains. A devout Muslim, al-Qassam wanted religious approval of this activity, but knowing the local clergy would refuse, he turned instead to a Syrian *sheikh* in Damascus who gave the stamp of religious approval to actions of this kind.[43] Before the gathering in Jaffa, al-Qassam had already contributed to the more violent aspect of the Palestinian struggle against the British and the Zionists. In April 1931, his unit killed three members of Kibbutz Yagur.[44] The following year they struck again, killing a man in the Jewish village of Balfouriya and another in Kfar Hasidim. Late that year, they slew a man and his small son in the village of Nahalal. Some members of the group were caught and hanged before the end of that year. Al-Qassam himself was put on trial, but there was no evidence to link him directly with the perpetrators.

Al-Qassam's unsavory acts attracted a great deal of attention during the rise of Nazism in Germany. The coming of the Nazis to power in Germany at the end of January 1933 focused Palestinian attention on Jewish immigration. In 1932 some 9,000 Jews arrived, and 30,000 came the following year. The Jewish presence was noticeable everywhere, not only because of the large numbers of new arrivals but also because of the rapid growth of economic activity, particularly in the urban areas, while the purchasing power of the Palestinian population dropped to about a quarter of the population.

But the anxiety of the Jews of Europe was not on the Palestinian agenda. In the 1930s, the Arabs of Palestine were afraid of becoming a minority in their homeland, of losing their workplaces and their land and even of large-scale evictions. Their main outlet was the Palestinian press, which from the summer of 1933 became wholly committed to resisting immigration. From the press, the protest moved into the streets, and by autumn there were massive demonstrations. They began with thousands marching in the streets of Jerusalem and spread throughout the country. In Jaffa the demonstrators

tried to break into the offices of the district governor and were fired on by
the police. In Jerusalem young Palestinians broke into Jewish neighborhoods,
and the police killed twenty-six and wounded many more.[45]

In October 1934 the Palestinian Executive called for demonstrations in
the desperate hope of changing the government's policies, but to no avail.
The government held the Husaynis responsible for the disorder and arrested
Jamal al-Husayni.[46]

When al-Hajj Amin returned from Jaffa, he immediately went into action.
Once again elections were held in Jerusalem, but this time the family did not
put forward a candidate of its own. On the advice of al-Hajj Amin, backed
after some hesitation by Jamal, the family supported the candidacy of Dr
Hussein al-Khalidi. Al-Hajj Amin threw himself into the campaign, and his
speeches denounced Raghib al-Nashashibi, the opposition's candidate for
mayor, as non-national and not pro-Islamic.[47]

Hussein al-Khalidi was a good choice – a gifted man, a good speaker and
an outstanding chief physician in the Department of Health. He resigned his
medical post so as to dedicate himself to politics and the city. He defeated
Raghib al-Nashashibi and restored the Husaynis to the position of power they
had lost with the advent of British rule fourteen years earlier. What is more,
he caused a split in the Nashashibi camp. The 1934 elections were decided
by the Jews, whose numbers in Jerusalem had grown to 30,000, thanks to
immigration. They withheld their vote from Nashashibi, mistaking him for a
nationalist extremist because he had taken part in the Palestinian delegation
to London in 1930. High Commissioner Wauchope also expressed displeasure at Raghib's obtaining another post.[48] It should be noted that Hussein
al-Khalidi helped the family even during the worst years of the revolt, and
in 1936 he joined the Husaynis' party.

As they had many times before, the Husayni women played an important
part in cementing the alliance. Hussein al-Khalidi's wife, Wahida, cooperated with Amina, the wife of Jamal al-Husayni: in 1929 they had recruited
twelve other women and formed a female Palestinian executive. It grew into
a women's congress, led by Salma, the wife of Musa Kazim, the first lady of
Palestinian nationalism (to borrow a modern American term).[49] Two hundred women, mostly from the families of the urban notables, attended the
opening session of the congress.

There was a dark passage in the life of the two families, however. Munif
al-Husayni, editor of *Al-Jamaa' al-Arabiyya*, fell in love with a young woman
of the Khalidi family, but her parents opposed the match. Munif was powerful enough to force them to accept the marriage, but in response some of

the Khalidis resigned from organizations controlled by the Husaynis. Rasim al-Khalidi quit the leadership of the Palestinian youth movements created by Jamal in 1932. But after a while the furor subsided, love flourished and the alliance survived.[50]

This passionate drama and all the other upsets were forgotten in the winter of 1934 when Musa Kazim died at the age of eighty-four. The last two demonstrations in which he took part hastened his demise. In Jerusalem he fell and was bruised, and in Jaffa he was battered in a bloody demonstration. Though al-Hajj Amin was the people's leader, Musa Kazim was the head of the family; perhaps even in the eyes of the people, his standing was higher than al-Hajj Amin's. After all, he was the president of the executive, and his ability to achieve a consensus created the impression of unity in the Palestinian camp.

Musa Kazim was the most highly respected of the Husaynis in the twentieth century – '*Sheikh al-Mujahidin*' ('Palestine's foremost warrior'), 'her greatest casualty', as the historian al-Dabagh described him. His funeral became a huge demonstration, the likes of which had never been seen in Jerusalem, and he was buried at al-Aqsa.[51] When he had fallen ill, the delicate alliances he had built fell apart: the Nashashibis became a real opposition, while the Husaynis became the mainstream and led the movement towards a head-on collision with the British authorities. But when Musa Kazim died, the two camps seemed to agree on a successor – Yakub Faraj, Musa Kazim's deputy (and a member of the opposition). Yet this moment of unity was, for all intents and purposes, the Palestinian Executive's swansong.[52]

### Family Statesmanship: The Second and Final Chapter

It is not known how al-Hajj Amin felt about the passing of the most admired Palestinian since the start of the mandate. In the early 1930s, the relationship between them had deteriorated after Musa Kazim accused al-Hajj Amin of falsely obtaining family funds to give to his supporters.[53] Jamal, who was on close terms with both of them, tried in vain to arbitrate. Now that Musa Kazim was dead, al-Hajj Amin had the national stage to himself. But it is doubtful that this state of affairs favored al-Hajj Amin, who always benefited from having to consider opposing opinions within his family.

With Musa Kazim gone, the family sought a new structure for its political and national action, particularly in response to the organizing skill of the Nashashibis, who created the National Defense Party in 1934. Therefore, the following year the Husaynis created the Palestinian Arab Party, whose avowed aims were ending the British Mandate, achieving Palestinian independence and abrogating the Jewish national home. In contrast to the Istiqlal, this new party's platform did not contain anti-British or anti-imperialist statements. Jamal was chosen to head the party with the help of a Greek Catholic deputy, Alfred Rock. A Greek Orthodox – Emil al-Ghori – served as general secretary, and his main function was to win the support of the Palestinian youth. To the Husaynis, the presence of Christians in the party leadership was not merely an indicator of national unity, it also reflected their political and intellectual outlook since the 1920s. This party became the political center of gravity in Palestinian intellectual life during the 1930s.[54]

Once again the family developed new skills in political organization and grew stronger. Only this time it missed out on a field of activity that might have given it a still greater role in the struggle for Palestine: guerrilla and military warfare. As a result, it lagged behind not only Izz al-Din al-Qassam but also the Jewish community. The Palestinians went in for demonstrations on the one hand and for al-Qassam's sporadic acts of violence on the other.

Meanwhile, the Jewish Agency prepared for a possible conflict with the Palestinians and built up a military infrastructure. In the course of 1935, it smuggled weapons into the country hidden inside civilian imports. On 18 October, while a shipment of cement was being unloaded from the Belgian vessel *Leopold* at the Port of Jaffa, a barrel fell on the dock and broke open, revealing a load of ammunition. The loud cry of a Jaffaite docker marked the start of a new and violent phase in relations between the communities in Palestine.[55] This time al-Hajj Amin did not hesitate to recommend that the executive declare a general strike.

At that time Izz al-Din al-Qassam was in Jerusalem trying to persuade al-Hajj Amin to launch a *jihad* against the British and the Zionists. He had established a base in the north of Nablus and was preparing for a sweeping guerrilla campaign. Al-Hajj Amin recognized the value of militant Islamic action, and that year he was also in touch with the Muslim Brotherhood, on which al-Qassam had modeled his group. Al-Hajj Amin had known Abd al-Rahman, the brother of Hassan al-Bana, founder of the movement; hence his familiarity with it and its methods.[56] But al-Hajj Amin's association with the al-Bana brothers did less for the Palestinians and remained just another chapter in the expansion of the Egyptian movement into a successful pan-Arabist one. So highly did the al-Bana brothers value the association that they published the extensive correspondence between Hassan and al-Hajj Amin as one of movement's most important texts. The Muslim Brotherhood did manage to hold some impressive pro-Palestinian demonstrations, but their movement was more focused on the struggle against the British occupation of Egypt than on any other issue.[57]

When face to face with Izz al-Din al-Qassam, al-Hajj Amin did not adopt the line of Islamic militancy. He maintained that the time was not yet ripe for such action. The solution had to be political rather than militaristic. A few days after they met, al-Qassam tried a different tactic to pressure al-Hajj Amin. He sent one of his men, Mahmud Salim, together with a Jerusalem notable named Sheikh Musa al-Azrawi, to inform al-Hajj Amin that he was about to start a revolt in the north of Palestine and to suggest that al-Hajj Amin launch one in the south. The fact that al-Qassam placed himself on equal footing with the *mufti* precluded any possibility of coordination between them as much as the *mufti*'s objection to such action did.[58] Al-Hajj Amin wanted to persuade the Arab rulers to pressure Britain to change its policy, and he believed that the Arab world needed to be united to achieve this.

Immediately after al-Qassam's visit, al-Hajj Amin set out on his travels, accompanied by Izzat Darwaza, the General Secretary of the Pan Islamic Conference in 1931 and of the Supreme Muslim Council in 1936, whose memoirs are the basis for the present account. Their first stop was Cairo. In his white turban, al-Hajj Amin was taller than his companions, who all wore Western suits. He stuck to his traditional black robe and carried a walking stick, thus clearly standing out as the leader.

From Cairo this extraordinary delegation went to the Arabian Peninsula. This was not a courtesy visit or merely a request for support but an opportunity for al-Hajj Amin to practice real statesmanship. He took part in a conciliatory mission between the Saudi king Abd al-Aziz and the Yemeni *imam* Yahya, inveterate opponents on the peninsula who remained enemies despite al-Hajj Amin's efforts.[59]

In the summer of 1935, al-Hajj Amin was still the most talked about and highly regarded Palestinian leader, as illustrated by the visit in August of the Tunisian leader Abd al-Aziz al-Thali, who came at al-Hajj Amin's invitation to open a new seminary for Islamic reform in the Abu Kabir quarter of Jaffa. But after the visitor departed, it was clear that a new star had risen in the Palestinian firmament.

In November 1935, al-Qassam launched his *jihad*. This time his men did not attack civilians but rather policemen near Ein Harod. They distinguished between Jewish police, whom they killed, and Muslims, whom they let go.[60] This action made a powerful impression on Abd al-Qadir al-Husayni, who at once organized a number of boys from the local Scouts movement into a guerrilla band and named it 'The Green Hand'. The actions of this band were unimpressive but very important in the collective memory of Abd al-Qadir's life. Izz al-Din al-Qassam's action, however, was a real guerrilla operation that raised his profile in the eyes of the Palestinian public and won him a reputation as one of the Palestinian national movement's foremost martyrs. The British police launched an extensive hunt for the group, and before the end of November British soldiers shot al-Qassam dead near Kufr Ya'abd.[61]

Al-Qassam's death seemed to balance out that of Musa Kazim. The huge wave of sympathy that swept over the country and found expression in a mass funeral in Haifa produced a temporary unity in the Palestinian leadership. 'Only the poor came to his funeral,' wrote the Palestinian author and fighter Ghassan Kanafani. At first al-Hajj Amin hesitated and did not attend the funeral or the memorial ceremony. But when the *sheikh's* posthumous reputation grew and he became a national martyr, al-Hajj Amin, urged by his advisers, called on the widow and gave her 10 Palestinian pounds. Jamal attended the memorial ceremony and made a speech at the Zaharat al-Sharq café before a crowd of 6,000 in which he prophesied – correctly – that 'al-Qassam's name will be remembered for ever and become a symbol in the history of the country'.[62] Hamdi al-Husayni went further still, publishing a panegyric to al-Qassam in the family newspaper.

Six days after al-Qassam's death, representatives of the five Palestinian parties called on the High Commissioner and handed him an unusually blunt memorandum. If they did not receive a satisfactory response, they warned him, 'the situation may deteriorate further and extremism will prevail'.

Neither al-Hajj Amin nor Jamal had ever imagined that the death of the unknown preacher from Haifa would spark a revolt in the north and turn the leadership's organized protests, strikes and demonstrations into an uprising against the British Empire. The timing was probably inauspicious – Britain had not yet felt any diminution of its imperial power and was faced with a possible worldwide conflict when the Palestinians chose to challenge them.

Had the political leaders among the Husaynis or their counterparts been able to sense the undercurrents, they might have controlled and diverted them into a more productive channel. But for that they would have had to be in constant touch with the Palestinian masses. Most of the members of the Palestinian Executive were landowners or merchants from the new bourgeoisie, both Christian and Muslim, who were similarly detached from the people and could not represent the peasant majority.[63]

The followers of al-Qassam, called the '*Qassamiyun*', offered a violent outlet to the very real hardships of the majority. Thanks to their organization, the armed activity continued in early 1936, and the Palestinian consciousness went on battling against British policies and the Zionist presence. The large-scale economic and social processes that had given rise to the extensive anti-government actions in 1929 intensified in the 1930s. The huge influx of Jewish immigrants, the increase in the Jews' purchasing power, the overwhelming spread of Jewish labor in the urban employment market and above all the sense that private and collective lands were being lost all heightened, or concretized, al-Qassam's message. The message ran counter to the understanding that the Husaynis and Nashashibis, in fact the entire Palestine leadership, sought to convey. Al-Qassam had rejected the possibility of a political solution, while the leadership pinned all its hopes on one. In 1936 al-Qassam became the guide, and al-Hajj Amin his disciple.

The British woke up late. The High Commissioner decided to renew efforts to create a legislative council and managed to throw the Palestinian camp into confusion. The Nashashibis and their allies favored the proposals, if only because they might put a dent in the dominance of the Supreme Muslim Council. The Husaynis were divided on the issue. Jamal thought it better to make use of the British authorities rather than fight them, because the country would soon be filled with Jews. Thus he justified his public image as the only leader who placed principled considerations above personal ones. Al-Hajj Amin vacillated and neither endorsed the proposal nor rejected it out of hand.[64]

The public wanted a clear-cut stance, but assuming that the press did not only harangue but also expressed public sentiments, then it appears al-Hajj Amin was faithfully representing what most Palestinians wished for at the time. He seemed to sense that the public was not eager to rise in battle. In February 1936, al-Hajj Amin summoned the religious dignitaries of Palestine, who must have felt that the public needed to be instilled with a fighting spirit, as their main resolution called for a unification of the *Qassamiyun* with the armed groups of young men organized by Abd al-Qadir al-Husayni.[65] But some politicians were still hoping to avoid a bloody conflict. That the leadership felt this way is illustrated by its attempts to reach an understanding with the Jewish Agency while deciding to confront the British.

Though that hot April in 1936 is thought to be the start of the Arab Revolt, no one knew it then. Events began to escalate, and we can only see their direction in hindsight. These were difficult days for al-Hajj Amin. The opposition was more radical than he, and the British High Commissioner apparently did not wish to maintain relations with the Palestinian leadership after the violent outbreak in Jaffa in April 1936. Yet at this time al-Hajj Amin chose to seek contact with the Jewish Agency. Some say that he feared for his position,[66] which may have been the case. But perhaps he thought that it might be possible to prevent the conflict.

In the middle of July 1936, the principal of the Quaker school in Beirut, Daniel Oliver, arrived in Palestine. Following consultations with Weizmann in London, he hoped to mediate between the Jews and the Arabs. Al-Hajj Amin told Oliver that the demand to stop immigration was not absolute but would remain in force pending a decision by an international commission of inquiry.[67]

But the initiative never got off the ground: the Jewish leadership was not interested, and the British Parliament, which had been informed of it, quickly dismissed it. This utter disregard, added to the economic and social hardships and al-Qassam's influence, was one of the immediate causes of the outbreak. But above all the uprising expressed the mounting bitterness and an intense desire to change the situation. As so often happens, the specific incident that triggered the revolt seems trivial in relation to the underlying causes. Historians are unsure which particular event set it off – an attack by the *Qassamiyun* in Nablus that left two Jews dead or a riot in Jaffa following the killing of two Palestinians by some Tel Aviv residents. Both events took place in April 1936.

Violence sparked still more violence, and by the end of the month the country was up in arms. The Arab Revolt, as it became known, had begun. Before the end of the month an eleven-member Higher Arab Committee was formed as a local Palestinian government replacing the executives of the various conferences. The Husaynis were once more at the forefront. Along with the *mufti*, who was chosen as chairman, Jamal and another member of the family, Ahmed Hilmi, were on the committee. Though the latter was closer to Istiqlal than to the family party, during the revolt he remained loyal to the family. An ally of the family, Hussein al-Khalidi, was on the committee, and the Nashashibis had two representatives as well. The only two Christian members belonged to the Husayni camp.

Thus at the moment of crisis there was national unity. Some months later, the newspaper *Filastin* depicted the elation felt at that historical juncture in a caricature showing Chaim Weizmann horrified by the sight of al-Hajj Amin al-Husayni and Raghib al-Nashashibi shaking hands.[68] But this charmed state of affairs did not last long.

After his election, al-Hajj Amin began to organize a countrywide strike that was meant to continue until Jewish immigration and land purchases had stopped and a representative national government was established. For the first time since the beginning of the mandate, he broke an explicit order from the High Commissioner forbidding him to travel about the country by taking the members of the committee on a tour. Their first stop was the tomb of Sheikh al-Qassam.[69]

Al-Hajj Amin had become a militant leader, spurred on not only by public opinion but by a new dynamic in internal Palestinian politics. The opposition encouraged a contest to see who was more national, the yardstick being the willingness to take on the British authorities. Al-Hajj Amin was called upon to resign from the presidency of the Supreme Muslim Council, since it was a mandatory government post. Raghib al-Nashashibi had already said as much to Jamal al-Husayni in March 1936. (We know this because of the eavesdropping and shadowing of the Jewish Intelligence Service, whose archive has been opened to Israeli historians but not to Palestinians, even though the bulk of its contents has to do with Palestinian history.)[70]

One person who did resign his post was George Antonius, a descendant of a Palestinian Christian family that had settled in Egypt. He had returned to his homeland in 1921 and until 1930 served in the local Department of Education. Dr Crane of the American King–Crane investigating team freed him from the colonialist department that perpetuated ignorance among the Palestinians, and hired him at the academic institution he directed in the United States.

Al-Hajj Amin's great faith in Antonius's wisdom and experience was not always reciprocated: Antonius was wary of the religious fervor that sometimes animated the *mufti*. However, at this critical time he agreed to help al-Hajj Amin and at his instigation opened a channel of communication with the Jewish Agency. He hoped its leaders would at least agree to limit Zionist activity, thereby preventing the bloodshed that might cost the *mufti* his position. But while Ben-Gurion was more accessible than the High Commissioner, he adamantly refused to make the smallest concession in matters he regarded as vital to the Jewish community – namely, unrestricted immigration and freedom to purchase every possible piece of land.[71]

In 1938 George Antonius wrote the finest essay written up to that point – some say to this day – about Arab nationalism. He was aware of the remarkable national awakening in Syria and Egypt during the 1930s, when young men laid down their lives for the national idea and urged conservative leaders to mount an all-out struggle against the British Empire. This nationalism had a dual nature, containing both a secular–liberal current and a religious–Islamic one. The situation in Palestine seemed similar, and as yet there was no telling who would lead the struggle. Antonius wanted to influence it in the liberal direction and hoped thereby to restrain Amin. But since his was

274 The Rise and Fall of a Palestinian Dynasty

a middle-class nationalism, and that of the Husaynis a notable nationalism, neither he nor others in the Palestinian leadership perceived that the driving force of the Palestinian uprising was the peasantry. The suffering of the *fellahin* and the laborers created the social-economic ground on which a national consciousness could grow. The Palestinian leadership did not make the effort to harness this power, which is one of several explanations for the failure of the revolt.

Only one of the Husaynis seemed to be aware of the peasants' plight and to understand the close connection between it and the national crisis. The writer Ishaq Musa al-Husayni wrote a book, published in 1943, titled *The Memories of a Hen* that became a classic of Palestinian literature. Bits of the story were published in the local press in the 1930s, and the family heard about it during the years of the Great Revolt. The first to hear of it was Khalil al-Sakakini, who since his return to Palestine had become Ishaq Musa's close friend. Sakakini – who adopted the nickname 'Human being, *inshallah*' – was still the family's revered teacher. When he approved of the book, Ishaq Musa proceeded to publish it.

The story is the history of Palestine from the viewpoint of a hen. At first, the hen belongs to a peasant family and is free to walk about the yard at will, has enough food to eat and lives a comfortable life. She observes that her peasant owners are content with what the soil produces, pay their taxes and do not fear the future. Then one day the hen finds that someone has set up barriers in the yard. To her amazement, she discovers that the peasants have sold their land to a rich stranger in order to pay their taxes. But the remaining land is insufficient to sustain the hen's owners, and they begin to sell their other property. After being sold to a shopkeeper in a nearby town, the hen is put in a cage and loses her freedom. Though she does not starve, food is not regularly available – some days there is plenty, others she goes hungry. The cage begins to fill up with other hens, and at best she can find only a narrow corner for herself. The new hens are a source of trouble: they speak a language that the older hens do not understand and manage to grab most of the food in the cage. Gradually she learns to understand their language and realizes that they intend to throw out the hens that were there first. Fortunately, the owner of the cage comes to their help and prevents their expulsion, but the hen-heroine notices that the number of strange hens keeps increasing, and her life is filled with tension and anxiety about the future.

As an official in the mandatory administration, Ishaq Musa had to publish his criticism in the form of fiction, but no one failed to understand his meaning. The great Egyptian novelist Taha Hussein honored the book with an introduction that interpreted the parable.[72] But no other Husayni produced a political document that expressed the sensitivity or insight that informed Ishaq Musa's book.

Moreover, the main strategy adopted by the Higher Arab Committee – namely, the general strike – not only failed to break the British authorities in the summer of 1936, it actually worsened the plight of the villagers and urban workers. The British responded with great brutality, destroying parts of ancient Jaffa, including the old port, ostensibly for reasons of sanitation but in reality as a collective punishment. The Zionists' watchfulness and energy were as impressive as always. As soon as the Port of Jaffa was destroyed, they sought and obtained permission to build one of their own. When it opened, it destroyed the livelihood of Palestinians in Jaffa.

In the opinion of Awni Abd al-Hadi, the Nablusite leader of the pan-Arab party Istiqlal, al-Hajj Amin was being too passive. Having received the consent, perhaps even the encouragement, of the High Commissioner, he went in September 1936 to Transjordan to see Amir Abdullah. The Hashemite *sheikh* – who had astutely converted the southern Syrian province into a separate state in 1921, thereby preventing its inclusion in the Zionist enterprise – was beginning to play an important part in the history of Palestine. His pro-British stance made him acceptable to the decision-makers in London. He agreed to intervene in the Palestinian crisis: he could hardly resist the chance of becoming the king of Palestine instead of the ruler of a desert kingdom with some 300,000 inhabitants. Moreover, the uprising in Palestine might have spread and infected his kingdom.

But Abdullah did not wish to appear to be the sole mediator, and so he enlisted two more kings: his kinsman, the young King Ghazi of Iraq, and his rival Ibn Saud of Arabia. Al-Hajj Amin had earlier sought the help of Ibn Saud to no avail – the British representative in Jeddah had advised Ibn Saud to turn down al-Hajj Amin's appeal.[73] Confronted with this triple intervention, al-Hajj Amin willingly agreed to call off the strike and to respond to a British attempt at conciliation. Britain allowed the Arab kings to mediate while it continued to use military force against the rebels and strikers, thereby expanding the local conflict into a regional one.

In November 1936, Lord Peel, a liberal politician and the son of the Conservative Prime Minister Sir Robert Peel, was appointed to head a commission of inquiry that would seek a solution to the problem of Palestine. It seems that the British government had been shaken by the fact that more Jews and Palestinians had been killed in a single month than during the entire period of the mandate. Though al-Hajj Amin called off the strike, he was not in position to cooperate with the commission. At first he tried, but he was insulted and withdrew. He was offended by the fact the commission met in the former Palace Hotel, which had been the apple of his eye before the King David Hotel opened. But chiefly he was angered by the attitude of Lord Peel, who must have forgotten that his purpose was to mediate, not to humiliate.

On 14 January 1937, al-Hajj Amin came to the hotel accompanied by many of the Higher Arab Committee. Said Qabani, one of the country's best interpreters, was assigned to him personally. From the moment he began to testify, Lord Peel needled him and challenged each and every one of his arguments, beginning with his claim that in 1922 General Allenby had promised the country independence and ending with the avowed 1930 British policy that was never implemented.[74]

Consequently, the Higher Arab Committee boycotted the commission. The reasons for the boycott were, of course, more profound. The committee's position was clear and would remain unchanged when the United Nations sent a Commission of Inquiry of its own in 1947: the cessation of immigration and land purchases were not subjects for negotiations but preconditions for negotiations, and the very willingness to negotiate should be seen as a concession on the part of those who were the original inhabitants of the country dispossessed by outside invaders.

But while boycotting the Peel Commission, al-Hajj Amin continued to seek channels of communication with the Zionists. This time it was Musa al-Alami, a member of a renowned family and a high official in the mandatory judiciary, who acted as intermediary. His contacts on the Zionist side were associates of Moshe Shertok (Sharett), the head of the political department, and were implicitly approved by Mapai (the dominant Zionist labor party). The contacts that took place in 1936 were intended to achieve a suspension of Zionist activity and a cessation of Palestinian resistance that would lead to substantive negotiations about the country's future.[75]

But this round also ended fruitlessly. In the meantime, al-Hajj Amin found himself, inadvertently and perhaps unwillingly, the sole leader of Palestinian politics. Some of the leaders of the opposition had left the country because of the violence. Public opinion was no longer confined to the press – people were now forming groups to fight the strikebreakers and individuals suspected of having a moderate attitude towards Zionism. The remaining members of the committee resigned in protest at the *mufti*'s 'mildness'. This criticism, and presumably the heated atmosphere, caused even Jamal to demand that the *mufti* take firmer action against the British.

This time it was Amin who was more cautious and who occasionally reined in Jamal's fighting spirit. Jamal's main activity was pressuring apolitical members of the family to join the national struggle. He persuaded the economist Muhammad Yunis to take on the directorship of the Agricultural Bank (a subsidiary of the Arab National Bank) and to join in on the effort to save Palestinian lands. He also convinced educator and journalist Abd al-Salam III to devote much of his time to national education and journalism.

Jamal remained a cautious leader even at the end of 1936, but not in his relations with opponents within the camp. One of the ugliest passages in the history of Palestinian internal politics began when the Nashashibis adopted a more extreme rhetoric and accused the *mufti* of cowardice. The newspaper *Al-Difaa* wrote:

> Antara and Hatim al-Tay [two famous Jahiliya poets] met on the road. Hatim asked Antara, 'What is courage?' Antara replied, 'Put your finger between my teeth and take my finger between your teeth. You bite hard and so will I.' They both began to bite down with all their might. 'Stop, enough!' shouted Hatim. 'Courage is patience,' said Antara. 'If you had waited a moment until I cried out with pain, you would have been a greater hero than I. But you cried out first, so I am a greater hero than you.' Oh, Arab! Your finger is in your enemy's mouth and his finger is in yours. Be Antara and wait.[76]

These charges of cowardice stemmed from al-Hajj Amin's refusal to adopt extreme measures, including an anti-British strike.[77]

The *mufti* did not support the strike and even managed to prevent government employees from striking. Nor did he support violent action, and until June 1936 he avoided inflaming the situation. Al-Hajj Amin also made a special effort to mitigate anti-Christian hostility, one of the bitter results of the fiery sermons of Izz al-Din al-Qassam. After the latter's death his followers called for a *jihad* against the infidel Christians. Al-Hajj Amin had intervened and, by touring the mosques and speaking movingly about the Christians who had laid down their lives for Palestine, managed to nip that morbid growth in the bud.[78]

But in 1936, wherever al-Hajj Amin went the Nashashibis provoked outbursts that embarrassed him – whether in Jaffa, or at the Haram al-Sharif.[79] Yet they did not undermine al-Hajj Amin's election as chairman of the executive.

In June 1936, al-Hajj Amin began to move against his opponents. It was not weakness but rather a new sense of power that drove his campaign. The sense of power was born the previous month, when he summoned all the national committees that had formed that year and led the uprising in all the towns and cities in Palestine. The headmen of the surrounding villages came and swore loyalty to each of these committees, confirming their standing.

This gathering, representing all the Palestinians in the country, testified to al-Hajj Amin's stronger position. He opened the meeting with the words, 'In the name of Allah the merciful and compassionate, we open this national gathering with greetings to our wounded, and I ask you to stand up in remembrance of our fallen and say together the *fatwa* for their souls.'

Before the year ended, al-Hajj Amin had to repeat these words several times. He explained to his audience that Britain had broken all its promises, notably the promise made by the British government in 1930 to implement the recommendations of the Hope Simpson Commission. The national committee from Hebron agitated for stronger measures, such as a boycott on Jewish products and non-payment of taxes, but al-Hajj Amin seemed more concerned to move against his opponents than against the British. After the spate of national rhetoric, he invited his friends among the Higher Arab Committee to dine at his house. Over his favorite dish of lentil soup, they planned a campaign that included violent acts of vengeance. At the end of the month, al-Hajj Amin took the members of the Higher Arab Committee on a tour of the country, and wherever they went they received an ecstatic welcome.[80]

Following the successful tour, al-Hajj Amin gave the green light to eliminating several of his opponents. This unprecedented fratricide lasted for two years, until the summer of 1938. Among the targets were Khalil Taha, one of the directors of the *waqf* in Haifa, who had supported the Husaynis before switching to Istiqlal. He was assassinated in September 1936.[81] Hassan Shukri, the mayor of Haifa, narrowly escaped assassination, unlike other less fortunate opponents. This chapter in al-Hajj Amin's biography marred much of what he had done before. It seems he was personally responsible for establishing internecine terror as a means of control.

Another casualty of the campaign was Arif al-Asali, who in the summer of 1937 published a booklet calling for Arab–Jewish understanding. He was abducted from his house by the *mufti*'s bodyguards, tried and condemned to death. Only after his father, a district governor in Transjordan, made certain that his son would never engage in political activity for the rest of his life did the *mufti* allow him to be taken out of the well in the courtyard of his office, where he had been held. He was expelled to Beirut, where he died in 1990.[82]

In the summer of 1937, Lord Peel published his recommendations to divide
Palestine up into a tiny Jewish state, an Arab state and a British protectorate,
and to annex the Arab state to the kingdom of Transjordan. The opposition
accepted the idea of a Hashemi annexation but rejected the partition. The
*mufti* refused to become a protégé of the Hashemite kingdom and represented
Palestinian public opinion well when he rejected the commission's recommendations outright. Most of the Husaynis agreed with him, but not all.

Unlike the *mufti*, Jamal had no objection to Abdullah. He had visited the
amir in May 1936 and persuaded him to demand the suspension of Jewish
immigration as a precondition for his intervention in the Palestinian crisis.
The amir's consent increased Jamal's confidence in the Hashemites. Indeed,
the last time in the 1930s that Jamal was invited to a tea party at the High
Commissioner's, he told the guests that if the country had to be partitioned,
it might be best for the Arab part to be given to Abdullah. 'If only the Arabs
and the Jews had known how to speak to each other,' he said, 'we would have
reached an agreement.' Al-Hajj Amin, on the other hand, adopted an openly
anti-Hashemite attitude. In February 1937, he went on a *Hajj* in order to seek
Ibn al-Saud's help against Abdullah, and he even asked the Hijazi tribes to
enter Transjordan.

Jamal spelled out for al-Hajj Amin the choices he was facing: either
negotiations with the Zionist movement, forming a common front against
the British, or an out-and-out fight against the British. Until August 1937
al-Hajj Amin allowed Jamal to try to get non-Zionist Jewish groups in the
United States and the Brith Shalom group in Palestine to support voluntary
Jewish restrictions on immigration and land purchases. That summer
Jamal also tried to persuade the mandatory government to recognize the
Palestinian leadership's passionate opposition to immigration, especially illegal
immigration. 'It is especially curious', he wrote to the government secretary,
'that it is through the ports under government supervision that most of the
illegal immigrants enter.' In reply, the secretary decried the importance of
the government-supervised ports.[83]

Almost without warning, the earth began to shake under al-Hajj Amin's
feet. It seems he was unaware how far the mandatory authorities were willing
to go in their attempts to silence him. In July 1937, al-Hajj Amin saw the first
indication that the British Empire regarded him as an enemy.

At daybreak on 17 July, armored vehicles of the British police surrounded
the offices of the Higher Arab Committee, blocked all the streets leading to
al-Hajj Amin's house and encircled the entire neighborhood. The telephone
lines were cut, and troops broke into the offices. Al-Hajj Amin had slipped

out in time and was lying low at his former residence in the Old City, which adjoined the Haram al-Sharif and was an integral part of the main complex around the mosque of al-Aqsa. He sealed all the openings of the house except the tunnel that linked it to the mosque. Apparently the British authorities knew where he was hiding but decided not to act against him yet. He was still able to establish contact with the world at large and the Arab world in particular, his last gambits before the mandatory government eventually resolved to act decisively against him.

His first move after this attack should be viewed in light of these efforts to survive. In August al-Hajj Amin again asked Nazi Germany for help (he had been refused before). The new German consul in Jerusalem, Wilhelm Dalle, was more interested in this contact than his predecessor had been. Rumors had been coming in from German embassies in the Arab world that the Nazis were changing their attitude towards the Palestine conflict, and Musa al-Alami went to Berlin to find out if they were true. He discovered that the Nazi government was showing no sign of support or even interest in the problem. For al-Hajj Amin this was one of several attempts to strengthen the Palestinians' international position. Israeli historiography would claim, with very little evidence, that by this time the *mufti* endorsed the Nazi ideology and was therefore looking for closer ties with Berlin. This accusation would be accepted in the West in general and in Britain in particular.[84]

When all these efforts failed, al-Hajj Amin attempted once more to rally the Arab world to the Palestinian cause, this time with more success than in the past. The growing Arab interest in Palestine neutralized Abdullah's involvement in the country, eliminated the Hashemites' clients (the Nashashibis) as an influential factor on the domestic scene and allowed al-Hajj Amin to maintain his position as the national leader of most Palestinians. Using the funds of the Supreme Muslim Council, in September 1937 al-Hajj Amin convened a pan-Arab conference at the Syrian resort of Bludan. Its 400 delegates supported al-Hajj Amin, assured him that he was a regional leader and urged him to launch an all-out revolt against Britain. It even helped him prepare an ambitious scheme for broad Arab support for military action.

It was an unofficial conference – in part because Britain and France had pressured Syria to disallow an official one – but it marked the beginning of external Arab involvement in Palestinian affairs. This involvement, however, consisted of much verbiage and little action, an impotency that contributed significantly to the disaster of 1948. The British apparently followed the conference with interest. Their consul in Damascus, Gilbert McGrath, had an agent in place who sent in daily reports in which he described the *mufti* as one of the empire's main enemies in the region. After the Bludan Conference, the rift between the Palestinians and Britain was irreparable, and it severely damaged the Palestinians' ability to influence London in their favor.

Though there are Palestinian testimonies from the conference, it is interesting to examine it through the reports of the correspondent of *The Times* of London, who acted as if he were (and maybe he really was) a British intelligence agent. The conference was a successful demonstration of loyalty to al-Hajj Amin that had been staged by his former opponent, the Haifaite notable Mu'in al-Madi (who would later change his spots and become a loyal supporter of King Abdullah). He had succeeded in bringing 400 delegates to Bludan – they were crammed into the main hall at the Grand Hotel, which could only hold 250 of them.

Foreign journalists were not permitted to enter the conference, which was one of the highlights of al-Hajj Amin's life even though it did not produce all the results he had hoped for. The *Times* correspondent managed to infiltrate the ranks of young members of Syria's National Bloc and get past the flags of Lebanon, Egypt and other newly independent Arab states. Though most of the delegates moderated the *mufti*'s strong anti-British proposals, there was broad agreement to reject the Peel Report, to demand an unpartitioned Palestine, the repeal of the mandate and of the Balfour Declaration and a halt to immigration and land purchases. The conference also called for a boycott of Zionist goods, threatened to call a boycott of British products and denounced Arabs who sold their lands.[85]

Though suspicions about the way al-Hajj Amin used the funds of the Muslim Council have never been dispelled, it should be noted that in Bludan he spent 1,500 Palestine pounds – a considerable sum – of his own money to cover the expenses of the delegates and the costs of the conference. Nevertheless, some of the participants did not pay their expenses, and the *Times* correspondent described angry and petty exchanges in the hotel lobby.

Al-Hajj Amin did not have long to relish being at the peak of success. The conference took place in August, and the following month the British District Commissioner of Northern Palestine, Lewis Andrews, was assassinated. It was a local initiative and had nothing to do with the *mufti*: Andrews had been associated with the Peel Commission, and the assassins regarded him as tainted by its recommendations. The murder enabled the British authorities to do what they had contemplated doing since early 1936: remove al-Hajj Amin from the political scene before he could use his strong position to lead an all-out struggle against them. After the assassination, they disbanded the Supreme Muslim Council and the Higher Arab Committee.

Before the Peel Commission's report, al-Hajj Amin had conducted a cautious policy. But his absolute opposition to the report led him to a head-on collision with the mandatory government. Though he did not launch an armed insurrection, his fate was sealed by the immense power of the British Empire. A month after the Bludan Conference, al-Hajj Amin had to flee Palestine accompanied by other leading members of the family – they would return, and he would not. Like a script with a foregone conclusion, it was the start of the political decline of the Husayni family as the Palestinian notables who were first among equals. However, this was a minor slide compared to the downfall of the entire Palestinian society a decade later.

## CHAPTER 10

# The Family in Exile

## The Husaynis and the Armed Revolt, 1937–8

Al-Hajj Amin realized that the die had been cast: as far as the British government in Palestine was concerned, he was *persona non grata*. On 12 October 1937, he moved to the Rawdat al-Ma'arif, and from there out of the city.[1] It is difficult in hindsight to know whether the British authorities in Palestine indeed contemplated arresting him that October. The documents show hesitation and indecision. The leading figures in the mandate knew that arresting the *mufti* might exacerbate the Palestine conflict. Yet they feared that if they allowed him to remain free, he could reinforce the leadership of the revolt. One way or the other, al-Hajj Amin had made up his mind to escape before he could be arrested.

The disbanding of the Supreme Muslim Council had led to the closing of the school. It had been very dear to al-Hajj Amin's heart – he had studied there, had managed it and renovated it and it was the last place he stayed in before leaving Palestine nearly for ever. (He would return once to East Jerusalem under rather strange circumstances, as we shall see.) The school was on the north side of the Dome of the Rock, an integral part of the northern wall of the shrine's courtyard. It had been built in the time of the Mamluk governor of Gaza and Jerusalem, Alim al-Din al-Sanjar al-Jauli (1284–1344), and was named '*al-madrasa al-jauliya*' after him. During the fifteenth century, it was the residence of the Mamluk governors of Jerusalem. The Ottomans, indifferent to its glory, housed a court and a jail in the building, and under Turkish rule it was called the 'Ancient'. As mentioned earlier, Muhammad Salih al-Husayni had opened a primary school on the premises, and after the Great War al-Hajj Amin bought it. When he was appointed head of the Supreme Muslim Council, al-Hajj Amin incorporated the school in the religious property of the Haram al-Sharif. In 1922 the Supreme Muslim Council appointed a directorship for the school, which had by then become a secondary school and taught up to eleventh grade, preparing students for matriculation. The school had a good library containing antique books in Arabic and English, as well as a mosque and a small stage for plays in Arabic – the directors insisted on Arabic being the school's official language of tuition. The British authorities closed the school, because during the first years of the Great Revolt Muslim religious scholars met there to promote anti-government activities and because they regarded the school's Scout movement as a potentially subversive organization. When the school was closed, its 100 students moved to the house of the late Musa Kazim in the Zahara Gate neighborhood, where they continued to study until 1948.[2]

Al-Hajj Amin went inside the school for the last time. Perhaps he remembered that it stood on the site of the Roman *praetorium* where Jesus Christ was sentenced to be crucified and that it was the first station of the Via Dolorosa. He had identified with Jesus in the past: when asked by the Shaw Commission about his part in the violent outbreaks of 1920 and 1929, he declared that he was innocent and hinted that he was being falsely accused. 'Why have you been charged?' asked the Jewish lawyer. 'For the same reason that 1,900 years ago, some 200 meters from where the honorable commission is sitting [the hearing took place at his house], Jesus was sentenced to be crucified. Then, too, the verdict was given to oblige the Jews.'[3] Perhaps al-Hajj Amin stood on the site of the stairs that had led to the rest of the stations – known as the Scala Sancta, they had been removed and taken to Rome in the first century AD. But even if he imagined himself in the role of Jesus Christ and the British governor as Pontius Pilate, al-Hajj Amin could not linger in the school to contemplate his destiny.[4]

As evening fell on 12 October, the *mufti*, dressed in Bedouin robes and bearing the identity of Muhammad al-Ja'afar, slid down twenty meters from the window of his house in the Haram into an orchard outside the wall. The owner of the orchard, who had been watching the British patrols day and night, signaled to the *mufti* that the field was clear. The *mufti's* close friend Rafiq al-Ajouni was waiting for him in a car and drove him to Jaffa. The car was stopped and examined several times en route. In Jaffa another friend, Yusuf Dhiya al-Dajani, met them and took them to his fine house on the shore. At midnight al-Hajj Amin left the Port of Jaffa in a small boat and reached the Port of Abu Zabura, forty miles north of Jaffa, at dawn. The following night he proceeded to Haifa, and the next night he left Palestine, which he would not see again until 1967, when King Hussein of Jordan invited him to Jerusalem. He reached Tyre, where he was caught by the French Coast Guard, who brought him before the French police chief Pierre Colombani. But the latter turned out to be a friend, and the *mufti* promised him that he would not stay long in Lebanon but would move on to Damascus at the first opportunity. Jamal fled after al-Hajj Amin. Before leaving, he edited the last issue of *Al-Liwa*, the Husaynis' second publication (after *Al-Jamaa' al-Arabiyya*). When the British came to arrest him, they found his office empty.

At first the British thought that al-Hajj Amin's flight to Lebanon was a convenient solution. He was staying at the house of Dr Samah al-Fahuri, the head of the Supreme Muslim Council in Beirut, and the French authorities obliged the British by stationing a military force beside the house.[5] The *mufti* occupied the top floor of the three-storey house. One of his first visitors was Akram Zuaytar, who found al-Hajj Amin in good spirits, encouraged by the warm welcome he had received from the local Muslims. Al-Hajj Amin asked his visitor how people in Palestine reacted to his flight, and Zuaytar did not have the heart to tell him that opinions were divided. Some argued that he should have remained in the country even if it meant confinement in the Haram, and others said that 'sacrifice is not made for its own sake' and that the main thing was to evade the British clutches. But Abd al-Qadir supported the *mufti*'s flight, putting an end to the public debate. Zuaytar assured al-Hajj Amin that everyone was behind him.

Al-Hajj Amin did not stay long in al-Fahuri's house, as the Lebanese wanted to hide him in a more secluded place. An old friend of his, the well-known Beirut socialite Maude Faragallah, approached the French High Commissioner and obtained a more convenient refuge for him. Though it was not easy to arrange a safe haven for a person the British considered to be a threat, she did eventually find him a house in Kassalik, a palatial residence that would one day serve as the presidential palace of Fuad Shihab.[6] It was not only convenient but also strategically located in a way that allowed him to be in touch with Palestine, where the revolt was not over yet. With the French authorities' knowledge, he was allowed to receive advisers and messengers. During the uprising al-Hajj Amin instituted the *kaffiyah* and *aqal* (cloth headdress and cord) as the national Palestinian headgear in place of the traditional tarbush.[7] He looked for ways to encourage the armed band of youths in Palestine that was trying to wage a guerrilla war against the British mandate in 1938. However, the band was crushed ruthlessly with the help of the Royal Air Force and a series of collective punishments that today would be considered war crimes.

With al-Hajj Amin ensconced in Lebanon and Jamal touring the Arab world, another Husayni briefly appeared on the stage of Palestinian history: Suleiman al-Husayni, also a scion of the Tahiri branch. He was working very closely with the better-known Ishaq Darwish, al-Hajj Amin's relation by marriage and his close adviser. They both established the headquarters of the Palestinian uprising in Damascus, and in many ways the success of the armed campaign before it was crushed was due to their skill in orchestrating such operations from far away.

While it lasted it was an impressive war of liberation – the kind the Palestinians would venture to wage again in 1987 and then in 2000. From October 1937 until the winter of 1938, the uprising raged all over Palestine, with guerrillas attacking British and Zionist targets. As mentioned, the British government responded harshly, imposing collective punishments and death sentences. Thanks to the efforts of Suleiman and Ishaq, the Husaynis retained their political power throughout the uprising. Even without the important posts of *mufti, naqib al-ashraf,* mayor, members of parliament, head of the Supreme Muslim Council or the Higher Arab Committee, the family remained at the heart of the political map – an impressive achievement.

The family determined the politics of the military leadership, but it could not direct the armed struggle. Indeed, few Palestinians were capable of doing so, and the first priority of the high command was to find an Arab, not necessarily a Palestinian, who could head it. The natural choice was Fawzi al-Qawuqji. A native of Tripoli in Syria, he had made his reputation by leading the Syrian rebellion against France. He had projected himself as the embodiment of pan-Arab solidarity in Palestine. His military experience had won him the post of military adviser to the Saudi king, but for some reason he fell out with the Saudi court and went back to serving in the French army even though it had sentenced him to death. In 1932 he had been in Baghdad, where he began to work for the armed struggle in Palestine. But he had chosen the Nashashibis as his political patrons, and here British and Husayni interests overlapped.[8] In 1936, he headed an army of volunteers that took part in some daring operations against the British forces. But he did not stay for long, and in October that year he left Palestine. He would return in 1948 and would become al-Hajj Amin's archrival in local politics. But in 1938, even if he had contemplated another entry to Palestine, he would have been barred by the Iraqi government, which was under pressure from the British to prevent him from returning to the Palestinian battlefield. For a brief moment, the British position meshed with that of the Husaynis since they both opposed the Nashashibis. And so Fawzi al-Qawuqji's candidacy fell at the first post.

Other candidates who were approached refused. Then Abd al-Rahim al-Hajj, one of the early leaders of the uprising who was still fighting in Palestine, accepted the position. But he was killed at the end of February 1939 in a battle against British forces. He was succeeded by two local commanders until the end of the uprising.

Even the local commander in the Jerusalem area was not directly connected to the Husaynis. Arif Abd al-Raziq was the district commander who directed operations starting in September 1938, when the rebels decided to launch an attack on the British forces in Jerusalem. For one day, 17 October 1938, the city was in the hands of the Palestinians, as the British district commander, Honig, reported to his superiors – a small triumph for a failure-haunted movement.[9]

The Husaynis were the uprising's foreign ministers, especially Jamal and al-Hajj Amin. Helped by Suleiman and Ishaq Darwish, the two diverted the headquarters of the revolt to the house of their friend Amir Said al-Jazairi, scion of the famous family that had led the Algerian uprising against the French. The family had been exiled to Damascus at the end of the nineteenth century, where it became allied with Faysal's regime and later with the Syrian National Bloc, which spearheaded Syria's struggle for independence. The amir recruited the veterans of the 1925 Syrian revolt against the French to help the Palestinians. In a rare moment of pan-Arab solidarity, these veterans formed a committee to aid the Palestinian uprising of 1936. It was the first significant step in the recruitment of Syrian volunteers for Palestine, which would continue until 1948.

Suleiman al-Husayni was the liaison between the committee in Damascus and the rebels in Palestine, while Ishaq Darwish was the liaison with the *mufti* in Lebanon. The two purchased a house for their exiled relatives in the Salihiyya Quarter on Muhajarin Street (another historical irony, placing the Palestinian exiles in 'the street of the migrants'). The house was used not only for gatherings but also as a refuge for exiles who could not afford to buy houses for themselves. No one could enter the place without giving the password. Meetings were held either in the early hours of the morning or late at night, in part because Suleiman and Ishaq were busy during the day. They met government officials or sat in the al-Qamahin Café (owned by Ibrahim al-Asal and Abu Abdu Qador, veterans of the 1925 revolt) recruiting volunteers and arms for the uprising. The arms they obtained were cached in the central Maydan Quarter, beside the great garbage dump that dated back to Ottoman times. The local gendarmerie cooperated, and arms smuggling into Palestine followed a predetermined route through sympathetic villages. The attempt to build a similar network inside Lebanon failed because the Lebanese police did not cooperate.

Most of the arms were collected in the Kurdish mountain region, where it was always possible to find weapons for sale. As in every complex political situation in the Middle East, the Palestinians were aided by diverse and conflicting interests. The Kurds helped because they hoped that the Palestinians would support their own struggle against Turkey in the future, and the Turkish consul in Damascus was happy to support any operation that would reduce the number of weapons in Kurdish hands.

Though nowhere near the battleground, al-Hajj Amin sought to depict himself as the supreme commander. He adopted the *nom de guerre* 'Sumuh' ('The Generous'), which was used by all his correspondents throughout his exile in Damascus to fool British intelligence.[10] The farther he was from his native land, the more al-Hajj Amin's delusions of grandeur intensified – in 1941 he presented himself in Germany as the leader of the entire Arab nation.

Al-Hajj Amin had an extensive network of connections in the Syrian administration. The Husaynis in Damascus were on close terms with Adil al-Azma, the general director of the Syrian Ministry of the Interior. This was a revived connection – in 1925 the Azma brothers had been involved in the Syrian revolt against the French and were periodically exiled to various places, among them Jerusalem. Upon their return home that year from their first exile, they received a letter from the *mufti* expressing his hope that they would continue their vital struggle. This letter must have won al-Hajj Amin a special place in the heart of this family.[11]

In 1936 Adil's brother Nabih, the minister for internal security, having represented Syria at the first Islamic conference, was exiled to Jerusalem for some time. On that occasion, he and al-Hajj Amin disagreed about the conference: Nabih wished to use it as a pan-Arab instrument to aid the Syrians in their struggle against the French, while al-Hajj Amin wanted it to serve the Palestinian cause almost exclusively. But their dissension was forgotten, and in 1936 Nabih came in person to Palestine to help organize the army of rebels and Adil made possible the dispatch of German rifles that had been bought from the Kurds and kept since the Great War. Adil also arranged to purchase arms in more distant countries, such as Italy and Germany. Being in charge of the border guard on the Syrian-Palestinian border made it easy for him to smuggle the weapons across to the rebels.[12]

While in Beirut, the *mufti* continued to advance the Palestinian cause with the assistance of the *mufti* of Lebanon. Other family members were also deeply engaged in rallying support throughout the Arab world. Al-Hajj Amin's nephew Munif al-Husayni was representative of the kind of commitment the family had shown. Due to his participation in the revolt, he was arrested and exiled to Damascus in the winter of 1937. From there he moved to Cairo, where he directed the Palestinian Information Office, distributing leaflets and holding meetings in private houses. But Egypt was still very much a British territory, and soon after his arrival Munif was caught by the British authorities. Along with a number of other Palestinians, he was detained in a British camp in the Seychelles. In 1939 he and the others were released, and he was soon as active as before.

Thanks to their status in the Arab world, the Husaynis were able to recruit prominent supporters in all these countries. In Egypt they were helped by the well-known author and intellectual Hussein Heikal, then a minister without portfolio in the Egyptian government, who committed his newspaper *Al-Siyasa* to the Palestinian cause. In Baghdad the family was helped by Naji al-Suweidi, a member of the ruling power. He was among a group of Iraqis who helped the *mufti* to move to Baghdad during World War II and turn it into a center of pro-Palestine activity.

The most successful stroke of the campaign was the opening of the Information Office in Damascus in 1938. Run by Akram Zuaytar and Izzat Darwaza and advised by Jamal al-Husayni, it published numerous manifestos. In exile the two Husayni leaders, Jamal and al-Hajj Amin, once again collaborated, with Jamal coordinating the work in the Arab capitals. Jamal traveled twice a week to al-Duq in Lebanon to see the *mufti*, and also looked after the finances. The funds were held in the Damascus branch of Misr Bank, in the accounts of prominent Syrians – it was essential not to keep them under Palestinian names. An elaborate network helped the Palestinians' finances. Ali Masud, a Christian Lebanese employee of the Italian consulate in Cairo, transferred the funds raised in Egypt to the assistant manager of the Misr Bank, another member of the al-Azma family, who would withdraw the money and give it to Jamal.

The complex financial arrangement tied the leading Husaynis even closer to the Germans and the Italians during the months before World War II. The relationship began when Jamal received some help from the Italian and German consulates in Damascus. The German consulate supported the activities of a Palestinian youth club located near the exiles' headquarters in the Salihiyya Quarter – a fine place with gyms, dance and game halls and a lecture hall. The British suspected that there were pro-Nazi Germans among the gym trainers, preparing the volunteers who were later smuggled into Palestine. But it seems it was mainly the Syrian authorities who usually supported such activities. The range of the projects aided by the Syrian government indicates that there was genuine solidarity between the government and administrative personnel, not merely fiery rhetoric as was the case with other Arab regimes at the time. So either the Husaynis were particularly successful in Syria in those days, or the Syrians, including the political elite, were less indifferent to the Palestinian plight than politicians in other Arab countries.[13]

Al-Hajj Amin's thinking was complex, as shown by his incessant exploration of other ways of resolving the conflict. While building up a logistical and financial infrastructure, examining the possibilities of help from the Germans and Italians and searching for additional allies in the Arab world, he sent his nephew Musa Abdullah al-Husayni to London to represent him at the talks instigated by the unusual British official, Stuart Newcomb. Newcomb continued to believe in a British-Palestinian alliance even during the uprising. Like his Anglo-Jewish friend Albert Haimson – who had held a post in the Palestine British administration between 1921 and 1934 and had gone from being a warm supporter of the Zionist movement to being a critic of Zionism and the British attitude towards it – Newcomb also believed in the possibility of a Jewish–Palestinian understanding. In the midst of the bloody confrontation in 1939, Newcomb and Haimson outlined a nine-clause program for the resolution of the conflict, calling on both sides to make far-reaching concessions in order to achieve calmer conditions for prolonged negotiations.

Contrary to their formal positions and the overall escalation, both the *mufti* and leading members of the Jewish Agency decided to give this initiative a chance. The Jewish Agency appointed Yehuda Magnes to represent it in this endeavor. Though this probably escaped the *mufti's* attention, Magnes's having been chosen was an indication that the Zionist leadership did not consider the initiative too seriously. A reformist American rabbi who served as the first chancellor of the Hebrew University in Jerusalem and as its president until he died in 1948, Magnes was a highly respected intellectual but was considered to be a naive politician. In the 1920s, he had adopted an interpretation of Zionism that led to him being ousted from the mainstream. He advocated the creation of a bi-national Arab-Jewish state in Palestine. Therefore any initiative he was involved in fell into the category of things the Zionist leadership considered insignificant but worth exploiting, less for the sake of coexisting with the Palestinians and more as means of sowing further discord between them.

The *mufti*'s choice for exploring this option was an equally respectful member of the family but one who was often regarded as a dreamer rather than part of the hardcore body of political decision-making. This was Musa Abdullah al-Husayni. He belonged to al-Hajj Amin's branch of the family (not that it mattered any more) and saw al-Hajj Amin as his 'uncle'. He is known in the West only as the chief plotter of the assassination of King Abdullah of Jordan in 1951, which will be covered later on. At this point, he was still a medical student, like so many others in the Tahiri branch, in London. Soon after his arrival he was attracted to the socialist ideology of the Fabian Society and he dreamed of leading a Palestinian leftist movement, hardly a typical Husayni vision. But he did not persevere in this direction. Being a political pragmatist like his uncle al-Hajj Amin, he looked for those he thought would have the power to help the Palestinians – and these were not the socialists. He decided that the future lay in Germany, where he moved when the war broke out, marrying a local woman and integrating into the local society for a while. But in 1936 his pinkish politics appealed to Yehuda Magnes and made a dialogue possible.

British intelligence depicted the whole affair as a subversive socialist attempt to undermine British power in Palestine and convinced the government to withdraw its support for the Haimson–Newcomb initiative. Their focus was now once more on the political and even physical elimination of the *mufti*. Their open hostility pushed him even further into the hands of Berlin and Rome.

But while this bizarre dialogue went on, it revealed that on both sides, for sincere or cynical reasons, some individuals were willing to offer far-reaching compromises and concessions. Speaking in the *mufti*'s name, though possibly without his knowledge, Musa Abdullah reported to Magnes that, in view of the crisis, al-Hajj Amin was willing to consider the establishment of a small Jewish state along the lines of the Peel recommendations, provided it did not include Haifa and Galilee. But first Jewish immigration had to be reduced to levels acceptable to the Palestinian population. The delighted Magnes rushed to report the news to the leader of the Zionist movement, David Ben-Gurion, who was known for having accepted the recommendation of the Peel Commission. But that had been a year earlier and was done to appease the British; it was not a sign of Zionist moderation, as Israeli historiography suggests. It was off the agenda in 1938, and Ben-Gurion showed no interest in the Palestinian position in general or the rather marginal Musa Abdullah in particular.[14]

But let there be no mistake – most of al-Hajj Amin's efforts were directed towards boosting the guerrilla struggle against British and Zionist targets in Palestine. The burden of the uprising fell mainly on the rural population, and many of the commanders on the ground were local men. Yet this brought them no political gains, which may have been the reason why they did not come forward when the Husaynis tried to rally them once more to the greater and more vital battle in 1947 and 1948.

Some of the Husaynis did fight. For these young men and women of the family it was a formative experience to find themselves in the vanguard of a national struggle. Romantic dreams mingled with the dark reality of bloodshed, casualties and imprisonment, and the experience released the frustration and rage that had built up since 1929. It was also the first time that members of the family had actually taken part in an armed conflict. At least the younger generation felt that they had a role in a wider struggle. Their actions were typical of popular uprisings against an occupying military force and foreign colonialist settlers: they threw rocks and Molotov cocktails at lorries, offices and government premises, and they attacked individual Jewish settlers and more rarely entire outposts. The results were much less important than their having participated in the struggle.

The two sons of al-Hajj Amin's cousin Muhi al-Din, Mustafa Nafiz and Ali, were involved in actual fighting, while other members of the family, such as Yaqub Abd al-Salam, helped Abd al-Qadir to direct the fight in Jerusalem. The young Fawzi, Jawad, Muhammad and Sami (the last-named was Abd al-Qadir's brother) took part in battles and in operations against British and Zionist targets in Jerusalem. Jamal's younger brother Daud organized the uprising in Jaffa, but before long he was put on the British wanted list and escaped to Damascus. He slipped back repeatedly, bringing arms for the rebels. It was said that during one of these forays in October 1938, he killed Sidqi al-Dajani, the Husaynis' traditional rival in Jaffa, but there is no evidence to support this suspicion or that the British authorities ever considered it.

The middle generation made its contribution mostly as organizers and advisers. Sawfat Yunis, director of the Higher Arab Committee, and the lawyer Ibrahim Said al-Husayni, the son of Said and director of the religious properties in Hebron, were responsible for smuggling arms to the rebels in Mount Hebron. Jamal's brothers were especially prominent. Hilmi acted as the liaison between Jamal and the rebels, even involving his wife in the dangerous missions. He was helped by the Haifaite Yaqub, who was a customs official and who used his position to organize operations in the Haifa area. Yaqub was caught in 1937 and like many of the Husaynis paid personally for the national cause.

A glance at the lists of detainees in the British camps shows which of them paid with his liberty for taking part in the uprising. In Aujat Hafir it was Ahmad Jamil and Munif, who were released in November 1936 but repeatedly rearrested. In Sarafand it was Jamil and Tawfiq Rafat; in Jerusalem Muhammad Yunis, director of the Agricultural Bank, who was arrested in 1938, and Rasim Yunis al-Husayni, who was arrested in 1937 and tortured. A few gave their lives for the cause – Salim's son Ali, Abd al-Qadir's right-hand man, fell in a battle with British forces in 1938, and Umar, an engineer, (the grandson of Hussein) who fell in the great battle at Bani Na'im (located between Hebron and Bethlehem) when Abd al-Qadir confronted the British army.[15]

Ali's father, Salim Hussein, the brother of Musa Kazim, was the last of the generation of 1920s leaders to remain in the country. (He must not be confused with the mayor of Jerusalem on the eve of the Great War, though of course he belonged to the same branch of the family.) His house was the meeting place for the rebels who had not yet been caught or exiled. In the early 1940s, he joined al-Hajj Amin in Europe but did not engage in any more political activity.

The women of the family also took part in the struggle for Palestine, notably Salma, the wife of Raja'i al-Husayni. She and other Palestinian women joined the pan-Arab women's conference that was held in 1938 at the initiative of the Egyptian feminist Huda al-Sha'arawi. Al-Sha'arawi became the most prominent woman writer in the Arab world and made an impact on the public status of Arab women. She and Asma, the wife of Syria's Nabih al-Azma, had helped promote the Bludan Conference. When the wives of the leaders of Syria and Lebanon formed the Women's Palestine Defense Committee in Damascus, it got off to a modest start. In September 1938, al-Sha'arawi called summoned the women of the Mashreq (the eastern flank of the Arab world) to Cairo to attend a conference for Palestine, which took place on 15 October. In the Palestinian delegation, each of prominent notable families had two representatives. We do not know whether this was on purpose or whether the worthy women regarded themselves as representing families. Wahida and Samiha al-Khalidi and Fatma and Zahiya al-Nashashibi joined Salma and Su'ad (the wife of Fahmi al-Husayni). The heroine of the occasion was Mamina, the widow of Sheikh al-Qassam.[16]

The involvement of Husayni women in politics, if belated, reflected the social transformation in the family as a whole. In the past, the women's political contribution had been confined to arranging the marriage ties that underpinned the alliances with other families. In the twentieth century, women were far more literate and self-assertive than the previous generations; some of them, like so many teenage girls all over the Middle East, were sent to Europe and America to marry or to join relatives who did well there. One such family member was Amina, the granddaughter of Salim al-Husayni and sister of Musa Kazim, who was married at age fourteen to her cousin Muhammad al-Husayni. She traveled with him to Germany, where he studied medicine and she studied X-ray technology. When they returned to Palestine she became the first Muslim woman to learn to drive and was seen driving her car in the streets of Jerusalem. (She was preceded by Asya al-Halabi, the first Christian Palestinian woman to drive a car.) Amina helped her husband with the X-ray machine, especially after he developed heart trouble. When her children grew up she worked for charity organizations, often in cooperation with Zaliha al-Shabani, the president of the first charity club in Palestine, whom she later succeeded. Amina began to engage in political activity only after 1948, and during the 1960s was a highly respected member of the Palestinian National Council as the representative of the women's organizations.

Amina was not the first woman in the family to break out of the confines of tradition. Fatma, the wife of Rafiq al-Husayni (son of Musa Kazim and brother of Abd al-Qadir), graduated from the English College in Jerusalem and went on to study at the American University in Beirut, where she completed her master's degree. From there she went to Iraq to teach. Tragically, one day while on home leave she stepped on a nail, developed blood poisoning and died at the age of twenty-seven.[17] Since this is a political biography, we are constrained to focus on the men of the family and leave to other researchers the strenuous reconstruction of the history of Palestinian women.

This complex group of men and women of the Husayni family had lost two of its leaders. Since al-Hajj Amin and Jamal were in exile, their places at the head of the family were taken by two others. The principal and best known was Abd al-Qadir, and the other was Tawfiq Salih. During the uprising Abd al-Qadir commanded the Jerusalem front in the rebellion, was wounded twice and was honored and admired by the fighting men. The first time he was wounded was in a battle against British forces near the village of al-Khadir, the first battle against British tanks. The Palestinian fighters managed to put one tank out of action, and though Abd al-Qadir was not personally responsible, the achievement is credited to him. At the end of that battle, he was caught and arrested. The highest price seems to have been paid by Abd al-Qadir's father, Musa Kazim, in 1933.

For Abd al-Qadir, 1938 marked a decisive shift in his view of the conflict and his attitude towards Britain. His trust in Britain was shaken beyond repair when he witnessed the outcome of the British punitive operations. The worst was the massacre in Atil, where British forces blew up and set fire to many houses with their occupants inside. Some women were reportedly raped and abused.[18] He was especially horrified by the British practice of tying a suspected nationalist activist with a rope to the door of his house and other ruthless methods used by the British army at the time.

Like other commanders of the uprising, Abd al-Qadir adopted the national anti-imperial discourse, mixing religious terms with the modern ones of the anti-colonialist struggle. *Jihad* became a national concept, and Abd al-Qadir often exhorted his men on the eve of a battle to give their all for the sake of the national anti-imperial holy war. The goal of the Palestinian national movement was now clearer than ever: complete independence.

In 1938, the ugly practice of killing village headmen who refused to shoulder the burden of the uprising reached its peak. Though Abd al-Qadir himself was not directly involved in these assassinations, his subordinates certainly were, notably Said Shuqair, a man from the vicinity of Ramallah, who carried out these acts of vengeance in Abd al-Qadir's name. One of the reasons the uprising failed may have been this dissension, in which Abd al-Qadir actively participated, in a badly organized and unclear chain of command.

This two-front war – fighting against the occupying force and at the same time waging an internecine struggle against collaborators or potential rivals in the chain of command – was plainly in evidence at the battle of Bani Na'im in December 1938. This large village in the district of Hebron was a stronghold of the opposition to the uprising – namely, the Nashashibi camp. Abd al-Qadir's men surrounded the village and tried to persuade the inhabitants to join the uprising, but the planned time of the attack was leaked and a large British force was waiting. The British air force launched a merciless assault on Abd al-Qadir's forces, and he himself was wounded.

Palestinian collective memory records every such battle as a clash with British forces, and together they are described as the first military campaign in the history of the Palestinian national movement. Abd al-Qadir's willingness to lay down his life for the homeland stands out. He had been mentally prepared for the revolt since 1931, when he organized the young men of Jerusalem to act against the British. Two years later he and Emile al-Ghuri, a friend of the family, created the first-ever Palestinian military organization, *Al-Jihad al-Muqaddas*. There were only seventeen members in that ineffectual and short-lived organization, but it signaled Abd al-Qadir's distinctive contribution to the Palestinian military inheritance. Nafiz, the son of Muhi al-Din, was just as active as his famous kinsman, but did not make it into the national history books. Khalid, a cousin of Abd al-Qadir's, was one of his seconds-in-command, thanks to his experience in the ranks of the British police force; he had reached the rank of inspector in the Jaffa police.[19]

So Abd al-Qadir was the first of two family members to fill the void that al-Hajj Amin and Jamal left behind during their exile. The other one is less known: Jamal's eldest brother, Tawfiq Salih, the director of the Muslim orphanage in Jerusalem who was greatly admired for his social work. He served in the British Immigration Department and tried his best to bar the entry of Zionists to the country. Al-Hajj Amin sometimes appointed him deputy head of the committee, but he had no official title.

Quite a different contribution was made by Ishaq Musa al-Husayni. The literary-minded Ishaq Musa persuaded his journalistic cousins to publish his early essays. The first discussed the weaknesses of Palestinian Arab society. It displeased the heads of the family, who ignored his warning of how unfit and ill-prepared the Palestinian leadership was to meet the dangers Zionism posed to them and to Palestinian society as a whole. Ishaq Musa was probably the most scholarly member of the family. He studied and then taught at the American University in Cairo, and in 1934 completed his doctoral studies at the University of London under the supervision of the renowned Orientalist Hamilton Gibb. After he returned to Jerusalem, he taught Arabic literature at the Arab College. During the revolt, he became the supervisor of Arabic language tuition in Palestine, a post that acquired special significance amid the uprising and the struggle against Zionism.

But not all the Husaynis enrolled in the fight. The most notable dissenter was Arif Yunis al-Husayni, a scion of the branch that had filled the post of *sheikh al-haram* for long periods. This post was restored to the Husaynis in the early twentieth century, but since it had lost its importance, the branch that held it was also minor. Whether for that reason or because he held strong views of his own, Arif Yunis opposed al-Hajj Amin's leadership, and did so publicly. The chief of police in Jerusalem became concerned for his safety and placed a permanent guard near his house, which foiled an attempt on Arif Yunis's life. Another member of the family who tended to the opposition was Abd al-Salam Shaker, the editor of the weekly *Al-Wahada*, which maintained a position similar to that of Musa al-Alami's camp.

However, most of the Husaynis supported the uprising and engaged in its daily undertaking. Out of all of them, al-Hajj Amin was the one most occupied with his personal fate: since he had been expelled from Palestine, his future was unclear. The uprising in Palestine broke out when he was looking for a refuge for himself. Political drama overshadows all other existential activity. Only when the historian examines the years of the revolt from the viewpoint of the average inhabitant does it become evident that the uprising did not affect the whole population all of the time. Even some of the Husaynis were engaged in other activities that, on the face of it, seemed less heroic at the time. But in retrospect these would become the kinds of struggles that Palestinians were engaged in as ordinary citizens of an occupied land throughout the twentieth and into the twenty-first century.

Such was the struggle of Arif Yunis al-Husayni. He confronted the Zionist municipality of Jerusalem head-on. Mayor Daniel Auster mixed municipal issues with wider ideological concerns. Under his leadership, the municipality wanted to widen various roads, gates and pavements. One of the spaces that fell within the widening project was Arif Yunis's garden, which contained some of the family tombs. Unlike the great national struggle, this one was concluded successfully. The non-nationalist Arif Yunis won, while the exiled al-Hajj Amin lost his inheritance not to the city but to the Zionists. Al-Hajj Amin's property in the Nahlat Ahim area was expropriated and given to the Jewish National Fund. Only the school that stood on that property was spared, and the municipality had it moved it elsewhere.[20]

Together with other Palestinian landowners, the Husaynis fought a rearguard battle against the rapid urban development driven by British officials and the Zionists. The population of Jerusalem in the 1930s was 150,000, and some of the neighborhoods were more crowded than the slums of London. Accelerated construction came at the expense of the green spaces and public parks. However, during the uprising the municipality took some steps to preserve the city's 'green lungs'.

But al-Hajj Amin lost more than his property; his political standing was no more secure. In the winter of 1938, the British government changed its tactics. Instead of trying to crush the uprising, it looked for ways to calm the country. Al-Hajj Amin was not part of their plans. A new commission of inquiry led by Sir John Woodhead recommended ditching the idea of partition (which Britain would again support in 1943) and severely criticized the conduct of the High Commissioner during the uprising. Chancellor was unceremoniously dismissed and replaced by the Orientalist Sir Harold MacMichael. Though an expert 'Arabist', MacMichael aggravated relations between Britain and the Palestinians and was largely responsible for the perception, etched in the Palestinians' collective memory, that Britain betrayed them even in the last years of the mandate. Al-Hajj Amin certainly regarded the British as the enemy, perhaps even more than the Zionists. [21]

An examination of Britain's wider politics at this time, however, reveals that this judgment is excessively severe. In 1938 Britain abandoned the idea of partition and attempted to freeze the demographic balance in the country, despite the increasingly desperate plight of the Jews in Nazi-occupied Europe. But this British U-turn came too late. When tensions mounted in Europe, the Germans marched into Czechoslovakia and British troops began to withdraw from Palestine, the leadership of the Palestinian uprising was more impressed by the reduction of Britain's military presence than by its change of policy. When the Woodhead Commission left, the uprising flared again. In response, the British government sent back some of the withdrawn forces and launched a frontal attack on the rebels – while continuing to tilt its policy in favor of the Palestinians. At this time, there was a wave of pan-Arab support for Palestine, prompting the British government to renew the diplomatic maneuvering. In February 1939, after nineteen years of rule over Palestine, the government brought the two sides to a roundtable conference at St James's Palace in London.

The government in Jerusalem wanted to determine the composition of the delegation. It suggested that Jamal be the *de facto* representative of the Palestinians, but Raghib al-Nashashibi would be its official head. (Jamal was still suspect due to his involvement in the revolt.) The *mufti* was *persona non grata* in London, not only because he had led the uprising but because he was tainted by his growing friendship with Germany and Italy. The connection between the *mufti* and the Damascus consulates of Germany and Italy – especially the latter – had begun during the uprising. The Germans tried now and then to send in weapons, but they were captured by the British. Most of the help came from the Italians. By and large, the Nazi regime did not meddle in the affairs of Palestine before the war, did not officially object to the Peel recommendations and until the outbreak of war did not prevent Jews from fleeing Germany to Palestine.

Syrian politician Adil Arslan urged al-Hajj Amin to form closer ties with the Italians. He not only talked to al-Hajj Amin about it, he published an exchange of letters between them in the newspapers *Al-Jamaa' al-Islamiyya* and *Filastin*.[22] The purpose of the correspondence was to show that Italy, unlike Britain, supported the Arab claims unreservedly. Arslan wrote the *mufti* that the Arab nation needed a European friend, and only Italy would fit the bill. Munif al-Husayni, the editor of *Al-Jamaa' al-Arabiyya*, was such an enthusiastic supporter of an alliance with Italy that the British suspected him of being its agent and some of his staff resigned on that account. The journalists did not regard Italy as a possible ally but as a colonialist power crushing the Tripolitanians' struggle for independence. The Nashashibi opposition used al-Hajj Amin's courtship of colonialist Italy to accuse him of betraying the pan-Arab cause, though no one in the opposition criticized his later friendship with Germany.[23]

The opposition behaved very shabbily when the St James Conference was convened. Fakhri al-Nashashibi was the most vocal in objecting to al-Hajj Amin's participation in the talks. He informed the British that not only did he himself support their policy, he had actually created 'peace bands' that fought against the rebels. It seems that this posture embarrassed the more nationalist elements in the Nashashibi camp, and for a moment it looked as if they would denounce Fakhri's action. Raghib even suggested inviting al-Hajj Amin to London as head of the delegation. Al-Hajj Amin must have felt for a moment that he was about to return to the center of politics in Palestine. To his great surprise, he was allowed by the British to travel to Egypt, only to discover that he had been brought there to be pressured by Egyptian prime minister Muhammad Mahmud to refuse Raghib's invitation and to give Jamal al-Husayni the position as a head of the Husayni representative in the delegation.[24]

Not everyone in the British government treated the *mufti* with such hostility. By March 1938, when the new High Commissioner MacMichael took up his post, voices were heard in the British government suggesting the *mufti* be allowed to return to Palestine. But MacMichael detested al-Hajj Amin and would not allow it. Throughout World War II, the decision-makers in London were divided on the question of the *mufti*. The Colonial Office led the opposition to his return, followed by the War Office, whereas the Foreign Office sought to keep an open channel to the person it regarded as the leader of the Palestinian Arabs.[25]

Thus in the days leading up to the conference in London, al-Hajj Amin could have felt that he had not lost his power to influence events. He closely followed his colleagues' efforts to convince the British government to convene the conference in the first place, and regarded the British agreement to do so as a very significant Palestinian achievement.

He succeeded in persuading an exhausted delegation to visit him to discuss the conference before returning to Palestine from London. Two of the delegates, Musa Alami and Izzat Tannus, wrote accounts of the meeting with al-Hajj Amin. They were hoping to get some rest before going on to Beirut to report to al-Hajj Amin, but on disembarkation they encountered the *mufti*'s car waiting for them at the Port of Tripoli. The car took them straight to the al-Zarq Hotel, where the impatient al-Hajj Amin had gathered the Palestinian exiles in Syria and Lebanon, including most of the membership of the Higher Committee. As Alami described it, Tannus as usual dominated the report to the *mufti*, until Amin al-Tamimi, a member of the executive, asked Alami humorously, 'But were you not in London too, *ya* Musa?' Alami nodded and said, 'What's more, I have the form of the agreement with MacDonald' (Colonial Secretary Ramsay MacDonald, who gave his consent in writing to convene the conference). He pulled the document from his inside pocket. According to al-Hajj Amin, 'Izzat Darwaza, another witness to that occasion, rose from his seat and with tears in his eyes embraced Alami, saying, "This is the declaration of Palestine's independence!"'[26]

Al-Hajj Amin instructed Jamal to travel through the Arab world building support for what he now saw as an enhanced Palestinian position. Jamal met Egyptian Prime Minister Ali Maher (Mahmud's successor), who complained that he still did not understand what the Palestinians really wanted. In reply, Jamal produced the agreement brought by Alami, adding in Egyptian argot, 'Anyone who holds such a document should dance and rejoice till he drops and thanks God.'[27] It is doubtful that the document clarified the Palestinians' position to the Egyptian prime minister, or caused him to dance till he dropped. Like other Egyptian politicians, Ali Maher thought that the Palestinians had little cause for rejoicing, mainly because they had failed to unite around a single, well-defined goal. In Egypt, too, there were disagreements, but all parties were united by the goal of an independent Egypt freed from its British overlords. But the Palestinians did not define their aim, whether they wished to be part of some other Arab country or truly independent. Their distinctive plight was not clearly understood by most of the politicians in the Arab world at the time, either because of their basic disinclination to study the question or their dismay at the petty discords within the Palestinian camp. The Egyptian prime minister's perplexity led to a pan-Arab initiative to help the Palestinians define their aims.

In the event, the Colonial Office and MacMichael succeeded in preventing al-Hajj Amin from taking part in the St James Conference but not from instructing the Palestinian delegation by telephone from Beirut. Exile weighed heavily on al-Hajj Amin, and witnesses reported that he waited impatiently for every scrap of information from London. He agreed to give Jamal a major role in the next moves. But he was too far from center stage to have an impact any more.

In fact, the Palestinian political elite as a whole ceased to play a significant role in Palestine's destiny. At the conference in St James's Palace, the Palestinian delegates were surprised to discover that Britain, Egypt, Iraq and Saudi Arabia had coordinated the search for a solution. The British government was eager to obtain the support of the Arab countries in case of a global war. After consultations with representatives of Egypt, Arabia and Iraq, but not with the Palestinians, the British Foreign Office drafted a planned solution: until 1944 a total of 75,000 Jews would be allowed to immigrate to Palestine, land purchases would be as restricted as possible and every Zionist project would require Arab consent. However, Arab independence in the whole country would require Zionist consent. Until then, of course, Britain would continue to rule over Palestine.

The plan was adopted as the government's official policy and incorporated in a 1939 White Paper. The Jewish community was united in rejecting it. The Palestinian leadership failed to take advantage of the opportunity and ultimately rejected the last chance offered by the British to save Palestine.

The Higher Arab Committee met in Lebanon to discuss the White Paper once they realized that the Arab states would support it. Four members of the committee did support it, but the *mufti* hesitated. There was nothing in the document to promise an independent Arab Palestine, which al-Hajj Amin had come to regard as the quintessence of the Palestinian goal. It is important to note that had he examined the plan in minute detail, he would have found that it was less a document about Palestinian independence and far more a corrective to the Balfour Declaration through its severe limitations on immigration and land purchases. As such, it kept alive the option of independence in the future. But al-Hajj Amin convinced the members of the committee to focus on the issue of an independent state, and they decided to send Izzat Darwaza to London to find out if Britain would be willing to accelerate the implementation of the promise to establish one. When Darwaza returned empty-handed, al-Hajj Amin forced the rest of the committee to reject the White Paper.[28]

Why did al-Hajj Amin fail to discern the opportunity when it came his way? Why did he not connect the great sacrifices made by the Palestinians during the uprising with what was actually a substantial achievement? Some historians ascribe al-Hajj Amin's rejection to personal vindictiveness, but there may be a better explanation.[29] The longer he was in exile, and the more he hobnobbed with the foremost figures of the Arab world, the greater his aspirations for himself and for his people became. When he was in Lebanon, he would not accept anything less than an independent state. By the time he went to Rome and Berlin, he was demanding the independence and unification of the entire Arab world.

After the failure of the St James Conference, al-Hajj Amin had to curtail his activity even more, though he did have some minor successes. He found himself in direct conflict not only with the British and the leadership of the Jewish community in Palestine but also with the enterprises of the Baron de Rothschild, primarily the Palestine Jewish Colonization Association (PJCA), which conducted its own policies and sought independent contact with the *mufti*. Its directors tried to reach al-Hajj Amin through Ibrahim Said, the son of Said al-Husayni who, as noted above, had once worked for the company in Jerusalem. When these attempts failed, they tried to frustrate the *mufti's* efforts to recruit Bedouin tribes in the Golan and Galilee to the Palestinian struggle. They persuaded Amir Faur, a Bedouin *sheikh* in Syria, to reject the *mufti* publicly. Al-Hajj Amin responded at once, denouncing Amir Faur as a traitor until the *sheikh* lost all his political power.[30] But these were minor triumphs, and on the whole al-Hajj Amin's activity was quite limited.

When World War II broke out and Britain and France declared war on Germany, al-Hajj Amin was placed under house arrest for not supporting the Allies.[31] He became increasingly gloomy, and his close advisers realized that he could not go on being inactive in Lebanon. In desperation he turned to the French chief of police in Damascus, Pierre Colombani, a dubious character who had been in the post after being accused of murdering a rival politician in France. In return for a bribe, Colombani arranged the *mufti's* escape from Lebanon to Damascus. On his advice, al-Hajj Amin disguised himself as a Lebanese peasant woman in traditional dress and veil, thus hiding his identity from the French officers at the border crossing in Maysalun.

On 13 October 1939, exactly two years after leaving Jerusalem, al-Hajj Amin was on Syrian soil. He did not remain in Damascus for long. Aided by Izz al-Din al-Shawa, a Gazan known for his bold actions, al-Hajj Amin fled again. This time he went to Baghdad to meet with Rashid Ali al-Gaylani, office chief of Abd al-Illah, Iraq's heir to the throne and *de facto* ruler. The *mufti* appeared in al-Gaylani's office on 16 October, signed his name in the visitors' book, received the heir apparent's blessing and went to meet Prime Minister Nuri al-Said. From there he went to a house on al-Zahwi Street, where he resided during his exile in Baghdad, being feted and treated royally the whole time.[32]

After al-Hajj Amin's arrival in the Iraqi capital, many other Palestinian exiles landed there, including Abd al-Qadir and his family. There, as in Damascus, they created various structures for independent action. It looked for a while to be a very pleasant chapter of al-Hajj Amin's life, compensating for the last harsh two years. He enjoyed prominence and prestige in Iraq's internal politics for a short period, and he measured his situation against the problem of Palestine. Whether in Baghdad or in Lebanon, he was unable to restart the uprising or even to persuade the British government to allow him to return home.[33] Baghdad was the preamble to the grandest stage of his life. But the grandeur was misleading: just when al-Hajj Amin imagined himself the leader of the entire Arab nation, his ability to act on behalf of his people would further diminish.

In the meantime, the national struggle in Palestine was carried on by less prominent members of the family, alongside the Khalidis and Alamis. Mainly it proceeded thanks to the perseverance of other social strata – farmers, merchants and professionals. But though these groups would later form political structures that better reflected their world and aspirations, this did not detract from the Husayni predominance in Palestine.

Al-Hajj Amin and Jamal preserved the family's primacy from abroad, while Jamal's older brother Tawfiq Salih did so at home. Munif, too, did his share. In 1939 he was released along with the other Palestinians from detention in the Seychelles and was royally welcomed by the Egyptian Wafd Party, led by Nahas Pasha. Munif became the family's ambassador to Cairo.

While the Husaynis led the Palestinian uprising, they were not sure how to evaluate it. Though the family guided the revolt against the British and their policies of enlarging the Zionist presence in the country, the uprising was doomed to end with a military defeat. Britain did change its policy and was serious about limiting Jewish immigration and land purchases – not to enable a Palestinian state but to freeze the conditions that prevailed in 1939. These seemed best suited to British interests – a small Jewish community, a leaderless Arab majority and a mollified Arab world. Under such circumstances, Britain could confront the Nazi war machine in Europe and the Japanese in Asia.

CHAPTER 11

# World War II and the Nakbah
## In the Midst of the Revolution in Iraq

In October 1939, the *mufti* was in the Iraqi capital. Within less than a year he would become a major factor in Iraq's internal politics and get involved in the senior officers' attempted pro-Nazi coup against the monarchy and the British protectorate. But before al-Hajj Amin moved against Britain, Britain moved against him.

Iraq's prime minister Nuri al-Said had tried and failed to get the *mufti* to issue a public statement supporting the Allies and was advised to place him in complete isolation. But Nuri al-Said did not dare to act against the man described in the Iraqi press as the most honest figure in the entire Arab world. The *mufti* had been enthusiastically welcomed in Baghdad, and the newspapers lauded him as 'the hero of the Arab nation', to his great satisfaction.[1]

In March 1940, his standing grew even stronger when a new government was formed in Iraq that included some of his personal friends. These friends took pains to increase the *mufti*'s financial subsidy and influenced their government to adopt a pro-Palestinian policy. Most of the money was meant for the budget of the Office for Palestinian Exiles, which ran the affairs of the large group of refugees from the uprising. Al-Hajj Amin had hoped to use the funds to restart the armed struggle, but there was not enough for that purpose.

For a short time, these connections made al-Hajj Amin a pivotal factor in the political power play in Iraq – at least that is what the contemporary British documents claimed. It may have been an exaggeration, but most historians have taken this claim at face value. There is no doubt that al-Hajj

Amin enjoyed a personal reputation of decency and probity – outstanding amid the endemic corruption in Arab politics in general and Iraqi politics in particular – extensively documented in the Arab press at the time.

Since al-Hajj Amin's position was so strong, the British government considered taking various extreme measures against him. The Colonial Office prepared a plan to abduct and even to assassinate him, but the Foreign Office scotched it. For one thing, it feared that an attack on the *mufti* would anger the Muslim community in India, which was still loyal to Britain, unlike the Hindu majority in the subcontinent. The Foreign Office even rejected a more moderate proposal by the intelligence office in Cairo to discredit al-Hajj Amin by publicizing his contacts with the Axis governments. This would actually have done him little harm, as Britain's international standing, like that of France, had been declining since some time before the war. This British vacillation would be seen again in 1945.

But in the summer of 1940, the British government changed direction and sought to conciliate al-Hajj Amin. The Nazis had just scored some major victories, and Rommel's advance towards Alexandria seemed unstoppable. The British government, particularly Colonial Secretary Lord Lloyd, decided to open channels to the exiled Palestinian leadership in Baghdad. Colonel Stuart Newcomb was dispatched to Baghdad and, through the mediation of Nuri al-Said, met with Jamal al-Husayni. Newcomb wished to know whether the Palestinians' attitude towards the White Paper they had previously rejected had now changed. He proposed a broader British plan for the future consisting of an independent state of Palestine, with guaranteed equality for all the inhabitants, irrespective of religion or race, and with each community enjoying considerable autonomy in running its own affairs.[2]

The proposal was discussed in Baghdad for two weeks, and Newcomb accepted Jamal's demand that the British government demonstrate its goodwill by implementing the White Paper as soon as the war ended, after consultation with the Arab governments. But this welcome signal from London was extinguished before it awakened any real hopes. Prime Minister Winston Churchill rejected the plan altogether, probably under massive Zionist pressure. Al-Hajj Amin himself, it seems, was less than enthusiastic about the new move, partly because the British government forbade Newcomb to meet with him.

The demise of this option impelled al-Hajj Amin to open intensive contacts with the Nazis, beginning on 15 July 1940. Al-Hajj Amin sent several emissaries to prepare the ground for a future understanding with Germany, among them Naji Shawqat, Iraq's minister of justice, who contacted Franz von Papen, Germany's ambassador to Turkey. The first approach included a letter addressed to Hitler, which opened with compliments to the Nazi Führer. Here al-Hajj Amin for the first time adopted the Nazi discourse – a move which would later cost him and his people dearly. He spoke of the dangers of international Jewry as a force that had recently appeared in Palestine, which meant that Nazism and the Palestinian nation had a common enemy. The communications channel through the German embassy in Istanbul was temporarily blocked by the German Foreign Ministry's instructions not to meddle overmuch in the 'Arab territory' – it was supposed to be Italy's sphere of interest, rather than Germany's.[3]

A month later, al-Hajj Amin obtained a permit for his personal secretary, Kemal Haddad, to visit Berlin. But once there Haddad met only minor officials. Al-Hajj Amin was trying to impress the Nazis by declaring that he had created a pan-Arab organization that was ready to cooperate closely with Germany. In return, he demanded a German–Italian declaration on the right to independence of Arab nations from Sudan to Syria, including Palestine. Such a declaration, al-Hajj Amin affirmed, would spur a pan-Arab revolt (financed by the Axis) against the British throughout the Middle East. This reflected al-Hajj Amin's ambitious notion of reenacting with new allies the revolt of Sharif Hussein, the grandee from Mecca who had rebelled against Turkey during the First World War and helped the British replace Ottoman rule with European colonialism. The Germans remained unimpressed.[4]

The third attempt, in January 1941, was more successful. Al-Hajj Amin's confidant in Damascus, Dr Said Fatah al-Imam, coordinated propaganda positions with the Nazis. The climax of these contacts was a letter al-Hajj Amin sent Hitler on 20 January 1941, dealing mainly with the disastrous consequences of Franco-British colonialism in the Middle East. The rather lengthy analysis included references to an insidious but abortive British plan to settle millions of Indians in Iraq, harsh criticism of the Franco-Syrian accord of 1936, the injustices of Britain's domination of Egypt and finally a reference to events in Palestine. Until he met Hitler, al-Hajj Amin did not appreciate the centrality of anti-Jewish hatred in the Nazi worldview. He devoted his entire letter to the Arab hostility towards Britain, even in connection with Palestine. Only one sentence echoed the Nazi discourse (though this theme would intensify as the relationship developed). He described world Jewry as 'dangerous enemies, whose secret weapon is wealth, corruption and intrigue'. Elsewhere he emphasized the Anglo-Jewish connections – the Jews of the world, he said, were intimately linked to England, and therefore 'the

Palestinian problem united the Arab countries in a common hatred against the British and the Jews'.[5]

The letter was taken to Berlin by al-Hajj Amin's secretary Haddad, who was instructed to add verbal explanations and clarifications. The *mufti* was asking for German assistance to withstand the massive aid given by the Jews of the United States. In return, he would commit the Palestinian people to support anyone who fought against the British–Jewish coalition, as Germany did.

But the clarifications did not help, and no real answer was ever given to the letter or to the verbal appeal. Until al-Hajj Amin went to Europe, the feelers he sent out on behalf of the Palestinian cause remained negligible. Nevertheless, this effort at cooperation with the Axis played an important part in the revolt against continued British rule in Iraq. It was largely inspired by the views of anti-British Iraqi politicians, and in effect the *mufti* helped the platform and agenda of pro-German Iraqi politics more than those politicians advanced the Palestinian cause.[6]

Al-Hajj Amin himself claimed that the idea of approaching Germany was raised by his Iraqi allies:

> 'They asked me to seek contacts with Germany. And why not? Our people were under the yoke of the British, not the Germans, and the Germans had shown us sympathy and friendship as far back as the time of Abdul Hamid II, which is why Hitler was so popular.'[7]

Al-Hajj Amin thought of it as forming a relationship with Germany rather than with Nazism – at least at this stage.

Al-Hajj Amin's main activity in Iraq was not approaching the Axis government but rather getting involved in local Iraqi politics. The outbreak of World War II heightened the opposition's hope that the pro-British Hashemite regime might be toppled. Facing the opposition for many years was Nuri al-Said, a hero of the Arab Revolt against the Ottoman Empire and a confidant of the Hashemites in Iraq. He was the strongman of Iraqi politics who had served as prime minister several times since 1930. At the outbreak of the war, he was again appointed prime minister but was challenged by a powerful anti-British opposition. In March 1940, he resigned, either to demonstrate to Britain the strength of the opposition or to prove to the Iraqi political establishment that he was indispensable.

The opposition was led by Rashid Ali al-Gaylani, flanked by four army officers who would later be known as 'the Golden Square'. Al-Hajj Amin worked wholeheartedly to help al-Gaylani and his 'square' become the core of Iraq's next government. The man who guided the *mufti*'s moves from the shadowy background was François Ganeau, a tall, sturdy man, and a secret agent of the Vichy government who would later be dubbed France's Lawrence of Arabia. In the few films shot in Iraq during this time, he is always seen at the *mufti*'s side, and it was he who would bring al-Hajj Amin to Il Duce's palace in Rome and to the encounter with Hitler.[8]

While in Baghdad, al-Hajj Amin created the Party of the Arab Nation to coordinate the struggle of all the Arabs against colonialism. The *mufti*'s neglect of the Palestinian issue in favor of the pan-Arab cause strained his relations with Jamal.[9] But there was no way to influence al-Hajj Amin now that he had become for the first time a key factor in pan-Arab politics. Al-Hajj Amin's progress to the summit of regional politics climaxed at the end of February 1941, at his temporary home in Baghdad, where the officers of the Golden Square and other supporters swore on the Qur'an to fight the enemies of the Arabs, beginning with Britain.[10]

But beyond a dinner party and moral exhortations, al-Hajj Amin could offer no magic formula for victory over the British Empire. The only material aid that might have countered Britain's might had to come from Germany and Italy, but al-Hajj Amin's contacts with those two powers were fruitless. In February 1941, the British forced Gaylani to resign. Nevertheless, in April al-Hajj Amin and his associates in the Golden Square succeeded, without German military help, in bringing off a military coup that restored Gaylani to power. The Germans did help with money – $35,000 reached Baghdad, but it was not enough. The group lacked weapons, and these did not arrive. In May 1941, the rebels, backed by most of the army but without enough weapons, faced the British army, which was reinforced with units from the Transjordan Arab Legion.[11]

But it seems that al-Hajj Amin did not lose heart at these critical moments while still on the summit of a pan-Arab revolution. He was euphoric about his involvement in a successful coup against the British Empire. As *mufti*, he cried '*Jihad!*' against the British, who once again swung against him and even schemed to abduct him. To this end, they released from prison David Raziel, the commander of the Zionist underground known as the Irgun, but Raziel was killed in Iraq before he could attack the *mufti*.[12]

The boldest of the Husaynis, Abd al-Qadir, did not limit himself to organizing the revolt but fought alongside the Iraqi rebels. He was caught by the British and held in detention for two years. When he was released, he went to the Hijaz, where he stayed for some eighteen months. His son Faysal, the future Husayni representative in the Palestinian leadership in the 1980s and 1990s, had been born in 1940 in a Baghdad hospital.

The coup held out for twenty-six days, until the end of May, when it was crushed by the British Empire. On 29 May, before Nuri al-Said was brought back to Baghdad by the British, al-Hajj Amin and Jamal fled the city. Before leaving, al-Hajj Amin pointed to the Jews of Iraq as the party responsible for the failure of the coup, an explanation that satisfied several officers and hundreds of soldiers in the Iraqi army. On 1 June, when a large group of Jews went out to welcome the returning British army, these units attacked them and then turned on the Jewish homes in Baghdad. In this pogrom, known as the Farhud, 179 Jews were killed and many houses and shops were pillaged.[13]

This was the first chapter in the *mufti*'s role in World War II. It made the Zionist Jewish community in Palestine hate him and placed him alongside Hitler in the collective Zionist memory of the enemies of the Jewish people. But the main chapter of that history was al-Hajj Amin's activity in the Nazi capital during the Holocaust.

## Courting Mussolini and Hitler

In May 1941, when the short-lived coup collapsed, al-Hajj Amin and his wife, Aisha, escaped to Tehran. They were accompanied by other Husaynis – among them Jamal, Salim Hussein and Safwat Yunis – as well as the leader of the revolt, Rashid al-Gaylani, and eighty of their comrades. The Italians sent a special emissary, Count Alberto Malini, to act as liaison with the *mufti* and to see to his needs. At first al-Hajj Amin was royally received by the pro-German *shah*, but when British forces invaded southern Iran and the Russians moved into its north, the monarch's position became precarious. Al-Hajj Amin had come to Iran at a bad time, just as the government changed and a pro-British orientation replaced the pro-German one.

Jamal's route was even less fortunate. He went straight into the British-occupied zone in southern Iran, was captured near the town of Ahwaz and was sent to a detention camp in Zimbabwe (then Rhodesia), where he remained until the end of the war. Al-Hajj Amin was luckier – he himself described how Malini came to the house where he was hiding in Tehran a few minutes ahead of the local police and spirited him away to the Japanese legation.

The British did all they could to capture the *mufti*. The anti-British *shah* fell in September, and a new *shah*, Muhammad Reza Pahlavi, took the throne, promising to favor the Allies in the war. This political reversal prompted the Reuters news agency to report that the *mufti* had been captured and would be brought to a swift trial in Baghdad.[14] So confident were the British that it would be a simple matter to capture him that they worried what they would do once he was in their hands. They discovered that it was doubtful his arrest would serve their purpose – he might become a martyr to his cause. Using him as hostage to pressure the Husayni leadership in Palestine, however, might be more productive. In the event, they failed to capture him.

Al-Hajj Amin remained in a small pavilion in the garden of the Japanese embassy for twenty days. He lost half his weight, which altered his appearance. In October he decided that this was insufficient and prepared for flight by shaving off his beard and moustache, dying his hair and putting on a Western suit. In this guise, he had a new passport photograph taken.[15]

It was his third flight in October, an ill-omened month in his life. Again he disguised himself as a woman and set out with an Italian passport bearing a woman's photograph. He mingled among the women of the Italian legation, who traveled on a local bus via Russian-occupied Iran to Turkey. He experienced some unpleasant moments at the border crossing, on the Iranian side, when the Russian officials became suspicious. But eventually he was allowed to proceed. He made the rest of the journey through Turkey in relative comfort on a train heading west to Istanbul.

Once again, the Azma brothers came to the *mufti*'s aid. Nabih, who was romantically involved with a certain lady in the Intelligence Department of the German Foreign Ministry, represented al-Hajj Amin's interests to the Germans. Even before the *mufti*'s flight, in July 1941, Nabih and Fawzi al-Qawuqji had been preparing a pan-Arab conference under Germany's aegis, hoping to promote a new national authority and declare an alliance between the Arab nation and Germany. The memoirs of the Azma brothers reveal that they shared al-Hajj Amin's hopes of reproducing the agreement Sharif Hussein had struck with Britain, but with a different power – an idea put forward by some senior figures in the German Foreign Ministry. Nabih's brother Adil had been with Fawzi al-Qawuqji in Berlin since the beginning of 1941. Nabih wrote to his brother that before he and al-Hajj Amin headed for Germany, they wished to know 'if the Arab nation would be supported'. If not, they would turn to the other side.[16]

While in Istanbul, al-Hajj Amin and his Azma friends heard that British foreign secretary Anthony Eden, while answering questions in Parliament about al-Hajj Amin's fate, had said that 'the *mufti*, the empire's great enemy, was almost captured in Tehran, and we are still pursuing him.'[17] Al-Hajj Amin did not stay long in Istanbul. His friends sent him on another long train journey – to Sofia, the capital of Bulgaria, and thence to Rome.

Once in Rome, al-Hajj Amin discarded all his disguises and put on his traditional robe and tarbush. It has been suggested that he put off meeting with Rome's fascist leaders until his beard grew back. He was always very conscious of the connection between his external appearance and the message he wished to convey. Now he wanted to personify religious authority and tradition, as well as national leadership. In Rome he was described as one of the leaders of the 'Arab nation', and on his arrival he expressed the wish to collaborate with the government of Italy, provided it publicly recognized a unified Arab nation with a distinct national character.

A virtuoso stage director, Mussolini housed the *mufti* in the splendid Villa Scarlani near Rome, a residence fit for a visiting leader. It is possible that al-Hajj Amin was dazzled by the grandeur – servants, a car accompanied by a brace of motorcycles – and forgot for a moment that in Palestine, the place nearest to his heart, he had become a marginal figure.[18]

Italian documents state that the *mufti* planned a fascist Arab state, but it is not known whether he said as much or whether this was an Italian paraphrase. Perhaps al-Hajj Amin said this to curry favor with his hosts, and if so he achieved his purpose. After a month in Rome, the Italian Foreign Ministry recommended that the government support al-Hajj Amin and provide him with funds and a liaison officer.[19] Al-Hajj Amin stayed in the Italian capital until the end of November and was joined by his faithful aide, Izzat Darwaza.

The highlight of this visit was al-Hajj Amin's meeting with Benito Mussolini at the dictator's palace in Venice. He was met on the stairs by Il Duce's personal secretary, who led him through one immense hall after another. In each hall sat a minor official behind a small desk who stood up and greeted the visitor with a fascist salute. Finally, in the doorway of the last hall, Mussolini awaited him, smiling broadly. Al-Hajj Amin would say later that he felt as if he was meeting Napoleon. Mussolini amazed him by his extensive knowledge of history and his manner of a Roman Caesar.[20] To al-Hajj Amin's dismay, however, their meeting was short. Al-Hajj Amin had expected a lengthy conference with a person he believed would soon be one of the rulers of the world, or at any rate the Middle East. Al-Hajj Amin conducted himself gravely as the leader of the Arab nation, which Mussolini's reception of him seemed to affirm. He had prepared a long, well-reasoned survey of each region in the Arab world, and even wanted to air his view of the situation of the Muslim population in the Balkans. The farther he was from Palestine, the more he took on the role of a modern Arab caliph and shed that of Palestine's national leader.[21]

Though Mussolini was more interested in speaking than in listening, al-Hajj Amin managed to make his first statement. He had just enough time to request Italy's support for an independent Arab state that would include Iraq, Syria, Lebanon and Transjordan, as the best way to counter the threat of the Jewish national home. Not once since leaving Baghdad and heading to the Axis states had al-Hajj Amin mentioned the demand for an independent Palestinian state. All his appeals had been on behalf of the entire Arab nation, as though he were an Istiqlali, an associate of Awni Abd al-Hadi, rather than the head of the Party of the Arab Nation. Perhaps he thought that nothing less would interest the Axis governments or perhaps he was temporarily in despair about the prospects for an independent Palestine.

Il Duce, for his part, talked almost exclusively about Britain and about the blood pact he had made with Germany against it. He agreed with his guest that the Jews had no right to Palestine, but emphasized that he was not anti-Semitic. He asked the *mufti* to guarantee the rights of the Christian Maronites in Lebanon. Al-Hajj Amin gave him his solemn word to do so – as though he were about to be crowned king of the Arab world.

In fact, al-Hajj Amin obtained nothing. At the very least, he had expected the meeting to yield a joint declaration, thereby confirming his standing as the new leader of the Arab nation. But the pompous Mussolini, or at any rate his advisers, understood that the *mufti* was incapable of unleashing the Arab world against Britain. At best he might be able to help Italy when the campaign for the Middle East began – that is, in 1940. Using the pretext that the Germans had to be consulted about it, Count Malini informed al-Hajj Amin of Mussolini's decision to postpone the joint statement for the time being. The only gains from the meeting were Il Duce's promise to arrange for the *mufti* to meet Hitler, and the promise of the Italian foreign minister, Count Ciano, to provide him with a radio station.[22]

Al-Hajj Amin reached Berlin in November 1941. After his stay in Rome, his penchant for grandeur and ceremony reached unprecedented dimensions. His entourage had increased to include several personal secretaries and the Italian diplomat Malini. He was met at the railway station by senior officials of the German Foreign Ministry, who took him to the palatial residence reserved for the ministry's important guests. Al-Hajj Amin at once began to polish the joint declaration that Mussolini had postponed, believing that he could persuade Hitler to endorse an Italo-German commitment to Arab unity and independence. He himself was convinced that such a declaration would rouse all Arabs, perhaps even all Muslims, to rebel. During their journey to

Berlin, Malini had – ingratiatingly or sincerely – encouraged al-Hajj Amin to believe that such a prospect was feasible.[23]

Two days after his arrival in Berlin, al-Hajj Amin heard that his greatest rival in Palestine, Fakhri al-Nashashibi, had been murdered in Baghdad. It is possible that he knew that this would be Fakhri's fate. The Germans, too, must have been pleased, as Fakhri had been energetically recruiting Palestinians to join the British forces. Though he was not very successful at that, he did recruit more men than al-Hajj Amin would do for the Axis (nearly 10,000 joined the British armed forces). When Fakhri went to Baghdad, where many of the leaders of the Palestinian uprising were still staying, a tribunal of rebels appointed itself a field court and sentenced him to death for organizing the 'peace bands', paramilitary groups that had fought for the opposition against the Palestinian guerrillas. He was shot and killed on 8 November 1941.[24]

Dr Musa Abdullah al-Husayni, then in his late thirties, informed al-Hajj Amin of the murder. In 1938, as has been said, Musa Abdullah had led the Husaynis' abortive contacts with Zionist leaders in Britain. He was still a socialist in 1938, when he went from London to Nazi Germany, and he was captivated by the Germans – or, at any rate, by the German Thea Maria, whom he later married. As soon as al-Hajj Amin arrived, Musa Abdullah became his guide and right-hand man.

But at this time al-Hajj Amin was not concerned with minor matters such as local politics in Palestine. He believed he was on the verge of international glory, and he eagerly anticipated his meeting with Hitler. First, though, he had a meeting with the Nazi foreign minister, von Ribbentrop. They conversed in French, and the talk was pointless. Finally, twenty days after his arrival in Berlin, he got his audience with the Führer.

Hitler's interpreter recalled that the meeting began badly. Upon his arrival, al-Hajj Amin was invited by the *chef de protocol* to review a small guard of honor that awaited him in front of the Foreign Ministry. Then he was taken to see Hitler, where the mishaps began. Hitler ignored al-Hajj Amin's outstretched hand and the interpreter's suggestion to offer coffee to the guest. The photograph taken of the two men sitting on the edge of their armchairs as though about to rise would be useful to all the enemies of the Palestinian national movement, from London to Jerusalem, who wanted to harm the *mufti's* reputation.

Al-Hajj Amin launched into a lengthy speech and, unlike his meeting with Mussolini, was given enough time to display his knowledge of conditions throughout the Arab world and to explain the importance of a joint statement. Hitler responded with pathos, referring to the Nazis' commitment to

Arab independence, but he spoke chiefly about the Jews. 'My main struggle is against the Jews,' he began. 'The elimination of the Jewish people is part of my overall campaign. They want to establish a state that will be the basis for the destruction of all the nations in the world.' It is possible that Hitler did not use the words 'eliminate the Jews,' but this is how it was engraved in the memory of the *mufti*. After this there was no stopping Hitler. It is doubtful if the interpreter translated everything, but the message was plain enough.

In 1969 al-Hajj Amin tried to reconstruct his response to that speech. By then he was aware of the damage that his association with Hitler had inflicted on the Palestinian image. He claimed that he was slow to answer because he felt cornered. 'I replied that I was convinced we had an ally in our struggle against Zionism and the British, and said nothing more.'[25]

At their second meeting, he recalled, he clarified his meaning. 'We regard the Zionists, not the Jews, as the destroyers of the world.' 'You are a sentimental people,' said the Führer. 'I invite you to visit my research center, and there I shall convince you of the global conspiracy.' In 1942 al-Hajj Amin spent three days in such a center in Frankfurt. In retrospect, he sought to depict himself as having accepted some of the Nazi analysis of the Jewish problem but not its solution. He similarly described a chilling discussion he had with the Nazi ideologue Alfred Rosenberg, whom al-Hajj Amin made no effort to persuade because 'he was like a religious man on this subject'.

Politically speaking, al-Hajj Amin gained little during this visit. Hitler did promise to support the Arab struggle but wanted to postpone publicizing the fact until German forces had reached the Caucasus. He made a dramatic point of revealing to his visitor Germany's secret plan to reach the southern Caucasus.

The Führer was interested in the military potential that al-Hajj Amin could rally. Al-Hajj Amin was embarrassed, as he could not hide his objection to the idea of sending Arab soldiers to fight against the Arab soldiers in the Allied armies. Did he feel that in Germany, as opposed to Italy, he was viewed as a representative of an inferior race, and therefore not a serious ally?[26] Whatever the case, the people around him testified that at this time he was still exalted, feeling that suddenly everything was about to happen.

His enthusiasm infected Rashid al-Gaylani, who had also fled to Berlin. In February 1942, the two met the King of Italy, who gave them the longed-for public statement about Italy's unreserved support for the Arab nation. In the summer of that year, the Axis forces won impressive victories in North Africa, seized Tobruk and moved towards Egypt's western border. That summer the *mufti* met Count Ciano, Mussolini's son-in-law and foreign minister, and suggested preparing the inhabitants of North Africa for the victory of the Axis powers. To that purpose, he published an open letter to the people of Egypt.[27] He began to work fast, feeling that this gamble had gone well.

But during his stay, the Azma brothers accused al-Hajj Amin of not keeping them in the picture. They complained that instead of adhering to the policy they had agreed upon, al-Hajj Amin was selling Arab support to the Axis powers too cheaply.[28] After some time, Qawuqji, too, began to feel that al-Hajj Amin was seeking glory at his expense, and began to avoid him in Berlin. Qawuqji's main complaint was that al-Hajj Amin did not involve him in discussions on military matters, in which the *mufti* had neither experience nor expertise. Al-Hajj Amin had several discussions with the Germans about the possibility of an anti-British revolt with Nazi help.

On one subject, Fawzi al-Qawuqji supported al-Hajj Amin. He and Rashid al-Gaylani helped the *mufti* to carry out an idea he proposed in 1943 – namely, the creation of a pan-Arab committee led by himself, with equal representation for members from Syria, Iraq and Palestine, and with Rashid al-Gaylani as its foreign minister in charge of contacts with the Axis powers on the future of the Arab Middle East.[29] This placed al-Hajj Amin at the center of a new pan-Arab project designed to bring about unity and independence with Axis help.

Al-Hajj Amin al-Husayni, Fawzi al-Qawuqji and Rashid al-Gaylani adopted much of the Nazi vocabulary. They often took part in propaganda broadcasts from Berlin and Rome, spouting anti-Semitic vituperation, which may have been their composition or, more probably, translated from the Nazi Propaganda Ministry material. They made one minor contribution – they taught the Nazi ideologues, such as Alfred Rosenberg, the difference between the term 'anti-Semitism', which offended them, and 'anti-Jewishness', which they supported.

Palestinian historiography was long uncomfortable with discussing these statements and their moral implications. However, recently they have openly and sensibly revisited this chapter of ill-fated liaisons, describing the players as a few individuals who were detached from Palestine and its politics and no longer attuned to the genuine predicament of the people there. This was not a formative chapter in Palestine's history, but it is one that cannot be ignored given how it has been manipulated by Israeli historiography to Nazify the Palestinian movement as a whole and to justify brutal oppression, ethnic cleansing and occupation. For the purposes of this narrative, these events are highly important as an indication of al-Hajj Amin's transformation from a bright, sensible leader of a movement into a hallucinatory figure losing touch with reality and assuming roles and capabilities far beyond those he actually possessed.[30]

The reversals suffered by the Germans and Italians in North Africa did not faze the *mufti*. He proposed that the Germans declare the independence of the Maghreb and recruit a Maghrebi army to fight on their side. But the Germans had promised the region to Marshal Pétain, the leader of Vichy France, and could not guarantee its independence. Al-Hajj Amin worked diligently for the Germans through 1943. He persuaded Muslim leaders in India to support anti-British action, organized a Bosnian division in the Balkans and military groups to help the Germans in the northern Caucasus and promoted the idea of creating a Muslim state in Bosnia-Herzegovina.

Then the idea arose of creating an Arab army division that would fight alongside the Axis powers. One hundred and thirty men began to train on the sands of Cape Sunion, not far from Athens, but the project fizzled out. In the Balkans, al-Hajj Amin wrote a booklet called 'Islam and Judaism', which could hold its own with the racist fliers distributed by the SS to German soldiers. Albania's Muslims honored al-Hajj Amin when he helped create a local SS unit that would later take part in murdering the Jews of the Balkans. In the Caucasus, too, al-Hajj Amin enlisted Muslims to the war effort, above all to the German SS units. The Nazi discourse suited his aims and helped his enterprise. Palestine and Jerusalem might be far away – even perhaps from his mind – but he was still convinced that he was riding on the wings of history and helping to free the Arab world and to unify it.

While al-Hajj Amin was rallying the Palestinians to the losing side, Winston Churchill acceded to the Jewish Agency's request to form a Jewish brigade in the Allied forces. The brigade did not take an active part in the battles, but it became the basis for the Zionist military effort and highlighted the Zionist commitment to the Allied war. (The final accounting shows that the British armed forces included 12,000 Arabs from Palestine and 27,000 Jews, including the Jewish brigade.)

But still al-Hajj Amin believed that the goddess of fortune was smiling on him and the Palestinians. He spent most of the war in Bari in southern Italy, now and then visiting Berlin to broadcast anti-British propaganda in Arabic on German radio. Only towards the end of the war, when the Nazi defeat became certain, did he realize that he had made a mistake. He was then in Berlin, and the Germans offered to send him in a submarine to an Arab country. However, a Swiss government radio broadcast offering political asylum to refugees convinced him to buy a small car and set out in May to the Swiss border. But the border was snowed in, and al-Hajj Amin and his companions could not proceed. The Germans offered to take him across in a light aircraft, but the Swiss government, ignoring the pleas of diplomats from Arab countries, did not want him.

Back he went to Germany, this time to Konstanz, in the French occupation zone. From here it was a short route to France, where he was held first in prison, then under house arrest and finally in fairly comfortable conditions. The soft treatment was due to France's annoyance with Britain at the end of the war. France, which had given al-Hajj Amin refuge in Lebanon in 1938, seven years later gave him refuge at home. And just as in 1938, the British government dithered about his treatment and did nothing. It could have asked for his extradition – but then what? Should he be put on trial? Lord Gort, the new High Commissioner in Palestine, wanted nothing to do with him, imprisoned or free.

For a moment it looked as though al-Hajj Amin would be tried alongside the Nazi leaders as a war criminal, as the Zionist organizations in the United States demanded. In the atmosphere that reigned after the war, this was not unthinkable: al-Hajj Amin's behavior during his stay in Europe showed that he warmly approved of every Nazi act against the Jews, including extermination. Adolf Eichmann's deputy, Dieter Wisliceny, claimed that al-Hajj Amin had acted in the countries adjoining the Nazi-controlled areas to bar the entry of Jews escaping from the concentration and death camps. But the context in which the *mufti* acted would have obliged the judges at Nuremberg to deal with the highly complex connections between the Holocaust and the Zionist movement, and between the latter and the future of Palestine. It is doubtful that anyone in the American Justice Department, let alone in Britain, cared to untangle them. The leaders of the Jewish community in Palestine also probably preferred these political and moral complexities not to be dragged into court. In any case, al-Hajj Amin's identification with the Nazi death machine made it difficult for him to reintegrate into Palestinian politics and overshadowed everything else he had ever done. Many historians in the world, especially in Israel, have depicted him, unjustly and inaccurately, as a mini-Hitler.

Al-Hajj Amin decided not to take a chance and fled once more with the help of French friends. The dates were again symbolic – he had fled Iran on 29 May 1941, and on 29 May 1945 he took on the identity of a member of the Syrian embassy in Paris and left for Cairo via Italy and Greece. Rumors about his movements caused excitement not only among the Husaynis, who were unable to find out much about them, but among the Palestinian population. It was said that he was on his way to Palestine, and people prepared to celebrate his return.

But al-Hajj Amin did not reach Palestine, and he would later feel obliged to explain why. He said Britain had banned his entrance and he did not want to risk it. Two years later he did make an effort to enter Palestine. At this time, he was living in Cairo, which had become his home thanks to King Faruq. The rotund king was anxious to show his people that he was an Egyptian and pan-Arab patriot, while showing the British government, particularly its local ambassador, that he was still an independent and crucial actor on the Middle Eastern scene.[31] Cairo was also home for al-Hajj Amin because other Husayni exiles were living there, notably Munif, who prepared an apartment in Heliopolis for al-Hajj Amin. Twenty days after his arrival, al-Hajj Amin had an audience at Abadin Palace, where the king urged him to move into another royal palace in Inshas and live there as long as he liked. The following day, the Egyptian government issued a statement welcoming the hero of the Arab nation.

At this time, there were still substantial British forces in Egypt, and the British ambassador conducted himself more like a colonial governor than a foreign diplomat. But the British were no longer omnipotent in Egypt, being constrained by a national government and a king who worked, albeit slowly and inefficiently, to bring an end to their dominance in their country. Consequently, al-Hajj Amin could count on the Egyptian government's protection as well as its hospitality. 'The King of Palestine' enjoyed a comfortable exile in the Inshas Palace, and when that venue seemed insecure, he was moved to Faruq's summer palace, Muntaza.

From this place of exile, al-Hajj Amin began to rebuild his position as head of the family and the Palestinian people. In the autumn of 1947, he discussed with local British officials the possibility of returning to Palestine, but to no avail.[32] Being out of Palestine, he lost some of his power. Jamal was playing a greater role in preparing the Palestinians for the most important battle of their history. Nevertheless, al-Hajj Amin remained the symbolic leader and would be blamed for the tragedy of 1948, though he was not the only leader of the national movement.

Jamal was well served by his brother Tawfiq Salih. Throughout the war, while al-Hajj Amin and Jamal occupied themselves with inter-Arab and pan-Arab politics, Tawfiq deputized as the president of the Palestinian national party, maintaining the family's primacy in local politics. In this he was helped by a family friend, Emile al-Ghuri, the suspended secretary of the Arab Higher Committee. Together they made the Husaynis' Party of the Arab Nation into a sound and efficient body that functioned throughout the country. They also acquired influence in the important newspaper *Al-Difaa* in Jaffa, which began to show support for the family and its party. The newspaper had been founded by Ibrahim al-Shanti in 1933 as a counterweight to *Filastin*, which often reflected the opposition. During the post-war years, the opposition showed signs of weariness and decline. The representatives of the former al-Istiqlal and the Defense Party attempted to create a counterforce but failed, though they remained strong enough to prevent unity.[33]

In December 1941, the British authorities brought back from exile three Husaynis of the uprising leadership – though not Jamal – in the hope of starting a new, more fruitful dialogue with the leading party. But this was insufficient. The opposition was disgruntled because the government had failed to use the opportunity to crush the Husaynis' political power.[34] The Husaynis grew stronger, or maintained their position, but the Palestinians as a political force began to lose important positions, such as the municipality of Jerusalem. In the 1940s, Daniel Auster was elected head of the municipality, and thus Mustafa al-Khalidi, Hussein's successor, became Jerusalem's last Palestinian mayor.

On the other hand, the family's position as a religious icon was waning. During the war, the Nabi Musa celebrations were neglected. Even when they did take place, for example in 1942, the ceremony was no longer a family affair. The governor of Jerusalem, Keith-Roach, became the custodian of the Prophet's flags and banners, which had formerly been kept by the Husaynis and were now stored in the Shari'a court. The family's stamp faded from the important festival, and the wings of the Husayni phoenix were clipped.[35] The festival was celebrated for the last time in 1947, and the custom of visiting Nabi Musa would only be revived forty years later, on 17 April 1987. The last Husayni to hold a religious position in the city was Sheikh al-Haram Arif Yunis al-Husayni. Though in his black robe and white tarbush he resembled the *mufti*, he actually kept away from politics and was on good terms with the opposition and the authorities.

It was not only Jerusalem politics that eroded the Husaynis' standing. The Judaization of Jerusalem continued apace, and the Husaynis fought in vain along with other Palestinians to block it. The struggle climaxed in 1943, when the municipality under Daniel Auster presented its comprehensive city plan. It included massive construction and the development of services, mainly on the Jewish side, and the expansion of an area near Mount Scopus that was designated a nature reserve at the expense of Palestinian landowners.

That year the municipality also wanted to assign enormous tracts in the Jerusalem area to housing for poor Palestinians. Said al-Husayni, honorary president of the Association of Palestinian Architects, led the opposition to the scheme and thwarted the publication of a tender for an alternative plan for those areas based on socialist and egalitarian principles instead of the interests of an aristocratic regime. Any move that could improve conditions in the overcrowded Palestinian neighborhoods was seen by the urban notables as a direct attack on their estates and their wealth, and as imposing a Jewish ideological character on the city.[36] The Husaynis viewed these proposals as continuing the plans of the 1930s, which discriminated against the Palestinian neighborhoods.

The aged head of the family, Ismail al-Husayni, had died in 1945. He had refused from the start of the British Mandate to play any part in local politics. He was the last of the Arab-Ottoman notables of Palestine, but this aristocracy was not viable under British rule, let alone under Zionism. Ismail had never become a notable of nationalism – its world was entirely alien to him. His one contribution to national Palestine was to found the Palestine Commercial Bank. But he died before it opened, and it had done little before the downfall of 1948.

Though they lost Jerusalem, Palestine was still predominantly Arab and the leadership was still the Husaynis. For two years after the war ended, Jamal was the central figure in Palestinian politics as a whole. With Ismail's demise, Jamal became the head of the family, as well as the head of its Tahiri branch. As has already been said, the political significance of the branches had ended with the Ottoman Empire. During the mandate they retained their meaning only in connection with marriages: wherever the family could impose its will, it ensured that the matches took place not only within the family but within the particular branch.[37]

After World War II, Ishaq Musa, who had always embodied the apolitical tendency in the family, began to take a greater interest and more involvement in the struggle for Palestine. He agreed to direct the Palestinian Cultural Committee. Launched in the summer of 1945, it mainly organized lectures to promote cultural awareness in the community and cooperated with similar bodies elsewhere in the Arab world. At this time, Ishaq Musa arranged an exhibition of Palestinian literature at the Orthodox Union in Jerusalem and published an extensive bibliography of the Palestinian literary contribution to Arab culture. The exhibition contained some two hundred works by Palestinian authors written during the mandate. Raja'i al-Husayni and eight other Palestinian intellectuals were members of the committee.[38]

But this was not the time of the intellectuals; it was chiefly the time of external diplomacy and internal organization. Jamal understood both missions. But to complete them he had to be released, which was not easy to achieve. Egyptian prime minister Nahas Pasha believed that the British would agree to release Jamal in time for the launch of the Arab League in December 1944. But they did not, and Musa al-Alami was appointed to represent the Palestinians on this important occasion. Jamal was finally freed at the end of November 1945.

In Palestine at this time, local and regional politics intermingled. It is doubtful whether the Husayni heritage, based as it was on 'politics of notables', could safely have guided the people's destiny in such a complex situation. Palestine's fate was about to be decided on the international stage, where the Nazi horrors had been exposed. The Palestinians had to present their case before international public opinion, through the new international organization, the United Nations, where Zionist positions were clearly favored. Now it was the United States and the USSR that determined the rules of the game. Since 1942 David Ben-Gurion had been busy rallying the Jewish vote and American sympathy, while al-Hajj Amin was courting the Nazis and Jamal was out of action in prison. Jamal returned to Palestine just before the arrival of hundreds of thousands of Jews to reinforce the Zionist community.

Together the newcomers and the more veteran settlers constituted a well-established and determined community. Its leadership had used the war years to build up an army and acquire experience in warfare, and it would be ready to take over the country once the British Mandate ended. Moreover, there were many indications that Britain would not be able to hold out much longer in Palestine, or in the Middle East as a whole. Worse, the Zionist leadership at that point had decided on its future policy toward the native Palestinian population. Vague past ideas about massive expulsions and ethnic cleansing began to transform into real plans and an overall strategy that would result in the expulsion of half of Palestine's indigenous population and the destruction of half of its villages and cities in 1948.

None of the Husaynis seemed to sense the pending catastrophe. Palestine in 1945 was dominated by the Arab League, a regional body that failed to achieve the goal of Arab unity but enabled its secretary general, Azzam Pasha, and other Arab leaders to use Palestine as the touchstone of the members' pan-Arab patriotism. In reality, it became the arena in which the Arab countries jostled for prominence in the Arab world, either with rhetoric or by actually grabbing chunks of Palestine.

*Palestine 1946: Districts and District Centres during the Mandate Period*

The league's first act was to try to create a representative body for the Palestinians, because the end of the war revived an attempt by the new Labour government in Britain to reach an agreed solution to the problem of Palestine. Prime Minister Clement Attlee and Foreign Secretary Ernest Bevin had promised Labour voters to solve the problem, but having no clear plan they could only react to events on the ground and did not initiate any forward moves. The effects of the war – acute economic hardship and widespread devastation – dictated the answer, which was to quit Palestine. Before doing so, the British made one last diplomatic effort, motivated by Bevin's desire to involve the Americans in the solution. (He wanted to obtain their commitment to a British presence in the Middle East and believed they could put pressure on the Zionist movement.)[39] As a first step towards this last attempt, the British government released Jamal to enable the formation of a local leadership, which was needed to turn over a new leaf.

When the war ended, the Arab League tried to unify the warring Palestinian camps by setting up a new Arab Committee. It passed a resolution at its first conference impelling the Arab nations to discuss the future of Palestine. In November 1945, even before Jamal's return, a League delegation led by Jamil Mardam, Syria's representative in Cairo, arrived in Palestine. The delegation set up a twelve-member committee consisting of five Husaynis (including Jamal), five leaders of other parties, and two independent members, Musa al-Alami and Ahmad Hilmi (an economist affiliated with Istiqlal). Jamal returned to Palestine in February 1946 and became the head of the committee and its dominant figure. By the end of March 1946 the five delegates from the other parties refused to recognize Jamal's position and conducted separate negotiations with the league. Then they formed their own Higher Arab Front as a kind of alternative to the Higher Arab Committee.[40]

During this predicament, Jamal needed al-Hajj Amin and kept the *mufti* in the picture. Working from his residence in Cairo, al-Hajj Amin and Jamal tried to rally diplomatic and military support to counter the growing Jewish power in Palestine and to fight the battle for Palestine when the Mandate ended. When their appeals to Arab governments failed, they tried to stir Arab public opinion. Though they received a great deal of support, it was not sufficient to save Palestine.

While the leadership of the Jewish community actively prepared for the takeover of Mandatory Palestine and the associated diplomatic struggle, strove to increase the influx of Holocaust survivors and made a fairly successful effort to build up a military force, al-Hajj Amin, Jamal and the rest of the Palestinian leadership continued to tread water. The international arena was left to Arab diplomats, who retreated before the moral vindication of Zionism provided by the Holocaust. Whereas in the past the Palestinian position had been listened to and its arguments in favor of protecting the natural and legitimate rights of the majority native population in Mandatory Palestine seen as valid, after the war Zionist diplomacy skillfully linked the tragedy of the Holocaust with the problem of Palestine and its solution, winning sympathy in quarters that had previously been indifferent or hostile. Europe wished to atone for Nazism at Palestine's expense, and the local political leadership, the Husaynis and almost everyone else did not possess the skills to face this travesty.

Nevertheless, one might have at least expected Jamal to concentrate on preparing Palestinian society. In contrast to the early discussions on the

Jewish side about possible scenarios at the end of the mandate, Jamal began very late and covered little ground. In May 1946, he raised the possibility that war might break out in Palestine and suggested that serious consideration be given to evacuating women and children.[41] But the women and children were not evacuated, and the men were not conscripted.

Jamal was also responsible for the failure to create a wider Palestinian front, and he overlooked the significance of the split in the local Communist Party. The Palestinian members who quit that party and formed the National Liberation League might have been deluding themselves about separating the Jewish laboring masses from the Zionist leadership, but they knew the Palestinian working class and had good connections with it. Instead Jamal accused Communist leader Jamal Nassar of collaborating with the Zionists, and so the Husayni leadership had no channels to the peasants or the urban workers.[42]

Jamal also tried to break up the close relations between the Liberation League and the Arab Workers' Congress, the largest Palestinian labor union, organized in 1925. He suggested that Sami Taha, the union's leader, form an alliance with him and offered to include him in the new Higher Arab Committee – showing that he was aware of the national leadership's disjunction from the workers. But Taha remained faithful to the principle of class solidarity and refused to forgo relations with the Jewish trade unions.

The series of dramatic events that began in 1947 with the British decision to quit Palestine put the kibosh on the delicate contacts between those diverse social forces, the Husaynis and the labor unions. By the summer of 1947, anyone who did not obey the Higher Arab Committee was regarded as an enemy. Thus on 12 September 1947 Sami Taha was murdered near his house in Haifa. The assassins were never caught, but no one had any doubt who had paid them.[43] A few weeks later, when the UN had passed the Partition Resolution and Zionist forces began the ethnic cleansing of Palestine, the relations between the Husaynis and the union leaders improved, largely thanks to Abd al-Qadir al-Husayni. When he fell in battle, the head of the Arab Workers' Congress wrote al-Hajj Amin a letter of sympathy. But this improvement of relations, so vital to the Palestinian interest, came too late.[44]

Jamal was also hampered by the absence of a clear division between the internal and external authorities, such as that which existed on the Zionist side. Consequently, he had to concentrate on repulsing the final diplomatic campaign in the country's history: the Anglo-American commission sent to study the situation in Palestine.

The commission was one of Ernest Bevin's worst failures. This British foreign secretary, who at his first press conference confidently declared that he would gamble his political future on a successful solution being found to the conflict in Mandatory Palestine, began to despair about Britain's involvement in the Holy Land. He enlisted the help of the United States, but misjudged President Truman's Zionist commitment following the Holocaust and the effectiveness of the pro-Zionist lobby surrounding the president. The result was that the Anglo-American commission, which was supposed to replace all the previous commissions and propose a solution to the problem of Palestine, did not reflect British interests and sang the tune composed by the Jewish Agency. The repeal of the White Paper and the recognition of the Jewish claim to a state were only two of its pro-Zionist recommendations.

Jamal, who had testified before the commission when it visited Palestine early in 1946, had not imagined such a setback. Now he began to work quietly on a new Palestinian course of action. He asked for the British Mandate to be prolonged and called for an attempt to reach agreement in the hopes that the uncompromising Jewish stance expressed by Ben-Gurion back in 1942 would be softened.[45]

When he came out after testifying before the commission, Jamal was surrounded by Jewish journalists, most of whom he knew, and was as always revitalized by such an encounter. 'What will be the outcome of the investigation?' the journalists asked. But Jamal preferred to discuss the situation on the ground, and he made a prognostication that would not be realized: 'If you believe that a Hebrew state will come about, you're mistaken. If you think that an Arab state will come about, you are again mistaken. Things will go on as before. If only the two sides, the Arabs and the Jews, had any sense, they would reach some sort of agreement.' 'Is it possible to reach an agreement?' asked one journalist. 'I believe it is,' Jamal replied, 'but on one condition – not with the existing Jewish Agency.' 'Nor with the existing Higher Arab Committee either,' another journalist remarked. 'Perhaps,' replied Jamal on a conciliatory note. That was his last friendly encounter with the country's Hebrew press.[46]

Jamal was mistaken: the Jewish state did come about, while the Anglo-American commission became a footnote in history. Except for one of its recommendations – to enable the immigration of another 100,000 Jews – it defined the difference between the British and American positions. Bevin made one or two further attempts to keep his promise to solve the conflict, then gave up. He convened another Anglo-American commission, resulting in the Morrison–Grady Report, which recommended dividing Palestine into cantons, such as those in Switzerland, an idea that both sides rejected outright.

To conduct the negotiations, the Arab League now appointed a body that gradually displaced the Higher Arab Committee and barred it first from taking part in the diplomatic struggle for Palestine and later from preparing for the military campaign. The Syrian resort of Bludan reappeared on the map of Palestinian history. But whereas al-Hajj Amin had been an honored participant there in 1937, in June 1946 the cause of Palestine was appropriated by the Arab League. When the League met in Sofar, Lebanon, to discuss the Palestinian struggle a few months later, it did not even bother to invite al-Hajj Amin. His dismay can only be imagined, given that he had formed a close association with the Arab League when he settled in its birthplace of Cairo.[47]

Jamal was more welcome in Bludan, though not more effective. He demanded that the Arab states provide military support for a revolt if an Anglo-American solution were to be forced on Palestine (based, he assumed, on the creation of an independent Jewish state). The representatives of Syria and Iraq declared their full support. Since the end of World War II, Syria had been in favor of aggressive action, though it did not support the Husaynis. The Iraqi delegates were two-faced. They supported the ambition of Transjordan's King Abdullah, the kinsman of their Hashemite king, to take over all or part of Palestine, assuming he could reach an agreement with the Zionists. At the same time, in pan-Arab gatherings, whether secret or open, they were the keenest supporters of comprehensive military action.[48] Jamal tried to impress the delegates by claiming, falsely, that he had recruited 30,000 young men for the revolt, but it is doubtful anyone believed him.

This diplomatic effort did yield some results that inspired false hopes in the Palestinian public. In January 1947, after years of conflict, the British government recognized the Arab Higher Committee (a few months later the committee was also recognized by the United Nations). But the gesture was almost meaningless, since over the following months, hit by a severe winter of austerity and economic crisis, the British government resolved to quit Palestine. The Palestinian leadership tried frenziedly to devise ways of dealing with the imminent power vacuum. The Jewish Agency, by contrast, had been preparing for this juncture since the 1920s. Jamal directed the team that struggled to create a Palestinian state out of nothing to replace the British Mandate. Perhaps he had the necessary qualifications, but he had neither the means nor the time in which to do this.

Nevertheless, he carried out some impressive operations. At his initiative, the Arab Higher Committee set up the Arab Treasury, the supreme financial institution of the national movement. It solicited funds from the Arab world and sought to nationalize the nation's capital. It was a good replica of the Zionist financial structure, but it was founded too late. The pace of organization had become more dynamic in May 1946, when al-Hajj Amin began to play an active part in these moves. Under al-Hajj Amin's direction, the committee began to function as a government-in-waiting, with ministries and collective responsibility. The general headquarters was in Cairo and the local headquarters in Jerusalem. Such a structure, which might have suited a European government in exile, only weakened the Palestinians' ability to act.[49] Al-Hajj Amin was more effective in obtaining and storing arms in various places in the Arab world.

The main burden fell on Jamal, who carried on as best he could. In April 1947, he nationalized the People's Fund, Istiqlal's private finance ministry headed by Ahmad Hilmi, a dim personality who would become the prime minister of a symbolic Palestinian government in Gaza at the end of 1948. But Jamal was unable to nationalize Musa al-Alami's Project for Saving the Land, and the organization of funds and infrastructures faltered.

After intense efforts, in June 1947 Jamal succeeded in unifying the two main youth movements, the Husaynis' *Futuwah* and Nimr Hawari's *al-Najada*. He placed Mahmud Labib, a retired Egyptian officer, at the head of the unified organization. But in August, Labib carried out a fairly successful operation against Jewish youth in Tel Aviv, and the British authorities expelled him. Hawari also harmed the common enterprise by reaching an understanding with the Jewish Agency. He then served the Hashemites until 1950 and finally settled down in Israel and became a justice of the peace. But all the operations together could not create a Palestinian fighting body, build a firm financial foundation for taking over the power bases in the country and sustain the diplomatic campaign.

The greatest obstacle on the diplomatic front was that, since February 1947, the British government had adopted the basic Zionist argument that a vast gulf existed between Jewish 'progress' and Palestinian 'backwardness'. In their eyes, this made it impossible, if only on social grounds, to let the Palestinians run the country – except under Jewish dominance and outside supervision. In vain Jamal tried to prove to the mandatory government that illiteracy in the Arab population had greatly diminished and that the Palestinians could no longer be described as an ignorant population by comparison with the Jewish community. Had he not been a member of a notable family, and had he been conversant with the ideology and discourse of nationalism, Jamal might have explained to the British government that 'progress' and 'illiteracy' were irrelevant to the question of who owned the country.[50]

Being outside Palestine, al-Hajj Amin probably could not help Jamal to impose his authority. The family – that is, the Tahiri branch – mistakenly believed that it stood at the center of events. In fact, al-Hajj Amin had to resort to violence to impose his authority and that of his family. Once again, though on a smaller scale, accounts were settled and enemies eliminated in the urban power bases that al-Hajj Amin valued. The murder of Sami Taha, the Palestinian trade unionist, has already been mentioned. Most of the actions were not as violent and consisted mainly of jostling to dominate the national committees. (These bodies ran the local struggle after having made their appearance during the great uprising.) Al-Hajj Amin tried to create new committees to replace them everywhere but succeeded in creating only three, and they did little to stop the Zionist determination to 'cleanse' Palestine.

One victim of the account-settling was a member of the family, Fawzi Darwish al-Husayni. Fawzi favored collaborating with the Zionists against the British and had founded a party called *Filastin al-Jadidah* ('New Palestine') for this purpose. In his opening speech before a mixed Palestinian and Jewish crowd at the party's founding, he said:

> Experience has shown that the official policy of both sides has brought nothing but harm and suffering to both. The Jews and the Arabs used to live together in amity and cooperation. I myself went along for many years with my cousin Jamal al-Husayni. I took part in the events of 1929, but over the years I realized that this road leads nowhere. The imperialist policy is fooling both of us, Arabs and Jews, and there is no other way but to unite and work shoulder to shoulder for all our sakes.

Fawzi was manipulated by Zionists such as Haim Kalvarisky and by more genuine peace seekers such as the leading members of Brith Shalom. The latter pressured the British police to find Fawzi's killers – believed by everyone, including the police, to be members of his family. The day before he was murdered, Fawzi had made a brave speech attacking Jamal for his uncompromising attitude towards the Jewish community:

> They will no doubt incite against us, perhaps even attack us, but if we can demonstrate cooperation with the Jews, useful and productive cooperation, the Arabs will follow us. Because many of those who are following Jamal are doing so from lack of choice.[51]

On 10 March 1947, the day Fawzi was killed, the newspaper *al-Wahada*, which favored Jamal, published a strong attack on all who cooperated with 'the alien invaders who had come to Palestine after 1918'.[52]

Fawzi stood out because he had chosen political cooperation with the Jews, but individuals who had personal relations with Jews were not affected. For example, Safwat's son, Fuad al-Husayni – an attractive man with whom many women, Muslim, Christian and Jewish, fell in love – had a long affair with a woman who would later become the wife of a prominent Israeli journalist. Their relationship was well known yet did not provoke particular annoyance or censure.[53]

These internal dissensions came at the expense of the most important campaign in the history of the Palestinians – in the diplomatic arena of the United Nations. The UN had been in existence for two years when it took up the question of Palestine. It was still an inexperienced organization wholly dominated by the United States. In May 1947, it handed the problem to a committee of experts, but unfortunately these experts knew nothing about the subject and some of them were indifferent to it. The UN Special Committee on Palestine (UNSCOP) sat on the issue from May until November and brought forth the Partition Resolution. In 1988, the Palestinians would still regard this resolution as a crime committed by the world against them: partition meant the recognition of a Jewish right to part of Palestine.

Fawzi would have accepted it, perhaps even Musa Kazim, but not Jamal or al-Hajj Amin. Had the Nashashibis been a major political power they might have supported it. But once it was known that Britain was about to quit, they attached themselves to King Abdullah, who thought that dividing the country between himself and the Jews was a good idea. The leadership of the Jewish Agency eagerly welcomed the proposition, and the absence of a formal agreement between them was due to Ben-Gurion's territorial aspirations to rule over most of the country, Abdullah's concern not to seem to betray the pan-Arab interest and the atmosphere of uncertainty before the outbreak of hostilities.

The two sides agreed informally that Abdullah would stay out of the territory of the Jewish state, and in return the Jewish state would let him annex large chunks of Palestine. This was how the West Bank was born, and the Jewish state was spared a direct attack by the Arab world's best-trained army. Pettiness and religious sensibilities prevented them from agreeing to the partition of Jerusalem – which they would do after the war – but otherwise their understanding prevailed.

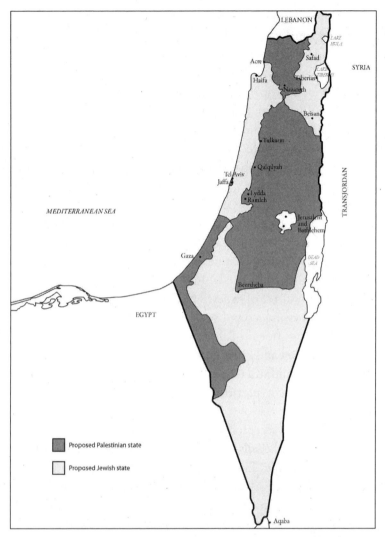

LEBANON

LAKE
HULA

Acre        Safad                SYRIA

Haifa      Tiberias

Nazareth

Beisan

Tulkarm

Qalqilyah

Tel Aviv
Jaffa

Lydda
Ramleh

MEDITERRANEAN SEA                                    Jerusalem
and
Bethlehem

Gaza                              DEAD
SEA

Beersheba

EGYPT

▓ Proposed Palestinian state

☐ Proposed Jewish state

Aqaba

*Palestine: United Nations Partition Recommendation, 29 November 1947*

In February 1948, after Bevin's main advisor on Palestine, Harold Beeley, was sacked, the British government also supported this agreement without reservation and directed the commanders of the Arab Legion to uphold it. The British, the Hashemites and the Zionists all objected strenuously to the establishment of an independent Palestinian state, believing that it would become 'the *mufti*'s state'. Thus al-Hajj Amin ended up as the *bête noire* of the three most powerful factors in the struggle for Palestine.

But worse was already happening on the ground in February 1948. That month a small group of Zionist leaders and military commanders, under the guidance of David Ben-Gurion, finalized a master plan for the massive expulsion of the Palestinians from any part of Palestine that they deemed to be the Jewish state. In February they evicted by force five villages, and in March they had already produced 'Plan Dalet', a systematic blueprint for the ethnic cleansing of most of Palestine. Neither al-Hajj Amin nor Jamal was aware of this or paid attention to what happened on the ground. It seems also that even if the Palestinians had taken a different position or a different Palestinian leadership had been in place, they would not have weakened the Zionists' determination or undermined their ability to cleanse Palestine of its indigenous population.

The only way Jamal and al-Hajj Amin could counterbalance Hashemite ambitions was to stick to Egypt. Jamal relied wholly on the Muslim Brotherhood in Egypt. As early as May 1946, when the movement launched a branch in Jerusalem, Jamal, as vice president of the Higher Arab Committee and al-Hajj Amin's deputy, honored them with his presence. In a way, the effort reaped some success: the Brotherhood provided half of the fighting force sent by Egypt into Palestine on 15 May 1948. However, this was not enough to avert the catastrophe.[54]

Jamal represented the Palestinians before the UN investigating committee that came to the country a few days after the '*Exodus* affair' made international headlines. The *Exodus* was a ship that came from Europe with many Jewish survivors of the Holocaust in a PR campaign meant to embarrass the British for their anti-immigration policy. As expected, the ship was refused entry and made its way back to Germany, a symbolic return that enraged and galvanized Western public opinion.

Jamal had to vindicate the Palestinians' moral position at a time when world public opinion tied the fate of the Holocaust survivors – like the passengers caught between hope and despair on board the *Exodus* – to the solution of the problem of Palestine. The case of the *Exodus* persuaded many about the Zionist argument that the Holocaust proved the necessity for a Jewish state in Palestine. Jamal was not at his best, perhaps because of the charged atmosphere. He also made the mistake of allowing the committee to invite a separate Christian Palestinian representative – as though there were two Palestinian peoples in the country. At least Henry Qatan, a Jerusalem lawyer, made a better presentation than Jamal.[55]

As we have seen, it was the Arab League that waged the diplomatic campaign on the future of Palestine, and it systematically prevented al-Hajj Amin from taking part in it. Al-Hajj Amin represented an independent Palestinian position, and the League, particularly its general secretary Azzam Pasha, used the opposition and the Hashemite king of Transjordan to undermine the *mufti*'s efforts to obtain substantial support for the struggle in Palestine. As noted, Abdullah had his own agenda and was supported by Britain, Iraq and the Jewish Agency.

Britain's diplomatic moves were all carefully coordinated with the Arab governments rather than the Palestinian leadership. Consequently, the Palestinian leadership objected on principle to the Anglo-American delegation and to the Grady–Morrison Report and Bevin's plan, which was based on it. It regarded them as attempts to undermine al-Hajj Amin's legitimate claim to represent the Palestinians. This was also the background for al-Hajj Amin's refusal to accept the UN Partition Resolution.

The British effort to exclude the *mufti* went furthest in January 1947 when, in a last attempt to solve the conflict on the basis of Bevin's plan to divide Palestine into cantons, it convened a meeting in London to discuss the proposal and barred al-Hajj Amin and his representatives from attending. When this conference failed, the British government decided to quit Palestine for good.

When the League first became involved in the Palestinian issue following Britain's decision to return the mandate to the UN, al-Hajj Amin was not worried. In September 1947, the league met in Sofar and gave al-Hajj Amin 180,000 pounds sterling to buy arms, but then it all turned into a prolonged nightmare as the League systematically undermined al-Hajj Amin's standing. His diminished prestige in the eyes of the league members was demonstrated in the seventh session of the League's council, which met in Aley, Lebanon, to shape their policy on the UNSCOP and Britain's imminent departure from Palestine. Not only did they fail to invite al-Hajj Amin, he was the subject of a minor debate instigated by King Abdullah and the Iraqi delegates about his 'subversive activity in Iraq and his part in the revolt of Rashid Ali al-Gaylani'. Feeling that things had gone too far, al-Hajj Amin went to Aley without invitation, stormed into the council session and was allowed to stay.[56]

This was one of the lowest points in al-Hajj Amin's career. Like others, he heard the Arab intelligence experts' reports about the strength of the Jewish community and warnings that the Arab world would be unable to present a serious military challenge to this power unless it mounted its maximum military force. He learned that the Arab statesmen preferred the extension of the mandate above all other political solutions. He was dismayed to find that his rival Abdullah had won, because he had been the only one to act on the diplomatic front. Al-Hajj Amin's own ally, Egypt, was less than eager to send an army into the battlefield – and without Egypt he was lost.

In Aley it became evident that it was mainly Hashemite Iraq and Transjordan that cooperated in limiting al-Hajj Amin's role, sometimes with regional support. The first independent Syrian government after French colonial rule ended, being a fairly democratic republican regime, was more loyal to Palestine than were the Hashemites, and more loyal than it has been given credit for in the history books. But it was not loyal to al-Hajj Amin – it pinned its hopes on Fawzi al-Qawuqji. As we have seen, al-Qawuqji was a leader of the Syrian uprising against France who during the 1930s took part in pro-Palestinian activities and directed the pan-Arab volunteer recruitment for Palestine. He was obedient to Damascus and therefore was presented as the *mufti*'s rival. He was even appointed commander of the Arab Salvation Army – a volunteer army created to fight for Palestine.

The first volunteers of al-Qawuqji's Arab Salvation Army arrived early in 1948. Most of them came from the margins of society in their own countries or belonged to fringe groups – people whom the Arab governments were quite happy to dispatch to the battlefield.[57] Al-Qawuqji found the Palestinian opposition easy to get on with, and thus inadvertently he helped to weaken the Palestinians further. Damascus's policy of opposing the *mufti* was not due to personal hostility, as was the case in Amman and Baghdad, but mainly to Syria's fear that al-Hajj Amin would embroil it in a hasty operation before the British actually departed and before the League exhausted attempts to prolong the mandate. Perhaps this was why the Syrian government held up permission for al-Hajj Amin to send young Palestinian recruits for military training in Syria in preparation for the imminent clash with the organized Jewish forces that had been training for the decisive battle since the end of World War II.

In vain, al-Hajj Amin begged the League in Aley to place him at the head of a government in exile and appoint him commander of a pan-Arab army. The League set up a military commission for the deliverance of Palestine, headed by an Iraqi general, Ismail Safwat, who was promised a budget of one million pounds sterling. However, only part of the money was provided, and when the general tried to coordinate the inter-Arab activity in preparation for the final British withdrawal from Palestine, he was hampered by a lack of genuine cooperation.[58]

Something similar occurred in Egypt. In December 1947, the League met in Cairo, and once again Iraq and Transjordan vetoed al-Hajj Amin's participation. The leaders of the Arab countries resolved to intensify efforts to help the Palestinians and increase aid, but the resolution meant little, as the Arab armies held no training exercises for the forthcoming battle. They still had not coordinated their diplomatic or military strategy, or significantly increased their arsenals. While the Jewish Agency went into high gear, al-Hajj Amin's proposals to prepare for the creation of a separate political framework for Palestine and for a civil takeover of the country were rejected. His plea for pan-Arab funding of the Higher Arab Committee was rejected because of the Arab League. The only outcome of the Cairo meeting was the division of Palestine into four command sectors; the Husaynis got one, the Jerusalem sector, headed by Abd al-Qadir, who made the best of the situation and recruited a relatively large force of thousands. This force gave him a higher status in the military enterprise than the League had assigned him.[59]

But al-Hajj Amin did not give up easily. He fought back against the League's intentions to neutralize him. Early in 1948, he proclaimed the establishment of a civil administration – in effect, the government-in-waiting that should have been formed in the 1920s. The League gave in a little and declared that every part of Palestine that was liberated would come under that administration. But this was al-Hajj Amin's only success in attempting to wrest a central role in salvaging Palestine for himself. He was so preoccupied by the vital struggle with the League that he hardly prepared for the British evacuation; and worse, he was unaware of the beginning of mass expulsions of the rural areas by the invading Jewish forces.

In Palestine, all these maneuvers gave rise to the feeling that the Arab world was sitting on its hands. The social and economic elite in Palestine was already preparing for a hasty collective departure. Some 70,000 Palestinians left, believing that no one could stand up to the Zionist movement; all of them meant to return, but did not want to find themselves in the battle zone. The rest of the population swung between hope and despair, unaware of the catastrophe awaiting them in the next few months.

In less than three months, between February and May 1948, large chunks of Palestine fell to a Jewish occupying force – mixed cities, major junctions and isolated villages. It began as a civil war, but around March that year it turned into *de facto* ethnic cleansing – the expulsion of the Palestinian population from the territory of the Jewish state. In the first stages of the war, the Arab volunteers did not distinguish themselves in battle against the Jewish forces. They would do better in later stages, but it would be too late. Before the Arab armies entered Palestine, more than 200,000 Palestinians, among them many Husaynis, found themselves in refugee camps. A few had fled out of fear of the war, but most were driven out by the Jewish forces. When the war broke out, they were joined by about half a million other Palestinians, most of whom had been expelled from the territory designated by the UN as the future Jewish state.

The ethnic cleansing was accompanied by some forty massacres. The Nakbah – the Palestinian catastrophe – happened while the Husayni family was leading the national movement. The dreadful stories about the expulsion and massacres reached the Husayni leaders, and their failure to raise an outcry about it would cost them and the other notables a heavy political price. They would no longer have the trust and support of their society.

The Husayni family's collective memory of the Nakbah is dominated by the heroism of Abd al-Qadir, above all on the date of his death, 8 April 1948, in what became known as the Battle of Qastel (a village west of Jerusalem on the road to the coast). He was eulogized by his second-in-command Kamal Iraqat, known as Abu Da'aya. Khalil al-Sakakini wrote in his diary that, 'The eulogy was one of the finest heard in that funeral.'

The masses that followed the cortege showed that the family was still popular among all strata of the population.[60] Abd al-Qadir was buried in a chamber on the Haram beside his father, Musa Kazim, and Sharif Hussein, the leader of the Arab Revolt during the Great War. They are enshrined in the pantheon of the Palestinians' collective memory, and in 1950 the respected periodical *Majalat al-Azhar* compared Abd al-Qadir to Salah al-Din al-Ayubi (Saladin). No other member of the family has been so lauded.[61]

Abd al-Qadir's son Faysal was only eight when his father was killed. 'I didn't know my father because he was always on the move and came home rarely, but I read and heard a lot about him,' said Faysal, who in the 1980s would become a leading political figure in the occupied West Bank. Though he barely knew his father, towards the end of the twentieth century Faysal continued Abd al-Qadir's legacy by adapting himself to the national mythology and committing his own family to the service of the national movement. The movement's organization, the Palestine Liberation Organization (PLO), made no such demand of any other Husayni, because no member of the family, not even Jamal and al-Hajj Amin, has retained a place to equal Abd al-Qadir's in the nation's pantheon.[62]

The day before Abd al-Qadir's death, Jamal al-Husayni, as representative of the Higher Arab Committee, and Moshe Sharett, the representative of the Jewish Agency, negotiated indirectly in New York. Jamal refused to meet Sharett directly, and messages between the two were passed by the president of the UN Security Council. Their purpose was to try to achieve a truce in the fighting in Jerusalem. Sharett and others in the Jewish Agency – with typical Zionist Orientalist prejudice – feared that the Jewish community in the city, being largely of Middle Eastern origin, might not be able to withstand the pressure. They therefore wanted a break in the fighting and even agreed to a temporary halt in immigration. Jamal's position was uncompromising: he demanded they stop the implementation of the Partition Resolution. The UN refused – once implementation had begun, no one in the international organization dared to propose reconsidering the resolution. It should have, however, as it was a resolution accepted by only one side and forced on the other (who were the majority and natives of the land). Reconsideration would have meant reopening the negotiations over Palestine on the basis of a settlement acceptable to both sides.[63]

But neither the death of Abd al-Qadir nor Jamal's firm stance – which had been so sorely lacking during the UNSCOP investigation – could save the Palestinian people from catastrophe. And when it came, it swept them all away: villages and towns alike, fields and houses throughout Palestine, including even the Husayni homes in the Husayniyya quarter in the city of Jerusalem.

## *The Nakbah: The Demise of the Local Aristocracy*

During the Nakbah, many of the Husaynis were living in the strategically important Husayniya neighborhood. Volunteers from the Arab world who came to save Palestine, together with the remnants of Abd al-Qadir's fighters under the command of another nephew of the *mufti*, Khalid al-Husayni, took up positions in some of the neighborhood houses – not Husayni residences, incidentally, but Nashashibi ones, notably Raghib's house. As early as March 1948, the Jewish armed force, the Hagana, tried to capture the family's stronghold but was foiled by British intervention. The neighborhood overlooked the road to Mount Scopus, and it was from there that a Zionist convoy to the Mount – the site of the Hebrew University and Hadassah Hospital – was assaulted in April 1948.

On 15 May, the Israelis launched a forceful attack on the neighborhood. Five houses were totally destroyed, but the Husayni homes remained standing. The Nuseibah family living nearby felt they had been abandoned. 'We were unarmed and undefended,' they wrote in their memoirs.[64] A British force was not far, in the *mufti*'s old house in Sheikh Jarrah – the house that had been built by Jewish contractors, which was now occupied by Katie Antonius, the widow of George Antonius, who had been renting it since 1943. The neighborhood's inaction made it look useless, yet it was kept inside the Arab territory by the Transjordan Arab Legion.

Not so with the Arab neighborhoods on the western side of the city, among them Baq'a, Talbiyyeh and Malhah, which fell to the Jews. Jerusalem fell, and with it most of Palestine. With Abd al-Qadir gone, the Husaynis took no part in the Palestinian armed struggle during the war, which was in any case feeble compared to the Jewish or the pan-Arab efforts. Khalid al-Husayni was not a charismatic figure, and al-Hajj Amin did not approve of his appointment as Abd al-Qadir's successor. In each neighborhood a different commander stood out – most of them from Iraq and Syria, or from the poorer classes, as for example the commander of Katamon, the above-mentioned Kamal Iraqat, aka Abu Da'aya.

For the leading figures in the family, Jamal and al-Hajj Amin, the war was entirely a political campaign, since they did not experience the fighting and did not become refugees, much less survivors of massacres. To many this meant that they had lost the moral and political right to lead the Palestinian people. This reversal did not happen all at once and was not perceived during the war, but by 1951 there was a man who thought of himself as the *mufti's* legitimate successor – a young student of engineering in Cairo, a member of the al-Qidwa family of Gaza, named Yasser Arafat. Another man, Ahmad, the son of the *mufti* of Acre As'ad al-Shuqayri, whom the Husaynis had known in the late Ottoman period, waited a few more years before he became the leader of the Palestinian people in the eyes of the Arab League. But that is a subject for another book and other studies.

During the war, al-Hajj Amin spent most of the day in a small office at the Arab League. He was profoundly embittered and probably did not believe the optimistic reports from the front that appeared in the Cairo newspapers in the first days of the war. In the winter of 1947, he had realized that the Arab states were either not interested in saving the Palestinians as much as in fulfilling their territorial ambitions, as in the case of Jordan, or unable to do so, as in the case of Syria and Egypt.[65] But though he probably did not expect a miraculous redemption, he had not imagined that the downfall would be so catastrophic.

His first secretary in Cairo was Dumiyya al-Sakakini, the daughter of Khalil al-Sakakini and the source for this part of the account.[66] Her father had left his house in Katamon when the fighting broke out and settled in Cairo. The connection between the Sakakini family and the Husaynis was renewed on 20 June 1948, this time as exiles. Dumiyya, her sister Hala and their brother Sari had been living in the Heliopolis Quarter of Cairo since January, not far from al-Hajj Amin's first residence in the city. One evening al-Hajj Amin visited the Sakakinis, and they talked about unsung heroes. Al-Hajj

Amin told them about a Palestinian fighter known as Abu Da'aya, who had been badly wounded in the battle of Ramat Rachel, south of Jerusalem, and had been airlifted from the battlefield straight to the Cairo military hospital. Abu Da'aya was a skinny young leader whose men told stories about him fit for the annals of any war of liberation. He was a goatherd from the village of Suraif near Hebron. This village had already played a part in the fighting – for example, in the attack on the Etzion Bloc convoy (he should not to be confused with the first Abu Da'aya, Abd al-Qadir's deputy). His bravery had been so impressive that the Jordanian commander of the Jerusalem sector mentioned him in the book he wrote about the war. When Khalil joined the conversation, his daughters urged him to go and visit the wounded fighter, who was completely paralyzed. Consequently, after al-Hajj Amin's visit, Sakakini took his daughters to visit Kamel Iraqat, who was the deputy of Abdul Qadir in Qastal, and took over command from him. A warm friendship grew between them. But the patient was transferred to Beirut, where he died from his injuries. Khalil began to write a book about him but did not finish it. Such was the encounter between al-Hajj Amin and the man who had fought in his name and had tried in vain to defend Palestine.

During the war some 750,000 Palestinians ended up in refugee camps. Some remained in Palestine, either in the territory seized by Egypt, in the State of Israel or in the West Bank. They were victims of what would today be called 'ethnic cleansing'. Behind them they left properties, villages and a homeland. By 15 May, al-Qawuqji's Arab Salvation Army and the thousands of volunteers had failed to defend the mixed cities and the main roads. Nor could they stop Jewish forces from seizing the centers of power, such as the customs, the ports, the treasury and most of the British army bases in the country. Now and then they managed to inflict heavy damage on isolated Jewish settlements and convoys making their way to besieged outposts north and south of the country.

After the Jewish state was declared, Arab armies invaded the country, raising the hopes of the population. (It also raised their concern about hasty surrender to the Jewish forces; they feared that a victorious Arab army would punish those who gave in too readily.) Most of the Palestinian inhabitants were unarmed and did not fight very hard, hoping that the Arab states would come to their aid.

In the first week of the war, Syrian units crossed into the north of the country and surrounded some isolated Jewish settlements but were unable to break through. The Arab Legion captured the Jewish Quarter of Jerusalem's Old City and Gush Etzion in the central sector, but, abiding by an unwritten agreement with the Israeli army, it did not advance beyond Jerusalem and the nearby villages.

In the following weeks the legion held back, abandoning the towns of Lydda and Ramleh, with their tens of thousands of inhabitants, to the Israeli forces. In Lydda the expulsion was accompanied by a massacre of the young men in the city's mosque, prompting the rest of the population to join the thousands from nearby Ramleh who had already been driven out of their houses in a march of death toward the West Bank.

The Legion also abandoned the Egyptian army, which became trapped in the Falluja enclave. This army was made up of Muslim Brotherhood volunteers, Sudanese troops and a regular Egyptian division. During the first week of the fighting, it made some impressive gains. It came close to Tel Aviv, having captured several kibbutzim en route. But its lines of supply became too stretched, its ordnance ran out and it could not fight off the Israeli forces. During the truce, the Israeli army recovered, rearmed itself with weapons from the Eastern Bloc and drove the Egyptians back onto the Sinai Peninsula.

The central part of Palestine fell in July. The north was lost in September and October, and by January 1949 the south of Palestine had also been occupied by Israel. Some 800 villages, six towns and more than a million Palestinians were divided between Israel, Egypt and Transjordan. The finger of blame was pointed not only at those who expelled them, or those who had promised to help and instead betrayed, but also at those who had insisted on leading and failed.

In the summer of 1948, while the Palestinian social and cultural life was totally destroyed, an absurd drama took place, involving many Husaynis. That July, the Arab League proclaimed the formation of a Palestinian Arab government. When Palestine had still been in one piece and al-Hajj Amin wished to establish such a government, he had been rebuffed. Now the League defied the harsh reality with a meaningless act of desperation. The inspiration behind this initiative was Jamal al-Husayni. He went to all the Arab capitals, and this time, unlike the months before May 1948, he was fully supported – except in Amman, where King Abdullah would not hear of it. Abdullah already knew that he stood to acquire a fair chunk of Palestine, not because he fought to save it but thanks to his agreement with the Jewish Agency before the outbreak of war.[67]

Only in October was the Arab League able to keep its promise to the Palestinians and call on the leading figures in Palestine to form a government in Gaza. These were al-Hajj Amin's last days of grace, though in fact he was functioning in an imaginary reality unrelated to the disaster on the ground.

The eighty-five men who took part in the opening session on 1 October formed the Palestinian National Council, which elected the All-Palestine Government. Al-Hajj Amin headed the council, and the government was led by Hilmi Pasha, one of al-Hajj Amin's men in the Higher Arab Committee. All that this futile exercise left behind were phrases and symbols. Al-Hajj Amin's opening words in Gaza were: 'Based on the natural and historical right of the Palestinian Arab people to freedom and independence, we hereby declare ...' – which would remain the central motto of all the Palestinian documents up to the Palestinian Declaration of Independence in November 1988.[68] The symbol that has survived from that time is the Palestinian flag, whose colors derived from the banner of revolt raised by Sharif Hussein in 1916. The black, white and green flag, with a starless red triangle on the left-hand side, has rallied Palestinians to their national struggle up to the present time.

There were several Husaynis in that virtual government: Jamal, in recognition of his deeds and abilities, was named Foreign Minister, and Said's son Raja'i, who had been active in politics after First World War but then withdrew to the sidelines, returned to the arena as Minister of Defense. On the face of it, these were the two principal ministries, but in reality they were of no importance whatever, as this government vanished in history's oubliette as abruptly as it had appeared.

King Abdullah swore to oppose this government to the end, and the British government instructed all its representatives in the region to do all they could to destroy it.[69] But it was the Egyptians who gave it the *coup de grâce*. Egyptian premier Mahmud Nuqrashi ordered al-Hajj Amin to return to his exile in Cairo. When he refused, an armed Egyptian officer came to his house and took him away by force. With al-Hajj Amin's political demise, the government fell apart. Raja'i, who became addicted to politics, accepted the post of Saudi Minister of Transport in 1949, perhaps the clearest signal of the family's disappearance from the country's leadership after the Palestinians had lost Palestine.[70]

Of course, the Husaynis did not cease to exist in 1948. While al-Hajj Amin lived, he was first at the heart of Palestinian activity, then on its margins. After his death in 1974, there were still some prominent Husayni public figures – for example, Dr Hatem al-Husayni, the director of al-Quds University, and the first lady of Palestinian nationalism, Amina al-Husayni, the widow of Abd al-Qadir and mother of Faysal al-Husayni. Faysal would make his appearance as the last remaining Husayni in Palestinian politics after the war of 1967. He soon discovered that to join the new leadership it was not enough to flourish the family's ancient lineage. The key to success was a faded document testifying to membership in Fatah – proof of personal sacrifice in the national cause.

In this history of the family, however, 1948 does mark the end. For in that year the curtain came down on the Husaynis as a social and political entity. When the war ended, it became clear that as well as losing their homeland, houses and properties, the Palestinian people had also lost their aristocracy. Other Arab nations lost their aristocracies as well, but under very different circumstances resulting from local radicalism, whether socialist or nationalist.

The author is no admirer of aristocracy – a leadership based on blood relations, enjoying many privileges and in almost complete control of the society's resources. But at a certain stage in the history of every nation, even opponents learn to appreciate the 'grandees' and 'notables'. Forming a bridge between past and present, between power and the people and between tradition and change, they enable social transformation to occur in a moderate fashion, and their destruction provokes revolutions. Their premature annihilation, before an alternative leadership has had a chance to arise, before the society has adjusted to a new reality, results in disaster.

This was the Palestinians' disaster.

# Epilogue

Though this account of the family's history has come to an end, the story is not over. In 1948 a chapter in the history of the country was closed, a long chapter that began at the start of the eighteenth century and ended with the Nakbah. The part played by the family throughout this period, most notably by al-Hajj Amin al-Husayni, will continue to occupy generations of Palestinian historians. But there are still other chapters involving the individual Husaynis who continued to play important roles in Palestinian politics after 1948.

Al-Hajj Amin was not allowed to participate in diplomatic contacts that occurred after the 1948 war. In April 1949, when the Palestinian issue was raised at the Lausanne Conference with the UN's bumbling attempt to revive the Partition Resolution – this time with Arab consent and Israeli refusal – al-Hajj Amin played no part at all. When he heard that on 13 May 1949 the Arab delegations in Lausanne had endorsed a protocol express-ing their willingness in principle to negotiate a peace settlement with the Jewish state, al-Hajj Amin wrote to his old acquaintance Adil Arslan, the Syrian foreign minister, 'Do not recognize Israel. Whoever says he intends to do so is committing grave treason.' In Syria, al-Hajj Amin concentrated on opposing every possible attempt at reconciliation with Israel, such as the one made by the Syria.n ruler Husni Zaim in April 1949.[1] His somewhat hostile Israeli biographer Zvi Al-Peleg described him as 'striving against the formation of a new reality'.[2]

Nevertheless, in the early 1950s, al-Hajj Amin was still the most politi-cally prominent member of his family. However, the connection between al-Hajj Amin's activities and the family began to evaporate. Other members of the family pursued various personal careers, some fairly successfully. For example, before his death in 1954 Yunis al-Husayni published three basic books on social and economic development in Palestine, on social thought in the world and on the cities of the Middle East.[3]

Al-Hajj Amin's main activity was behind the scenes, mainly trying to prevent the Jordanization of that part of Palestine, the so-called West Bank, that had fallen to the Hashemite kingdom. Demographic reality in the enlarged kingdom made it into a *de facto* Palestinian state. Al-Hajj Amin hoped that this would challenge the legitimacy of Hashemite rule, if not across the Jordan, at least in the West Bank. King Abdullah's almost open peace negotiations with Israel, and his 1949 concession of the 'little triangle' (an area of the West Bank) to Israel, were added reasons to undermine the Hashemite ruler. Finally, although it should be said that there is no clear evidence connecting al-Hajj Amin to the murder of King Abdullah, those directly involved were very close to him. It is likely, but not easy to prove, that he decided that the king should pay with his life for the peace moves and for his betrayal during the war (the abandonment of Lydda and Ramleh in particular). Perhaps he also thought that such a dramatic event would destabilize Greater Jordan and lead to a new geopolitical configuration.

As always, Jamal worked in the opposite direction from al-Hajj Amin's. He toiled above all to encourage the population of the West Bank to preserve its distinct identity and strive to create an independent Palestinian entity. Jamal's messages often included the term *qiyan* (entity), a vague word that substituted for 'state' until the aims of the Palestinian national movement were defined. But beyond all this, the Husaynis made little contribution to the movement's reawakening in the 1950s and 1960s.[4]

Al-Hajj Amin's collaborators were Transjordanians and Palestinians who wanted to settle accounts with King Abdullah, perhaps also with the dynasty. Of the family, only al-Hajj Amin's kinsman Dr Musa Abdullah al-Husayni was directly involved in the plot. In Germany, Musa Abdullah had been al-Hajj Amin's right-hand man. After the war, he was detained in Belgium, before he was exiled to the Seychelles in 1947. After his release, he taught at Beirut University and soon afterwards moved to Amman.

In Amman, Musa Abdullah joined the forces of Abdullah al-Tal, the commander of the Arab Legion in the Jerusalem sector, and appeared to be a keen proponent of the Transjordanian scheme to annex the West Bank and integrate it into the Hashemite kingdom. It later became clear that he had worked his way into the Hashemite establishment in order to undermine it. He had a chance to display his acting ability at the Jericho Conference – convened by King Abdullah to compel the West Bank grandees to call for the unification of the two sides of the Jordan River and declare him king of the joint entity – by expressing great enthusiasm for the scheme. The palace rewarded him with the post of liaison officer with the Red Cross, a kind of honorary consul to the international body with a senior political and diplo- matic status. His amiable personality won him the favor of the monarch for whose assassination he would be chiefly responsible.

But perhaps we are doing Musa Abdullah an injustice by depicting him as a schemer who wormed himself into the king's favor in order to kill him. Perhaps he truly wanted to integrate into the Hashemite world, and it was only his bruised ego when he failed to be elected to the Jordanian Parliament in 1949 that changed his feelings and caused him to contact al-Hajj Amin and volunteer to act against the Hashemite monarchy. Be that as it may, after his parliamentary setback, Musa Abdullah opened a travel agency in East Jerusalem and worked in close cooperation with an Israeli travel agency, organizing pilgrim tours on both sides of the city.[5]

By the time he returned to Jerusalem, he was already in close contact with his exiled relatives in Egypt: al-Hajj Amin, Rajai and Ishaq Darwish. The four joined forces with Abdullah al-Tal, who had turned against the king because of Abdullah's attempts to reach a separate peace treaty with Israel. Together they laid plans to bring him down. Musa Abdullah became the pivotal player in the conspiracy, his mission being to strengthen his connection to the palace and to charm the king. He also located a potential assassin, a twenty-one- year-old apprentice tailor in Jerusalem, Mustafa Shukri Ashu, provided him with a handgun and instructed him to wait for the right opportunity.

On 21 July 1951, the king was scheduled to visit the towns of the West Bank and Jerusalem, and Musa Abdullah joined him in Nablus. James Lunt, a senior officer in the Arab Legion, was greatly impressed by Musa Abdullah (then forty-odd years old), his British education (as noted before, he had graduated from London University) and above all by his obvious devotion to the king.[6] Musa Abdullah accompanied the king in his car on the way to prayers at the Haram al-Sharif. Once there, he hastened to open the car door for the king, bowing demonstratively. A few minutes later the king told his bodyguards to move aside so he could wave to the cheering crowd. Mustafa Shukri Ashu was already there. He seized the moment, fired at the king and killed him.[7] Musa Abdullah's physical proximity to the king just before he was killed immediately drew suspicion to him.

Jordanian security services at once hunted down all the members of the al-Husayni family who were active in Jordan and arrested them. In Cairo al-Hajj Amin published a statement denying all connection to the murder. Musa Abdullah was questioned and tortured, and he admitted to planning the assassination. Later in court he declared he was innocent, but was found guilty. On 6 September 1951, he was hanged, together with others who were convicted with him. Other members of the family, Tawfiq Salih and Daud al-Husayni, were arrested on the day of the murder but were released for lack of evidence.[8]

Despite suspicions of complicity, al-Hajj Amin still wielded considerable influence in Jordan during the 1950s. His erstwhile follower Sheikh Taqi al-Din al-Nabhani founded the Islamic Liberation Party to rival the Muslim Brotherhood. In 1958 Jordanian intelligence suspected that al-Hajj Amin and Jamal were still active in local politics and financing the party.

Al-Hajj Amin was also suspected of collaborating with Iraq's revolutionary leader, Abd al-Karim Qasim, who came to power in a military coup in July 1958. Soon after coming to power, Qasim set about creating a Palestinian army and an independent organization for the liberation of Palestine. These moves did little for the country, but in the long run prompted Gamal Abd al-Nasser to create the PLO with Ahmad al-Shuqayri.[9] Through him and the new organization, forces in Palestinian society, mainly from the refugee camps, were pushing forward the concept of the 'Palestinian entity', which was blessed officially by a special meeting of the Arab League Council (the Foreign Ministers Assembly) that took place in Shtura, Lebanon, in May 1960.

These moves sidelined al-Hajj Amin altogether. But he was still the leading ambassador for the Palestinian cause in the mid-1950s. It was to his credit that the Palestinian issue appeared high on the agenda of the Afro-Asian bloc that emerged to challenge the rigid Cold War dichotomy forced on the world by the US and the USSR. At the 1955 Bandung Conference, al-Hajj Amin was accredited as an observer and helped make the situation in Palestine one of the major issues discussed.[10]

But al-Hajj Amin failed to recognize the centrality of the refugees in the new movement.[11] He waged a Sisyphean struggle against the reversal in Palestinian politics and the transfer of the leadership to the refugees. He organized demonstrations against the PLO's proclamation of the independent Palestinian entity in 1964, having tried some years earlier to play a major role in creating a new, independent Palestinian organization, instigated by Qasim.[12]

Nasser's protégé, Ahmad al-Shuqayri, tried to mollify al-Hajj Amin and offered him the presidency of the nascent Palestinian National Council. But al-Hajj Amin and the organization to which he remained attached, the Higher Arab Committee, refused to take part in the launching conference in

Jerusalem. 'The conference is illegal', the Higher Arab Committee declared in a public statement, 'because it does not represent the Palestinian people and its goals.' Four years later Ahmad al-Shuqayri tried again through another Husayni, Daud, to conciliate al-Hajj Amin, but the ex-*mufti* demanded that the new concept of the 'entity' be identified with him. He was quite out of touch with reality. Not only had he lost his political authority, in the eyes of certain Palestinian historians he also lost his moral sway.[13]

The conflict with Ahmad al-Shuqayri diverted al-Hajj Amin from the national path to such a degree that when a conflict erupted in 1967 between the PLO and King Hussein of Jordan, Amin supported the young king. 'The forces of evil' is how he referred to the PLO in speaking to the Hashemite monarch, though luckily for his image, these words were not recorded in the Palestinian history books.[14]

Thanks to Hashemite support, al-Hajj Amin was able to visit Jerusalem – a small consolation. Early in March 1967, he was received in the city as an important personage and visited the scenes of his childhood and youth that he had not seen for thirty years. Inside the al-Aqsa mosque he asked to withdraw into the *mihrab*, the Muslim prayer niche, of Salah al-Din al-Ayubi, as he used to do as a boy in the early years of the century. 'The mosque is the same as it was in 1937, when I left it,' he said to a journalist a couple of years later.[15] After two weeks, he left the city. 'When the plane circled above Jerusalem's airfield I saw the Dome of the Rock smiling at me. I left a bit of myself in every corner of the city, on every one of its hills.'[16] He never returned to Jerusalem, not even after his death. Israel refused permission to bury al-Hajj Amin in his native city. Even in death, he remained Zionism's worst enemy.

'Do you hate the Jews?' he was asked by the Egyptian journalist Zuhair Mardini at his Beirut residence in Mansuriya in 1969. As was his custom from youth, al-Hajj Amin delayed answering. He summoned his servant – as always, by his first name – and asked for another cup of tea. What was he thinking about before he gave his answer? Pictures of the refugees, or more remote scenes of his deportation from Palestine? 'I'm a Muslim and my position is based on the holy Qur'an,' he said. Then he added, 'I do not dip my pen in the ink of hatred.' Mardini waited, knowing it was not the whole answer. The former *mufti* pedantically tidied the books on his desk. Most of them dealt with the problem of Palestine, and he gazed at them as if searching for the reply. He gave a very indirect and winding answer: 'How much can one man, whatever his status, change an existing situation? All the efforts that were made did not lead to a solution. All we know is that emotions alone cannot solve a crisis. We're in the midst of a bloody conflict, and we have no choice but to pursue it.' Mardini had the impression that al-Hajj Amin was not moved by hate and was facing reality with reason and common sense.[17]

By the 1970s, nothing was left of al-Hajj Amin's status. He had been pushed to the margin of Palestinian action and memory. Another member of the Husayni family remained engraved in that memory as a heroic figure, to some extent balancing out criticism of the former *mufti*.

Others – mainly the Husaynis who remained in Jerusalem – were not content to shape their image for posterity but returned to public life in the spheres of welfare and education. A notable example was Khalid al-Husayni, Abd al-Qadir's brother who succeeded him as commander of the Palestinian forces in Jerusalem until the end of the war of 1948. Afterwards he became the director of the United Nations Relief and Works Agency (UNRWA) in the district of Nablus and made his home in that town. He was perhaps the only Husayni who worked directly with the refugees, but apparently they were not grateful. Towards the end of February 1951, he was twice attacked by an armed refugee in Nablus; the second blow was fatal. He was projected as the main culprit in the Palestinian catastrophe. The family believes that the Hashemite secret service was behind his assassination, and it has been said that the murder of King Abdullah was an act of revenge.

In the 1990s, Khalid's work was continued by his son Sharif, who worked in Orient House. One of the few Husaynis who engaged in political activity during the 1980s, he joined the Palestinian leadership in the Occupied Territories.

The story of Ishaq Musa al-Husayni, who made a name for himself in the 1950s, is quite different. He became a known spokesman for the Palestinian cause in the region and beyond. At first he went to Aleppo in Syria and in 1949 settled in Beirut, where he taught at the American University until 1955. Like other members of the family, he was impressed by Gamal Abd al-Nasser, and in the late 1950s he moved to Cairo and taught at the American University there. During those years he wrote one of the pioneering studies on the Muslim Brotherhood. In the 1960s, he contributed to the cause by writing books about the Arab character of Jerusalem and Palestine.[18] During the following two decades, he was regularly invited by leading universities in the West to lecture on Arabic literature. He returned to Jerusalem in 1973, almost thirty years after he had left it, and to the subject of Palestinian literature as distinct from Arab literature as a whole. He has done a good deal to strengthen higher education in East Jerusalem. He died in 1990 at the age of eighty-six.

## *Faysal al-Husayni*

The best-known member of the family at the end of the twentieth century was Faysal al-Husayni, the son of Abd al-Qadir. He played a major role in the Palestinian leadership in the Occupied Territories and in the Palestinian Authority. In May 2001 he died of a heart attack while on a frustrating political mission to Kuwait in an abortive attempt to secure a reconciliation with the Kuwaiti regime in the wake of Arafat's unequivocal support for Saddam Hussein in the First Gulf War.

Since the Palestinian Authority, to which Faysal belonged, did not enjoy the full support of the Palestinian people, and since the future of Palestinian politics remains obscure, it is not yet possible to define Faysal al-Husayni's place in his people's history. The climax of his political career was probably the eve of the Madrid Conference in 1991, where he was a senior member of the Palestinian delegation at the peace talks with Israel. But he lost his seniority to Mahmud Abbas, aka Abu Mazen, who succeeded Arafat in 2004 as President of the Palestinian Authority.[19]

Faysal al-Husayni was born in Baghdad in 1940, when his father Abd al-Qadir was staying there with al-Hajj Amin. But soon afterwards, he moved with his family to Cairo where he spent his first twenty years until he returned to Jerusalem as a young man in 1961. He was very active as a student in Cairo, and in 1958 he founded the General Union of Palestinian Students, which became one of the pivotal institutions in the PLO.

In Jerusalem he was attracted to the Palestinian nationalism propagated by Fatah, and he worked in the organization's office in East Jerusalem before the June 1967 war. At the age of twenty-seven, he wished to be even more active and asked to be recruited to Fatah's fighting units. When the 1967 war broke out, he was attending a course offered by the Palestinian Liberation Army, the military organization created by the Arab League, and he returned to Jerusalem in secret.

In November 1967, he was arrested for possession of weapons, which he had received from Arafat, who commanded Fatah in the territories and was trying in vain to start a popular uprising against the Israeli occupation. Before giving the slip to the Israeli army and crossing to Jordan, Arafat held a brief meeting in Ramallah with Faysal al-Husayni. At his trial, Faysal said that he himself did not believe in the efficacy of the armed struggle and wanted to dedicate himself to the political path. This statement led the judges to sentence him to only one year in prison.

When he was released, he married his cousin Najat al-Husayni, who bore him a son and a daughter. For years he engaged in private business, then worked in his uncle's X-ray institute in East Jerusalem, helped with the development of the lands at Ayn Siniya and in 1979 returned to public life, founding and directing an academic institute of Arab studies. He made an important contribution to the collection of archival and academic material that enabled young Palestinian historians to reconstruct the history of the country and to recreate almost from nothing the Palestinian collective memory that had been effaced by Israel since 1948. Not surprisingly, the Israeli authorities would not accept him as a purely academic figure and several times placed him in administrative detention.

When the First *Intifada* broke out, Faysal was in Abu Iyyad's camp in Fatah, which was looking for a political way to realize the gains of the uprising. He had led the advisory team of PLO delegations at various meetings in the Arab countries that drew up a well-defined Palestinian position and consequently took part in the Palestinian delegation that went to Madrid in 1991 to discuss a comprehensive peace settlement of the Arab-Israeli conflict.[20]

But there was little in Faysal al-Husayni's modern biography to connect him to the family history. 'The son who did not follow in his father's footsteps', said the Israeli journalist Pinhas Inbari, meaning that Faysal had worked to bring about Israeli-Palestinian peace, whereas his father had fought against Zionism and paid with his life. But it must be remembered that the family had ceased to be a meaningful political body in Faysal's life and in Palestinian politics as a whole. It was Faysal's younger brother Ghazi who believed he was following in his father's footsteps when he joined the Islamic Jihad movement, whose name echoes that of the organization created by Abd al-Qadir, *al-Jihad al-Muqaddas*.[21]

Let us conclude this book not with Faysal al-Husayni, but with al-Hajj Amin. Towards the end of his life, al-Hajj Amin occupied himself more and more with the pan-Islamic world, since he had been deposed from all significant positions in Palestine and the pan-Arab arena had faded since 1967. He tried to participate in the first pan-Islamic conference in Rabat, Morocco, in 1969 but was prevented by the strenuous protests of the PLO, which wanted to eliminate him as a representative of Palestinian nationalism. When the second conference was held in Lahore, Pakistan, in 1974, al-Hajj Amin was invited, since by then he had become weak and his health had deteriorated. The conference took place in February, and in July of that year al-Hajj Amin died of a heart attack in the Mansuriya quarter of Beirut in Lebanon.[22]

The following year, the civil war erupted in Lebanon and the former *mufti*'s house was burned down by the Maronite-Christian Phalangists. Mona Bori, today a refugee in Texas, was a neighbor and managed to photograph some of the archives in the house that burned down. Some of the missing material was seized by the Phalangists, and no one knows where it is or what was contained in the material that perished. But whatever it was, it was not likely to diminish al-Hajj Amin's grave responsibility as head of the family for his people's tragedy.

At al-Hajj Amin's grave, his only son heard the leaders of the PLO praising and eulogizing his father (his six sisters did not come to the funeral). But Salih remained in Spain and did not follow the family's political tradition. Nor did the fulsome eulogies last very long. After al-Hajj Amin's death, the question of his place in Palestinian historiography was raised. He himself had tried as early as 1954 to engrave the 'official' version of his life and role into Palestinian history. In newspaper articles and anthologies, he repeatedly described his positive role in the struggle for Palestine, hoping that the catastrophe would appear as a terrible concatenation of irresistible hostile forces. At the heart of his historiographical analysis was the British betrayal. His mixing of rational thinking with demonic mythology served to diminish his historical stature rather than enhance it.

The discussion continued without him and focused on his responsibility for the Nakbah. Even before he died, Palestinian historians and intellectuals of the left severely criticized the role of the upper class, with the Husaynis at its center. 'The urban upper class remained alien to the armed struggle throughout the period of the mandate,' argued Hisham Sharabi. 'This class especially benefited through that period.' The problem of the Husaynis, Sharabi stated in 1969, was that they perceived Zionism not as the ultimate danger but as a nuisance, while to the peasants and the workers Zionism was a tangible threat.[23]

During the 1980s, the discussion became clearer and more focused. The attack on al-Hajj Amin was led by the Palestinian historian Samih Shaqib, and the opposite viewpoint was presented by the historian Husni Jarar. In 1988 the two conducted a thorough debate that left the *mufti*'s historiographic image in tatters.[24] In the next decade, the picture became more balanced when Philip Mattar published the first comprehensive Palestinian biography of al-Hajj Amin, offering a balance-sheet of achievements and failures.[25]

Only Abd al-Qadir al-Husayni's reputation has remained impeccable, and perhaps it was natural that his son Faysal, rather than al-Hajj Amin's son Salih, went on to play a part in Palestinian politics. It also redounded to the Husaynis' credit that Yasser Arafat, the unquestioned leader of the Palestinian revolution from 1969 to 2004, was related to their family on his mother's side. Furthermore, he always made a point of telling everyone that in 1948 he had been Abd al-Qadir's personal secretary.

Above all, al-Hajj Amin should not be confused with his family's pivotal role in the history of Palestine, for good or for worse. Its achievements and failures – and those of the other notable families – were those of Palestinian society as a whole. And since the Husaynis, more than any other family, were at the center of Palestinian politics on the eve of the 1948 catastrophe, they bear heavy responsibility for its occurrence. And yet, one should not for a moment forget the nature of this responsibility. It was the inability to defend and organize a community that was the object of an ethnic cleansing ideology and praxis. It is very difficult to assess whether an alternative leadership would have fared better in the face of such a calamity.

By 1948, the family had declined not only because of the Nakbah but also because the Arab-Ottoman world to which it belonged was gone for ever. In the words of the English travel writer Colin Thubron, who visited Jerusalem in the 1960s: 'The Husaynis no longer rule over the city's religious life, nor do the Nashashibis rule over the municipality. A whole generation has departed from the highway followed by their ancestors for centuries.'[26]

The Husaynis are not what they had been. Their history shows that they were part of a culture, an experience and a life that vanished in 1948. The desire to resurrect them lies at the heart of the historical-political thought of all Palestinians, wherever they may be. This thought animates the struggle over this country, and if it were understood by the other party in the conflict it could lead to reconciliation.

# Family Trees (1700–1948)

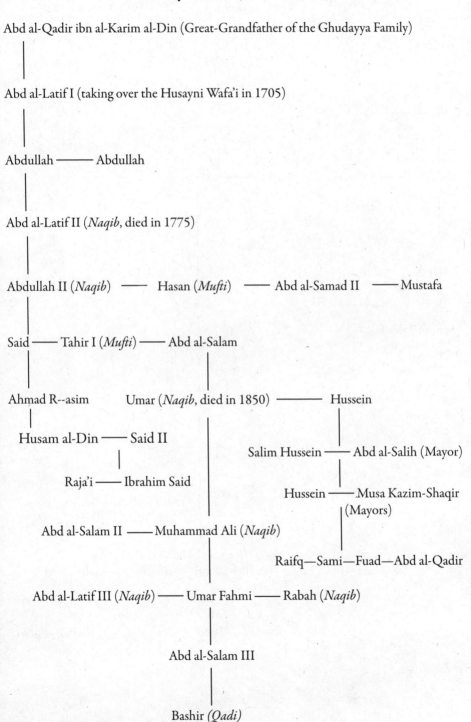

Abd al-Qadir ibn al-Karim al-Din (Great-Grandfather of the Ghudayya Family)

Abd al-Latif I (taking over the Husayni Wafa'i in 1705)

Abdullah ——— Abdullah

Abd al-Latif II (*Naqib*, died in 1775)

Abdullah II (*Naqib*) —— Hasan (*Mufti*) —— Abd al-Samad II ——Mustafa

Said —— Tahir I (*Mufti*) —— Abd al-Salam

Ahmad R--asim    Umar (*Naqib*, died in 1850) ——— Hussein

Husam al-Din —— Said II

Salim Hussein —— Abd al-Salih (Mayor)

Raja'i —— Ibrahim Said

Hussein ——Musa Kazim-Shaqir
(Mayors)

Abd al-Salam II —— Muhammad Ali (*Naqib*)

Raifq—Sami—Fuad—Abd al-Qadir

Abd al-Latif III (*Naqib*) —— Umar Fahmi —— Rabah (*Naqib*)

Abd al-Salam III

Bashir *(Qadi)*

*The Tahiri Branch*

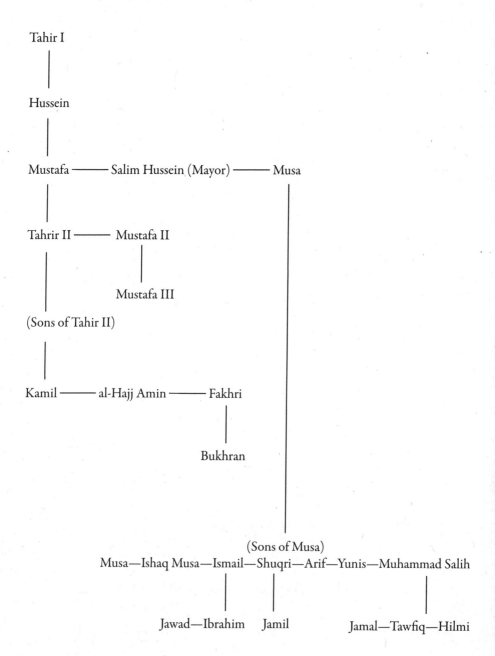

Tahir I

Hussein

Mustafa ——— Salim Hussein (Mayor) ——— Musa

Tahrir II ——— Mustafa II

Mustafa III

(Sons of Tahir II)

Kamil ——— al-Hajj Amin ——— Fakhri

Bukhran

(Sons of Musa)
Musa—Ishaq Musa—Ismail—Shuqri—Arif—Yunis—Muhammad Salih

Jawad—Ibrahim    Jamil          Jamal—Tawfiq—Hilmi

# Endnotes

## Preface

1. R. Springborg, 'Patterns of Association in the Egyptian Political Elite' in George Lenszowski (ed.), *Political Elites in the Middle East*, Washington 1975, p. 93.
2. B. Doumani (ed.), *Family History in the Middle East: Household, Property, and Gender*, New York 2003.
3. One such work is D. Ze'evi's *An Ottoman Century: The District of Jerusalem in the 1600s*, Albany 1996.

## Introduction

1. A. Raymond, *Cairo,* Cambridge 2000; K. Cuno, *The Pasha's Peasants: Land, Society and Economy in Lower Egypt, 1740–1858*, Cambridge 1992; A. Marcus, *The Middle East on the Eve of Modernity: Aleppo in the Eighteenth Century*, New York 1989; J. Reily, *A Small Town in Syria: Ottoman Hama in the Eighteenth and Nineteenth Centuries*, Oxford and New York 2002; L. Fawaz, *Merchants and Migrants in Nineteenth Century Beirut*, Cambridge 1983; M. Reimer, *Colonial Bridgehead: Government and Society in Alexandria, 1807–1882*, Cairo 1997; D. Khoury, *State and Provincial Society in the Ottoman Empire: Mosul, 1540–1834*, Cambridge and New York 1999.
2. E. Toldenao, 'The Emergence of Ottoman-Local Elites (1700–1900): A Framework for Research' in M. Maoz and I. Pappé (eds), *Middle Eastern Politics and Ideas: A History from Within*, London and New York, 1997, pp. 146–7.
3. Ibid., p. 150.
4. Ibid.
5. I. M. Lapidus, *A History of Islamic Societies*, Cambridge 1988, pp. 640–1.
6. A. Hourani, 'Ottoman Reform and the Politics of Notables' in A. Hourani (ed.), *The Modern Middle East*, London and New York, p. 87.
7. Ibid.
8. Ibid.
9. G. Baer, 'Jerusalem's Families of Notables and the Waqf in the Early 19th Century',

in D. Kushner (ed.), *Palestine in the Late Ottoman Period*, Jerusalem 1986, p. 110.

10. S. Pamuk, 'Money in the Ottoman Empire' in H. Inalcik (ed.), *An Economic and Social History of the Ottoman Empire, 1300–1914*, Cambridge 1994, pp. 966–7.

11. O. Peri, 'Waqf and Ottoman Welfare Policy: The Poor Kitchen of Khasseki Sultan in Eighteen Century Jerusalem', *Hamizrach Hehadash*, vol. 34, issues 133–6, pp. 64–76. Quote from page 68, note 17.

12. Ibid., p. 111.

13. Baer, *Jerusalem*, p. 111.

14. Quoted in Peri, 'Waqf', note 23, Sijjil Jerusalem 279, pp. 36–7.

15. Albert Hourani, *A History of the Arab Peoples*, London 1991, pp. 252–5.

16. Peri, *Jerusalem*, p. 72.

17. Ibid., pp. 75–6.

18. Baer, *Waqf*, p. 114.

19. Ibid., p. 118.

20. Hourani, *A History of the Arab Peoples*, pp. 252–5.

21. A. Scholch, *Palestine in Transformation, 1856–1882: Studies in Social, Economic and Political Development*, Washington 1993, p. 119.

22. By 1920, they owned 50,000 *dunams*; see J. Kano, *The Problem of Land between Jews and Arabs, 1917–1990*, Tel Aviv 1992, p. 137.

23. Lapidus, *A History*, p. 641.

24. Hourani, 'Ottoman Reform', pp. 83–111.

25. Lapidus, *A History*, p. 641.

26. Hourani, 'Ottoman Reform', pp. 83–111.

## Prologue

1. On the period in general and the background for the revolt see M. al-Muhibi, *A Summary of the Notables' Lives in the 11th Hijjra Century*, vol. 2, Cairo 1868 (Arabic); Arif al-Arif, *The History of Jerusalem*, Cairo 1950 (Arabic); A. Cohen, *Palestine in the 18th Century: Patterns and Administration*, Jerusalem 1973, pp. 170–5. See also extensive parts of Y. Ben-Zvi's *The Settlement of Eretz Israel*, Jerusalem 1976 (Hebrew). My descriptions of the city and some of the personalities of the period that appear in the prologue and chapters dealing with the eighteenth and nineteenth centuries are based on several travelogues, most notable of which are C. R. Conder, *Palestine*, 1891; J. Finn, *Stirring Times or Records from Jerusalem Consular Chronicles*, London 1878; A. P. Stanley, *Sinai and Palestine*, London 1887; W. P. Lynch, *A Journey to the Dead Sea and the Jordan River*, New York 1984; M. A. Rogers, *Daily Life in Palestine*, London 1984; Y. Schwartz, *The Harvest of the Land*, London 1845 (Hebrew); A. Yelin, *The Memoirs of a Jerusalemite*, Jerusalem 1924 (Hebrew); and A. Yaari, *Travels in Palestine*, Ramat Gan 1976 (Hebrew). Other collections were helpful: M. Ish-Shalom, *Christian Pilgrimage in the 19th Century*, Tel Aviv 1965 (Hebrew); Y. Ben-Areyh, *Palestine in the 19th Century and Its Rediscovery*, Jerusalem

1970; Z. Vilnai, *Investigative Tourists in Palestine*, Tel Aviv 1984 (Hebrew); Y. Shavit (ed.), *The Wonders of the Holy Land*, Jerusalem 1981 (Hebrew); and N. Shore, *The Book of Palestine's Travelogues in the 19th Century*, Jerusalem 1988 (Hebrew).

2. The description of the *naqib* revolt is based on A. Manna, 'The Naqib al-Ashraf's Revolt in Jerusalem (1703–1705)', *Cathedra* 64 (April 1992) (Hebrew), and M. Rosen, 'The Naqib al-Ashraf's Revolt in Jerusalem, 1702–1706', *Cathedra* 22 (January 1982) (Hebrew). Manna's article is important in particular as it is based on the *sijjilat*, the Shari'a court protocol during those years. On p. 73, Manna mentions a possible marriage connection between the al-Ghudayya and al-Wafa'i families. In a lecture he gave in the Truman Institute in Jerusalem on 4 February 1999, he reported further advances in his research and a deeper conviction about the connection between the two families. Another important source that quotes extensively from the *sijjilat* is Arif al-Arif, *The Concise History of Jerusalem*, Jerusalem 1961, pp. 355–7 (Arabic).

3. Al-Asali's *Jerusalem in the Arab and Muslim Travelogues* (Amman 1992) (Arabic) is an anthology of manuscripts of Muslim travelers frequenting the city in various centuries. The anthology includes manuscripts that appear on microfilms in Syrian and Jordanian universities.

4. Ibid., pp. 110–5.

5. M. K. al-Muradi, *A Guide to the Notables of the 12th Hijjra Century*, Istanbul 1882, vol. 3, p. 89 (Arabic).

6. Al-Nabulsi, p. 245.

7. The above description is a fusion of information derived from al-Nabulsi's previous visit, ibid., p. 255; Mustafa Ibn Kamil al-Bakhri's manuscript as it appears in al-Asali, *Jerusalem,* p. 111; excerpts from description of Muhammad ibn Abd al-Rahim's visit, 'The Sunna's Tales of Jerusalem's Origins' (Abd al-Rahim was *Sheikh al-Islam*, responsible for the appointment of the Hanafi *Muftis*); and from Mustafa Asad al-Qaymi al-Damaiti's book *Thoughts of People I Met on My Trips to the Valley of Jerusalem* (Arabic) (al-Damaiti was an Egyptian visitor to Jerusalem in 1724). These two last sources are quoted in al-Arif, *Concise History*.

8. G. Winegart, 'The Religious Muslim Life in 18th Century Jerusalem', *Cathedra* 49 (September 1988), p. 79 (Hebrew).

9. Al-Asali, *Jerusalem*, p. 264, and A. Hourani, *A History of the Arab Peoples*, New York 1993, p. 247.

10. The above description is a fusion of a second travelogue composed by al-Nabulsi – A. al-Kurdi (ed.), *Ismail al-Nabulsi: Fiction and Reality in a Trip to the al-Sham Countries and Hejaz,* Cairo 1986, pp. 110–38 (Arabic) – with a description of al-Bakhri's travels in al-Muradi's book *A Guide*, vol. 4, pp. 124–6. I also referred here to the entry 'Al-Bakhri' in the Palestinian Encyclopedia, *Al-Mawsuat al-Filastiniyya*, vol. 4, Damascus 1982, p. 227 (Arabic).

11. M. al-Hanabli, *The Magnificent Man*, Cairo, no date (Arabic).

12. Al-Muradi, *A Guide*, vol. 4, pp. 124–6.

13. B. Abu-Manneh, 'The Husaynis: The Rise of a Notable Family in 18th Century Palestine' in D. Kushner (ed.), Palestine in the Late Ottoman Period, Jerusalem 1986, pp. 93–108, and I. M. al-Husseini, The al-Husseini Family, Jerusalem 1988, pp. 1–2 (Arabic). Both sources connect the 1703 revolt with the family.

14. The Shariʿa court, Jerusalem, *Sijjil*, vol. 272, p. 147. The Zionist Central Archives, the Mufti Files, Biography.

15. In his book *Historiography and Nationalism* (Jerusalem 1995), which is based on Jewish sources, Yacov Barani mentions a totally different hierarchy of the notable families. On the importance of the three posts held by the family see Y. Porath, 'Al-Hajj Amin al-Husseini, The Jerusalem Mufti – His Rise and the Consolidation of his Position' in G. Baer (ed.), *The Ulama and the Religious Problems in the Muslim World*, Jerusalem 1979, p. 223 (Hebrew).

## Chapter One

1. This description and most of the chapter was inspired by the very important and comprehensive research of Butrus Abu-Manneh (Abu-Manneh, *The Husaynis*, pp. 93–106) and on the basis of his 'A New Light on the Husaynis' Ascendance in the Eighteenth Century' in A. Cohen (ed.), *Chapters in the History of Jerusalem in the Early Ottoman Period*, Jerusalem 1979 (Hebrew). This last article and conversations with its author triggered my original interest in the subject.

2. The details on the eunuchs are taken from M. Penzer, *The Harem*, London 1967. The description of the Topkapi Palace is based on a visit to the place and on a tourist booklet published by the Turkish Ministry of Tourism. See *The Topkapi Palace*, Net Turistik Yayinlar, Istanbul 1987.

3. The text is taken from Abu-Manneh, *The Husaynis*. He bases it on the Jerusalem *sijjilat*. It stands to reason that the *sijjil* did not record precisely the things that had been said, but I presume this is a reasonable reconstruction of the exchange, if indeed it was said.

4. The Jerusalem *Sijjil*, vol. 269, document 92, pp. 102–4, 1203 *hijjra* (1788). I wish to thank Dr Mahmoud Yazbak, who guided me in working on these documents in the Haram.

5. This passage is reconstructed with the help of a genealogical tree given to Philip Mattar by Dr Mahmoud al-Naqib al-Husayni, Amin's physician and relative. See P. Mattar, *The Mufti of Jerusalem*, New York 1988, p. 6, note 23. See also M. Khadduri, *Arab Contemporaries: The Role of Personalities in Politics*, Baltimore 1973, p. 69; G. al-Jabarti, *The Wonders of Biographies and Chronicles*, Cairo 1879, vol. 1, pp. 374–5 (Arabic).

6. Quoted in al-Asali, *Jerusalem*, p. 38.

7. Al-Muradi, *Guide*, vol. 3, p. 90.

8. On Dahir al-Umar, see U. Heyd, *Daher al-Umar*, Jerusalem 1963; C. P. Volney, *Travels in Syria and Egypt in the years 1783, 1784 and 1785*, London 1787. Other sources used as background are M. N. al-Dabbagh, *The History of Shaykh Dahir al-Umar al-Zaydani*, Harisa 1927 (Arabic); B. Doumani, *Rediscovering Palestine*,

Berkeley 1995, pp. 95–7; and Thomas Philipp, *Acre: The Rise and Fall of a Palestinian City, 1730–1831*, New York 2001.

9. On al-Umar's wish to occupy Jerusalem, see A. Cohen, *Palestine*, p. 92. I assume that not only the family had thought to contact al-Umar.

10. This description is based on documents in A. Cohen, A. Simon-Picali and O. Salameh (eds), *Jews in the Muslim Court*, Jerusalem 1996, pp. 14, 163 (Hebrew).

11. Based on the biography of the family as it appears in H. A. Abd al-Latif, *The Jerusalemite Biographies in the 12th Hijjra Century*, no date (Arabic).

12. A. Rafeq, *The Province of Damascus*, Beirut 1970, p. 21.

13. Al-Asali, *Historical Documents from Jerusalem*, Amman 1989, vol. 3, p. 45 (Arabic). There he quotes in full from the *sijjil* of Jerusalem, vol. 271, p. 4, 1204 *hijjra*. In page 48, note 31, al-Asali brings in the record in the *sijjil* and reports that in 1202 *hijjra*, the governor of Damascus imposed an unregistered tax on the population of Jerusalem (*Sijjil*, vol. 269, p. 33). See also S. Pamuk, 'Money in the Ottoman Empire' in H. Inalcik (ed.), *An Economic and Social History of the Ottoman Empire, 1300–1914*, Cambridge 1994, pp. 966–7.

14. The funeral rites are described in K. Salibi and Y. K. Khoury (eds), *The Missionary Herald: Reports from Ottoman Syria, 1819–1870*, Washington 1991, p. 267.

15. Abu-Manneh dealt extensively with that period as well: Abu-Manneh, *The Husaynis*. Inspired by this article, others researchers as well as myself have read the manuscript of Abd al-Latif. See Abd al-Latif, *Biographies*.

16. At the end of the nineteenth century, the American consul reported that the genealogical tree was hung in the notables' houses. See E. S. Wallace, *Holy Jerusalem*, New York 1898, p. 341.

17. In the following chapters, I used valuable information found in the biographical lexicon composed by Adel Manna. The information here is taken from A. Manna, *The Worthies of Palestine in the Late Ottoman Period*, Beirut 1995, p. 109 (Arabic).

18. Manna, ibid., p. 87. It is argued that Hassan was appointed as *mufti* in 1773.

19. Al-Asali, *Documents*, p. 34, document 19; the proclamation of the Damascus governor, the Shari'a court *sijjilat* of Jerusalem, vol. 271, p. 56, 1201 *hijjra* (1789).

20. Ibid., p. 34, document 20; *Sijjil*, vol. 287, p. 41, 1211 *hijjra* (1797).

21. Ibid., p. 35, document 21; *Sijjil*, vol. 287, p. 70.

22. Ibid., p. 33, document 17. According to Abu-Manneh, the decision on the name was taken in 1790. Abu-Manneh, *The Husaynis*.

23. Ibid.

24. Manna, *Worthies*, p. 87.

25. Al-Asali, *Documents*, p. 53, document 38: *Sijjil*, vol. 272, pp. 7–8, 1205 *hijjra* (1790). The document mentions Saliyat bint Khalil, a Mutawali (appointed) woman for the endowment (*waqf*). See also ibid., p. 83, *Sijjil*, vol. 270, p. 118, document 60: *Sijjil*, vol. 270, p. 118, 1204 *hijjra* (1789).

26. Cohen, Simon-Picaly, Salameh, *Jews*, pp. 111, 163.

27. *Sijjil* Jerusalem, vol. 267, p. 3, 1200 *hijjra* (1785).

28. A. Shihabi, *The History of Ahmad Pasha Al-Jazzar*, Beirut, no date (Arabic).

29. Manna, *Worthies*, pp. 104–8.

30. We do not posses confirmed information on the Husaynis in this context. But in the *sijjil*, the reference is to the *A'ayans* who were headed by the Husaynis. See al-Jabarti, *The Wonders*, vol. 3, pp. 527–8.

31. *Sijjil* Jaffa, vol. 15, 1216 *hijjra* (al-Muharram 1801). I wish to thank Dr. Said Hassan for providing me with copies from the *sijjil*.

32. A. al-Awda, *The History of Suleyman Pasha the Noble*, Tyre 1936, pp. 77, 88–9 (Arabic).

33. *Sijjil* Jaffa, vol. 5, 1219 *hijjra* (Safar 1804).

34. *Sijjil* Jaffa, vol. 29, 1219 *hijjra* (Rajab 1804).

35. Al-Awda, *The History*, p. 83.

36. L. M. al-Yassui, *The History of Syria and Lebanon, 1782–1841*, Beirut 1912, p. 20 (Arabic).

37. Al-Asali, *Documents*, vol. 3, p. 38, document 25; *Sijjil* Jerusalem, vol. 293, p. 210, 1224 *hijjra* (1809).

38. On al-Kanj's camp see al-Arif, *Jerusalem*, p. 309.

39. R. Curzon, *Visits to Monasteries in the Levant*, London 1851.

40. Al-Asali, *Documents*, p. 37, document 22; *Sijjil* Jerusalem, vol. 293, p. 210, 1224 *hijjra* (1809).

41. This account of Tahir's piety is derived from a fusion of what can be found on him in Abu-Manneh, *The Husaynis*, and the travelogues collected in al-Asali, *Jerusalem*.

## Chapter Two

1. Abu-Manneh, *The Husaynis*, p. 23, note 13.

2. Abu Nabut's revolt is described in R. A. S. Macalister and E. W. G. Master-man, 'Occasional Papers on the Modern Inhabitants of Palestine', *The Palestine Exploration Fund Quarterly* (1906), pp. 34–6. On al-Jazzar's heirs, see al-Nimr, *The History*, vol. 1; al-Awda, *The History*; F. A. Chateaubriand, *Itinéraire de Paris à Jérusalem*, Paris 1811; and J. Crane, *Letters from the East*, New York 1996, p. 126.

3. G. Baer, 'Jerusalem's Families of Notables and the Waqf in the Early 19th Century', in D. Kushner (ed.), *Palestine*, ibid., and B. Abu-Mannah 'Jerusalem in the Tanzimat Period, the New Ottoman Administration and the Notables', *Die Welt des Islams*, 30 (1990).

4. Al-Awda, *The History*, pp. 202–97.

5. Manna, *Worthies*, pp. 113–6.

6. This description appears in her husband's book; see G. Belzoni, *Narrative of the Operations and Recent Discoveries in Egypt*, London 1882, p. 285.

7. Al-Arif, *Jerusalem*, p. 127. For a general article on the period, see Mordechai Abir, 'Local Leadership and Early Reforms in Palestine, 1800–1834' in Moshe Maoz

(ed.), *Studies on Palestine in the Ottoman Period*, Magnes: Jersualem 1975, pp. 20–35.

8. Khoury, *The Missionary*, pp. 182–4.

9. Manna, *Worthies*, ibid.

10. S. N. Spyridon (ed.), *Annals of Palestine, 1821–1841: Manuscript of Monk Neophytos of Cyprus*, Jerusalem 1938, pp. 674–83.

11. Al-Arif, *Concise History*, p. 197.

12. B. Kimmerling and J. S. Migdal, *Palestinians: The Making of a People*, New York 1993, pp. 3–36.

13. Al-Dabagh, *The History*, vol. 10, part 2, p. 15.

14. Salibi and Khoury, *The Missionary*, vol. 1, pp. 395–7.

15. Al-Arif, *Jerusalem*, p. 359.

16. On the debt owed to Abdullah in 1824, see S. N. Spyridon (ed.), *Annals of Palestine, 1821–1841; Manuscript of Monk Neophytos of Cyprus*, Jerusalem 1938, pp. 674–83.

17. Salibi and Khoury, *The Missionary*, p. 396.

18. Al-Arif, *Jerusalem*, p. 109.

19. We assume that Abd al-Samad carried the letter, but we do not know for sure. Also its content has been surmised from other sources.

20. Y. Schwartz, *The Harvest*, London 1845, pp. 450–1 (Hebrew).

21. Based on al-Arif, *Jerusalem*, p. 277. With him came 40,000 soldiers.

22. L. M. Salem, *The Egyptian Rule in Syria, 1831–1841*, Cairo 1989. This book by an Egyptian scholar includes many documents from Dar al-Watha'iq, the Egyptian archive. This document is from file 56, vol. 1 (al-Sham), correspondence 6, Rajjab 1247 *hijjra* (1831), p. 248, note 20. It appeared in the British Public Record, FO 78/803, Finn to London, 19 May 1949. On the issue of Hussein Abd al-Hadi's to Ibrahim, see Schwartz, *The Harvest*.

23. On Ibrahim's visit with the *mufti* in the Holy Sepulchre, see Spyridon, *Annals*, pp. 87–8.

24. R. Asad, *The Egyptian Royal Archives*, Cairo 1946, vol. 2, p. 391 (Arabic).

25. Al-Arif, *Jerusalem*, p. 280.

26. Asad, *The Egyptian*, vol. 1, p. 724.

27. Ibid., vol. 2, p. 233, puts Tahir's signature on the document. On the peasants' revolt in the days of Muhammad Ali, see A. Kinglake, *Eothen*, London 1845. On the revolt in Egypt in 1834, see al-Arif, *Jerusalem*, p. 112. On the letter captured by Muhammad Ali and according to which the sultan planned to attack him, see S. J. Shaw, *Between Old and New: The Ottoman Empire Under Sultan Selim 3, 1789–1807*, Cambridge 1971, pp. 32–3.

28. Abu-Manneh, *Jerusalem*, p. 6; Finn, *Stirring*, vol. 2, pp. 188–9.

29. Q. Pasha al-Muhis edited an anonymous memoir, *Historical Memoirs* (Harisa Lebanon, no date), p. 95; the information was also drawn from a series of lectures given at the University of Damascus, which were published in A. Ghariba, *Syria in the 19th Century, 1840–1876*, Damascus 1969 (Arabic).

30. Another anonymous writer composed 'The Wars of Ibrahim Pasha', vol. 2, p. 38.
31. Asad, *The Egyptian*, vol. 2, pp. 191–391.
32. Kimmerling and Migdal, *Palestinians*, and S. Abu Izz al-Din, *Ibrahim Pasha in Syria*, Beirut 1929, p. 169.
33. Kimmerling and Migdal, ibid.
34. Al-Arif, *Jerusalem*, p. 113.
35. Abu Izz al-Din, *Ibrahim*, pp. 173–4.
36. Al-Arif, *Jerusalem*, p. 114.
37. A. Paton, *History of the Egyptian Revolution*, London 1870.
38. 'The Wars of Ibrahim', vol. 2, pp. 100–1.
39. Asad, *The Egyptian*, vol. 2, pp. 404–24.
40. Abu Izz al-Din, *Ibrahim*, p. 174.
41. On Tahir's connections with al-Azhar, see A. Manna, 'Cultural Relations between Egyptian and Jerusalem "Ulema" in the Early Nineteenth Century' in G. Gilbar and G. Warburg (eds), *Studies in Islamic Society*, Haifa 1974, p. 141.
42. Asad, *The Egyptian*, vol. 2, file 188.1, quoted on p. 9.
43. Ibid., vol. 3, p. 230.
44. Ibid., vol. 4, pp. 294–309.
45. Ibid., vol. 4, p. 336, file 330.2.
46. Al-Arif, *Jerusalem*, p. 116.
47. As comes out from the description in M. al-Abadi, *Foreigners on Our Land*, Amman 1947 (Arabic), and in Z. Gorgi, *The Famous Personalities of the East in the 19th Century*, Cairo, no date, vol. 2, p. 52 (Arabic).
48. Abu-Manneh, *Jerusalem*, p. 2, note 6.

## Chapter Three

1. Abu-Manneh, *Jerusalem*, p. 2, note 6; al-Arif, *Jerusalem*, p. 119.
2. Al-Arif, *Jerusalem*, p. 118.
3. B. Lewis, *The Emergence of Modern Turkey*, Princeton 1961, p. 95.
4. B. Abu-Manneh, 'The Rise of the Sanjak of Jerusalem in the Late 19th Century' in I. Pappé (ed.), *The Israel/Palestine Question*, London and New York 1999, p. 43, note 13.
5. The discussion is in Abu-Manneh, ibid.
6. M. Russel, *Palestine*, London 1834, pp. 17–8.
7. B. Anderson, *Imagined Communities*, London 1991, pp. 1–9.
8. Al-Dabagh, *The History*, vol. 10, p. 35.
9. Adel Manna relies on documents of the al-Khalidi family; see Manna, *Worthies*, pp. 141–2.
10. Manna, *Worthies*, p. 118; Abu-Manneh, *Jerusalem*, pp. 19–20; PRO, FO 78/540, Consul Young to Consul Rose in Beirut, 15 July 1843, 4 August 1843 and 2 October 1843; PRO, FO 78/625, Consul Young to London, 21 April 1844.
11. Manna, ibid., p. 115.

12. Ibid., p. 112.

13. Ibid., p. 118.

14. Abu-Manneh, *Jerusalem*, p. 22.

15. Y. Porath, *The Emergence of the Palestinian National Movement, 1918–1929*, Tel Aviv 1976, pp. 1–17 (Hebrew).

16. PRO, FO 78/839, Jerusalem to London, 27 September 1850.

17. Abu-Manneh, *Jerusalem*, p. 30, note 141.

18. PRO, FO 78/839, Finn to London, 13 September 1848.

19. Z. al-Peleg, *The Grand Mufti*, Tel Aviv 1989, p. 8 (Hebrew).

20. Spirydon, *Annals*, p. 124.

21. PRO, FO 78/874, Jerusalem to London, 15 July 1851.

22. Kimmerling and Migdal, *Palestinians*, pp. 36–64; see PRO, FO 78/755, Finn to London, 5 February 1848.

23. Al-Arif, *The Concise*, p. 259.

24. Al-Arif, *Jerusalem*, p. 119.

25. S. Landman, *The Jerusalem Notables' Neighborhoods Outside the Wall in the 19th Century*, Jerusalem 1984, pp. 66–8 (Arabic).

26. Al-Dabagh, *The History*, part 2, vol. 10, p. 210.

27. Landman, *The Jerusalem*, p. 17; Abu-Manneh, *Jerusalem*, p. 3, note 12.

28. *Ha-Magid*, July 1860, p. 116 (Hebrew).

29. Manna, *Worthies*, p. 119.

30. On clashes with Europeans, see A. Scholch, 'European Penetration and the Economic Development of Palestine, 1856–1872' in R. Owen (ed.), *Studies in the Economic and Social History of Palestine in the Nineteenth and Twentieth Centuries*, Oxford 1982, pp. 10–87, and A. Scholch, *Palestine in Transformation, 1856–1882*, Washington 1993.

31. A. Droyanov (ed.), *Letters on the History of the Love of Zion and the Settlement of the Palestine*, Odessa 1919, part 1, chapter five (Hebrew).

32. A. Hourani, 'Ottoman Reform and the Politics of Notables', in W. R. Polk and R. L. Chambers (eds), *Beginnings of Modernization in the Middle East: The Nineteenth Century*, Chicago 1968, p. 52.

## Chapter 4

1. A. Hourani, 'Ottoman Reform and the Politics of Notables', in W. R. Polk and R. L. Chambers (eds), *Beginnings of Modernization in the Middle East: The Nineteenth Century*, Chicago 1968, p. 52.

2. Uthman Taba', *The Strong Men of Gaza*, part 1 (Arabic). This manuscript is in the Jerusalem Shari'a court and is quoted in part in Manna, *Worthies*, p. 119.

3. D. Kushner, 'The "Foreign Relations" of the Governors of Jerusalem Toward the End of the Ottoman Period', in D. Kushner (ed.), *Palestine in the Late Ottoman Period*, Jerusalem 1986, p. 316, note 32.

4. See Rokah's letter to Pinsker, 24 Nissan [Hebrew Calendar] 1886, in Droyanov, *Letters*, part one, pp. 768–70.

5. H. Spoer, 'Das Nabi Musa Fest', *Zeitschrift der Deutshen Palestine-Vereins*, vol. 32 (1909), p. 215.
6. Ibid.
7. Al-Arif, *Jerusalem*, vol. 4, p. 224.
8. Doryanov, *Letters*.
9. I. M. al-Husayni, *Abd al-Latif al-Husseini's Treasure*, Jerusalem 1985, the introduction (Arabic).
10. M. I. Darwazza, *Memories and Notes: One Hundred Palestinian Years*, Damascus 1986, vol. 1, p. 109 (Arabic).
11. This information was collected by Dr. Mazen Qatatu from the family's women for this research in the year 1994.
12. Landman, *The Jerusalem*, p. 90.
13. Al-Dabagh, *The History*, part 2, vol. 10, p. 210.
14. Y. Shiryon, *Memoirs*, Jerusalem 1943, p. 177 (Hebrew).
15. Manna, *Worthies*, p. 120, based on an interview by the author with Ishaq Musa al-Husayni.
16. R. Karak and M. Oren-Nordheim, *Jerusalem and Its Environs*, Jerusalem 1993, p. 274 (Hebrew).
17. Ibid., p. 163.
18. Ibid., p. 114.
19. S. al-Khalidi, *Visits in al-Sham*, Jerusalem 1946, p. 107 (Arabic).
20. Landman, *The Jerusalem*, p. 8.
21. Karak and Oren-Nordheim, *Jerusalem*, pp. 120–9, and Ben-Aryeh, *Palestine*, p. 476.
22. Darwazza, *Memories*, vol. 1, p. 47.
23. Al-Qayatli did not mention in which year he visited the city, but he did visit more than once. But as he mentions Mustafa al-Husayni it must have been around 1890 to 1893. See M. A. al-Qayatli, *The Flavors of al-Sham in the Al-Sham Travelogues*, Beirut 1981, pp. 96–7 (Arabic); Al-Arif, *Concise*, p. 308.
24. J. Qatul, *The Education in Palestine*, Jerusalem 1974, part 1 (Arabic).
25. R. Khalidi, *Palestinian Identity*, Berkeley 1997, p. 69.
26. Karak-Oren Nordheim, *Jerusalem*, pp. 120–9.
27. B. Spafford Vester, *Our Family in the Holy City: 1881–1949*, Jerusalem 1950, pp. 192–4; S. Mardin, 'Religion and Secularism in Turkey' in A. Hourani, P. S. Khoury and M. C. Wilson (eds), *The Modern Middle East*, London 1993, pp. 347–74.
28. Spafford Vester, *Our Family*, p. 179.
29. According to 'The Report of the Ottoman Education Ministry' of 1898, pp. 1,246–9, there were five classes. The report is brought in full in al-Dabagh, *The History*, part 2, chapter 10, p. 135.
30. Y. Al-Hakim, *Syria in the Ottoman Period*, Damascus 1950, pp. 190–201 (Arabic).
31. This was in fact reported in *Al-Hilal*, vol. 22 (1913–14), pp. 1, 603–5 (Arabic).

32. A. Yelin, *The Memoirs of a Jerusalemite*, Jerusalem 1924, pp. 172–3 (Hebrew).
33. From A. al-Aswad, *The Imperial Visit to the Ottoman Empire*, B'abada 1898 (Arabic).
34. Ibid., p. 113.
35. Ben-Aryeh, *Palestine*, p. 481.
36. Al-Aswad, *The Imperial*, p. 129.
37. Spafford Vester, *Our Family*, pp. 246–7.
38. Porath, *The Emergence*, p. 11.
39. Mattar, *The Mufti*, p. 46.
40. A. Yaari, *Memories of Palestine*, Ramat Gan 1974, part 1, pp. 198–203 (Hebrew).
41. A. al-Husayni, *Diwan Shi'r*, Anthology of Poems: a manuscript in al-Aqsa without a date (Arabic).
42. Porath, *Hajj Amin*, p. 226.
43. Ibid., note 11.
44. Y. Porath, 'Social Aspects of the Emergence of the Palestinian National Movement' in M. Milson (ed.), *Society and Regime in the Arab World*, Jerusalem 1977, p. 13 (Hebrew).
45. J. McCarthy, *The Population of Palestine*, New York 1988, pp. 7, 15.
46. PRO, FO 78/5285, Dickson to London, 14 November 1903.
47. Al-Dabagh, *The History*, part 2, vol. 10, p. 49.
48. I. Agmon, 'Foreign Trade as a Transforming Factor in the Arab Economy in Palestine, 1897–1914, *Cathedra* 41 (1986), pp. 107–32 (Hebrew).
49. N. Gross, 'Economic Reforms in Palestine at the End of the Ottoman Period', *Cathedra* 2 (1977), pp. 102–25 (Hebrew).
50. Al-Arif, *Jerusalem*, p. 125.
51. A. Hyamson, *The British Consulate in Palestine*, London 1940, part 2, p. 461.
52. Landman, *The Jerusalem*, p. 68.
53. Central Zionist Archives, S/25, File 2911, Sokolov to Kish, London, 19 June 1930.
54. See 'The Wailing Wall Trial, The Report of the International Wailing Wall Committee' (Tel Aviv, 1931), p. 40, quoted in Ben-Aryeh, *Palestine*, p. 420.
55. Y. Yehoshua, *The History of the Arabic Press in Palestine: The Ottoman Period, 1908–1918*, Jerusalem 1974, p. 10 (Arabic).
56. PRO, FO 78/5497, Beirut to Istanbul, 12 January 1901.
57. For a discussion, see in I. Pappé, 'Understanding the Enemy: A Comparative Analysis of Palestinian Islamist and Nationalist Leaflets, 1920s–1980s' in R. L. Nettler and S. Taji-Farouki (eds), *Muslim-Jewish Encounters: Intellectual Traditions and Modern Politics*, Amsterdam 1996, pp. 223–63.
58. From *Al-Muqtataf al-Mufida*, part 4, issue 22, April 1897, Gaza (Arabic).
59. Appeared in *Al-Manar*, vol. 1, issue 6, no date, pp. 107–8 (Arabic).
60. *Al-Manar*, vol. 1, issue 41, p. 810.

61. M. Asaf, *Arab-Jewish Relations in Palestine, 1860–1948*, Tel Aviv 1970, p. 52, note 243 (Hebrew); Manna, *Worthies*, p. 131.

62. Ibid., p. 76, note 401.

63. Mattar, *The Mufti*, p. 14.

64. PRO, FO 78/5353, Jerusalem to London, July 1904, three letters.

65. Yehoshua, *The History*, p. 10; Manna, *Worthies*, p. 129; T. Jabara, *Studies in the Modern History of Palestine*, Jerusalem 1986, p. 33 (Arabic).

66. Central Zionist Archives, W/125, a letter from Hussein al-Husayni to the president of the Anglo-Palestine Society in London, 10 February 1905.

67. H. Ram, *The Jewish Community in Jaffa*, Jerusalem 1996, p. 168 (Hebrew).

68. H. Hamburger, *Three Worlds,* Jerusalem 1946, p. 74 (Hebrew).

69. *Al-Manar*, vol. 1, issue 3, April 1897–April 1898, p. 88, and also vol. 1, issue 17, pp. 312–3.

70. Abu-Manneh, *Jerusalem,* p. 25.

71. See A. C. Inchbold, *Under the Syrian Sun*, London 1906, pp. 412–35. A note on the reconstruction: according to their date of birth this could be valid for Jamal as well as for Amin, and maybe Inchbold was in someone else's celebration. According to the testimony of Amina al-Husayni, such were the rites in her family and this why we used this description as an archetype.

72. Darwazza, *Memories*, part 1, pp. 114–7.

73. Manna, *Worthies*, p. 131.

74. An interview with Haidar al-Husayni, Amin's aide, conducted by Philip Mattar; see Mattar, *The Mufti*, p. 7, note 26.

75. S. Graham-Brown, *Palestinians and their Society, 1880–1946*, London 1980, picture 154, pp. 29–30.

76. Ibid., picture 17, p. 17.

77. See Rokah's letter to Pinsker, 24 Nissan [Hebrew Calendar] 1886, in Doryanov, *Letters*, part one, pp. 768–70.

## *Chapter 5*

1. S. Hanioglu, 'The Young Turks and the Arabs Before the Revolution of 1908' in R. Khalidi et al. (eds), *The Origins of Arab Nationalism*, New York 1991, pp. 31–49.

2. Ibid.

3. Lewis, *Emergence*, p. 170.

4. I. Tannus, *The Palestinians: A Glorious Past and a Wonderful Future*, Beirut 1982, pp. 22–3 (Arabic).

5. Darwazza, *Memories*, p. 174. Muhamad Izzat Darwazza was born in Nablus to a middle-class family. Although he never graduated, he was well educated and learned. Some of the information here is taken from an interview with Darwazza in G. Abu Ghazzala, *The National Culture in Palestine During the British Mandate*, Beirut, no date, p. 37 (Arabic).

6. W. al-Khalidi, *Before the Diaspora: A Photographic History of the Palestinian People, 1876–1948*, Beirut 1987, pictures 6 and 7 (Arabic).

7. Darwazza testified that he loved reading papers; see Darwazza, *Memories*, vol. 1, p. 172.

8. Ibid., p. 171.

9. *Filastin*, third year, 26 November 1916.

10. A. al-Said, *The Great Arab Revolt*, Beirut, no date, vol. 1, pp. 7–6 (Arabic); A. Nuhayd, 'A Man in Palestine: Khalil al-Sakakini', *Filastin* 17 July 1995 (Arabic).

11. H. al-Sakakini, *This Is Me, Gentlemen*, Jerusalem 1990, diary entry: 12 November 1908 (Arabic).

12. Manna, *Worthies*, p. 127.

13. Darwazza, *Memories*, vol. 1, pp. 174–6.

14. K. al-Sakakini, *This Is Me, Oh World!*, Jerusalem, 1955, pp. 33–4 (Arabic).

15. Darwazza, *Memories*, p. 174.

16. Hanioglu, *The Young*, pp. 174–7.

17. Porath, *The Emergence*, p. 17.

18. *Filastin*, 4 May 1912.

19. Jabbara, *Studies*, p. 38.

20. *Al-Karmil*, vol. 19, issue 336, September 1913, p. 1.

21. Based on family material edited by Manna. See Manna, *Worthies*, p. 124.

22. Khalidi, *Palestinian*, p. 296.

23. *Al-Karmil*, vol. 186, third year, 18 October 1912.

24. Darwazza, *Memories*, p. 181.

25. See the appendix in B. N. al-Hut, *The Political Leaderships and Institutions in Palestine, 1917–1948*, Beirut 1981, p. 849 (Arabic).

26. Z. Mardini, *Palestine and Hajj Amin al-Husseini*, Beirut 1986, p. 28 (Arabic).

27. I. M. al-Husayni, *I Learned from the People*, Jerusalem 1968, p. 6 (Arabic).

28. Tannus, *The Palestinians*, p. 54.

29. Among them, 'The Captain's Daughter' by Pushkin was published in *Al-Manar* in 1898. *Anna Karenina* by Tolstoy that was published in *Al-Nafais*. His most famous book was *Al-Warith (The Inheritor)*, which was published in *Al-Nafais al-Asriyya*, forth year, and in 1921 appeared as a book printed by a Jerusalemite publisher.

30. Al-Sakakini, *This Is*, 21 September.

31. *Manjala* in Arabic, a pincher holding the coal for *nargilehs* and heating the water. This description was taken from Inchbold, *Under*, p. 213.

32. R. Memimel, *The Remedy of My People*, Berlin 1883 (Hebrew).

33. Asaf, *Arab-Jewish*, p. 62.

34. Y. Lamdan, 'The Arabs and Zionism, 1882–1914' in Y. Kolat (ed.), *The History of the Jewish Settlement in Palestine since the First Aliya*', Jerusalem 1990, p. 233 (Hebrew).

35. R. Hichens, *The Holy Land*, London 1910, pp. 260–76.

36. Al-Dabagh, *The History*, p. 151.
37. M. H. Mansa, *The History of the Modern Arab East*, Beirut 1976, p. 150 (Arabic).
38. Darwazza, *Memories*, p. 188.
39. On 15 March 1911, *Al-Ahram* wrote on the connection between Jawdat Pasha and a French bank concerning the sale of land for Jewish owners. On 7 February 1913, *Al-Ahram* told its readers that the French-language paper *The Young Turks* was owned by the Jewish minister in charge of public affairs.
40. Lamdan, *The Arabs*, p. 231.
41. M. J. Mandel, *The Arabs and Zionism Before WWI*, Berkeley 1976, p. 112.
42. Porath, *The Emergence*, p. 19.
43. Al-Hut, *The Political*, p. 20.
44. Lamdan, *The Arabs*, p. 248.
45. H. Winner, 'The Zionist Policy in Turkey until 1914' in Y. Kolat (ed.), *The History of the Jewish Settlement in Palestine since the First Aliya*', Jerusalem 1990, p. 338 (Hebrew).
46. Y. Yehoshua, *The Fruit of Jerusalem*, Jerusalem 1974, vol. 3, appendix on p. 128 indicates that the original document is to be found in the national library in the Hebrew University, Jerusalem (Hebrew).
47. On 9 and 10 April 1914, *Al-Ahram* reported the birth of Abd al-Qadir; see K. H. Muhsin, *The Mother Palestine and her Noble Son Abd al-Qadir al-Husseini*, Amman 1986, p. 135 (Arabic).
48. K. A. Salwadi, *Dr Ishaq Musa al-Husseini*, Jerusalem 1991, p. 35 (Arabic).
49. Al-Husayni, *I Learned*, p. 30.
50. Darwazza, *Memories*, vol. 1, p. 128.
51. Tannus, *The Palestinians*, pp. 14–7.
52. Amin al-Husayni's file in the Central Zionist Archives, file 104999 in S25.
53. A. Rupin, *My Life*, Tel Aviv 1968, vol. 2, pp. 164–5 (Hebrew).
54. Y. al-Awdat, *Palestine's Thinkers and Authors*, Amman 1976, p. 109 (Arabic); for an interview by Philip Mattar with Zaynab al-Husayni, Amin's daughter, see Mattar, *The Mufti*, p. 10, note 30.
55. Izzat Tanus, *The Palestinians*, p. 28.
56. Ibid.
57. Ibid., p. 31.
58. Jamal's memoirs are quoted in Tannus, *The Palestinians*, p. 218.
59. A. Palmer, *The Decline and Fall of the Ottomans*, London 1992, p. 234.
60. Al-Sakakini, *Diary*, 28 September 1914.
61. G. Antonius, *The Arab Awakening*, London 1961, pp. 178–200.
62. Mattar, *The Mufti*, p. 11, note 14.
63. Al-Peleg, *The Mufti*, p. 9.
64. P. Kahanov, 'The Jerusalem Trade Fifty Years Ago', *From Early Days*, 1 (1935), p. 142 (Hebrew).
65. Al-Awdat, *Palestine*.

66. Tannus, *The Palestinians*, pp. 212–4; Al-Peleg, *The Mufti*, p. 9.
67. *Filastin*, 15 May 1914, quoted in Y. Lunz, 'The Sources and Origins of the Palestinian National Movement on the Eve of the First World War' in M. Maoz and B. Z. Kedar (eds), *The Palestinian National Movement: From Confrontation to Reconciliation?*, Tel Aviv 1996, p. 35 (Hebrew).
68. Jamal's memoirs as they are quoted in Tannus, *The Palestinians*, p. 218.
69. *Filastin*, 24 May 1913; Tannus, *The Palestinians*, pp. 258–9; and P. Brockelman, *Geschichte der Arabischen Litteratur*, vol. 3, Leiden 1970, p. 431.
70. T. A. Baru, *The Arabs and the Turks in the Constitutional Ottoman Era*, Cairo 1960, pp. 310–8 (Arabic).
71. George Antonius claims that young al-Hajj Amin played a crucial role in recruiting volunteers to the Arab revolt and that their numbers reached a few thousand. Dawn disagrees about the number. See the debate in Porath, *The Emergence*, p. 61. On Lloyd George, see D. Lloyd George, *The Truth About the Peace Treaties*, London 1938, pp. 1,027–40.
72. Mattar, *The Mufti*, p. 6.
73. The tale of Baydas's escape is described in al-Awdat. The description of Said al-Husayni's house is based on Landman, *The Arabs*, pp. 35–6. The rest of the descriptions are from al-Hut, *The Political*, p. 63.
74. Tannus, *The Palestinians*, p. 48.
75. Al-Sakakini, *Diary*, 2 February until 15 March 1915.
76. Tannus, *The Palestinians*, p. 54

## Chapter 6

1. See P. Wavell, *The Palestine Campaigns*, London 1927, pp. 165–7.
2. The surrender is described in several sources. Izzat Tannus received the letter of surrender from Bishop Najib Qabain, who kept it after receiving it from Michail Abu Khatum in Jerusalem in December 1918. See Tannus, *The Palestinians*, p. 50.
3. E. al-Ghori, *Palestine During Sixty Years*, Beirut 1973, vol. 1, pp. 25–7 (Arabic).
4. This description of the people in the delegation was reconstructed with the help of a picture that appears in several sources. But only one book includes detailed information about them: N. al-Nashashibi, *The Last Giant Came from Jerusalem: The Story of the Palestinian Leader Nasr al-Din al-Nashashibi*, Jerusalem 1986, picture on p. 31 (Arabic). The tale on the two sergeants appears in several sources: al-Hut, *The Political*, p. 64; Khoury, *The Modern*, pp. 283–4; in British sources, it appears in Wavell, ibid., p. 66. See also T. Canan, 'Two Documents on the Surrender of Jerusalem', *Journal of the Palestine Oriental Society*, 10 (1930), p. 27.
5. Newton, *Fifty*, p. 120.
6. The description of Allenby's entrance into Jerusalem was reconstructed with the help of al-Hut, *The Political*; Wavell, *The Palestine*; and pictures 15 and 16 from Walid Khalidi's album (see al-Khalidi, *Before*, 1987).

7. The archbishop's speech appears in Newton, *Fifty*, p. 109. It is possible that the sentence about ending the crusaders' era was not said, as it appears in an unreliable source.

8. The description of the first meeting between Hussein and Kamil appears in R. Storrs, *Orientations*, London 1938, pp. 278–90. On Kamil's attitude towards the British, see Porath, *The Emergence*, p. 61. The Arab Office's memo on the Husaynis is mentioned in B. Wasserstein, *The British in Palestine: The Mandatory Government and the Arab-Jewish Conflict, 1917–1929*, London 1979, p. 15, note 57.

9. This description is based on sources mentioned in the previous note.

10. On the significance of passing so many posts to Kamil, see Porath, *Al-Hajj*, p. 227, note 16.

11. Karak and Oren-Nordheim, *Jerusalem*, p. 273.

12. The theory that Faysal was not the actual conqueror of Damascus was developed by Elie Kedourie, *The Chatham Version and Other Middle Eastern Studies*, New York 1984, pp. 33–51.

13. The remark on the nonprofessional members can be found in N. Ziyaddah, 'Ishaq Musa al-Husayni', *Majalat al-Dirassat al-Filastiniyya*, vol. 9 (1992) (Arabic).

14. The pieces on the military rule are based on Emery Papers, Private Papers Collection, The Middle East Centre, St Antony's College, Oxford, box 1, file 1.

15. On the significance of the 8 November 1918 declaration, see Porath, *Al-Hajj*, p. 223.

16. Kamil's first meeting with Ussishkin is described in I. al-Sifari, *Arab Palestine Between the Mandate and Zionism*, Jaffa 1937, vol. 1, p. 29 (Arabic).

17. Y. Eilam, 'The Political History, 1918–1922' in M. Lissak (ed.), *The History of the Jewish Community in Palestine Since the First Aliya*', Jerusalem 1984, p. 148 (Hebrew).

18. Al-Peleg, *The Mufti*, p. 10.

19. Porath, *The Emergence*, pp. 104–5.

20. The description of the various Palestinian organizations and their preparations for the first conference is based on al-Hut, *The Political*, pp. 87–100 (which is in turn based on an interview with al-Hajj Amin al-Husayni and the private collection of Akram Zuaytar); Porath, *The Emergence*, pp. 56–110; al-Sakakini, *Diary*, 2 February to 15 March 1915.

21. Z. Al-Peleg, *From the Mufti's Point of View*, Tel Aviv 1995, p. 10 (Hebrew).

22. Al-Said, *The Great*, pp. 35–7.

23. The protest telegram of the first Palestinian Congress against the intention of making Palestine a Jewish national homeland was sent to the Paris Peace Conference on 3 February 1919 and appears in al-Kayali, *The Documents of the Arab Palestinian Resistance, 1918–1939*, Beirut 1988, document 2 (Arabic).

24. The suspicion that Storrs contributed to the agitation is mentioned in al-Sakakini, *Diary*, 22 March 1919.

25. This chronicle of the King-Crane Commission is based on al-Hut, *The Political*, pp. 110–1; Antonius, *The Arab*, pp. 276–325.
26. On Zionist activity at Versailles, see C. Weizmann, *Trail and Error*, New York 1949, pp. 240–52.
27. On the appointment of Palestinians in the Faysal government, see al-Said, *The Great*, pp. 35–7.
28. S. Schama, *The House of Rothschild and Palestine*, Jerusalem 1980, p. 166.
29. Ibid., p. 256.
30. Al-Sakakini, *Diary*, 4 April 1919.
31. Antonius, *The Arab*, pp. 149–64.
32. Ibid.
33. The description of Clemenceau's meeting with Lloyd George in Deauville is taken from Z. N. Zeine, *The Struggle for Arab Independence*, Beirut 1960, pp. 85–107.
34. This is based on Philip Mattar's interview with a member of the Nashashibi's family; Mattar, *The Mufti*, p. 10, note 40.
35. Porath, *The Emergence*, p. 43.
36. I. M. al-Husayni, *The Doyen of the Arabic Language: Muhammad Isaf al-Nashashibi*, Jerusalem 1987, p. 55 (Arabic).
37. I. M. al-Husayni, *I Learned*, p. 16.

## Chapter 7

1. Among other sources, I learned about the severe winter and early spring from pictures in S. Graham-Brown, *Palestinians and their Society, 1880–1946*, London 1980. All McCracken's reports, including the photos, appear in W. D. McCracken, *The New Palestine*, Boston 1922, pp. 227–23.
2. McCracken, ibid.
3. Ibid.
4. The welfare organization of Madam Jamal al-Husayni is mentioned in M. E. T. Mogannam, *The Arab Woman and the Palestine Problem*, London 1936, p. 76.
5. On Kamil's participation in the ceremony, see Asaf, *Arab-Jewish*, p. 84.
6. On Said in Damascus, see al-Dabagh, *The History*, part 2, vol. 10, p. 381. The call for a peaceful demonstration against Zionism appeared in the paper *Mirat al-Sharq*, 10 March 1920.
7. On Jamil al-Husayni's and Arif al-Arif's objections to exploiting the Nabi Musa feast for a political protest, see Porath, *The Emergence*, pp. 71, 81.
8. Storrs, *Orientations*, pp. 350–400.
9. The story of the theft appears in Storrs, ibid., p. 400.
10. On the history of the Nabi Musa festival, see K. G. al-Asali, *Nabi Musa*, Jerusalem 1981 (Arabic); al-Peleg, *The Mufti*, p. 12, note 13. The festival's description appears in Y. Drori, 'The Origins of Nabi Musa', *Sali't*, vol. 1/5 (1972), pp. 203–8 (Hebrew). For the pictures and description in Walid Khalidi's album,

see al-Khalidi, *Before*, picture 58 and onwards; for Graham-Brown's album, see Graham-Brown, *Palestinians*, pictures on p. 139.

11. The description of March and April 1920 is taken from Israeli documents found in the Central Zionist Archives, 3/L, file 222, an intelligence report, and the Palin Report in PRO, FO 371/5121, E9379, p. 4.

12. Whittingham's report appears in G. N. Whittingham, *The Home of Fadeless Splendor*, London, no date, pp. 183–213.

13. All of Adamson's observations are in an Easter report he wrote in 1920, found in his private collection: Private Papers Collection, Middle East Centre, St Antony's College, Oxford.

14. Ibid.

15. Storrs, *Orientations*, 1938.

16. See Khalil al-Baydas's speech in Awdat, *Thinkers*.

17. The bluntest accusation of Jabotnisky's involvement is found in Newton, *Fifty*, p. 134.

18. Whittingham, *The Home*.

19. The reports of the American consul appear in G. Biger, 'The American Consulate in Jerusalem and the Events of 1920–1921', *Cathedra* 49 (September 1988), pp. 133–139 (Hebrew).

20. Izzat Tannus claimed that Musa Kazim was fired because he refused to declare Hebrew an official language in the county. This is also corroborated by Jewish sources from the period. See Tannus, *The Palestinians*, p. 100; Porath, *The Emergence*, p. 82.

21. On Storrs's response to Allenby's apology, see Storrs, *Orientations*, p. 332.

22. The Palin Commission was made up of Anglo-Egyptian officials; see Newton, *Fifty*, p. 134.

23. On Baydas's arrest, see Awdat, *Thinkers*. The manuscript of *Hadith al-Sajun* was not found until recently.

24. Al-Kayali, *The Documents*, pp. 147–8.

25. On the second conference, see al-Hut, *The Political*, p. 118; Porath, *The Emergence*, pp. 71–2.

26. On Kamil's attitude towards the British, see Porath, *Al-Hajj*, p. 227, note 15. On Kamil's encounters with Jewish leaders in February 1920, see Mattar, *The Mufti*, p. 16.

27. N. Rogel, 'Weizmann's Man in Damascus: The Case of Dr Moshe Palman's Mission to Faysal's Court, September 1919–July 1920', *Ziyonut* 9 (1983), p. 302 (Hebrew).

28. In Walid al-Khalidi's album, there is a photo of Allenby's arrival in Jaffa (picture 79) with details of how he was brought to Jerusalem. OTEA stands for 'Occupied Territory of Enemy Area'.

29. On the clash with Frumkin, see G. Frumkin, *The Way of a Judge in Jerusalem*, Jerusalem 1946, pp. 288–9 (Hebrew).

30. Ibid.

31. On Samuel's visit to al-Salt, see Mattar, *The Mufti*, pp. 20–1; J. B. Schechtman, *The Mufti and the Fuerher: The Rise of Haj Amin al-Husseini*, New York 1965, p. 1920.
32. Musa Kazim's speech to activists in July was added here following a conversation with family members. The citation is taken from the Central Zionist Archives, Z4, file 2800/2, report 138, 5 August 1920.
33. The reports of the American consul appear in G. Biger, 'The American Consulate in Jerusalem and the Events of 1920–1921', *Cathedra* 49 (September 1988), pp. 133–9 (Hebrew).
34. On the third conference, see al-Hut, *The Political*, p. 139. She bases her account on Akram Zuayter's private collection. See also Porath, *The Emergence*, pp. 86–8.
35. Mardini, *Palestine*, p. 51.
36. Porath, *Emergence*, p. 140.

## Chapter 8

1. Porath, *The Emergence*, p. 86.
2. Based on Mattar's interview with Ishaq Musa al-Husayni; see Mattar, *The Mufti*, p. 21, note 13. See also Karak and Oren-Nordheim, *Jerusalem*, p. 64.
3. S. Attiyeh, *The Arab Palestine Party and the National Defense Party, 1934–1937*, Jerusalem 1985, p. 74 (Arabic).
4. The archive of the Palestine government secretariat, file 245, a CID report on the secretary's assistant for political affairs, 23 March 1921.
5. Al-Peleg, *The Mufti*, p. 14.
6. S. Hamada, *The Consciousness and the Revolution: A Study in the Life of the Shahid Izz al-Din al-Qassam*, Jerusalem 1985, p. 133 (Arabic).
7. Al-Ghori, *Palestine*, vol. 1, p. 57.
8. *Mirat al-Sharq*, 27 November 1923; Tahir III's conversation with Yizhak Ben-Zvi, 2 April 1930, in the Central Zionist Archives, S/25, file 3006.
9. PRO, CO 733/3, CO 24596, report from 9 May 1920.
10. Ibid.
11. P. H. Kisch, *A Palestine Diary*, Jerusalem 1939, vol. 1, pp. 40–2.
12. Al-Hut, *The Political*, p. 118.
13. Izzat Darwaza, personal Diary quoted in Mattar, *The Mufti*, p. 27, note 27.
14. J. Laval, *Al-Hajj Amin and Berlin*, Tel Aviv 1996, p. 15 (Hebrew).
15. Al-Kayali, *The Documents*, p. 94.
16. Kedourie, *Chatham House*, pp. 64–5. I wish to thank Daniel Monk for the documents and references.
17. Ibid.
18. Porath, *The Emergence*, pp. 153–4.
19. The Peel Report, p. 117.
20. The Israeli State Archives, Files of the Mandatory Government's Secretariat, file 245, Quingley to the secretary's assistant, 12 May 1921.
21. *Bait al-Muqadas*, 18 April 1921.

22. The Israeli State Archives, The Executive Committee Files, file 2700, Jamal al-Husayni to the High Commissioner, 27 August 1923.
23. Central Zionist Archives, S25, file 517, interview with Tahir III, 30 April 1925.
24. Interview with Amin al-Husayni.
25. 18 June 1921.
26. Porath, *The Emergence*, p. 51.
27. Centre for Arab Research, The Orient House Archive, document 177.
28. The Anglo-American Committee, pp. 900–1. See also S. Bar Elkana, 'The Rise of Hajj Amin to the Muslim Leadership in Palestine', in *Bar Ilan University's Year Book*, Ramat Gan 1972, pp. 37–83 (Hebrew).
29. Porath, *The Emergence*, pp. 159–61; Kimmerling and Migdal, *The Palestinians*, p. 85.
30. Al-Peleg, *The Mufti*, p. 19.
31. Porath, *The Emergence*, p. 164; Issa Khalil Muhsin's interview with Mahmoud Sad al-Din al-Husayni in 1983, Muhsin, *The Mother*, p. 139.
32. For a report on the Supreme Muslim Council, see PRO, CO 733/45, CO 26756, report 1922–23.
33. Porath, *The Emergence*, pp. 117–20; Muhsin, *The Mother*, p. 136.
34. Kedourie, *The Chatham*, pp. 75–7. See the Central Zionist Archives, Files of the Executive Committee, file 2480, Jamal al-Husayni to Musa Kazim al-Husayni, 5 August 1923.
35. P. Offer, 'The Crystallization of the Mandatory Regime and the Laying of Foundations to the Jewish National Home, 1921–1931', in M. Lissak (ed.), *The History*, p. 230.
36. *Mirat al-Sharq*, 27 June 1923; *Al-Karmil*, 5 July 1922.
37. N. Caplan, *Futile Diplomacy*, vol. 1, London 1983, p. 73.
38. Porath, *The Emergence*, pp. 189–92.
39. The Centre for Palestinian Research, file 220.
40. Darwaza, *Memories*, vol. 1, p. 46.
41. PRO, CO 733/68, Herbert Samuel to SoS for the Colonies, 23 May 1924.
42. PRO, CO 733/52, Political Report for November 1923, High Commissioner to SoS for the Colonies, 14 December 1923.
43. *Al-Karmil*, 19 July 1924.
44. F. Tuqan, *An Arduous Trip*, Acre 1985, pp. 28–9 (Arabic).
45. *Al-Karmil*, 6 February 1927; *Mirat al-Sharq*, 6 February 1927. See also Rubinstein, 'The Arab Question in the Aftermath of the 1929 Events and the Establishment of the Unified Board of the Jewish Community Institutions: Political Aspects', in I. Pappé (ed.), *Arabs and Jews in the Mandatory Era: A New Look at the Historical Research*, Givat Haviva 1992, p. 130 (Hebrew).
46. Quoted in *Haaretz*, 6 February 1927.
47. S. Dotan, *The Communist Party in Israel*, Kfar Saba 1991, p. 10 (Hebrew).
48. The Executive Committee's Protocol, J1/7229, July–August 1927.
49. P. Khoury, *Syria under the French Mandate*, Princeton 1987, p. 553.

50. The Egyptian paper *al-Hilal* provided an extended description of the visit.
51. Rubinstein, *The Arab,* pp. 65–102.
52. Photos from the inquiry commission, the Shaw Commission, Tel Aviv 1929.
53. PRO, CO 733/98, SoS to Clayton, 2 May 1918.
54. Pappé, *Understanding,* pp. 87–108.
55. Al-Hut, *The Political,* pp. 218–21.
56. *Davar,* 2 October 1925. See PRO, CO 733/163, Shucburgh to Chancellor of the Exchequer, 1 January 1929.
57. Most of the committee's publications appeared in Amin's paper *Al-Jamaa' al-Arabiyya;* see Porath, *The Emegence,* p. 214.
58. PRO, CO 733/160, Lock to Amery, 13 October 1928; *Davar,* 25–8 September 1928.
59. Mattar, *The Mufti,* pp. 35–7.
60. *Doar Ha-Yom,* 28 September 1928.
61. The Shaw Commission Report.
62. On Bentwich, see Pappé, *Understanding.*
63. Mattar, *The Mufti,* p. 37.
64. Al-Peleg, *The Mufti,* pp. 25–6.
65. Shaw Commission Report, general impression.
66. I. M. al-Husayni, *Facts,* Beirut 1956, p. 10 (Arabic).
67. Mattar, *The Mufti,* pp. 41–2.
68. B. Katinka, *From Then to Now,* Jerusalem 1961, pp. 255–63 (Hebrew).
69. Shaw Commission Report, general impression.
70. PRO, CO 733/163, High Commissioner to SoS for the Colonies, 10 May 1929.
71. Mattar, *The Mufti,* p. 46, notes 69 and 70.
72. The Shaw Commission, session 46, p. 94.
73. Ibid., session 31, p. 16.
74. The Israeli State Archives, 65/2804, report from 23 August 1929.
75. Al-Peleg, *The Mufti,* p. 27.
76. Porath, *The Emergence,* p. 218.

## Chapter 9

1. Attiyeh, *The Arab Palestinian,* p. 125.
2. Y. Reiter, 'The Supervision on Managing the Muslim Waqf Affairs in Jerusalem Since the Mandatory Period, (1918–1990)', *Ha-Mizarch Ha-Hadash,* 34 (1992), pp. 17–8 (Hebrew).
3. The Shaw Commission, session 46, p. 92.
4. Ibid., p. 103.
5. Ibid.
6. Kimmerling and Migdal, *The Palestinians,* p. 106.
7. An image from Darwaza, *Memories,* vol. 2, appendix. See Y. Porath, *From Riots to Revolt, 1929–1939,* Tel Aviv 1978, p. 39 (Hebrew).

8. Ibid.

9. *Al-Jamaa' al-Arabiyya*, 12 November 1931; S. Hamada, *The Consciousness*, p. 188.

10. The speech quoted in *Journal of the Central Asian Society*, vol. XVII (January 1910), pp. 93–8.

11. Portah, *From Riots*, p. 55.

12. Ibid., p. 20.

13. M. Kupferschmidt, 'The General Muslm Congress of 1931 in Jerusalem', *Asian and African Studies*, vol. 12 (1971), pp. 132–3.

14. PRO, CO 733/197, Interview of the High Commissioner with the Mufti, 5 October 1930.

15. Landman, *The Arabs*, p. 23.

16. M. Kramer, *Islam Assembled*, New York 1996, p. 126.

17. K. Qasmiyyeh, *The First Arab Pioneer: The Lives and Papers of Nabih and Adel al-Azma*, Damascus 1991, p. 209 (Arabic).

18. Al-Sifari, *Arab*, p. 178.

19. Porath, *Riots*, p. 26; Al-Peleg, *The Mufti*, p. 33.

20. Porath, ibid., p. 27.

21. Kramer, *Islam*, p. 127.

22. Khoury , *Syria*, pp. 539, 553.

23. Kramer, *Islam*, p. 132. On the biographer's embarrassment, see Muhsin, *The Mother*, p. 139.

24. Al-Peleg, *The Mufti*, p. 32.

25. A. H. Ghana'im, 'The Pan-Islamist Congress, 1931', *Shuun Filastiniyya*, 25 (September 1973), pp. 124–5 (Arabic).

26. The Shaw Commission.

27. Quoted in T. Mayer, 'Egypt and the General Islamic Conference of Jerusalem 1931', *Middle Eastern Studies*, 18/3 (1982), p. 311, note 46.

28. Kramer, *Islam*, p. 127.

29. According to an informant's report in Central Zionist Archives S25/3557.

30. Offer, *The Crystallization*, p. 332.

31. The French Report.

32. K. Stein, *The Land Question in Palestine, 1917–1939*, North Carolina 1985, pp. 233–5.

33. I wish to thank Dr Mustafa Abasi for providing me with the letter.

34. Mattar, *The Mufti*, p. 245.

35. Al-Dabagh, *The History*, part 2, chapter 10, p. 387.

36. Muhsin, *The Mother*, pp. 149–52; based on an unpublished MS by Qasim al-Rimawi, *A Biography of Abd al-Qadir*.

37. This description is taken from Muhsin, ibid., pp. 142-144, and Qasmiyyeh, *The First*.

38. *Filastin*, third year, no. 23, January 1923, pp. 8–10.

39. Ghana'im, 'The Pan', p. 258.

40. The committee's report, p. 31.

41. Laval, *Al-Hajj*, pp. 29–30.

42. Y. Ohana-Arnon, *A Sword at Home*, Tel Aviv 1981, p. 26 (Hebrew).

43. The Hagana Archives, section 47, file 7, 20 September 1937.

44. B. Dinnur, *The Hagana Book*, vol. 2, part 1, Tel Aviv 1967, p. 451 (Hebrew).

45. Ohana-Arnon, *Sword*, p. 250.

46. Attiyeh, *The Arab*, p. 130.

47. PRO, FO 371/78, file 178, Jerusalem to London, 15 October 1934.

48. Nashashibi, *The Last*, p. 24.

49. Mogannam, *The Arab*, p. 76.

50. Porath, *Riots*, p. 150.

51. *Filastin*, third year, no. 23, September 1923, pp. 8–10.

52. Porath, *Riots*, pp. 66–7.

53. Central Zionist Archives, S25/4127, and Ohana-Arnon, *Sword*, p. 102.

54. Offer, *Crystallization*.

55. Dinnur, *Hagana*, vol. 2, part 1, p. 540.

56. R. P. Mitchell, *The Society of Muslim Brothers*, London 1969, p. 154; Z. Abu Amru, *The Origins of the Political Movements in the Gaza Strip*, Jerusalem 1989, p. 63.

57. I. Gershoni, 'Muslim Brothers and the Arab Revolt in Palestine, 1936–1939', *Middle Eastern Studies*, 22/3 (1986), p. 337.

58. C. Yasin, *The Great Arab Revolt in Palestine, 1936–1939*, Cairo 1959, pp. 21–2 (Arabic).

59. A. Arslan, *The Memoirs of Prince Adel Arslan*, Beirut 1983, vol. 1, p. 43 (Arabic).

60. Hammad, *The Consciousness*, p. 72.

61. Kimmerling and Migdal, *The Palestinians*, p. 61.

62. Ghassan Kanafani's 1935 article was translated into Hebrew in *Derech Ha-Nizotz*, 4 August 1988, p. 10.

63. T. al-Nashef, 'Political Elite in Palestine', PhD thesis, New York 1974, pp. 86–8.

64. Y. Herzog, 'Contacts Between the Jewish Agency and the Palestinians, 1936–1939, The Arab Side: An Alternative or Integrative History?', in I. Pappé (ed.), *Arabs and Jews in the Mandatory Era: A New Look on the Historical Research*, Givat Haviva 1992, p. 12.

65. PRO, FO 371/20018, E1717, Report of the Chief of Police to the SoS for the Colonies, 2 March 1936.

66. Herzog, 'Contacts', p. 13.

67. Central Zionist Archives, S25/4146, Yeidot Yossef, 20 July 1936.

68. Kimmerling and Migdal, *The Palestinians*, p. 105.

69. Ohana-Arnon, *Sword*, p. 35.

70. Herzog, 'Contacts', p. 5.

71. Ibid., p. 6.

72. Al-Husayni, *I Learned*, p. 73.
73. M. Cohen, *The British Decision to Evacuate Palestine: 1947–1948,* New York 1987, p. 18, note 49.
74. A. Zuaytar, *The Diaries of Akram Zuaytar,* Beirut 1980, p. 220 (Arabic).
75. Herzog, 'Contacts', p. 15.
76. 13 July 1937; I wish to thank Yizhar Herzog for sharing this information with me.
77. Porath, *Riots*, pp. 198–204.
78. Kimmerling and Migdal, *The Palestinians*, p. 116.
79. Mattar, *The Mufti*, pp. 72–6.
80. Zuaytar, *Diaries*, pp. 90–8.
81. Y. Klein, *The Arab Community in Haifa in the Mandatory Era*, Haifa 1982, pp. 17–8 (Hebrew).
82. Yehuda Litani, *Al-Hamishmar*, 31 December 1993.
83. Israeli State Archives, The Mufti's Personal File, a letter from Jamal to the High Commissioner, section 65, 376/2613.
84. Laval, *Al-Hajj*, pp. 40–1.
85. Kedourie, *The Chatham*.

*Chapter 10*

1. Mardini, *Palestine*, p. 102.
2. J. and D. Kimche, *Both Sides of the Hill: Britain and the Palestine War*, London 1960, pp. 86–9, 98–9, 107. This source argued that the school was closed in 1936.
3. The Shaw Commission, session 46, p. 109.
4. J. Nevo, 'Al-Hajj Amin and the British in World War II', *Middle Eastern Studies*, 20/1 (January 1984), p. 4, note 6.
5. Zuaytar, *Diaries*, p. 336.
6. I want to thank Nadim Shadeh, the director of Lebanese Studies, Oxford, for this information. M. Fargeallah, *Visages d'une époque*, Paris, no date, p. 77.
7. Y. R. al-Radayi, *The 1936 Revolt: A Military Study*, Acre 1986, p. 50 (Arabic).
8. Laval, *Al-Hajj*, p. 34.
9. Honig Report, 19 October 1938, in PRO, CO 733/379, document 75528/74/38, 24 August 1938.
10. Qasmiyyah, *The First*, p. 327.
11. Ibid., p.185.
12. From an undated British Intelligence document in the Ben-Gurion Archives, Sdeh Boker, file 7-S-2. On the Azma brothers, see Qasmiyya, *The First*, p. 38; on the debates, see pp. 53–4.
13. Arslan, *Memoirs*, 24 April 1935.
14. Laval, *Al-Hajj*, pp. 44–5.
15. Zuaytar, *Diaries*, p. 552.
16. Ibid., pp. 398–487.

17. An interview with Salma al-Husayni (conducted by Dr Qatatu).

18. E. Danin, *The Arab Gangs,* Jerusalem 1981, p. 13 (Hebrew).

19. J. Nevo, 'The High Commissioner and the Mufti: Harold MacMichael and Hajj Amin Al-Husayni', *Cathedra* 64 (Apirl 1992), pp. 127–39 (Hebrew).

20. City of Jerusalem Archive, session no. 20 of the Committee for Planning and Urbanization, 19 April 1937, and session 50, 29 March, 1939.

21. Arslan, *Memoirs*, pp. 215–6, January 1939.

22. Porath, *Riots*, p. 161.

23. Ibid., p. 89.

24. M. Abd al-Hadi, *The Palestine Question and Its Political Solutions,* Beirut 1975, p. 62 (Arabic).

25. Porath, *Riots*, ibid.

26. Ben-Gurion Archives, file 7-S-2, ibid.

27. Arslan, *Memoirs*, vol. 1, 22 March 1939, p. 240.

28. Al-Hut, *The Political*, pp. 746–66; I. M. al-Husayni, *Akhbar al-Yawm,* 19 October 1957.

29. Kimmerling and Migdal, *The Palestinians*, p. 128, note 58.

30. Schama, *Rothschilds*, p. 292.

31. Mattar, *The Mufti*, p. 89.

32. A. Zuaytar, *Diaries*, pp. 608–9.

33. Nevo, *The High*, pp. 93–114.

## Chapter 11

1. PRO, FO 371/23240, Baghdad to London, 2 November 1939.

2. Darwaza, *Memoirs*, vol. 1, p. 226.

3. Laval, *Al-Hajj*, p. 50.

4. Ibid., pp. 52–3.

5. Ibid., pp. 56 –7.

6. W. Churchill, *The Second World War*, vol. 3, Boston 1952, p. 658.

7. Mardini, *Palestine*, p. 138.

8. The description here is taken from a program on TV5 (French television) on Françoise Ganeau, 20 July 1996.

9. Schechtman, *The Mufti*, pp. 96–8.

10. Kedourie, *Chatham*, pp. 165–6.

11. K. Hadad, *The Rashid Ali al-Galyani Movement of 1941*, Sydon 1950, pp. 9–10 (Arabic); G. Muhafazza, *The German-Palestinian Relationship, 1841– 1945*, Beirut 1981, p. 234 (Arabic).

12. Al-Peleg, *The Mufti*, p. 63.

13. Ibid., p. 65.

14. Laval, *Al-Hajj*, p. 64.

15. Ibid., p. 65.

16. Qasmiyyeh, *The First*, pp. 99, 103.

17. Mardini, *Palestine*, p. 107.

18. Laval, *Al-Hajj*, pp. 68–9.
19. G. Carpi, 'The Germans' Plan to Occupy the Middle East through the Caucasus', *Et-Mol*, 9/2 (1982), p. 14 (Hebrew).
20. Mardini, *Palestine*, p. 171.
21. Laval, *Al-Hajj*, pp. 69–70.
22. Muhafazza, *The German*, p. 244; M. al-Ris, *The Golden Book of the Arab Revolutions: The Iraq War 1941*, Damascus 1977, pp. 72–4 (Arabic).
23. Laval, *Al-Hajj*, p. 76.
24. Al-Nashashibi, *The Last*, p. 167; Kimmerling and Migdal, *The Palestinians*, p. 133.
25. Mardini, *Palestine*, p. 183.
26. Al-Ris, *The Golden*, p. 225.
27. Ibid., pp. 258–60.
28. Qasmiyyeh, *The First*, p. 100.
29. Ibid., p. 104.
30. Laval, *Al-Hajj*, p. 89.
31. Nevo, *The High*, p. 106.
32. Al-Peleg, *From the Mufti's*, p. 79.
33. Nevo, *The High*.
34. PRO, CO 733/439, Jerusalem to London, 26 December 1941.
35. Al-Asali, *Nabi Musa*, p. 137.
36. Al-Dabagh, *The History*, part 2, vol. 10, p. 378.
37. City of Jerusalem Archives, session 144, 14 December 1943.
38. Salwadi, *Dr Ishaq*, p. 25, note 10; Kimmerling and Migdal, *The Palestinians*, p. 55.
39. I. Pappé, *Britain and the Arab-Israeli Conflict, 1948–1951*, London and New York 1988.
40. A. Sela, 'The Palestinian Arabs in the 1948 War' in M. Maoz and B. Z. Kedar (eds), *The Palestinians*, p. 130.
41. A. al-Shuqayri, *Forty Years in the Arab and International Life*, Beirut 1969, p. 268 (Arabic).
42. Z. Lockman, *Comrades and Enemies*, Berkeley 1996, p. 324.
43. Ibid., p. 340.
44. J. Beinin, *Was the Red Flag Flying There?*, Berkeley 1990, p. 48.
45. D. Ben-Gurion, *At War*, vol. 4, part 1, Tel Aviv 1949, pp. 102–5 (Hebrew).
46. *Hadashot Ha-Erev*, 27 March, 1946.
47. PRO, FO 371/39990, E6328, Nahas Pasha to King Abd al-Aziz ibn Saud, 9 August 1944.
48. *Filastin*, 26 November 1946.
49. Sela, 'The Palestinian', p. 131.
50. Jamal's correspondence with the government's secretary: The Israel State Archives, CS, section 770.4, file 6, June 1947.
51. *Be'ayot*, third year, vol. 5, issue 1–2, pp. 31–4.

52. Gabriel Bear, *Be'ayot*, vol. 15, issue 3–4, p. 188.

53. I thank the late Professor P. J. Vatikiotis for this information.

54. I. M. al-Husayni, *The Muslim Brotherhood*, Beirut 1953, pp. 80–1 (Arabic).

55. Arslan, *Memoirs*, vol. 2, p. 723, 18 October 1947.

56. Al-Peleg, *From the Mufti's*, pp. 83–5.

57. Sela, 'The Palestinians', p. 155.

58. I. Pappé, *The Making of the Arab-Israeli Conflict, 1947–1951*, London and New York 1992, pp. 7–86.

59. Kimmerling and Migdal, *The Palestinians*, p. 144.

60. Dani Rubinstein, 'From Gush Etzion to Apropo', *Haaretz*, 13 April 1997, p. B3.

61. H. R. Rahman, 'The Concept of Jihad in Egypt: A Study of Majalat al-Azhar' in G. R. Warburg and U. M. Kupferschmidt (eds), *Islam and Nationalism and Radicalism in Egypt and the Sudan*, New York 1983, p. 254.

62. *Haaretz*, 22 March 1986, in an interview with Dani Rubinstein; see also, S. Shakib, 'The Mufti's Personality and His Activities', *Shuun Filastiniyya*, 186 (September 1988), pp. 87–90 and H. A. Jarar, *Haj Amin al-Husayni: The Commander of the Struggle and the Hero of the Palestine Question*, Amman 1987 (both in Arabic).

63. Y. Freundlich, *From Destruction to Resurrection*, Jerusalem 1994, p. 240 (Hebrew).

64. H. Z. Nusseibah, *Palestine and the UN*, London 1982, pp. 26–30.

65. Kimmerling and Migdal, *The Palestinians*, pp. 135–6.

66. H. al-Sakakini, *Jerusalem and I: A Personal Record*, Amman 1990, p. 126, 20 June 1948 (Arabic).

67. M. Abd al-Hadi, *The Palestine*, p. 169.

68. T. Jabara, *Studies in the Modern History of Palestine*, Jerusalem 1986, p. 173 (Arabic).

69. Pappé, *The Making*, pp. 81–9.

70. K. al-Budeiri, Sixty Years in the National Palestinian Movement, Beirut 1974, p. 140 (Arabic).

## Epilogue

1. Arslan, *Memoirs*, part 2, p. 881, 4 April 1949.

2. Al-Peleg, *From the Mufti's*, p. 112.

3. Al-Dabagh, *History*, part 2, vol. 10, p. 390.

4. E. Beeri, *The Palestinians under Jordanian Rule: Three Issues*, Jerusalem 1978, p. 11 (Hebrew).

5. Laval, *Al-Hajj*, p. 223.

6. J. Lunt, *Hussein of Jordan*, Berkeley 1996, p. 6.

7. T. Royle, *Glubb Pasha*, London 1992, p. 406.

8. Laval, *Al-Hajj*, p. 226.

9. A. Cohen, *Parties in the West Bank Under Jordanian Rule, 1948–1967*, Jerusalem 1980, p. 209 (Hebrew).

10. Al-Peleg, *The Mufti*, p. 128.
11. Cohen, *Parties*, pp. 121–3.
12. Ibid., p. 205.
13. Y. Sayigh, *Armed Struggle and the Search for a State: The Palestinian National Movement*, Oxford 1997, pp. 170–2.
14. Al-Peleg, 1989, *The Mufti*, p. 144.
15. Mardini, *Palestine*, p. 25.
16. Al-Peleg, *The Mufti*, p. 146.
17. Mardini, *Palestine*, pp. 19–21.
18. Al-Husayni, *The Muslim Brotherhood*.
19. T. G. Abed, 'The Palestinians and the Gulf Crisis', *Journal of Palestine Studies*, vol. 20/2 (1991), p. 134.
20. P. Inbari, *Broken Swords*, Tel Aviv 1994, pp. 27–82 (Hebrew).
21. Ibid., p. 97.
22. Al-Peleg, *The Mufti*, p. 155.
23. H. Sharabi, *Palestine and Israel*, New York 1969, p. 186.
24. *Haaretz*, 22 March 1986, in an interview with Dani Rubinstein; see also, S. Shakib, 'The Mufti's Personality and His Activities', *Shuun Filastiniyya*, 186 (September 1988), pp. 87–90, and H. A. Jarar, *Haj Amin al-Husayni: The Commander of the Struggle and the Hero of the Palestine Question*, Amman 1987 (both in Arabic).
25. Mattar, *The Mufti*.
26. C Thubron, *Jerusalem*, p. 170.

# Bibliography

Primary Sources

Ben-Gurion Archives, Sdeh Boker.
Centre for Arab Research, the Orient House Archives, Jerusalem.
City of Jerusalem Archives.
Public Record Office: CO 733, FO 78, FO 1521 and FO 371.

Official Reports

The Anglo-American Committee of Inquiry.
The French Report.
The Shaw Commission.
St Antony's College Middle East Centre's Private Papers Collection (The Emery and Adamson Papers).
The Central Zionist Archives, S/25, W/125, Z4 and the Mufti Files.
The Hagana Archives, Tel-Aviv.
The Israel State Archives, The archive of Palestine government secretariat, Archives of the Arab Higher Committee Executive.
The Shari'a court Records, Jerusalem.

Collections

A. Arslan, *The Memoirs of Prince Adel Arslan*, Beirut 1983 (Arabic).
R. Asad, *The Egyptian Royal Archives*, Cairo 1946.
K. G. Al-Asali, *Historical Documents form Jerusalem*, Amman 1989, (Arabic).
A. Cohen, A. Simon-Picali and O. Salameh (eds), *Jews in the Muslim Court,* Jerusalem 1996 (Hebrew).
M. Al-Kayali, *The Documents of the Arab Palestinian Resistance, 1918-1939*, Beirut 1988 (Arabic).
K. Salibi and Y. K. Khoury (eds), *The Missionary Herlad – Reports from Ottoman Syria, 1819-1870*, Washington 1991.

Newspapers

*Al-Ahram* (Cairo).
*Bait al-Muqadas* (Jerusalem).
*Davar* (Tel-Aviv).
*Doar Hayom* (Jerusalem).
*Filastin* (Jaffa).
*Al-Jamma'* (Jerusalem).
*Hadashot Ha-Erev* (Tel-Aviv).
*Al-Hilal* (Cairo).
*Al-Karmil* (Haifa).
*Al-Manar* (Cairo).
*Mirat al-Sharq* (Jerusalem).
*Al-Muqtataf al-Mufida* (Gaza).

Contemporary and Eyewitness Reports

M. al-Abadi, *Foreigners on Our Land*, Amman 1947 (Arabic).

H. A. Abd al-Latif, *The Jerusalemite Biographies in the 12ᵗʰ Hijjra Century*, no date (Arabic).

A. al-Asali, *Jerusalem in the Arab and Muslim Travelogues*, Amman 1992 (Arabic).

G. Belzoni, *Narrative of the Operations and Recent Discoveries in Egypt*, London 1882.

D. Ben-Gurion, *At War*, Volume 4, part 1, Tel-Aviv 1949 (Hebrew).

K. al-Budeiri, *Sixty Years in the National Palestinian Movement*, Beirut 1974 (Arabic).

T. Canan, 'Two Documents on the Surrender of Jerusalem', *Journal of the Palestine Oriental Society*, 10 (1930), pp. 27–30.

F. A. Chateaubriand, *Itinéraire de Paris à Jérusalem*, Paris 1811.

W. Churchill, *The Second World War*, Volume 3, Boston 1952.

C. R. Conder, *Palestine*, London 1891.

J. Crane, *Letters from the East*, New York 1996.

R. Curzon, *Visits to Monasteries in the Levant*, London 1851.

M. I. Darwazza, *Memories and Notes – One Hundred Palestinian Years*, Damascus 1986 (Arabic).

A. Droyanov (ed.), *Letters on the History of the Love of Zion and the Settlement of the Palestine*, Odessa 1919 (Hebrew).

J. Finn, *Stirring Times or Records from Jerusalem Consular Chronicles*, London 1878.

G. Frumkin, *The Way of A Judge in Jerusalem*, Jerusalem 1946 (Hebrew).

E. al-Ghori, *Palestine During Sixty Years*, Beirut 1973 (Arabic).

Z. Gorgi (Jurji), *The Famous Personalities of the East in the 19ᵗʰ Century*, Cairo, no date, vol. 2, p. 52 (Arabic).

H. Hamburger, *Three Worlds*, Jerusalem 1946 (Hebrew).

M. al-Hanabli, *The Magnificent Man*, Cairo, no date (Arabic).

A. Haymson, *The British Consulate in Palestine*, London 1940.

R. Hichens, *The Holy Land*, London 1910.

A. al-Husayni, *Diwan Shi'r*, Anthology of Poems: a manuscript in al-Aqsa without a date (Arabic).

I. M. al-Husayni, *Abd al-Latif al-Husayni's Treasure*, Jerusalem 1985.

I. M. al-Husayni, *The Husayni Family*, Jerusalem 1988 (Arabic).

I. M. al-Husayni, *I Learned from the People*, Jerusalem 1968 (Arabic).

G. al-Jabarti, *The Wonders of Biographies and Chronicles*, Cairo 1879 (Arabic).

P. H. Kisch, *A Palestine Diary*, Jerusalem 1939.

A. al-Kurdi (ed.), *Ismail al-Nabulsi; Fiction and Reality in a Trip to the al-Sham Countries and Hejaz*, Cairo 1986 (Arabic).

D. Lloyd George, *The Truth About the Peace Treaties*, London 1938.

W. P. Lyntch, *A Journey to the Dead Sea and the Jordan River*, New York 1984.

A. S. Macalister and E. W. G. Masterman, 'Occasional Papers on the Modern Inhabitants of Palestine', *The Palestine Exploration Fund Quarterly*, (1906).

R. Memimel, *The Remedy of my People*, Berlin 1883 (Hebrew).

M. al-Muhibi, *A Summary of the Notables' Lives in the 11th Hijjra Century*, vol. 2, Cairo, 1868 (Arabic).

M. K. Al-Muradi, *A Guide to the Notables of the 12th Hijjra Century*, Istanbul 1882 (Arabic).

N. al-Nashashibi, *The Last Giant Came from Jerusalem – The Story of the Palestinian Leader Nasr al-Din al-Nashashibi*, Jerusalem 1986.

A. Paton, *History of the Egyptian Revolution*, London 1870.

B. Qatinka, *From Then to Now*, Jerusalem 1961 (Hebrew).

M. A. al-Qayatli, *The Flavours of al-Sham in the Al-Sham Travelogues*, Beirut 1981 (Arabic).

M. A. Rogers, *Daily Life in Palestine*, London 1984.

A. Rupin, *My Life*, Tel-Aviv 1968 (Hebrew).

H. al-Sakakini, *Jerusalem and I – A Personal Record*, Amman 1990 (Arabic).

H. al-Sakakini, *This is, Oh World*, Jerusalem 1990, Diary entry: 12 November 1908 (Arabic).

Y. Schwartz, *The Harvest of the Land*, London 1845 (Hebrew)

A. al-Shuqairi, *Forty Years in the Arab and International Life*, Beirut 1969 (Arabic).

I. al-Sifari, *Arab Palestine Between The Mandate and Zionism*, Jaffa 1937 (Arabic).

B. Spafford-Vester, *Our Family in the Holy City – 1881-1949*, Jerusalem 1950.

H. Spoer, 'Das Nabi Musa Fest', *Zeitschrift der Deutshen Palestine-Vereins*, vol. 32 (1909).

S.N. Spyridon (ed.), *Annals of Palestine, 1821-1841; Manuscript of Monk Neophytos of Cyprus*, Jerusalem 1938.

A. P. Stanely, *Sinai and Palestine*, London 1887.

R. Storrs, *Orientations*, London 1938.

I. Tannus, *The Palestinians – A Glorious Past and a Wonderful Future*, Beirut 1982 (Arabic).

C. P. Volney, *Travels in Syria and Egypt in the years 1783, 1784 and 1785*, London 1787.

E. S. Wallace, *Holy Jerusalem*, New York 1898.

P. Wavell, *The Palestine Campaigns*, London 1927.

C. Weizmann, *Trail and Error*, New York 1949.

G. N. Whittingham, *The Home of Fadeless Splendour*, London, no date.

Y. Yehoshua, *The Fruit of Jerusalem*, Jerusalem 1974 (Hebrew).

Y. Yehoshua, *The History of the Arabic Press in Palestine – the Ottoman Period, 1908-1918*, Jerusalem 1974, (Arabic).

A. Yelin, *The Memoirs of a Jerusalemite*, Jerusalem 1924 (Hebrew).

A. Zuaytar, *The Diaries of Akram Zuaytar*, Beirut 1980.

Secondary Sources

M. Abd al-Hadi, *The Palestine Question and its Political Solutions*, Beirut 1975 (Arabic).

T. G. Abed, 'The Palestinians and the Gulf Crisis', *Journal of Palestine Studies*, vol. 20/2 (1991), pp. 132-144.

Z. Abu Amru, *The Origins of the Political Movements in the Gaza Strip*, Jerusalem 1989.

G. Abu Ghazzala, *The National Culture in Palestine During the British Mandate*, Beirut, no date (Arabic).

B. Abu Manneh, 'A New Light on the Husaynis' Ascendance in the Eighteenth Century' in A. Cohen (ed.), *Chapters in the History of Jerusalem in the Early Ottoman Period*, Jerusalem 1979 (Hebrew), pp. 95-104.

— 'The Husaynis: The Rise of a Notable Family in the 18th Century Palestine' in D. Kushner (ed.), *Palestine in the Late Ottoman Period*, Jerusalem 1986, pp. 93-108.

— 'Jerusalem in the Tanzimat Period, the New Ottoman Administration and the Notables', *Die Welt des Islams*, 30 (1990).

— 'The Rise of the Sanjak of Jerusalem in the late 19th Century' in I. Pappe (ed.), *The Israel/Palestine Question*, London and New York 1999, pp. 43–56.

I. Agmon, 'Foreign Trade as a Transforming Factor in the Arab Economy in Palestine, 1897-1914, *Cathedra* 41 (1986), pp. 107–32 (Hebrew).

Z. Al-Peleg, *From the Mufti's Point of View*, Tel-Aviv 1995 (Hebrew).

Z. Al-Peleg, *The Grand Mufti*, Tel-Aviv 1989.

G. Antonious, *The Arab Awakening*, London 1961.

A. al-Arif, *The Concise History of Jerusalem*, Jerusalem 1961 (Arabic).

A. al-Arif, *The History of Jerusalem*, Cairo 1950 (Arabic).

M. Asaf, *Arab-Jewish Relations in Palestine, 1860–1948*, Tel-Aviv 1970.

K. G. al-Asali, *Nabi Musa*, Jerusalem 1981 (Arabic).

S. Attiyeh, *The Arab Palestine Party and the National Defense Party, 1934–1937*, Jerusalem 1985 (Arabic).

A. al-Awda, *The History of Suleyman Pasha the Noble*, Tyre 1936.

Y. al-Awdat, *Palestine's Thinkers and Authors*, Amman 1976 (Arabic).

G. Baer, 'Jerusalem's Families of Notables and the Waqf in the Early 19th Century', in D. Kushner (ed.), *Palestine in the Late Ottoman Period*, Jerusalem 1986, pp. 103–13.

S. Bar Elkana, 'The Rise of Haj Amin to the Muslim Leadership in Palestine', *Bar Ilan University's Year Book*, Ramat Gan 1972, pp. 37-83 (Hebrew).

Y. Barani, *Historiography and Nationalism*, Jerusalem 1995 (Hebrew).

T. A. Baru, *The Arabs and the Turks in the Constitutional Ottoman Era*, Cairo 1960 (Arabic).

E. Beeri, *The Palestinians under Jordanian Rule – Three Issues*, Jerusalem 1978 (Hebrew).

J. Beinin, *Was the Red Flag Flying There?*, Berkeley 1990.

Y. Ben-Areyh, *Palestine in the 19th Century and Its Rediscovery*, Jerusalem 1970.

Y. Ben-Zvi's, *The Settlement of Eretz Israel*, Jerusalem, 1976 (Hebrew).

G. Biger, 'The American Consulate in Jerusalem and the Events of 1920–1921', *Cathedra*, 49 (September 1988), pp. 133–9 (Hebrew).

P. Brockelman, *Geschichte der Arabischen Littrature*, Leiden 1970,

N. Caplan, *Futile Diplomacy*, Volume 1, London 1983.

G. Carpi, 'The Germans Plan to Occupy the Middle East Through the Caucus', *Et-Mol*, Volume 9/2 (1982), p. 14 (Hebrew).

A. Cohen, *Palestine in the 18th Century – Patterns and Administration*, Jerusalem 1973.

A. Cohen, *Parties in the West Bank Under Jordanian Rule, 1948–1967*, Jerusalem 1980 (Hebrew).

M. Cohen, *The British Decision to Evacuate Palestine – 1947–1948*, New York 1987.

K. Cuno, *The Pasha's Peasants: Land, Society and Economy in Lower Egypt, 1740–1858*, Cambridge 1992.

M. N. Al-Dabagh, *The History of Shaykh Dahir al-Umar al-Zaydani*, Harisa 1927 (Arabic).

E. Danin, *The Arab Gangs*, Jerusalem 1981 (Hebrew).

B. Dinnur, *The Hagana Book*, Volume 2, part 1, Tel-Aviv 1967 (Hebrew).

S. Dotan, *The Communist Party in Israel*, Kfar Saba 1991 (Hebrew).

B. Doumani (ed.), *Family History in the Middle East; Household, Property, and Gender*, New York 2003.

B. Doumani, *Rediscovering Palestine*, Berkeley 1995.

Y. Drori, 'The Origins of Nabi Musa', *Sali't*, Volume 1/5 (1972), pp. 203–8 (Hebrew).

Y. Eilam, 'The Political History, 1918–1922' in M. Lissak (ed.), *The History of the Jewish Community in Palestine Since the First Aliya*, Jerusalem 1984, pp. 145–58 (Hebrew).

L. Fawaz, *Merchants and Migrants in Nineteenth Century Beirut*, Cambridge 1983.

Y. Freundlich, *From Destruction to Resurrection,* Jerusalem 1994 (Hebrew).

I. Gershoni, 'Muslim Brothers and the Arab Revolt in Palestine, 1936–1939', *Middle Eastern Studies*, volume 22/3 (1986), pp. 337–41.

A. H. Ghana'im, 'The Pan-Islamist Congress, 1931', *Shuun Filastiniyya*, 25 (September 1973), pp. 124–5 (Arabic).

A. Ghariba, *Syria in the 19ᵗʰ Century, 1840–1876*, Damascus 1969 (Arabic).

N. Gross, 'Economic Reforms in Palestine in the end of the Ottoman Period', *Cathedra* 2 (1977), pp. 102–25 (Hebrew).

K. Hadad, *The Rashid Ali al-Galyani Movement of 1941*, Sydon 1950 (Arabic).

Y. al-Hakim, *Syria in the Ottoman Period*, Damascus 1950 (Arabic).

S. Hamada, *The Consciousness and the Revolution – A Study in the Life of the Shahid Izz al-Din al-Qassam,* Jerusalem 1985 (Arabic).

S. Hanioglu, 'The Young Turks and the Arabs before the Revolution of 1908' in R. Khalidi et al. (eds), *The Origins of Arab Nationalism*, New York 1991, pp. 31–49.

Y. Herzog, 'Contacts Between the Jewish Agency and the Palestinians, 1936–1939, The Arab Side: An Alternative or Integrative History?', in I. Pappe (ed.), *Arab-Jewish Relationship in Mandatory Palestine*, Givat Haviva, 1992 (in Hebrew), pp. 14–23.

U. Heyd, *Daher al-Umar,* Jerusalem 1963.

A. Hourani, *A History of the Arab Peoples,* New York, 1993.

A. Hourani, 'Ottoman Reform and the Politics of Notables', in W. R. Polk and R. L. Chambers (eds), *Beginnings of Modernization in the Middle East – The Nineteenth Century*, Chicago 1968, pp. 52–67.

A. Hourani, 'Ottoman Reform and the Politics of Notables' in A. Hourani (ed.), *The Modern Middle East*, London and New York, pp. 87–98.

I. M. al-Husayni, *The Doyen of the Arabic Language: Muhamad Isaf al-Nashashibi,* Jerusalem 1987 (Arabic).

I. M. al-Husayni, *The Muslim Brotherhood,* Beirut 1953 (Arabic).

B. N. al-Hut, *The Political Leaderships and Institutions in Palestine, 1917-1948,* Beirut 1981 (Arabic).

P. Inbari, *Broken Swords,* Tel-Aviv 1994 (Hebrew).

M. Ish-Shalom, *Christian Pilgrimage in the 19ᵗʰ Century,* Tel-Aviv 1965 (Hebrew).

T. Jabara, *Studies in the Modern History of Palestine,* Jerusalem 1986 (Arabic).

H. A. Jarar, *Haj Amin al-Husayni: The Commander of the Struggle and the Hero of the Palestine Question*, Amman 1987 (Arabic).

P. Kahanov, 'The Jerusalem Trade Fifty Years Ago', *From Early Days,* (1935), pp. 142–50 (Hebrew).

R. Karak and M. Oren-Nordheim, *Jerusalem and its Environs*, Jerusalem 1993 (Hebrew).

E. Kedourie, *The Chatham Version and Other Middle Eastern Studies*, New York 1984.

M. Khadduri, *Arab Contemporaries – The Role of Personalities in Politics*, Baltimore 1973.

W. Khalidi, *Before the Diaspora – A Photographic History of the Palestinian People, 1876–1948*, Beirut 1987 (Arabic).

D. Khoury, *State and Provincial Society in the Ottoman Empire: Mosul, 1540-1834*, Cambridge and New York 1999.

P. Khoury, *Syria under the French Mandate*, Princeton 1987.

J. and D. Kimche, *Both Sides of the Hill: Britain and the Palestine War*, London 1960.

B. Kimmerling and J. S. Migdal, *Palestinians – The Making a People*, New York 1993.

Y. Klein, *The Arab Community in Haifa in the Mandatory Era*, Haifa 1982 (Hebrew).

M. Kramer, *Islam Assembled*, New York 1996.

M. Kupferschmidt, 'The General Muslm Congress of 1931 in Jerusalem', *Asian and African Studies*, vol. 12 (1971), pp. 132–3.

D. Kushner, 'The Foreign Relations of the Governors of Jerusalem Toward the End of the Ottoman Period', in D. Kushner (ed.), *Palestine in the Late Ottoman Period*, Jerusalem 1986, pp. 315–26.

Y. Lamdan, 'The Arabs and Zionism, 1882-1914' in Y. Kolat (ed.), *The History of the Jewish Settlement in Palestine Since the First Aliya'*, Jerusalem 1990, pp. 233–4 (Hebrew).

S. Landman, *The Jerusalem Notables' Neighborhoods Outside the Wall in the 19th Century*, Jerusalem 1984 (Arabic).

I. M. Lapidus, *A History of Islamic Societies*, Cambridge 1988.

J. Laval, *Al-Hajj Amin and Berlin*, Tel-Aviv 1996 (Hebrew).

Z. Lockman, *Comrades and Enemies*, Berkeley 1996.

J. Lunt, *Hussein of Jordan*, Berkeley 1996.

Y. Lunz, 'The Sources and Origins of the Palestinian National Movement on the eve of the First World War' in M. Maoz and B. Z. Kedar (eds), *The Palestinian National Movement: From Confrontation to Reconciliation?*, Tel-Aviv 1996, pp. 33–45 (Hebrew).

A. Manna, 'Cultural Relations between Egyptian and Jerusalem "Ulema" in the Early Nineteenth Century' in G. Gilbar and G. Warburg (eds), *Studies in Islamic Society*, Haifa 1974, pp. 141–53.

A. Manna, 'The Naqib al- Ashraf's Revolt in Jerusalem (1703–1705)', *Cathedra*, 64 (April 1992) (Hebrew).

A. Manna, *The Worthies of Palestine in the Late Ottoman Period*, Beirut 1995 (Arabic).

M. H. Mansa, *The History of the Modern Arab East*, Beirut 1976, (Arabic).

A. Marcus, *The Middle East on the Eve of Modernity: Aleppo in the Eighteenth Century*, New York 1989.

S. Mardin, 'Religion and Secularism in Turkey' in A. Hourani, P. S. Khoury and M. C. Wilson (eds), *The Modern Middle East*, London 1993, pp. 347–74.

Z. Mardini, *Palestine and Haj Amin al-Husayni*, Beirut 1986 (Arabic).

P. Mattar, *The Mufti of Jerusalem*, New York 1988.

J. McCarthy, *The Population of Palestine*, New York 1988.

T. Mayer, 'Egypt and the General Islamic Conference of Jerusalem 1931', *Middle Eastern Studies*, 18/3 (1982), pp. 311–21.

R. P. Mitchell, *The Society of Muslim Brothers*, London 1969.

M. E. T. Mogannam, *The Arab Woman and the Palestine Problem*, London 1936.

G. Muhafazza, *The German-Palestinian Relationship, 1841–1945*, Beirut 1981 (Arabic).

K. H. Muhsin, *The Mother Palestine and her Noble Son Abd al-Qadir al-Husayni*, Amman 1986 (Arabic).

T. Al-Nashef, 'Political Elite in Palestine', Ph D. Thesis, New York 1974.

J. Nevo, 'Al-Hajj Amin and the British in World War II', *Middle Eastern Studies*, Vol. 20/1 (January 1984), pp. 3–13.

J. Nevo, 'The High Commissioner and the Mufti: Harold MacMichael and Hajj Amin Al-Husayni', *Cathedra* 64 (April 1992), pp. 127–39 (Hebrew).

A. Nuhayd, 'A Man in Palestine: Khalil al-Sakakini', *Filastin* 17 July 1995 (Arabic).

H. Z. Nusseibah, *Palestine and the UN*, London 1982.

P. Offer, 'The Crystallization of the Mandatory Regime and the Laying of Foundations to the Jewish National Home, 1921-1931', in M. Lissak (ed.), *The History of the Jewish Yishuv in Eretz Israel since the First Aliya*, Yad Ben Zvi (in Hebrew), pp. 230–46.

Y. Ohana-Arnon, *A Sword at Home*, Tel-Aviv 1981 (Hebrew).

A. Palmer, *The Decline and Fall of the Ottomans*, London 1992.

S. Pamuk, 'Money in the Ottoman Empire' in H. Inalcik (ed.), *An Economic and Social History of the Ottoman Empire, 1300–1914*, Cambridge, 1994, pp. 966–76.

I. Pappe, *Britain and the Arab-Israeli Conflict, 1948–1951*, London and New York 1988.

I. Pappe, *The Making of the Arab-Israeli Conflict, 1947–1951*, London and New York 1992.

I. Pappe, 'Understanding the Enemy: A Comparative Analysis of Palestinian Islamist and Nationalist Leaflets, 1920s–1980s' in R. L. Nettle and S. Taji-Farouki, (eds), *Muslim-Jewish Encounters – Intellectual Traditions and Modern Politics*, Amsterdam 1996, pp. 223–63.

M. Penzer, *The Harem*, London 1967.

O. Peri, 'Waqf and Ottoman Welfare Policy: The Poor Kitchen of Khasseki Sultan in Eighteen Century Jerusalem', *Hamizrach Hehadash*, Vol. 34, Issues 133–6, pp. 64–76 (Hebrew).

T. Philipp, *Acre; The Rise and Fall of a Palestinian City, 1730–1831*, New York 2001.

Y. Porath, *From Riots to Revolt, 1929–1939*. Tel-Aviv 1978 (Hebrew).

Y. Porath, 'Al-Hajj Amin al-Husayni, The Jerusalem Mufti – His Rise and the Consolidation of his Position' in G. Baer (ed.), *The Ulama and the Religious Problems in the Muslim World*, Jerusalem 1979, pp. 223–30 (Hebrew).

Y. Porath, 'Social Aspects of the Emergence of the Palestinian National Movement' in M. Milson (ed.), *Society and Regime in the Arab World*, Jerusalem 1977, pp. 10–23 (Hebrew).

Y. Porath, *The Emergence of the Palestinian National Movement, 1918–1929*, Tel-Aviv 1976, pp. 1–17 (Hebrew).

K. Qasmiyyeh, *The First Arab Pioneer – the Lives and Papers of Nabih and Adel al-Azma*, Damascus 1991 (Arabic).

Y. R. al-Radayi, *The 1936 Revolt – A Military Study*, Acre 1986 (Arabic).

A. Rafeq, *The Province of Damascus*, Beirut 1970.

H. R. Rahman, 'The Concept of Jihad in Egypt – A Study of Majalat al-Azhar' in G. R. Warburg and U. M. Kupferschmidt, *Islam and Nationalism and Radicalism in Egypt and the Sudan*, New York 1983, pp. 250–61.

H. Ram, *The Jewish Community in Jaffa*, Jerusalem 1996 (Hebrew).

A. Raymond, *Cairo*, Cambridge 2000.

J. Reily, *A Small Town in Syria: Ottoman Hama in the Eighteenth and Nineteenth Centuries*, Oxford and New York 2002.

M. Reimer, *Colonial Bridgehead: Government and Society in Alexandria, 1807–1882*, Cairo 1997.

Y. Reiter, 'The Supervision on Managing the Muslim Waqf Affairs in Jerusalem since the Mandatory Period (1918–1990), *HaMizarch HaHadash* 34 (1992), pp. 17–8 (Hebrew).

M. al-Ris, *The Golden Book of the Arab Revolutions – The Iraq War 1941*, Damascus 1977 (Arabic).

N. Rogel, 'Weizmann's Man in Damascus – The Case of Dr. Moshe Palman's Mission to Faysal's Court, September 1919–July 1920', *Ziyonut* 9 (1983), pp. 302–22 (Hebrew).

M. Rosen, 'The Naqib al-Ashraf's Revolt in Jerusalem, 1702–1706', *Cathedra* 22 (January 1982) (Hebrew).

T. Royle, *Glubb Pasha*, London 1992.

A. Rubinstein, 'The Arab Question in the Aftermath of the 1929 Events and the Establishment of the Unified Board of the Jewish Community Institutions – Political Aspects', in I. Pappe (ed.), *Arabs and Jews in the Mandatory Era: A New Look on the Historical Research*, Givat Haviva 1992, pp. 125–36 (Hebrew).

D. Rubinstein, 'From Gush Eztion to Apropo', *Haaretz*, 13 April 1997, p. 3B.

A. al-Said, *The Great Arab Revolt*, Beirut, no date (Arabic).

L. M. Salem, *The Egyptian Rule in Syria, 1831–1841*, Cairo 1989.

K. A. Salwadi, *Dr. Ishaq Musa al-Husayni*, Jerusalem 1991 (Arabic).

Y. Sayigh, *Armed Struggle and the Search for a State; The Palestinian National Movement*, Oxford 1997.

S. Schama, *The House of Rothschild and Palestine*, Jerusalem 1980.

J. B. Schechtman, *The Mufti and the Fuerher – The Rise and Fall of Haj Amin el-Husseini*, New York 1965.

A. Scholch, 'European Penetration and the Economic Development of Palestine,

1856–1872' in R. Owen (ed.), *Studies in the Economic and Social History of Palestine in the Nineteenth and Twentieth Centuries*, Oxford 1982, pp. 10–87.

A. Scholch, *Palestine in Transformation, 1856-1882*, Washington, 1993.

A. Sela, 'The Palestinian Arabs in the 1948 War' in M. Maoz and B. Z. Kedar, *The Palestinians*, pp. 126–139.

S. Shakib, 'The Mufti's Personality and His Activities', *Shuun Filastiniyya*, 186 (September 1988), pp. 87–90 (Arabic).

H. Sharabi, *Palestine and Israel*, New York 1969.

Y. Shavit (ed.), *The Wonders of the Holy Land*, Jerusalem 1981 (Hebrew).

S. J. Shaw, *Between Old and New – The Ottoman Empire Under Sultan Selim 3, 1789–1807*, Cambridge 1971.

A. Shihabi, *The History of Ahmad Pasha Al-Jazzar*, Beirut, no date (Arabic).

N. Shore, *The Book of Palestine's Travelogues in the 19th Century*, Jerusalem 1988 (Hebrew).

R. Springborg, 'Patterns of Association in the Egyptian Political Elite' in George Lenszowski (ed.) *Political Elites in the Middle East*, Washington 1975.

K. Stein, *The Land Question in Palestine, 1917–1939*, North Carolina 1985.

E. Toldenao, 'The Emergence of Ottoman-Local Elites (1700–1900): A Framework for Research' in M. Maoz and I. Pappe (eds), *Middle Eastern Politics and Ideas: A History From Within*, London and New York, 1997, pp. 146–57.

B. Thubron, *Jerusalem*, London 1969.

F. Tuqan, *An Arduous Trip*, Acre 1985 (Arabic).

Z. Vilnai, *Investigative Tourists in Palestine*, Tel-Aviv 1984 (Hebrew).

B. Wasserstein, *The British in Palestine – The Mandatory Government and the Arab-Jewish Conflict, 1917–1929*, London 1979.

G. Winegart, 'The Religious Muslim Life in 18th Century Jerusalem', *Cathedra*, 49 (September 1988), pp. 79–90 (Hebrew).

H. Winner, 'The Zionist Policy in Turkey until 1914' in Y. Kolat (ed.), *The History of the Jewish Settlement in Palestine Since the First Aliya'*, Jerusalem 1990, pp. 330–8 (Hebrew).

A. Yaari, *Travels in Palestine*, Ramat Gan 1976 (Hebrew).

C. Yasin, *The Great Arab Revolt in Palestine, 1936-1939*, Cairo 1959, pp. 21–2 (Arabic).

L. M. al-Yassui, *The History of Syria and Lebanon, 1782–1841*, Beirut 1912 (Arabic).

D. Ze'evi, *An Ottoman Century; the District of Jerusalem in the 1600s*, Albany 1996.

Z. N. Zeine, *The Struggle for Arab Independence*, Beirut 1960.

N. Ziyaddah, 'Ishaq Musa al-Husayni', *Majalat al-Dirassat al-Filastiniyya*, vol. 9 (1992) (Arabic).

# Index